Collected Poems 1949-1987

Also by Edwin Morgan

EDWIN MORGAN

Collected Poems

CARCANET

First published in Great Britain in 1990 by
Carcanet Press Limited
Conavon Court
12-16 Blackfriars Street
Manchester M3 5BQ

Paperback edition 1996

A CIP catalogue record for this book
is available from the British Library.
ISBN 1 85754 188 X

The publisher acknowledges financial assistance
from the Arts Council of England.

Set in 9½pt Palatino by Bryan Williamson, Darwen
Printed and bound in England by SRP Ltd, Exeter

Funded by
THE
ARTS
COUNCIL
OF ENGLAND

Contents

9

11

12

13

Preface

This volume reprints the complete text of *The Vision of Cathkin Braes, The Cape of Good Hope, The Whittrick, The Second Life, The Horseman's Word, From Glasgow to Saturn, The New Divan, Star Gate, Sonnets from Scotland,* and *From the Video Box,* and selections from *Newspoems, Emergent Poems, Gnomes, Instamatic Poems, Selected Poems,* and *Themes on a Variation.* It also includes *Dies Irae,* which was to have been published by Lotus Press in their Acadine Poets series, but when the series foundered through lack of finance, never appeared; it was intended as a complementary volume to *The Vision of Cathkin Braes* – rather like the tragic and comic masks of drama. I have not included work which would have required colour reproduction: *Bestiary* (1968), *Proverbfolder* (1969), *Nuspeak* (1973), and *Colour Poems* (1978).

About fifty uncollected and unpublished poems have been added, ranging in date from 1939 to 1990. The concluding poem, 'Seven Decades', was written for a seventieth birthday celebration organized by the Third Eye Centre (Glasgow), who have published it, together with other pieces written for the occasion, in a pamphlet, *Felt-tipped Hosannas.*

E.M.

Beti zeru urdin zati bat dago: bila ezazu.

Prologue: Sculpture

Now the stoned ocean shudders,
The shape of the sea is the wax of a ghost
In time bound, the tame bend
Of the bone-team-beaten tide is tensed
To the bolt of duration's chances,
The stance of the waters is wax.

Zadkine on the pebble pedestal
Turns, dreaming of marble seas.
Arms, breasts, temples and carolling hair
Fly from the still prison, steel pressing
On the still delicate lineaments to change
The unchangeable, royal water pattern.

1939

Dies Irae
1952

Dies Irae

It was the blaze and maelstrom of God's wrath.
So frightfully was never islanded
Mortal voyager in the far flood of the north
When growling berg became his acre and burgh
And sheets of freezing grey lay all his world
As I within the sea of time was lost
And thrown upon the groaning shores of wrath.
My ship long since had struck its rock, and sunk,
My compass the voracious surge had sucked,
My clothes were sodden, rotting with the wet,
My pockets void of knife, or fire, or bread,
My boots kicked off in swimming through despair,
My feet cut fiercely by the biting beach,
My eyes half-blinded by the harsh salt spray,
My throat choked hoarse in the raw haul of the waves.
Cower among the pebbles I could not for the cold,
But in my flapping jacket faced the blast
And set my bloody steps along those rocks
That did not wince to break my flesh anew.
So, buffeted by the blustering hosts of the air,
Shot by sharp batteries of frozen rain
Whose ice congealed my streaming hair and hailed
Torrents of pitilessness upon my face,
Mocking my poor coat threadbare with their lash;
Whirled in that jealous gale with twigs, and sand,
Splinters of hissing rock, smashed shells, crabs' husks,
Thin downlike urchins scooped hollow by the tide,
And tiny sea-birds with stiff starlike feet
And eyes of ice, hurled senseless of the storm;
The boomerang drum-roll doubling and redounding a hundredfold,
The blistering fulgor fire-runnelling the livid vault,
The thunder and the blaze of heaven I bore.

It was the murmur and blame of meditation,
God's grinding reef of chiding and condemnation,
His maelstrom threatening for mortal retrogression.
He cast me from the plunging shiprail, he
To the boiling welter of waters felled me howling
And with his billows and fireballs dashed my ship to the abyss;
He bade me fight the wild and beastlike seas,
Flail with my arms the bodiless froth, and climb
Up from each slippery trench with failing strength,
Combing the ungraspable gulf; he flung my flesh
To crack its lungs for gusts of blessed breath
Upon these tearing and offensive teeth

21

And razorlike sighing shingle of the shore,
And there I dragged, through rain and hail and wind,
My terror and my abasement over that ground,
My legs through stinging bent and bushes forced,
My feet in blood upon the blade-edged stones;
He was that blaze and meditation in the sky
That pierced and scoured the spaces of the air
And showered and shook those lightnings quick and keen
Over my island and the savage waters;
He was that meditated thunder and thought
That opened up the clouds and rolled them back
Far into reverberating wrath
Ragged with mutters in that hurricane's heaven;
He was the anger and the blast: he was that heaven.

How will I tell then how the dark came down
And in the moaning of the wind I slept,
Crouched in the shivering refuge of a bush,
By weariness within that storm to rest?
Although my eyes were blind to trough and foam,
My ears no longer sang with the fretted sands,
I saw and heard in the gazing of a dream
Within my mind, and tempest there beheld.
So thought has wave in wave, deep behind deep,
Sea beyond sea stretched out far over the world,
Where we set sail, and founder, or to haven tremble,
A ship of glass among the bluffs to gamble.
I saw there other seas, and vaster storms,
Glimmering armadas of a million sails
Veered in a wake of blood, the confusion of hosts
Crushed in the slow slumbrous clash of arms,
Cries rising up like smoke, far, thin, and clear,
Above the tumult and enormous mass
Of the imponderable vessels triumphing there.
Some bugle sadly shook the hanging air,
And sombre flags I saw to fluttering set,
Which clung to the masts like just-fledged feeble moths,
Unstirring in the silence and the space.
Now such a calm as smooths the frowning dead
Was laid on the waters, and they shone with light,
Wide, burnished in the stillness of the sun.
The heavy ships moved slowly through the glare,
The sails were mingled with fire, the masts and spars
Vanished in that dissolving dazzle and hush,
And flag, hull, bugle, anchor, and hosts,
Enemy and sea-friend, captain, armourer, boy
Turned to embrace the tranquil morning gold,

Leaving the shining sea and sky serene
One glory, steady, holy,
One gazing eye, one meditation and blaze.
It was God's steadfast meditation and peace.
I wept upon the fading of the ships,
And shut my eyes against that blazoned grace;
I feared to see that glory face to face.
And though the light had crept upon my clothes,
Gilded my hand and hair, and on my lips
Diamonds and watery sapphires quivering cast,
Yet back and farther back I cringed, and shaded
My lids against the multitudinous flood
And searing soundless furnace-fall of sunlight,
Sobbed and cried out, wrung my burning hands,
Panting in heat too shadowlessly poured,
My blood set seething in the gentle veins
And in my body the heart and regiment
Shrivelling in the dominion of the flame,
Till terror came, that I might be consumed.
Niche, angle, cranny, arch, or shade was none,
Nor tree, nor cloud, nor wall or shelter of stone,
Nor sign of rain, nor noise, nor any change,
But where I stood was focussed all the stillness,
And all the searching glory bent on me,
A gaze too straight, a silence too severe.
Yet as I writhed, my chapped lips salt with sweat,
My coat in singed and charring flakes, there rolled
Suddenly a voice in splendour all around
Resounding from the battlements of light
God, God, God, God;
And I was taken into the blaze and the recession,
My flesh forgot to burn in mortal transgression,
I was not divided from his meditation.
It was a dream of meditation and grace
Where we were gazing fearless face to face.

It was a dream; bitterly then I woke
With the hoar chill of dawning on the sea
And shrieking of the wind and savage gulls,
The shudder of that surge along the cliffs,
The black and shivering tempest-blasted scrub
And nodding reed where I had curled and slept,
All freezing, glistening in the crude daybreak
With ice, cold dew, hard light, and driven spray.
And now the hurricane of the wrath has passed,
And this bare island, the tide and ebb, the sky
Polished and chased by streamers of the wind,

Rainbows, auroras, solar haloes dim
And clouds like the armadas of my dream
Remain, and I in this place content to be
As harsh necessity decides, the will of God
To that end he alone directs and sees.
Until his time and storm revolve new fate
A lee of stone I'll have, shellfish my food
And sea-birds' eggs and crackling tops of weed,
And fire begin from branch and rock and breath;
Nor rail against the maelstrom and the blaze
His anger raised against my voyaging
Nor loss of ship, and goods, and worldly course,
His cause in all things being ever best
And seen in truth when bitterness has ceased.

So may God bless this meditation and poem.
I made it to intercede at his murmur and blame,
And I pray he may gaze upon it in the endless doom.

Stanzas of the Jeopardy

It may be at midday, limousines in cities, the groaning
Derrick and hissing hawser alive at dockyards,
Liners crawling with heat-baked decks, their élite
Drinking languid above the hounded turbines,
Doorways and crossroads thronged with a hundred rendezvous,
Places low over spire and cupola with screaming
Jet-streams or soaring inaudible in disembodied calm,
Plough-teams on headlands in the sweat of noon, the warm
Earth up-ruffled swarming for crow and gull,
Boys whistling and calling at play in the sea-caves,
Cables humming, telephonists sighing, sirens
Wailing twelve from workshop and factory, tar
Bubbling in the skin of the street, shopfronts shimmering,
In Times Square, Leicester Square, Red Square – that the roar, the labour,
The onset and the heat, the engine and the flurry and the errand,
The plane and the phone and the plough and the farm, the farmer
And the stoker and the airman and the docker and the shopper and the boy
Shall all be called to a halt:
In the middle of the day, and in the twinkling of an eye.

24

It could be at midnight, braziers smouldering on wharves,
Watchmen dozing by the tar-boiler's hulk, warehouses
Planted gloomily in bloodless night-idleness,
Desolate siding and shed and circuit littered
With the truck and trash marooned by ebbing daytime,
Astronomers at their mirrors in zodiacal quiet, dancers
Swept through the rosy fantasy of muted waltzes,
Children speaking to the wind and stars in dream,
Great lakes of darkness mountain-locked and moonless
Breaking to the meagre splash of angler's oar,
Badger and hedgehog rooting among the beech-mast, gardens
Swirling with scents disessenced by the dawn,
Lovers lying in the dunes of summer, swimmers
Flashing like sudden fire in the bay – that the play,
The sleep and the pleasure, the tryst, the glow, the tranquillity,
The water and the silence, the fragrance, the vigil and the kiss,
The fishermen and the slumberers and the whisperers and the
    creatures of the wood
Shall craze to an intolerable blast
And hear at midnight the very end of the world.

'Shall the trumpet sound before the suns have cooled?
Shall there not be portents of blood, sea-beds laid bare,
Concrete and girder like matchwood in earthquake and whirlwind?
Shall we not see the angels, or the creeping icecap, or the moon
Falling, or the wandering star, feel veins boiling
Or fingers freezing or the wind thickening with wings?'
The earth may spin beyond apocalypse;
Long before entropy the worlds may stop.
The heart praises its own intentions, while the moment,
The neighbour, the need, the face of love and the tears
Have passed unseized, as some day they will pass
Beyond all action, beyond despair and redemption,
When matter has uttered its last sound, when the eye
That roved around the universe goes blind, when lips
To lips are numb, when space is rolled away
And time is torn from its rings, and the door of life
Flies open on unimaginable things –
At noon, at midnight, or at no time,
As you receive these verses, O Corinthians.

'What waves have beaten...'

What waves have beaten on the glass
Through darkness rolling such dazed foam
As now where light should bravely pass
Blinds the eye of this white room?

The moon drew up a sea of frost;
The stars in blackness sparkled back
From crystal characters embossed
While midnight drove the polar rack.

An iris and a rose of ice,
A wren picked out in diamond rime
I read in this minute device
Which gladdens the calm morning-time,

And as I gaze, I wish the sun
Would be this day so cool and wan
That not one claw or vein might run
From beauty rarely feasted on.

A Warning of Waters at Evening

What river-growl appals my flesh?
Night shakes the hounded streams with fear.
What waters roaring plunge, burst, crash
This chafed and shuddering weir?

Fog has hulled the fruited oak
Whose leaves and galls fly in the foam;
Twigs scatter like a starling-flock
Down to their howling home.

Dense as hidden Eden's cloud,
Black as the ravished mine of gold,
Such air refells the dancing blood
Back to blindness and cold.

I see neither tree nor wave;
The dark is full of tongues that bay
Their breathing and invisible drove
Along the glades of prey.

The hunt is neither pack nor fox.
The kill is in the seething firth.
I hear the bell upon the rocks
Where the sea fills the earth:

Swinging in the booming main,
Streaming with the tears of hail,
Singing like the all-damned man
That cries through fire's vale.

What sparkling mountain-spring was there?
The birth of snow and sun is ended.
All feeds the welter of the shore,
To rain-dark gulf descended.

I fear that tempest and that night,
I fear this river at my feet.
I fear the bitter salt far out
Where sin and wrath must meet.

The Sleights of Darkness

One nightmare after cinderfall
Idiocy in a slumber took me aside
To see my friend in his golden fell
Stumble at the handle of fiends'-hovel
By the feral riverside.

Blown like a quill to that fell lintel
He fumbled with bolts to mingle loneliness
With the waiting loneliness till little by little
Meeting by his fever the lascivious toll
He should feel fiend-homeliness.

And yet if all flesh was standing
As thick as smoke from wall to wall
And if love like gold was seen ascending
Through the valley of the blood and the understanding
What would suffice of it all

To my friend in his fleshly desolation?
Misery strides along my daydream
Whenever I re-unlatch his destruction.
His face at the fiends' sill is confusion,
Pale as the breaking stream.

27

Bitter vision, not of wishes!
Let me not find his heart at bay
Or laid with innocence in ashes,
Or if I must, let our lost riches
Of trust be all we must pay!

Slates flash out on the tawny gable;
Windows strain to the sinking sun;
The mavis drowses on its fable
Of the glory of day till the last feeble
Knot of its song is undone.

I strain and flash and fable too,
From the valid twilight before surrender.
Against the Night that scars the true
And mocks the lonely two by two,
Now love be my defender!

The Sleights of Time

Memory and phantasmagoria of memory
Shuffling feet at the love-catafalque
    The sun falls on the choristers
Through tears who can see the chains
Through smoke the burning, through spray the waves
    Broken at the rock of the causeway? –

Brilliant assignations, preparations
For dance and satiety at the revel-table
    Lust was lifted like a torch
And rebellious shame in ruffled hair
Surrendered laughing to the bloodrace ways
    Of hallucinating touch –

Attachments and enchantments too, the avowals
In far-off firelight, dreams of arrivals
    Faithful through a thousand snows
Till the fire is scattered, till the hearth is cold
Till the winds that sweep the dancing-floor
    Freeze, freeze unliving bones –

Buried and remembered, heads in happiness
I shall never know and disinheriting
    My dead may never give:
Son unborn, never to be born,
Wail at the back of time unknown
    With longing till longing is life!

Sleight-of-Morals

A death in the ditch of libertinism!
The last ditch is the last discipline.
The wounded ganymede glows like Gabriel,
Wolves have fetches that are unferal;
Put your sickness to mystic school.

I saw Traherne on a chestnut branch
Watching the woodsmoke wind and vanish
From the stamped-out fire, the friends had departed.
He spread his hands on the finger-patterned
Chestnut sprays, the candours were partnered.

Eckhart by the dying well
Spoke of divining and festival.
'Dig deep to find the dragon's food
In a shaft like flesh to a source like blood
– From the centre how far the stars have soared!'

They row in the bay, they linger in forests,
They know of the tempests, they think of the frosts.
Love is water and betrayal is bread,
The prison's walls are as vast as the world,
The sentence is life, let the walls be rolled.

Trundled before the cold juries
Hearts are crimes to heart-abjurers.
May judge and witness sweeten on the apple,
See through the braille of good and evil,
And put their sapience to mystic school.

Harrowing Heaven, 1924

Tell the archangels in their cells of divinity
They must levitate like larks, for LENIN is coming.
Break it to the ogdoad under the bo-tree
Their parched symposiums exploding in concinnity
From unity to trinity, with a Second Coming,
Have come to poverty, lock stock and poetry.

By candle of Tolstoy he can darken consuls,
By book of Marx he judges Jonahs,
And by bell of Blok repeals your lyres.
Vain to offer him heavenly consols,
Vain the emption, incredible the bonus;
On the opium standard beggars are buyers!

Preaching to sparrows of the fall of man:
Preaching to man of the fall of a sparrow:
This he will spare you, as unmanly folly.
But Dante will be his Caliban
When the lights are named, and charity may harrow
Your hell-proof hierarchy to common melancholy.

'Drill up your multicarated streets!
Dowse your neon-and-topaz noons!
My dialectics is mesembrian and sapphirical.
For dust shall blanch the sainted seats
And instead of saints iguanodons
Shall walk on your enormous wall.

A vision of bread without theophagy,
A handful of salt in the hands of humanity,
And wine that makes but is not blood:
Naked of sacrament, stranger to effigy,
Food for the Magellans of nature's infinity:
Such is the substance of my word.'

Cherubs in ziggurats, watch for Vladímir!
When world's-dreamer is heaven's undreamer,
Saints in their chains may murmur 'redeemer'.

From the Anglo-Saxon

THE RUIN

Wonder holds these walls. Under destiny destruction
Splits castles apart. Gigantic battlements are crumbling,
Roofs sunk in ruin, riven towers fallen,
Gates and turrets lost, hoarfrost for mortar,
Rain-bastions beaten, cleft, pierced, perished,
Eaten away by time. Earth's fist and grasp
Holds mason and man, all decayed, departed.
The soil grips hard. There a hundred generations
Of the people have dwindled and gone. This wall bore well,
Moss-grey and reddened, the revolutions of kingdoms,
Stoutly withstood tempests. That great gate fell...
Magnificent rose the fortresses, the lavish swimming-halls,
The profuse and lofty glory of spires, the clangour of armies,
The drinking-halls crammed with every man's delight,
Till that was overturned by steadfast fate.
The broad walls were sundered, the plague-days came,
The brave men were rapt away by the bereaver,
Their war-ramparts razed to desolate foundations,
Their city crumbled down. The restorers lie asleep,
Armies of men in the earth. And so those halls are wastes,
The old purple stone and the tiles and wood are lying
Scattered with the smashed roofs. Death crushed that place,
Struck it flat to the hill, where once many a man
Brilliant with gold and adazzle with costliest war-trappings,
Happy, proud, and wine-flushed, glittered there in his battle-armour,
Gazed over his treasures, on the silver and the curious stones,
On the rich goods and possessions, on the preciously cut jewels,
And on this splendid city of the far-spread kingdom.
The stone courts stood then, the hot stream broke
Welling strongly through the stone, all was close and sweet
In the bright bosom of the walls, and where the baths lay
Hot at the heart of the place, that was the best of all...

THE SEAFARER

This verse is my voice, it is no fable,
I tell of my travelling, how in hardship
I have often suffered laborious days,
Endured in my breast the bitterest cares,
Explored on shipboard sorrow's abodes,
The welter and terror of the waves. There

The grim night-vigil has often found me
At the prow of the boat when gripped by the cold
It cuts and noses along the cliffs.
There my feet were fettered by frost,
With chains of zero, and the cares were whistling
Keen about my heart, and hunger within me
Had torn my sea-dazed mind apart.
The theme is strange to the happy man
Whose life on earth exults and flourishes,
How I lived out a winter of wretchedness
Wandering exiled on the ice-cold sea,
Bereft of my friends, harnessed in frost,
When the hail flew in showers down.
There I heard only the ocean roar,
The cold foam, or the song of the swan.
The gannet's call was all my pleasure,
Curlew's music for laughter of men,
Cries of a seagull for relish of mead.
There tempests struck the cliffs of rock,
And the frozen-feathered tern called back,
And often the eagle with glistening wings
Screamed through the spindrift: ah what prince
Could shield or comfort the heart in its need!
For he who possesses the pleasures of life
And knows scant sorrow behind town-walls
With his pride and his wine will hardly believe
How I have often had to endure
Heartbreak over the paths of the sea.
Black squalls louring: snow from the north:
World-crust rime-sealed: hail descending,
Coldest of harvests –
                                        Yet now the thoughts
Of my heart are beating to urge me on
To the salt wave-swell and tides of the deep.
Again and again the mind's desire
Summons me outward far from here
To visit the shores of nations unknown.
There is no man on earth so noble of mind,
So generous in his giving or so bound to his lord
That he will cease to know the sorrow of sea-going,
The voyages which the Lord has laid upon him.
He has no heart for the harp, or the gift of rings,
Or the delight of women, or the joy of the world,
Or for any other thing than the rolling of the waves:
He who goes on the sea longs after it for ever.

When groves bloom and castles are bright,
When meadows are smiling and the earth dances,
All these are voices for the eager mind,
Telling such hearts to set out again
Voyaging far over the ocean-stream.
With its sad call too the cuckoo beckons,
The guardian of summer singing of sorrow
Sharp in his breast. Of this the prosperous
Man knows nothing, what some must endure
On tracks of exile, travellers, far-rangers.
And now my own mind is restless within me,
My thought I send out through all the world
To the floods of ocean and the whale's kingdom,
Until it comes back yearning to me
Unfed, unquenched; the lone flier cries,
Urges my desire to the whale's way
Forward irresistibly on the breast of the sea.

And keener therefore when they strike my heart
Are the joys of the Lord than this mortality
And loan of life; it is not my faith
That the riches of the earth will be everlasting.
One of three things to every man
Must always loom over his appointed day:
Sickness, old age, or enemy's sword
Shall drive out life from the doomed man departing.
And then it is best that those who come after
And speak of the dead should be able to praise him,
That he in this world before his end
Should help the people with deeds of courage
Against the malice of foes and the devil,
So that afterwards the children of men
Will exalt his name, and his praise with angels
Will remain for ever, everliving glory,
Bliss among the hosts. Great days have gone,
Pomp and magnificence from the world's dominions.
Now there are neither kings nor emperors
Nor gold-givers such as once there were
When in their realms they dealt with the utmost
Honour, and lived in the nobility of fame.
Fallen is all this chivalry, their joys have departed.
And the world is wielded by shadows of men
Ruling under affliction. Oh glory brought low,
Splendour of this earth grown withered and old
Like man himself now through all the world!
See age come up to him, and his face go pale,
A grey head in grief recalling friends gone,

The children of men given back to the earth.
Nor can body of flesh when life has fled
Taste for him any sweetness or be sensible of sorrow,
Nor will hand have touch, nor the mind its thought.
And though he should strew the grave with gold
Where his own brother lies, with numberless treasures
In a double burial, none will go with him
On that voyage, nor can gold avail
For the soul with its sin before God's wrath
Who hoards it here while he still has breath.

Dreadful is the terror of the Creator, when the world has turned
        through time.
He established the great abyss, the leagues of the earth and the sky.
The fool has no fear of the Lord: death falls on him unwarned.
The blessed man lives in humility: on him heaven's mercies descend:
He trusts the power of his Maker in the battlements of his mind.

THE WANDERER

The solitary man lives still in hope
Of his Maker's mercy, though with anxious mind
Over the ocean-roads he has long to go,
Rowing in his boat on the rime-cold sea,
Voyaging out his exile while fate is fulfilled.

The words of the wanderer recalling hardships,
Savage encounters, felling of kinsmen:
'In the doom of loneliness dawn after dawn
I lament my cares; there is none now alive
To whom I might dare reveal in their clearness
The thoughts of my heart. It is true I know
That the custom shows most excellent in a man
To lock and bind up all his mind,
His thought his treasure, let him think what he will.
Nor can the wearied work against fate,
Nor painful remembrance have present aid;
Those after glory must often hide
A dark thought deep in their mind.
So I in my grief gone from my homeland
Far from my kinsmen have often to fetter
The images of the heart in iron chains,
For now it is long since the night of the earth
Lay over my lord and I then forlorn
Wintered with sorrow on freezing seas,

34

Seeking in sadness some gold-giver's dwelling,
If only I could find whether far or near
One to show favour to me in the mead-hall,
One to give solace to me friendless,
To treat me with kindness. He who has felt it
Knows how care is a cruel companion
To the man deprived of his dear protectors:
Wandering is his, not winding gold,
A breast of grieving, not world's glory.
He remembers the retainers at the giving of treasures,
And how he in his youth was feasted and pleasured
By his friend and lord; that joy quite gone!
This is his suffering who has so long missed
The counselling voice of his cherished prince,
When sorrow and daydream often together
Seize the unhappy man in his solitude:
It all comes back, he embraces and kisses
The lord he is loyal to, lays on his knee
Hands and head as he did long ago
When he knew the triumphs and treasures of the throne.
Then the unfriended man wakens again,
Watches in front of him waves of grey,
Sea-birds swimming and flashing their wings,
Snow falling, hoarfrost thickened with hail.
Then the heart's wounds are the more harrowing,
Graver is his longing for that loved man.
Grief is revived when the vision of kinsmen
Gathers in his mind and he greets them with joy
And eagerly searches the dear faces;
But fighters and retainers float off and dissolve,
And the mind receives from these seafarers
Scant song of speech; care comes again
To him who must send his ceaseless heart
In its weariness over the frozen waves.

There is no cause indeed in all the world
Why my thoughts here should not grow dark,
When I ruminate the life of noble men,
How they suddenly left the halls in death,
Warriors in their pride. And so this earth
From day to day declines and decays,
Nor is any man wise before his due
Of worldly years. Wisdom is patience:
To be neither too temperless nor too sharp of tongue,
Nor too feeble in fight nor too heart-heedless,
Nor too deep in fear, in pride or in greed,
Nor ever boastful of things unknown.

35

A man should be wary in uttering his vows
Till he stands proud in sure knowledge
Of where thought and mind are ready to bend.
The wise man perceives how terrible is the time
When all the wealth of the world lies waste,
As now scattered throughout this earth
Walls are standing where winds howl round
And hoarfrost hangs, in crumbling courts.
Wine-halls are sinking, kings are at rest
Bereft of joy, all the flower of men
Has fallen by those walls. War took some,
Bore them from the world; one the winged ship
Drove over the deep; one the grey wolf
Gave to death; and one sad-faced
A man buried in a cave of the earth.
So the Maker of men laid waste this globe,
Till those old cities, the labour of titans,
Stood in their desolation silent after revelry.

He then who ponders wisely in his mind
And goes over this life in its darkness and its origins
With insight of heart recalls the carnage
Of far-off myriads and speaks these words:
"Where has the horse gone? the rider? the treasure-giver?
The halls of feasting? Where are man's joys?
The dazzling goblets! The dazzling warriors!
The splendour of the prince! Ah, how that time
Has gone, has darkened under the shadow of night
As if it had never been! Now in the place
Of that beloved chivalry a wall is standing
Marvellous in height, sculptured with serpents.
The men have been seized by the strength of spears,
By death-hungry weapons, illustrious destiny,
While tempests beat on this steep stone,
The blizzard falling binds the ground,
The terror of winter roaring in darkness
When the night-storm blackens and sends from the north
Fierce hail-showers in malice to men.
All the kingdom of the world is in labour,
Earth under heaven revolves through its cycle.
Here riches will pass, here friends will pass,
Here man will pass, here woman will pass,
And the whole foundation come to dissolution."'

So spoke the wise man in his mind, sitting in meditation by himself.
Good is the man who holds faith: he must never too readily tell
The grief he has in his heart, unless he has solace before him

In the daring a man may win. Blessed is he who implores
His grace and comfort from heaven, where the dooms of us all are
   shored.

FOUR RIDDLES

Swallows

Borne over the braesides,
A tiny folk, a swarthy folk,
Through the air in their black coats,
Gladly-singing companies
Calling loudly through the groves
Or in the houses where they go
Of the sons of men –
Name you them!

Swan

My garment sweeps the world in silence,
Whether indoors or troubling the waters.
Watch me taken over human houses
By my armour-trappings and by soaring airs:
See how the power of the clouds carries me
Far and wide above men. My adornments
Loudly and melodiously sound and resound,
Sing bright and clear, when I rise from my rest,
A spirit moving over field and flood.

Bookworm

A meal of words made by a moth
Seemed to me when I heard the tale
Curious and phenomenal:
That such a mite like a thief in the night
Should swallow up the song of a poet,
The splendid discourse and its solid setting!
But the strange robber was none the wiser
For all those words and all that eating.

Sometimes my master miserably binds me,
Sends me under the vast swell
Of the flourishing fields and forces me to be still,
Drives down my strength supine into darkness,
Furiously into a den where the earth presses
Crouching on my back. From that monstrous place
No way of turning I know but to trouble
And stir the home of man: Heorots
Rock, dwelling-houses, walls tremble
Terrible above hall-counsellors. Tranquil they seem,
Sky over landscape, sea in its silence
Till I drive upward, rise from my prison,
In the hand of him who guides me, who gave me
In the beginning my bonds and fetters, bound me
Never to bend but the way he beckons!

Sometimes from above I shake the waves,
Wreathe the ocean-stream, throw to the shore
The flint-grey flood: foam's in the fight
Of wave against sea-wall: mountainous above the main
It looms in darkness, and black on its track
Its neighbour travels in the water-tumult
Till they clash breaking at the brink of land,
At the soaring bluffs. There the ship seethes
Through the sailors' clamour, the steep rock-falls
Quietly stand for the sea's assailing,
For the crash in the stone-split when crested mass
Crowds to crush cliffs. There over the boat
A hard strife hangs if the sea should seize it
With its freight of souls in fearful hour,
Torn if it should be from course and command
Riding foam-white with its life outfought
On the back of the waves. Unblest, awesome,
Manifest to men, each terror I unwrap
Adamant in my wayfaring, and for whom will it be still?

Sometimes I career through what clings to my back,
The black wave-pourers, press far apart
The sea-feeding cloud-brims and suddenly let them
Slap again together: it is the king of sounds
Bursting above cities, boldest of crashes
When cloud on cloud edge to edge
Cracks dark and sharp. Creatures of blackness
Scurrying in the sky shower down fire,
Fire-pallor, fire-flare, with tremors roll on

Dull, din-resonant above the distraught,
All battle forward, letting fall
Rustling from their breast wet mist and gloom,
Rain from their womb. The dreaded arm
Advances in its feud, fear arises,
A great anxiousness among mankind,
All places are appalled, when the quicksilver phantom
Shoots in flashes with his sharpest weapons.
The fool fears nothing of those mortal spears,
But the fool lies dead if the living God
Lets an arrow fly to him from the far whirlwind
Right to his heart, through the falling rain
A falling bolt. Few remain
Whom lightning pins at weapon's point.

I establish that strife in its origins
When I go out among the cloud-congress
Forcing through its press with my vast host
On the bosom of the stream – the lofty war-thong
Breaks into great sound. Then again I bow
Low down to land in the hollow of the air
And load on my back what I have to bear,
Admonished in the majesty of my own master.
So I act and battle, a servant but glorious,
Now beneath the earth, now beneath the waves
Sunk in humility, now over the main
Rousing the ocean-streams, now risen up
Flinging the sky-wrack far and wide
In my vigour and race. Say what is my name,
Or who shall raise me when I cannot rest,
Or who shall support me when I must be still.

From the Early Middle English

THE GRAVE

Your dwelling was doomed   before you were born,
Your ground was in mind   from your mother's womb,
But it was not prepared   or its depth measured
Or the length considered   that your body would need.
Now you are borne   where for ever you will remain,
Now you must be measured   and your earth after.
Not at all proudly   is your house established,

For the ceiling is mean   and the walls are low,
A low place and mean   for a man to lie in,
And your breast will be cramped   by that roof of loam:
In the ground for ever   cold will be your home.

In dimness, in darkness   that lair rots on,
Doorless is that dwelling   and it is black within;
There you are closed fast   and death has the key.
That earth-home is loathsome   and dreadful to dwell in,
But there you must be   while the worms divide you.
There you must be laid,   a horror to your lovers;
No friend you have   will visit you there,
Will ever look to see   if your dwelling delights you,
Will ever lay open   that door for you again...
For soon you are hateful   and ghastly to gaze on,
Soon all your head   is bereft of its hair,
The fairness of your hair   is suddenly shed,
When no fingers on earth   will caress the dead.

The Vision of Cathkin Braes
1952

The Vision of Cathkin Braes

It was evening and June as I strayed in the red red rays
Of the lingering sun with my love on Cathkin Braes.
Rosy and warm in the gloaming lay those fields
Where love on summer nights his sweetness yields;
The drowsy mavis burbled from her bush,
The bats were hunting in the purple hush,
And rabbits popped from every tuft of grass.
We wandered, my honey and I, as far as we could pass
Into the trees and thickets eerie and dim,
And there in a green green glade we sat us down
And watched till the sinking sun was dwindled and done.
Then in that twilight fastness as we turned to kiss
Suddenly we heard a whistle and a hiss,
A high and rambling shriek, and then a voice
That split the happy stillness of that place
With wheezy cachinnations ancient and hoarse:
'I'll learn ye, little foxcubs, foxgloves, I'll nuzzle ye,
Sweet tongue-tip-kissers, lip-adepts, I'll muzzle ye,
How like ye this?' – And through the startled glade
A three-legged stool went hurtling past my head.
And now we saw, among the crowding trees,
Glowering at us across the open space
Of that green glade, limned in the pale moonlight,
Gaunt JENNY GEDDES, the minister's delight.
A pea-green mutch she wore, wellington boots,
A paisley shawl with painted buds and fruits,
And in her hand she clasped the Holy Book.
My love had terror of her holy look,
But Jenny, frowning, passed our shadowed nook,
And vanished like a time-expirèd spook.
Still there were whispers in that forest-house
Like wind through keyholes when the ghosts carouse,
And soon we saw a monstrous ruddy bull,
Sweating and snorting but truly beautiful,
A beast of most magnificent furniture
And lacking in no point of armature.
Upon his heaving back there sat a poet
(His eye was rolling, that is how I know it)
With one hand on the left horn firmly fixed,
One on a song-book with lusty pictures mixed,
And as the bull came on, we heard him sigh
(And would have beat his breast, but no hand free):
'Alas, O fortunate lovers, I am McGONAGALL,
And to you maybe a figure somewhat comical,
But as you see here I am riding a dangerous beast

43

With two horns, innumerable teeth, internal combustion, and a wild
    tail, to say the least.'
This poet fetched a sigh of such profundity
From his store of that wither-wringing commodity
That the grim rufous noble makariferous bull
Started out of his dream of the beautiful
And bore his weeping rider into the wood.

Then followed fast and in the clearing stood
A coalblack horse whose mane was hung with bells;
His hoofs were painted scarlet, and foumarts' fells
With the striped whittrick caparisoned his back;
His rider wore a huge and coalblack sack,
Red cowl and girdle, and socks with scarlet clocks,
And when he spoke, we knew it was JOHN KNOX.
'Woe, woe unto ye, Jezebel and your minion,
Think ye to hide among the true congregation?
I see ye clipping and plotting there in the dark,
But be assured I will come roaring upon that wark
And smite ye utterly within your tabernacle.'
And so he gave his bridle-bells a jangle,
Spurred on that sooty horse, and with anathemas
Careered away to prick the infamous.

But what was that soft fragrance breathing up
To fill the glade with musk and buttercup?
What was that faint and tingling melody
With which some voice so low made harmony
That almost an aeolian lyre it seemed
Or else the wind among the branches dreamed?
A heavenly vision then came through the trees
In peach-blush satin clad from breast to knees;
Her white white throat and shoulders floated on
Like some fair bird, and like the halcyon
Her eyes and teeth would flash in that grey glade.
The rippling satin answered each move she made,
And as she moved she plucked a mandoline
And sang all huskily, so sweet and so serene
That my dear love was jealous for her skill
And slew her on the spot, if looks could kill.
Who has not heard of LAUREN BACALL'S grace?
But I have looked upon her face to face.
Most fervently she sang: 'Come live with me
And be my love, and make my morning tea,
And we may all the silken pleasures prove
Of bearskin rugs, bear-hugs, and bunny-love.'

So sang that mouth which like a red red rose
Swayed in the dusk; and passed – where no man knows.

Behind her came another lovely lady,
Not Lauren named, but plainly gentle MARY,
And she with slow sad steps passed into view,
Smiling through tears; from her fair shoulders grew
Two subtle wings of grospoint Flanders lace,
But all the attire she carried with such grace
Was one starched tent-stitched straight-sleeved Scottish shroud,
And QUEEN OF SCOTS she was, though nothing proud.
She had a little lamb, and where she went
This lamb would always go, with great content,
Led by a cord of carbuncles and pure chrysoprase,
A blue bow round his neck, and living sprays
Of juniper tied to his gentle fleece.
He was a lucky lamb, and lived in ease.
But Mary knew no ease or luck at all,
And she complained thus, standing white and tall,
With low clear voice: 'O sisters have I none,
Yet that one's father was my grandfather's son.
If you should love, to Italy you go,
Scotland will blast the rose with knocks and snow.'
Almost we wept, so piteous was her plaint,
But on she walked, the lamb a smiling saint.

With that a horrible shout rang through the wood
And laughter fit to curdle milky blood,
With tolling of a deep and hollow bell
Like cattle at the bottom of a well,
And brazen clangings as of dungeon-chains
And gabble of choughs and rooks, and heavy strains
Of harping swimming slowly through the air.
And then we saw the venerable hair
Tonsured about a priestly polished dome,
The red red face, like sun at harvesthome,
The coarse and hairy rope-tied godly gown,
The sandals, topee, and double-barrelled gun
Of great and glorious ST MUNGO PARK,
Whose bird and fish became a Noah's ark.
(This holy man explored the jungle and coast
Where fishes flew, birds swam, bells grew, but most
Important of all, trees rang with balls and chains,
And these he brought and planted on our plains,
Called then Bar-Linnet, Wormwood-Shrubs, Garden-Evil,
And cages for the birds that never sing.)
He had a lion on an iron ring

Which never roared, and a vast key he bore
Which never opened any mortal door.
A flask he carried, with red-biddy filled
And as he harped he hazily quadrilled
Between the trees, laughing to burst his face,
Startling his cage of birds, his lion, and his page
Who struggled to bear his leaden bell behind,
And roaring this most anciently designed
Rank drunken mongering of crambo-clink:
'O it gars me greet when Glasgow . drouthy is of drink
After adventures in Africa . I pine for a pint
Lusty lovers if ye be at all . I call ye unkind
If ye blow me not a bawbee . for a half and a half
Glasgow to go round and round . I stir it with my staff
On Saturday at the Saltmarket . or at bloody Brigton
You may behold it belongs all . to me Mungo Bigtoun.'
There was a pocket in his harp for alms,
And so I gave him sixpence, and from harms
And bans, alarms and ruins, he blessed us free
And stumbled on with his strange minstrelsy.

Upon the instant when these clamours faded
Thick heavy stillness all that glade invaded
And in the silence silently appeared
A dancer for all solemnities prepared.
She was but veiled in an eye-teasing stuff
Shot like the rainbow it seemed fashioned of,
Her hair like smoke lay curled within a net
Of twisted gold, a glittering carkanet
That might have graced the daughter of a queen.
Fair, fair she was, and with her gauntlets green
And creamy thigh and quick feet made her fame
In divers lands; SALOME was her name.
She bore a casserole that seemed a pie
But out there jumped a man not one foot high
And danced upon the dish, and Salome began
To dance with all her body that pavan
Which twirled the heart of Herod on its pin.
And as she danced in silence the man would sing:
'Salome, Salome, take me in your arms Salome,
Dancing is not the only debt you owe me.'
But then she said: 'Young man, you're far too spry,
It's time I snapped you back within that pie.'
Yet still he danced and sang upon the dish,
And still she danced, but granted not his wish.
'True lovers then beware,' to us he cried,
'Trust not a woman who will dance and glide

46

And move to music with a heart of stone;
Now all my dancing and my love are gone.'
And so she took her veils beyond that wood
And left us pondering on her womanhood.

But last of all there came a proper man
Huge as a cloud, and leading by the hand
A little girl of perhaps five years old
Who snuffled like a spaniel with the cold.
Plus-fours with silver buckles this man wore,
White woolly stockings, gaiters on the lower
Reaches of his oaklike limbs, a funeral hat
Unbrushed for five long winters, and a spat
Upon his right boot, but the left was bare,
All bright and glittering in the smokeless air.
His grand and ceaseless mutter filled the glade
Like rolling becks and rills, and ever made
The snivelling child to weep within that shade.
But when he spoke in language used by men
The maid was dumb, the very woods again
Returned to their first stillness, and the moon
Shone on his face like butter on a spoon.
'Dear girl,' he said, 'fear not the forest grim,
For WORDSWORTH fears it not, and thou with him
Dost wander through the mystery of things
That to the innocent heart such solace brings
As the last drenchings of the evening sun,
The ragged peaks suffused, which slowly run
Glimmering along the reaches of the lake
In waves of that illuminated Form
Whose voice rolls through all things, all storm,
All stillness, all woods and waters, rills and ghylls,
All bodies, and all the everlasting hills
And always wanders on and on and on...'
Such was the poet's consolat=i=on
That that small child to sleep had almost gone,
But soon he shook her, and they travelled on.

We thought at last love's silence overbore
That glade, and turned to ruminate love's lore;
My love no tender kisses then forbore:
But lo! the glade became a dancing-floor,
For two by two these spirits hand in hand
Came back to dance a solemn saraband.
LAUREN and MUNGO with mandoline and harp
Leaned to a tree, and made those clear and sharp
Sweet honey tones which slowly round resounded,

47

For stately measured revelry intended.
And there was JENNY, steady in her boots,
Cocking her ear for Presbyterian flutes
But hearing only that grave melodiousness
So warming her heart to meritoriousness
That she to WORDSWORTH curtsied with due grace,
And he (though erring) thought it no disgrace
To dance with Jenny in that haunted place
(The child he had disposed of in the wood).
And next, in flower of her maidenhood
SALOME through the intricate figures swayed
Of that most dreamlike dance, and with her led
Stout KNOX down from his high black horse descended
And dancing as if those strains in heaven ended.
His partner he handled as if at the confession
Of ladies in his chamber and the ministration
Of private and unparalleled absolution;
His eyes half-closed, no doubt on heavenly vision.
What need to say how sleek Salome danced?
John in her moving veils she held entranced.
Then in that serious and majestic round
The grieving QUEEN OF SCOTS well blessed the ground
With her light foot and shroud of linen fine
And little merry lamb which danced to time.
Whether to laugh or weep she was not sure
So clearly rang that music solemn and pure,
And with the gaunt McGONAGALL she joined
As if she there fraternal spirit had found.
He gave not up his book of verse for that
But yet he danced, his arms stretched like a bat,
One on the book, and one on that pale queen.
Such dancing on this earth is seldom seen.

But now the music was winding to its close,
The dancers slowly and more slowly froze
And in the plagal cadence took their repose.
We heard a sleepy crowing from the farms,
That sound by which the roving spectre arms
And girds himself against his hellish return,
And the first faint grey light we could discern
Misting the cold stiff bush and distant trees;
The haunting of the night must surely cease.
And then as we shivered in the gathering dawn
And rose to go down among the houses of men
And stirring dewy fields, these shapes we lost,
Turned as might seem to oak-bole deep-embossed,
To shrub and grass and crumbling lichened stone,

Vanished, to leave us wondering there alone.
And the last we saw of these blithe spirits was
The horse of KNOX nosing the hoary grass,
While MUNGO took fair LAUREN on his knee,
And BLOODY MARY sang Abide with me.

A Courtly Overture

Most wintry reel,
My frozen court,
Hoarfrosted floor
Of the gay, my flora,
My pick of dancers,
Dancers of my humour,
Humour of ice,
Till the viols are still
Dance with me, dance.

Sway on so,
Dancer of glass
In the arms of glass,
Mad but no nearer,
Cold in unchastity
Still. The violcry
Lashes the crystal
Of your back as it turns
And gleams turning
In these arms of ice.
Dance with me, dance.

Stark the orchestra,
Steely the strings,
Distant the castanet
In a dark hand,
Darkest the hands
That trouble the troubler
The drum. Coast,
Dancers with skill
The drumberg boom.
Glass are the ships,
The fools are glass.
If fools on this floor
Spacious and specious
Gamble foundering

In musical hurricanes
Dance with me, dance –

On into silence,
Gaveston, silence,
Gaveston, Gaveston.
(I hear in the wake
The wail of viols
When we die to the storm
And away from the fools
Sway in our harmony
Harbourward to calm.)
Flash in these courts, and
Glide from these ports, and
Dance with me, dance.

Ingram Lake, or, *Five Acts on the House*

(Five contemporary dramatists find themselves in the same company at a literary stag party. They are persuaded to engage in a play-making game, each being responsible for one act and each being required to carry on from whatever situation his predecessor has left him. As the dramatists wore masks during this procedure at the festivity, their names have correspondingly, though not opaquely, been masked in this transcription.)

ACT I
WILLIAM TENNISSIPPI

Gentleman, the tragedy of Ingram Lake,
A modern tragedy, and a lesson for us all;
Man in the city, man in this century;
Actuality, and the need of pity:
At forty-two half self-confessed
Of dying dream and growing ignominy,
Hack of the pulps, horror, detective,
Scientifiction, a writer and a soak,
A Scott Fitzgerald without the genius;
A lean man, dark, a kind of Cassius
But with scant danger except to himself.
Jane is his wife, once handsome, now
Sagging, inert, colourless, and hated;
Fay their daughter, sharp-witted, twenty;

And at eighteen Rod the callow son
Wonders whether it is good to be born.
– All this the opening act must show
When the curtain rises on their sordid kitchen.
And let Fay have a boy-friend, and come back late
To be nagged by her mother for her corduroy lover
Who has read his Proust and is thought to be queer.
To fan the quarrel to rumpus heat
Let the father roar and knock at the door
With bottle in jacket and necktie flying
And nag at his wife for nagging the child
Who as Jane well knows can take care of herself
And hell, this Francis is only nineteen
And has good brown eyes and maybe some day
Will write a novel like Proust's – Or Lake's?
Pat comes the snap psychology in a sneer
As his wife interrupts the rambling apologia,
And the veins on Ingram's neck throb up
And he stumbles closer to the greasy table
With the city liquor fire in his eyes
But the home trembling in his frame and hands –
Fuddles, and sits, and drops his head
Wearily on the tabletop, among the crumbs
And the meagre chaos of cutlery and crockery…

ACT II
EARL SAUTERNE TOTTLE

But the end of one act is only the beginning
Of another act, and action is endless.
After this girl has murdered her mother
(A girl of twenty, with her life before her)
She begins to learn there is something more
Than the time behind her and the time before.
Grilled beneath the pitiless lights,
Sitting in the courtroom, in the prison cell
And in the condemned cell, and on her way to the chair
(The last chair of all, the electric chair)
She hears the voices, she hears the frou-frou,
She hears the footfalls of the Zombies.
They twitch in the alcoves, they pour libations,
They mutter to the judge, but they mutter more
To the girl whose deed has made her fey
And Fay indeed: for penance makes whole.
– Now watch Ingram, old before his time,
(But when is one's time? Time is endless),
Maudlin over bourbons for his Jane and his daughter

51

And in bursts of sobriety praying for his daughter
But not for the wife who bore him that daughter.
This second part of the second act
Visiting the sins of the daughter on the father
Will show in a cycle of recollections
The origin of his ruin and the mainspring of his humility.
The stranger he speaks to in Lazzetti's bar
Is Joe his college friend long forgotten;
And a music shop as he passes plays
A record of – how many years ago?
Till he stands again on the sunny campus
And hears the laughter and the ribaldry and the song
And sees through a mist the pages of books
And the pages that waited for his pen in vain
(This part is really quite sentimental).
And always and anywhere, in the bar, in the street,
Or when speaking to his son in their sordid kitchen,
Or awake in bed as the neons flicker,
Between the telephone and the rap on the door,
Alert in his chair or flat on the floor,
Faculty-free or lurching in liquor
He hears the sound of the wood-axe, crmp,
Thbdt, no more than that, as Jane
Becomes time past and perhaps time future –
But at anyrate is taken off his hands.
There is more of horror than there is of sorrow.
The end was happy, but the means was mortifying.
And so let us leave him looking for humility,
Sitting in thought at his greasy table,
Writing a letter to California....

ACT III
SOÛL-JEÛN PARTERRE

The mystic has arrived by interstate bus.
He carries a flaskful of desert, a folding
Bo-tree, and a spirit lamp; his hands
Are in gloves, for the sight of them disgusts him.
He has made his way to the Lakes' district
And the curtain goes up on his knock at the door.
It is answered by Rod (whom you may remember,
Though both my colleagues gave him short shrift)
And a lengthy colloquy on the state of man
Ensues as this attractive youth
Held by the eyes of Mr. Audley
(Such is the mystic's name) helps him
To unfold his bo-tree and to light his lamp.

52

Soon Mr. Audley suggests a séance
To which his father and the dead girl's Francis
Must at once be summoned. They are both got hold of,
The stage is darkened, and their sordid kitchen
Becomes the setting for supernature.
The four men sit round the greasy table
Which begins to mutter as the Zombies muttered,
Till the thin and ghastly voice of Fay
Scratches on silence like a worn-out record.
'So many people...too many people...
There are others in hell. Maybe hell is others.
Dad, now that you have asked me to come back
I will make this room grow cold, grow cold...
Wherever I come, a little hell
Is left behind, like a ticking parcel,
For my sorrowing friends. Rod, Rod,
Can you hear me, innocent baby, can you blush
Still? Have you told Dad about that hammock
We found in the cellar, and slung up, and tried
One hot June night in the darkness – have you?
And Francis, is it you, is it you my sweet?
How is Hank these days, Hank with his fur coat
Going to ball games with a bangle on his wrist?
And does Teddy sometimes visit you still?
He was so cultured, to the way he walked...
– But I fade, I leave you...Dad, remember me...'
The session is over. The dead was contacted.
Now Mr. Audley turns on the lights
And beams with expectation and benignance
On Ingram. Rod is as white as cheesecloth.
Ingram totters haggard from the table;
Hell lies about him, till he sees his son
And the shrinking Francis, and looks for the breadknife.
Mr. Audley hurriedly leaves for California.
– Ah gentlemen, this scene is excoriating.
The audience might almost *be* in hell...

ACT IV
SIMON KONSTANTPETEROFF

– But only from a bourgeois point of view.
There is nothing tragic in the act of justice.
Rod and Francis are decadent products
Of a certain time and a certain place,
And Ingram would only be asserting his rights
As father and man to remove them therefrom.
Anyhow, they escaped with a fright, and fled,

And he never saw either one again.
This fourth act now reveals the gradual
Rehabilitation of Ingram Lake.
He has nothing to lose; he has no hate left
(His daughter was obviously the victim of circumstances.)
So he gives up drink and science fiction,
And he goes to Joe who takes him in hand
(Fortunately Joe was a member of the Party)
By recommending the right Left literature
And egging him on to write Left himself.
It's a red-letter day when Joe and his wife
To clinch their approval (and to mitigate his loneliness)
Move in on Ingram with all their possessions
And plank strange baggage on that greasy table,
Strangeness of the wheel that has come full circle,
Since 'Stranger Than Truth' was the scientifictionist's
Boast, and now that fiction is replaced
By the strangeness of truth, by the Collected Works Of.
And typewriters chatter (for they all have their own)
And articles flow by night and by day –
'A Case of Victimization in Dallas,'
'How Long Shall There be a Bar in the South?'
'Strike while the Iron Drive is Hot!'
– It is the cause, it is the cause, gentlemen.
The neighbours get no sleep; it is the cause.
I shall not name it to you, gentlemen.
Ingram grows innocenter week by week,
He stands foursquare in the Study Circle,
He has got around to becoming a peg
Set squarely in the progressive whole.
And then one evening, when the meeting has dispersed
And the comrades have left with their fragrant intelligence,
Joe's wife crowns this simple story
With a question shot to Ingram by the fire,
'Have you ever tried your hand at a novel?
I have thought of a theme that is really terrific,
Symphonic – and only in one movement.'
So the fire creeps back to Ingram's eyes
As he looks in the fire and sees his book...

ACT V
FRITTER CRYSTOP

How unamenable to the statutory statistics
Are the relativities of theatrical chance!
That same very night (and remember that this
Is the final act) the house catches fire,

54

The greasy table goes up like brushwood,
Smoke countersullies that sordid kitchen,
The living escape, but the books are burned,
The books are burned, *all* the books burned.
The dispossessed are succoured by neighbours,
They live on hospitality, they scan the advertisements,
Till one day a widow with a cottage in the country
Offers to share it with two or three.
– The scene is the cottage, with its shining kitchen
And white scrubbed table, the homeless arrive,
Terms are agreed, and coffee is proffered.
'Now that my husband is dead,' says the lady,
'I intend to return to my maiden name,
Since Audley is a slight improvement on Tonks,
And people will know I have a famous brother
Who practises – well, he is in California.'
Now this strikes Ingram very forcibly
As something approaching uncommon coincidence,
But he bears no malice, and Stella Audley
Sees him as almost a distant relation
(And widows take slowly to presbyopia).
Spring and summer swing over the earth,
Joe and his wife succumb to the sunlight,
To pleasure and constitutional weather,
They groan for their doctrine and are fed on cornflakes,
They ask for the Word and are given gum;
In a month they cannot quote the paras.,
In two months the volumes, in six the Author.
They are broken reeds, they are punctured pumpkins.
Joe takes to growing runner beans,
His wife sells socks for Veterans' Benefit.
– After a year there arrives an evening
Popping with celestial visitations
And humming with the bird-sweet tangle of May
When Ingram sniffing the lilies with Stella
In their gorgeous dooryard whispers a proposal
And listens to her 'Yes' and returns her kiss
As the moon blandly rises and silently explodes
In light through the stage to the whirring curtain.

– The comedy, gentlemen, of Ingram Lake.

A Snib for the Nones

Who ever starved in solitary?
There's water, darkness, bread, silence, air.
What is this story of 'No pity'!
Does taking silk involve speaking silk,
Acting silk, with a moiré mercy
Running at every shot from justice?

You can't read bibles, grow roses there?
What is this extraordinary
Exclamatory 'Calamity'!
You've no Harry James, no Henry James,
No matadors and no Matterhorn?
No matter; what sang when you were born!

It is the unquerulous in the
Discipline who appear born again.
They fed on patience in darkness or
On darkness in patience; on the bread
Of silence, on the bread of silence
Deep in the battery of justice.

Verses for a Christmas Card

This endyir starnacht blach and klar
As I on Cathkin-fells held fahr
A snaepuss fussball showerdown
With nezhny smirl and whirlcome rown
Upon my pollbare underlift,
And smazzled all my gays with srift:
Faroer fieldswhide frosbloom strayfling,
Froral brookrims hoartrack glassling,
Allairbelue beauheaven ablove
Avlanchbloomfondshowed brrumalljove.

O angellighthoused harbourmoon,
Glazegulfgalaxeval governoon,
Jovegal allcapellar jupiterror
And you brighdsun of venusacre,
Respour this leidyear Phoenixmas
With starphire and restorying dazz
Bejeweleavening cinderill
To liftlike pace and goodquadrille.
All men reguard, from grace our fere,
And sun on us to kind and chere.

A Song of the Petrel

(translated from the Russian of Maxim Gorky, 1868-1936)

Wind-called clouds crowd up to cover
The grey wave-waste. Wheeling between
The pride of the cloud and the press of the sea
Is the proud petrel, black-lightning-bolt.
He screams skimming the scattered surf,
He cries in the clouds climbing like an arrow,
And the bold call of the bird comes
To the cloud's ear as clear gladness.
Cry of thirst this, thirst for tempest!
A cry is in the clouds of fury's force,
Of fire in passion and trust to triumph.
Seagulls in the storm shudder to moaning,
Moan in their seafaring, and in their surfseeing
Are ready to bury sea-bottom-deep
Their terror of the tempest. The loons too mourn,
The blows of thunder burst their hearts,
Battle-pleasures of unapproachable life.
The poor fearful penguin scuttles
With his plump plumage to the rocks. Alone
The proud petrel is poised free,
Bold above the foam-pale sea.
Still lower bowed, still blacker loured,
The clouds are closing over the waves;
The waves are whistling, and their whipped crests
Mount with thought to meet the thunder;
To thunder-grumble wave-rage-groaning
Speaks in the teeth and strife of the wind;
See the wind seize in embrace of force
Its flocks of billows and rush them on the rocks
With wild spite and swing, bursting
The be-emeralded sea-mass to dust and spume!
The petrel planes, black-lightning-bolt,
And cries as he climbs to the clouds like an arrow,
And sings as he swoops on the foam of the waves.
Some spirit of blackness he as he soars:
Spirit of the storm, laughing, sobbing,
Laughing at the clouding, sobbing with rejoicing;
Spirit sensitive through that threat of thunder
To long-waiting weariness upon the waters
But waiting in will for the sure unshrouding,
The assured unshrouding and unclouding of the sun.
Winds howl to thunder's growl;
Clouds piled blazing in pyre of blue

Flock above the unfathomed sea;
The sea seizing the lightning-streaks
Quenches them plunged into its caverns,
And the javelin-images over the waves
Quiver as they vanish like vipers in fire.
The storm is breaking into full being!
There flies the fearless petrel in his pride
Through lightning and over the wave-wrath-roaring
And there like a prophet cries triumphing
'Let the tempest be unloosed to its last tide!'

The Cape of Good Hope
1955

The Cape of Good Hope

I THE CAPE

Lands end, seas are unloosed, O my leviathan
Libertinism, armoured sea-shoulderer, how you broke
Out over foam and boulder! Break, ascetic man
Like seas to cringing crag-hang home. Mainward
My freedom looks, towards everything that is nature alone,
Looks from the rotting groyne and the drainwater-rusted
Concrete sea-wall and the plucked-up entanglements and the steps
Cut for safe cliff-walking, from the peeling danger-posts
Whipped by the wind and from the callow love-graffiti
Of the gullies whipped by the tide that sheets them inhumanly,
Out past the floating fish-crate slat and the creel-fragment,
Out over the petrol-film, the oil-drift, the gull trap that
Sheets them humanly; out by the sweet islet
With a mine's horns on its shingle, out by the buoy
Which carries the metaphysical mark of shipwrecked
And burned fingers and the physical bloodmarks given
With lives that clung one lashing wartime hour –
Out from the landfall smell of law, the landmarks
Of wedding and fidelity, pylon, aerial, radar-ear,
Hangar and customs-shed, junction and terminal, the handclasp
Handclasp and kiss that stave off the shrieking whistles
As the train steams in its pit, and the streaming face
As the window darkens and dwindles; from departures
Out by the last (except the departure of death),
Out from the heart and the spirit and humanity and love
Over matter alone, and into the sea of matter
Moves out, till everything that is is nature.

Lighthouse and skerry swim in haze.
Dissolve, dissolve, havoc of the cape!
Ship, grow grey in your silken haven.
How clear and faint the cries of boys
Fishing at nightfall in that far bay –
So shrill entranced so sweet: receive
Those echoes, home and love! Dissolve
Both boy and cry from me, both home and love!

The seething undersuck draws back,
The wake hisses as the stars flash,
The inshore rollers shimmer crashless
To receding sense. The kittiwake slews.
We are out. The heart of land beats low.
Take the shipyard, twilight arms;

Bind the lovers in your beams
O lighthouse stabbing faithful as their dreams!

Vanish faithful, vanish faithless,
Hide the desultory with the deathless,
Lay the darkest ghost of breath.
Soon the squall and waterspout
Will blot all landlocked spirit out
With rain more sensual and true.
Where is the lie, the tear, the vow?
The jest, the moving, the union, where are they now?

Great Lucretian deep,
Wean my libertinism
Pillow my nescience
Cradle my revolt.
I chose the emptiness
When fullness appalled me,
I ran to the barrens
When the warrens choked me.
The rose-spray is bartered
For the spray of the sea.
The land rose withers
As the land fruit rots
But I barter autumn
For what is seasonless
As the dazzle by day
On meadows without petals
Or the phosphorescence
That glimmers like the bloom
Of majestic fruit –
The dark sea jungle
And those ever unflowering
Fields that machete and heel
Cannot disturb or cull
And yet are never still.

II MID-OCEAN

When the grey cloud-haunches crouch, when the squall, the nightloper
Snarls to the sea, and the sea-blood shudders and curdles,
And the growling and challenge burst from the throat of darkness,
How glorious the beast's-coat of the constellations
Wrinkling fierily to pounce, how splendid the fangs
Bared with lightning that splinters the dense cross-drizzle
And snaps above the shrinking troughs! Ah ferocity

Felicity of libertinism, filling a midnight battlefield
With howl and clash this side of Cassiopeia
But only waves to be wounded, and the wind to fall!
Slowly, slowly the sleeping muscles of the sea
Are taunted up, ripples of pure force, energies
Bulldozer-ponderous, vertebrate, batteried
In dynamo-rooms unspeakable, abyssal,
Sharks' courts, ship-graves, playground of devilfish –
Rolling to meet the jetlike whine of the tempest
With poundings as of the earth's giant heart.
The low black cloud strikes; bristling and hungering
Jaws lunge down to the spindrift; claws catch
Air, spume, ocean; ocean springs, unleashes
Arm and sinew and water-grip; water-claw closes
On cloud-claw, the sea tornado is born:
Vice-clasp and hiss and fury, wrestlehold of matter,
Matter against matter, swelling, forcing, dizzying,
The exulting assault descending on the unassailable,
The world armed against the nature of the world.

Fountains and manna, feed my heart.
Power, from wave and rain-cloud call
To the stirring of the blood's report,
Be gale and danger to the blood's fleet,
Sustain with storms my will.

If strength so far from tenderness
Should make me falter, give me joy
Whose anodyne is turbulence,
And let me read destruction's face,
'Life!' in a lying eye.

Cone and cinder and lagoon
Sleep in the chaos the sea keeps.
Age was unheeded, order was vain,
To sea-ash and sea-atoms gone.
Open these atoms' lips!

Dismay the gaunt encrusted wreck;
Terrify the terrifiers
Barracuda, moray of the rock;
Blow through pit and pock and crack
As stops, the subsea fires.

Power that mulls the sleet of chance,
Power that feeds the well of change,
Materiality, dark sense

Like blindness that stirs fiercely once
To make a cosmos cringe

And sleeps in nightmares all the years:
Be the element and be the seas
Where I shall find the wanderers
At their eternal barriers,
Mariners by those ways.

   Darkness
As in the beginning
Moves on the waters
And the waters move
Folding darkness
Within darkness
Oldest of music
Brother to silence.
   Dark waters,
     Rock my heart.

   Out of the darkness
A gleam, an inhuman shimmer
That is neither spirit of god
Or demon nor lantern of ship
Glides in inhuman beauty
From hold to hold of the night.
The very faintest song,
No more than a breath, of the sea
As it stirs in the dream of nature
Rises and falls in the folds
And looming walls of the light.
   Dark waters, turn
     And return, and rock my heart.

The gleam breaks to a blaze.
Sudden unclouded moonlight pours
Scintillations on a self-scintillating
Kingdom of ice, on a king iceberg
White from the white and terrible barrier
Travelling the streams to warmth and death.
Crystal and diamond and sapphire and pearl
Would be weak to flash on that dazzling flesh
That shoulders the velvet and murmuring dark.
Harder than flesh and brighter than jewels,
Mindless, meaningless but for the almost
Intolerable aspect of an incorruptible
Vanishing loveliness in the gloom of the world,

It vanishes until the end of the world
And only in words is proved incorruptible.
　　Dark waters, turn in its wake
　　And return, and rock the rock of my heart.

III   A DREAM AT THE MYSTERIOUS BARRICADES

Leonardo rose
Crushing with his fist
The created thing,
Monster of a day's
Blackhearted wisdom:
Wire and fur and gum,
A bleak head twisted
From the pithless kelt
Dying in the stream,
Sombre cave-cold wings
Smelling of bat-hate
Transylvanian
Preternatural,
The backbone gilded,
The flanks hideous
Mole-quilted, snake-patched,
Daubed alizarin,
The tail a sheaf of
Rustling beetle-shards –
He stood abhorring
The work of his hands.
Woman to man to
Androgyne, cretin,
Goitre-freak, leper
To caricature
To écorché to
Skeleton-puppet
To beast and phantom,
Lion and dragon,
Fish of the shallows,
Barbastelle, viper –
Even the monster
He made, he unmade:
Even now too near
Life, and the heart's blood,
And the hostile soul
Warm, goading, tireless
Unanatomized.
'Plunge, loneliness, plunge!

Absolute zero
By the steps I know –
Godlike, hominoid,
Feral; parasite,
Sporebag; fossil, peat,
Coal and the desert
Rock, the desert rock.
What I love, I hate;
What I make, unmake.
It is as much love
When these arms embrace,
As much creation
When I plan bronzes
Or princes' bridges
As you will find love
In the beating surf
That is spent on sand
Or generation
In the slide and cling
Of blue glacier
And cold bridal hill.
Sometimes before me
I see these dreadful
Paths, and the country;
I see volcanoes,
Battles, deluges,
Waterspouts, judgements:
Ah what fires, what cries!
Man dies, nature roars
New with matter, new
Earth and heavenless,
Nothing on Patmos
Nothing in Florence
Only the lava
The smouldering gulch
The dune with its ash
The berg with its snow.
This is my vision
For which forgive me
God or gods unknown.'
– But as the shadows
Gathered, and the room
Opened like a shell
To pain, memory
And humanity
Broke like seas crying
'O Salai, Salai!'

Once Michelangelo
Paused in the Sistine and
Brushes flew to the floor
As he grasped the scaffold
Gazing with unwilling
Terror into the eyes
Of Christ millenary
Who abhorred his power
To paint Eve harridan
And in Adam's slumber
And the faces of youths
Plant gratifications
To his eternal guilt.
Lust and suppression are
The Rose, the scent circles
The heart mantling in proof,
The cheek shines cloth-of-gold
And the shoulder, the thigh
Plunge in their rippling nets,
The groin mine groans with gold,
Meditation is choked,
Mine-shaft, granary-wall
Crack gold, strain grain-of-gold
Swelling by love's lintel
In lust's wastrel jostle,
Ore and passion to paint
On night's chapel the Thorn
That scars meditation
For ever where the Rose
Fell – where the royal scent
Became bitter as death,
Where the scaffolding shook,
Where the Judgement Eyes were
Pupilled with the Thorn, where
In ogni loco God
As prayed for came, and gazed
Into desolation,
Into a heart, into
Michelangelo: once.

Newton lost the key of peace.
At fifty and in London
He watched the swarming pavements
Rise up like atomic shot
Where he walked, the carriage-wheels
He heard roaring angry law,
The running midnight link-boys

Like comets down corridored
Arcade horrors of arcane
Space flashed as portents, and he
When he dared two steps at noon
Felt the rack of gravity
Twist him between stone and sun.
What fellowship had this mind,
And what key lay by his heart?
'The order of the stars, God
The Sonless and Ghostless force
Obedient to far fiat,
Light and darkness of God's word,
Hermetic apocalypse
And translucent paradox:
But this crystal fellowship
That held my wine of science
Shattered when I drained the wine.
The pieces lie gleaming yet,
In my lonely candlelight:
Which is no key to my heart.
– I lay last night unsleeping
With my inhumanity
My bride awake at my side,
I knew alienation
Consummated half-deranged
In faint constellationlight
That shrivelled my coverlet
My covert till I shivered
Like beast at bay and embraced
That cold last consolation.
O unhallucinated
Happy sleeping human kind!
Neither monk nor misanthrope
Has moved from this world so far
As I in cell of study
In desert of garden-close
With number and law have moved.
Before woman I loved light;
England was too cramped a home;
Rainbow, moonray travelled once
Opened to those thoroughfares
Where I found the stellar day;
Feeling, that chaos, I sold
For abstract tranquillity.
Now the straw is on my back
And dust rises from the track
And the stellar day is black

And knowledge is my burden
I stumble in my garden
I fear the roar of London.
Walking in the universe
I have lost the key of peace.'

Rapturous release! Beethoven
Shouted to the titanic oaks.
His incomprehensible joy
Like a wind that dared the whole world
To dance, and dance, and dance once more
Before its great pulse froze in space
Swept helter-skelter through the glades,
And dance of corn and dance of grass,
Dance of glitter on the river,
Dance of swallow and kingfisher,
Dance of the brier, dance of vine
Ran through his restless nerves like fire,
To dance again as melody,
Irresistible harmony;
Art, and irresistible joy.
The sixth behind him, this to come
A symphony more towering
Than lyric, but of happiness
Of happiness still uttering
Its rapt and dazing secrets in
A voice like justification –
To nature's inhuman splendour
Ceaselessly projected in its
Energies, the throbbing crater,
The gust, the tide, the breaking vine
And the breaking grain and the light
That breaks through cloud and hail, poundings,
Outbursts, processions and returns
All in the figure of a dance
It might be dedicated by
That lonely and that human hand.
– He moved from the forest, the air
Grew still, in the ebb of the heart
He gazed on mill and farm and spire.
Sweet wisps of cottage smoke, the tang
Of turnip-field, clover and rose!
The tranquil labour, the evening;
The lamplit window, children's heads
Flaxen and eager, the farmer
With his wife, the fireside table ·
Flashing from shadow as he passed!

A boy came, shouldering a scythe
And whistling, but he heard no sound,
Saw only that he could not hear,
And then that whistling mingling with
The homes of others, the soft dusk,
The unheard words exchanged, the smiles
And the love, the communion
And the simplicity of love
Unknown like the voices unheard
Flooded his patience, and he wept.

Melville smiled and closed his eyes. 'Call me
Ishmael.' Nothing but a whale would do.
He felt the teeming mental sea-log
Swirl and swim in his understanding,
Symbols perched in the humming rigging,
Fought in the tryworks, made the wake speak,
Sounded and blew through the gleaming seas.
But royal was Moby Dick, deeper
Diving than symbol or sleight of thought;
The joy of making that great heart beat
Broke to words in a moment of time
From all he had despairingly been.
Powers frustrating his own powers
Here exorcised, and his quest dissolved
In that soaring word-libertinage
Grounded gladly on a great bondage
As a passacaglia lifted in
Delight between silence and silence.
Strange freedom, stranger zest, where he dreamed
In his chair in the grey twilight hour
The whale, the chase, the immolation!
Images of solitariness
Swept like sharp winds whistling through his mind,
Driving the ship to the hunt, the hand
To the sharp harpoon, the sharpness of
Death to the hearts of drowned sea-comrades,
Till Ishmael becomes Ishmael once more,
Zabulus Zabulus as of old.
He saw the vortex and the revenge
And the ambush laid for man's valour
And man's love that is dashed bitterly
Away like tears from eyes of the soul.
He saw the singing throat choked with sea,
The too stoic brow go down, the lips
That praised their ships freeze by the ships wrecked.
Within the whirlpool, at the whale's side,

Appalling fellowship of cities,
Estranging innocence and frankness,
Inverting spirituality,
The blind malevolence of the world
Loomed like God's judgement hulk, and he moved
With all voyage-lights to that blanched hold
As a man in the guilt of joy moves
To waken destruction at its close.
– He rose, and lit the lamps; solitude
Would return, solitude would return.

Mayakovsky, the revolver, the room.
He stopped his caged pacing, he stood gazing
Desperate, proud, through the weakly barring
Window-glass that blocked him from the stirring
And sparrow-jaunty Moscow streets of spring
As the more mysterious barricades
Locked his desire from the vision of love.
Who forbids our love? And when men turn to
Men, or the sea, or phantom images
Of art, or science with its secret face
Unmoralled and terrible, or music,
Whose vaults, whose vaults burst with that pain and cost?
'When I was twenty-two the leaves were green
But not more green than these. Good April sun
Beat on this mask, sun-comrade, comrade life
Eternally invoked and revered, knock,
Break on this anger, let me see my own
Pity as a stranger at the window.
– Restless, I lit the restless fuse of class;
Scapegoat and joke of love, I turned my love
To millioned scapegoat man, communism
To the crack of the world my love, without
Communism no love, no place, no life;
To myself hard, and receiving pity
Never, pity uncourted, uncared-for,
I drove my spellbound proletariat,
Browbeat bureaucrat and technocrat, strode
With scorn on my shoulder that was satire,
Pity, tears, pride and the suppressed crying
Out to Russia and time of my good hope
For all men which was fading for myself.
I see that those who praise life most are lost,
Although their praise may keep whole worlds in faith;
This sacrifice I understand at last.
The long voyage! – home, if home can be seen
In these useless walls and table, that gun

71

Waiting to blow me perhaps to other
Seas, other beaches, other pains; or out
Simply from this frantic house, this mind. O
Sleepless reminiscence of the voyage –
Friends, for whom the millennial cities
Of my prophecy should be present lights
Astounding the desert and the icefield –
Places: Yalta's fruits, factoried Kharkov,
Skyscrapered subway-riddled Manhattan,
Brooklyn Bridge the pledge and audacity
Of a century – Lenin's catafalque
And after, my own pledge and elegy
In a bridge of poetry: poetry
From heart to heart when I am history
(But for me there is no bridge, there's no land) –
Atlantics, Hudsons, Yeniseis, Baikals! –
To Moscow and to spring.
                                    My solitude
Returns in the midst of millions, bearing
In this intolerable life its death.
Soviet, city, and friend, remember
My voice and verse, and pardon in the hope
The despair, for by the despair I spoke.'

IV   THE RETURN

O my brothers in the throat of desolation, my brothers!
Round the dead world desert-of-sea great echoes
'Never return, never return, never return!'
Break, and mingle with the moan and bluster of morning.
It is the dawn heartlonging, a valediction like a cry,
A cry like a rope thrown to matter and life by
Agony I stirred when I stirred the dead in my search.
I am tugged at sunrise as their night hands are turned
To the winds they simulate, and their vast barrier hearts
Sleep sealed as before in the cold boom of the sea.
What can appal libertinism but love? Tears fall
As white fog swirls from the pole, and icehell phantasms
Twisting in eternal blind-man's-buff call world
To world, desert-of-sea to desert-of-land
Recall, and desert to field, and the field to be filled:
They strain through the mist to speak as I strain to see them:
The flurry takes them, and only the echoes, the echoes
In everlasting paradox swing out and remain,
With here in the sleet where ships are wrecked 'Return!'
And along the ice-cliff in the sun 'Return!' and from all

Liberty, in the petrel-haunted glimmer 'Return!'
Canvas, symphony, mural, poem, and law
As searchlights swept from islands far off in life
Stab and flush the echo-wakened memory
And waken again its acknowledgement of solitude overcome
In the work: for the bitterest maker's hand moved in
Love, and in the worst loneliness or unknown
Strayed gladdening unknown thousands unborn.
The throat of desolation is silent as I turn
Through the great world of matter to my heart.

Out of this element
Vision rocks to its end.
The rocked buoys toll
Time to the swooping gull.
Shadows of land ride
Reefs that comb the tide.
The cove alive with voices
The harbour with its faces
The waving from the houses
This the heart chooses
And its time is measured
Not by the splendours
Of zodiac in sky
Or sun's hand on the sea
But in the common phases
Where a dear breast rises
In its hope-caught breath
Running to the birth
Of joy in a meeting
Or leaden in its waiting
Dulls to the counting
Of the hours retreating.
Patience I saw sent
Out of this element.

In the roar what patience?
Poor vision and pittance!
Overarching the shore
Still shall the ocean roar
And beat in the field at my feet
And seethe in the dryest street.
It rings the soaring promontories
With its deep music and sorrows;
If I go by the highest snows
I hear its profoundest voice.
It speaks in the cave, in the mine,

73

Or by quietest fireshine.
Memory makes strong
What must endure long.
The roar along the bone
Brings my heart home.
When the friend has ceased to be true,
When the hand is powerless to do
And the eye to rest, when the mind
Is sick, and the threads unwind
From its flying reel into darkness –
Command and dissolve my sickness,
Flood me with recollections
Roar of more than patience!

I stand as the walls stand
Under the light of land.
Here is the creaking dock
And the dog barks from the rock.
Cable and mast and oil
Glide to human soil.
Common and lovely is the light
That falls on human sight.
Eyes were never so bright!
Against our tears we fight
When we mount from ourselves to see
The face in its mystery,
A dreaming child's in its cot,
A fisher-boy's at his net,
A girl's wakening to desire
And the old face by the fire.
As the fire on old hands
Flickers, we understand.
As the lamp glows to the bride
The bridegroom's eyes have smiled.
As the child sleeps, we know.
And the lad with fingers and brow
Is intent like adamant
And stands as the walls stand.

I heard a voice in the camp of fear
That spoke of liberty, and sang of hope,
Liberty tragic as the sea
Until it embraces necessity,
And hope that is born when the heart turns home.
Home was the neighbour, another harbour
At another cape, an alien camp
With its own hope, sentinels, and sleep.

The voice persisted; the hope was good.
This in an old gospel was known
And the question answered, Who is my neighbour?
Impossible answer, still unfulfilled!
Tragedy is earth, is magnet, is mass,
Tragedy is ambience and lung to history,
Tragedy is hard, but harder is hope
That is sent as a voyager to rove by the stars.
Faith of humanity shall break out from tragedy.
This is the war of tragedy and charity
That these are the times for, and that now begins.

    'Riveters' choir, choristers' choir,
    The hull swells as the cathedral founders
      Hope shall not founder

    Moonbent rocket, rocket warhead,
    Houses shudder but the heavens are revealed
      And faith will anneal you

    Shockwave and flashburn, forcewave and flashforce,
    The future has flashed, O destroyers, O martyrs
      If you will have charity'

This is the love that materiality
Must learn, and this is the materiality
That love must seize to be saved from despair.
There is always one to explore the night
Of his own loneliness or the world's course.
The darkness cannot be too black,
The rigours cannot be too stark,
The stars too far, or the years too quick,
For out of casting off he wins
Arrival, and where he left his hope
Trussed in the common human chains
He journeys into the whole of verity
Beyond the reach of vanity
And hears in verity the evangel of joy
According to hope and according to the world.

The Whittrick:
a Poem in Eight Dialogues
1961 (published 1973)

The Whittrick:
a Poem in Eight Dialogues

It is Cardan...who has also fundamentally transformed mathematical science by the invention of imaginaries. Let us recall what an imaginary quantity is. The rules of algebra show that the square of any number, whether positive or negative, is a positive number: therefore, to speak of the square root of a negative number is mere absurdity. Now, Cardan deliberately commits that absurdity and begins to calculate on such 'imaginary' quantities. One would describe this as pure madness; and yet the whole development of algebra and analysis would have been impossible without that fundamental – which, of course, was, in the nineteenth century, established on solid and regular bases. It has been written that the shortest and best way between two truths of the real domain often passes through the imaginary one.

– Jacques Hadamard

> *Silence awhile. Robin, take off this head.*
> – *A Midsummer Night's Dream*

DIALOGUE I: JAMES JOYCE AND HUGH MACDIARMID

MacDiarmid

Fill yir gless, Icarus! Thae nichts'll no revert!
The warld, for aa that it's gruppen wi sair decreets
O physics, stound and steid, will preeve to you and me
Yon auld camsteerie ghaistlie place Lucretie thocht
He had exilit fae the nature o things. Nicht
Will dwine and flee and leave anither you and me
Happit in relativitie's raggit yestreen.
Let aa we were and aa we sall be ming and mell
In this ae lowe o the unfremmit hours, my freen!

Joyce

Friendly and propitious be the salutation,
Happily lachrymary the candelabra,
Thick the crepuscular phantasmagoria.
The crimson curtain swells: the night-wind's in my glass.
Its golden level tilts, and reason is a dog,
It's had its day. It bays, but now it must obey.
The wild swift wolf its brother loping in moonlight,
The white-fanged London-jack imagination, leaps
Upon the dusty curtain, slinks by the candles,
Snuffs at the crystal and laps at the fire-water.

79

Pookahauntus! Nevertiti! Brahan Boru!
A toast to the guthering shadies. Toast the host.
The elements have crossed the Alphs, and Kubla can.
– A thousand banners, a broken prince, the time-stream.
A thousand princes by the breaking stream, banners
Broken by time. Galahad sees the Golden Horde.
Boadicea shouts at Balaclava's gates.
– Well may the candle gutter! It's the wind of time
That blows into this room from beyond the great grave
Of the dead; its bugle is desolating but
Incomparable are the old caparisons.
The jinn are out of the candles, flicker-flacker
Up the walls and across the ceiling, Finn MacCool
Fifing on a bollard, Arthur at his truffle,
Diving Grendel and a gun-grey dragon. Bottles
Have jinn as well as candles, and as I uncork
This gentle johnny, watch the shadows. – How they jumped!
Something we hardly saw leaped out – animal or
Vegetable lamb or mineral spring: what sprang?
A drink to all the unknown jinn of history.
Whisky always makes me think about history.

MacDiarmid

Whiskery? D'ye ken what it was that loupit?
Yon wes a whittrick, a rictum-tictum whittrick,
Auld putty-humphie, wi an egg in its plaidie
And a jouk in its jumper. Aye, and it minds me
O a ferlie I saw langsyne, or thocht I saw
In Glesca toun.
                    It wes the Schipka Pass, the gas
Wes peeferin-pufferin in and oot, blue licht
That gied a dwaiblie warsle wi the grey grekin
O fowr o'clock i the mornin. Sheddas flauchtert
Skairlike ower the stanes. I heard an unco fuffin
But it wisna fae the gaslicht, and it wisna
Fae my ain breist; it wes a whittrick-fuffin. Hoot-
Toot and hadna my steps stummelt here on a wake,
A whittricks' wake, for yonder I saw the cratur
Ligg on a peever-scartit stane as stiff's a rake!
Maist horridable wes the caunle they had set
In the deid yin's gruntle: thon wes a tozie glim.
Aa roon aboot in their solemneezin stacher
Scampert ten jinkin hiccupin cousin-whittricks,
A queer ill-sortit sosherie o usquebaugh,
Lugubriositie, and fancy-fuddickin.

– Noo ilka bodie suddent-like stood mim and quaet,
Cried oot their name, gied a bit birl, and lauchit sair,
Aa haudin up their gless to me in my daurk neuk.
'Is it not the great Grieve that has fallen on us?'
'Weep for MacTearmid!' 'Brother, are you still a wake?'
– Rax me a gag for thae unloosome grunyies! Yet,
Sall I gie ye their names, James? Collicider, Sproopshch,
Plintskong, Zumberquib, Ragatchkle, Ibidemblem,
Waverfolla, Trnosploss, Boljugstoy, Fazmattrex:
Ten o the friskiest dustifit shennachies
This side o Ardnamurchan: and bonnie on them!

Joyce

Surely no Christian tongue – Choctaw, Chukchaw? Glescaw?

MacDiarmid

Nicht's interlingaw, dorogoy Mezzofanti!
– Ah weel, ilkyin cried oot yince mair, streetched up his gless,
And poured his whisky ower the corp fae snoot to coots.
Oot gaed the caunle. Then fae the clortit thrapple,
Eerie as a wind fae Whipperginny, there cam
A girnin and a whingein and a wee fuff-fuff,
And the deid corp began to thresh and thraw, and cry
Like its ain Frankenstein for metamorphosis,
To come wi bluid into the warld o day and pain.
I steekit my een in wonder. Wha suld command
A whittrick to be resurreckit? Wha'd commend
The resurrection, ferlie though it be? For wha
Says life disna dae richt to dee? Aa's negleckit
When ferlie and flim-flam haud the hegemonie.
– But noo the licht wes weel advanced in Schipka Pass,
And wi the bat o an ee as I blenkit oot
I caught a flisk, a gliff, a glent o – what it wes
That glentit, gliffit, fliskit: fud o the whittricks
Or mot in my ee or a mystical cantrip
O the non-Eucliderium, I dinna ken!
Naethin wes left bar gutter and cobbles, naethin
O the wake or the corp or the yammer or wan
By-ordnar thing. I saw a wee broon curlie tyke
Cockin its lug at me as I gaed slawlie hame.
– And there's a true and solemncholie spell to pit
Intil yir lairdlie novelle!

81

Joyce

                    History, like hell,
Is murky, but these flashes are never murdered,
For they explode the gloom into divine questions.
The whittrick on the wall, the whittrick in the street,
Fireball, snowfall, tsunami, lava, or nova,
A word on a palm-leaf, trumpets out of silence,
Whisky on the candle in the muzzle of a –
Whittrick in the street or a whittrick on the wall.
A mighty cuff in Zen is sermon, comment, law.
An absence turns the heart into a mighty eye.
A whittrick gives the mighty slip to history.
– All whisky is a little historical, but
This whisky is mystical. I am wide awake,
Golden, and smooth. My name is MacCool. I'm a Finn,
And I swim in the wake of Cybele. Midnight
With all its suns is dead, and the dawn is chilly.
See: the frost's keen. A wake it is. A glass to day.

MacDiarmid

Aye, the gless I pledge ye's to the great day o time
In whase enormous hairst o miseries and love
The gowden truth o things liggs like a lowe and flegs
The gods and dogmas wi its wild begaried fires.
Awake yes, for the winnock's big wi licht! The yird
Is streetched oot fair for the cock that craws through the haar,
And green for the gleg whittrick that loups by the whins.

Joyce

Auspicious to the awakened be this aubade,
Benignant our nocturnal circumcolloquy,
Sweet the top of the morning and round as the world.

DIALOGUE II: HIERONYMUS BOSCH AND JOHANN FAUST

Faust

    I sold my soul in Krakow – a strange city,
    Dark with architecture and filled (as it seemed)
    With kings and astronomers. One afternoon,

82

Peddling my elixirs by the Vistula
I watched a withdrawn man watching me – a man
Of a quite unspeakable fascination.
He came to me as I packed my trumpery,
Invited me to dine and drink at his house.
I and my boy followed him, saying little –
It was a fascination that brought silence.
He had such courtesy as might have warned me,
For who buys vagabonds with innocent wine?
But there we were; he smiling, and I drinking,
My lad asleep in a corner. What he said
Concerned the equilibrium of powers:
For much to be received, much must be given.
He called me a vessel into which great good
Might pour, if I could first be emptied and scoured.
He could reward me: what would I sacrifice?
By his face I was drugged, if not by his wine.
I lay in his shadows, his voice was a spring
Playing in coolness, the eternal promise
Fell from my lips. And at last came the foretaste.
I slept, and a dream of all earthly delights
Filled sleep: sleep was alive with delight. I woke
To a sort of death. The dream was a craving
That made me grovel and shout at his feet – shout
Till he showed me the paper starred and sprinkled
With the vow of my blood to renounce all good.
The dream I can have, 'but at the end is hell'.

Bosch

I am an old man, and you must forgive me
If I seem to wander, and yet the truth is
That truth wanders, and these wanderers may meet
At the place where even this maze has its heart,
And hear that heart beat. The drugged sip may be sweet,
But neither then nor in sleep is the soul sold
Unless you believe it sold, and act the rest.
I am not persuaded that you are unblest.

Faust

You have not been damned by a dream more real than –

83

Life? Well, there are dreams and dreams, and some men say
That I in my imagination have dreamed
What only a devil-elect could gaze on
Sane, and paint as a tale that is told! You smile?
Here is a picture, a panel, not long dry.
What do you think an old eye's dream is set on?
A peering eye, and knuckles stiff as a claw
Clasped to the gaunt brush? Clear were my reveries
But they were not of home and child, or youth, or
Woods blown through by April, here or in Krakow,
And they were not of love, they were not of love.
This is a panel of my decrepitude.
The years are crumbling, but not towards sainthood.
To connoisseurs the painting will still be good.
It is called 'God Creating the World of Hell',
And if you bring the candle nearer – careful,
It shivers in the draught there – and just look down
Into this world that I have given life to,
Tell me if I have given life to a dream,
Have I made myself see, or have I seen?
                                            Here
Are the darkening angels falling burning,
And what they fall down into is being made
Hell. It is their land and sea and fire to come.
It twists and knots and bridles and strains and swells,
Its cruel births are Etnas, tidal waves, ash
That drifts over five cratered peninsulas.
Angels twist through the ash, you see their anguish.
They drift like starfish over each ash-white shore.
They are turned into starfish, to flakes of ash,
To an ash-white hand walking the crater-floor.
A forest drifts there: the miserable bark
Is angels' backs, hacked, huddled, flayed by the winds,
And I have made one oaken face twist screaming,
It is deathless, grafted into searing marl.
Angels are deathless, pain flays them to the soul
But cannot peel the soul from its ill. – Yonder
You see the first monsters, coming up like moles,
Bluish in the twilight magma, a winged snout,
A sac with claws, a lamprey-headed beagle.
These are the angels' mates and the loves of hell.
One is already enticed, and his horror
Crouches before him; he will never leave it.
In the very midst of these creatures – polecats,
Dogfish, dogs, catfish, sea-dogs, lap-slugs, wombats –

I once had a whittrick, now painted over,
A tiny whittrick, very lithe and smiling.
No, you won't find him anywhere now, he's gone.
Yet he became the focus of this picture,
I built the turbulence round his irony,
I saw the monstrous place fixed by his bright eye.
And then my brush had covered him up as if
He had played his part only to disappear.
The painting was complete. And now fantasy
And reality, the energies of work
And the energies of imagination
Swirl in me so hauntingly, so mockingly
That I wonder, was the whittrick ever there?
Wandering figments of my seventy years
Walk these unkempt floors, pucks, kobolds, pumpkin-men
Whistle and gesture to the easels, easels
As I doze in my chair collapse, snap, go pop
Like pods of broom, my broom will swish at midnight –

Faust

Perhaps the whittrick went pop with the easel?

Bosch

Ah, you were never damned in Krakow, Johann!
Or if you were, an old man's spell has freed you.

Faust

Yours has been a different fascination.
You have shown me my fate if my fears are true,
And yet I fear it less. Images, colours,
Oils, shapes on a wooden panel – yes, cover
Its horror again, I shall not forget it –
I know that these things in a sense you have been
As well as seen, and although you deny love
All art is a sort of love, and you therefore
Are in love with strangeness and danger and dread,
And your dream may be something more than a dream
As mine may only seem.
                                    – I touch your table,
Did I touch his wine? And when tomorrow comes,
Shall I have touched your table?

                            Sleep here tonight.
The bed, poor as it is, is ready for you.
Listen to the rain, and take your candle through.
– No protests, think of the weather and the hour.
From where you lie you will still see my shadow
Flickering awhile on the wall, but nothing
Need distract you from sleep. I have a few things
To put away, and then all will be quiet
I promise you. And meanwhile, here is some wine.

DIALOGUE III: QUEEN SHAHRAZAD AND KING SHAHRIYAR

Shahriyar

Pull up the quilt. Are you so cold, my dear?
Sheets must be fresh from night to night for kings!
It is the cold moon in the lattices,
Cold points of stars, and the bars of moonlight
Scimitaring our vast undrowsy bed.
It is the night itself, the night beyond
The thousand and first night; we move in it
As if this palace room lay on the moon
And we lay watching the earth rise, strangers
Suddenly to it and to ourselves. Love,
Trust, reconciliation – is it these,
After three years of fear, that now you fear?
Lean into the deep of my heart, my dear.

Shahrazad

I lean in love. I shall be warm, my lord.
It was a new state that I trembled at.
You have banished unnatural perils
Which almost became nature; forgive me.
– I can still hear music in the distance.
It floats from your fading celebration
Of the day and the evening like a smoke,
And someone sings. The hovels of the poor
Have a little bread. The coins you gave danced
As the day burned and the gilded banners
Mingled with trumpets and smiling sultans.
The lutes were like the doves of heaven, the
Scented fountains drenched the mimosas, and

Everyone was dancing in the twilight,
You and I were dancing in the twilight,
Dancing in the half-light of the fire-flies.
I saw my happiness then in your eyes.
– And now I have used the perilous word.
Happy I am, happy I am, my lord.

Shahriyar

If you are happy, and not yet sleepy,
The time has come for another story,
But not a story of dear Shahrazad –
Tonight the listener turns teller, the
Teller's taciturn, the tables are turned.
Now, have you heard the 'Tale of the Whittrick'?

Shahrazad

Never; I do not even know what a –

Shahriyar

Good, we can begin! Once upon a time
There lived in Baghdad a youth who enjoyed
Both innocence and poverty; Amlek
Was his name, he worked for an old cobbler.
One day a girl passed by his shop, gazing
A moment curiously at the shoes –
A dark head, eyes of a gazelle, timid
Yet rather young than shy; they glanced, and loved.
In the street of the silversmiths she lived.
They met, while summer moved in dust, and breath
From the dunes drove sand against the hour-glass
That stood among the silverware to show
Time pass, and in a silver looking-glass
The girl watched Amlek turn the hour-glass. No,
She said, I must have time to think, and time
To be sure of your love. There is one thing
You must do to prove you love me: a gift
You must give me: just one thing I want, a –

Shahrazad

Whittrick? For it must come in soon –

87

Shahriyar

                                    – whittrick,
My love, and patience! But where will I find,
Said Amlek, something I have never seen
And cannot even imagine? The girl
Was silent, but she smiled, and left him there.
– Week after week Amlek wandered the land
In search of the whittrick. The streets and streams
He asked, the stars and palm-trees, to tell him,
Beggars and sages, where the whittrick hid.
The streams and streets laughed: Nearer than you think!
The palms and stars were nodding: Yes, be quick!
Sages and beggars sighed: Gone, in a blink!
He asked a blind man with a flute: he played
His flute. He asked the women at the ford:
They thumped their clothes. He asked the gate-keeper:
He unlatched the gate and let him enter.
One day he came at last to a cavern
Deep in foothills of sulphur and gypsum
And slept out of weariness in white arms
Of stone; the dead white dust was glimmering,
Shapes were stirring in waves of heat. He dreamed,
And saw in his dream a great white jinnee
With hair and beard of sulphur, and one eye.
The jinnee swelled and fumed and growled: Get from
My cave, you honorary tramp, up from
My bed, you snoring dog-eared boot-smith, out
And leave me in peace! One wish, if you leave
This cave and forget you were ever here!
And Amlek made his wish, and the jinnee
Grunted, When you wake you'll see the whittrick,
And blinked his single eye, and disappeared.
And Amlek woke up with a start, and then
As the jinnee had promised, he saw it,
The whittrick. He gazed in astonishment –

Shahrazad

I don't believe there was anything there!
I don't believe you –

Shahriyar

                    – he ran from the cave,
And back to Baghdad in triumph he came,

And at dusk in the street of silversmiths
Showed to the girl the gift she had desired.
And thus the girl was won with the whittrick.
And thus she won her Amlek, whom she loved.
And in the street of shoemakers they lived.
– This is the king's tale, and must be believed.

Shahrazad

My lord, what was the fate of the jinnee?

Shahriyar

He slept in his cave; his secret was kept.

Shahrazad

And what then was the fate of the whittrick?
Did they keep it in a box, did it live?
Was it ever living, or did Amlek
Pick it like a nugget? Did it snuffle,
Could it swim, was it given bell or lead?
Did they eat it with a knife, was it cold,
Was it rough, was it tender, was it blue?
Did she sleep with it under her pillow?
Did he make it at last into a shoe?
By your smiling I see I am not warm.
O this is a story out of Egypt
Where ibises write books, and the scribes fly –
And yet you shake your head, your fantasy
Is true? I am to guess? I cannot guess,
My lord, I lie in your arms, you wrap me
In the dark reasonless content of love.
I whisper in the moonlight like a girl.
O kiss me now. The palace is silent,
The music has ceased. What breath of jasmine
Has blown in gently by the south lattice!
The air just moves, and if the nightingale
Is there, he will sing as the jasmine stirs.
– What was it that he gave her, my lord?

Shahriyar

This.

Charlotte

Emily, what are these marks on the sill,
Like scratches? Don't go away, my dear!
I have shut the window for the rain.
I just came in to find my duster,
I knew I'd dropped it in your bedroom,
And then I saw these curious marks
Where you had left the window open.
It might have been the dog, I suppose?
Emily? Could it have been the dog?

Emily

No.

Charlotte

Well, you should know, but what was it then?
No one in this house speaks, nobody
Tells me anything – except Branwell,
And what he says I'd as soon not hear.

Emily

Never mind Branwell.

Charlotte

But I do mind,
I must mind. If I didn't, who would?
Anne sits writing, you are ironing,
While he grows stupid at the Black Bull.
At least he knows what I think of him.
I have to hold you all together,
I am responsible. He is free,
He's a man, he abuses that right.
O do you think I have not cried too
That he might shake off all that folly
Of claiming to be persecuted,
A genius in shackles – folly

That drives him like a bad ship far out
To founder beyond our walls, our arms!
And do you think I cannot see Anne,
For all that she is placid, pining,
Pining – for what? Who would not pine here
In Haworth in the grey rain and cold?
I feel it more, far more, than Anne. I
Am not placid, I can hardly bear
To look at these few wet trees and tombs
And say, This is life, this is the world.
I do nothing, life passes away,
Life passes and the rain beats and beats,
I do nothing and you do nothing
Emily my sister, but keep house still
By the heath, with the sleet, and the dead.
– Look at me, Emily. Is this our life?
What you are thinking I never know.
You never fall into Anne's sadness,
Yet you are not placid, you are strong,
And while I fret, something sustains you.
Something sustains you that I can't see.

Emily

Is that a question?

Charlotte

        I suppose not.
I should have stopped asking you questions
When silence was the response I got.
And that was years ago. It is strange.
You were not always silent, but now
You are like a flower that has closed
As if the sun had hurt it, and yet
No rain crumples it, no wind kills it,
Its petals shield it like purest steel.
– You look past me, at the window, still.
If only the rain would stop! This house
Is thick with phantoms, sick with the past,
Littered with our childish brain-children,
Notebooks filled with dungeons and dangers,
Impossible enslavements, longings
Worse than slavery, laments, revenge,
Riding and luridness and defeat.

Imagination looms through this rain
Like a great message – a dead rider
With his cold fingers on a letter...
What would imagination matter
If we looked out on reality?

Emily

A lot.

Charlotte

You would stay like this, stay here?

Emily

Yes.

Charlotte

The way you say that frightens me.
Am I not natural, not normal,
Wanting the things anyone would want?
If I am lonely, am I happy?
Must we be stoics, or take to the
Psalms, or drink? No, I am a person,
Emily, and my heart would nearly break
If some unsought-for, ordinary
Kindness laid its warm hand on my arm.
You have no place for kindness, have you?
Kindness for our own kind, I mean – not
For dogs, fledgelings, waifs, wretches, strangers.
Pity makes such kindness too easy.
Pity is what you feel. – It is not?
O if I could read that piercing glance!
If it was not pity it would be
Love, and then in love's equality
You would yourself be that stranger –

Emily

Yes –

92

Charlotte

The wretched thing –

Emily

Yes –

Charlotte

And that waif –

Emily

Yes –

Charlotte

A fledgeling of the nest –

Emily

Yes –

Charlotte

And last,
A dog –

Emily

I was, and am, these things.

Charlotte

No!
If I believed you I would go mad.
Love is not sorrow for suffering.
Love is not interchanging of pain.

93

Love is not sympathy with outcasts.
For you might as well say you love fire
Or sea, the wind that batters the tombs,
The harebell, the snow, the very dust!
These are wild. From what are you outcast?
No, I don't ask you. For the first time
I feel fear for what you might tell me
As you stand there with that awful light
In your eyes and your fist clenched like stone.
I know the truth: you are not alone.
More than that had better stay unknown.

Emily

The rain has stopped, I think. The trees drip.

Charlotte

Well, let us open the window now.

Emily

The world glistens and rustles alive.

Charlotte

There's a thrush singing. The clouds break up.

Emily

The darkness in the north drifts away.

Charlotte

Sun after rain is an old story.

Emily

See how it sparkles on the wet sill.

Charlotte

Those scratches seem already like scars.

Emily

You know I sleep so lightly, a breath –

Charlotte

A pounce, quick as a whittrick, a face –

Emily

And my face to the pane when it moved!

Charlotte

If only daylight could fold about
Our house for ever in its great arms,
As all this brilliance strikes through the graves
Of the churchyard now, blazes on glass
And slab and glows where the shadows stood!
– If Anne would sit in the sun in joy,
And Branwell sang with his busy pen,
If I could bury my discontent
And you came back to us all again –
O no, it would be too bright, too good!

DIALOGUE V: MARILYN MONROE AND GALINA ULANOVA

Marilyn

Celebrities? There's nothing else here.
Three hundred celebrated persons,
And doesn't it sound like three thousand?
I guess London is always crowded,
But this is really packing them in.
I hope you tasted the caviare
Before mass circulation started?
After all, the reception is for you –

I know I should say 'for the Bolshoi'
But let it stand. I saw your dancing.
A great experience, believe me.
– Now, if we can make that corner seat.
Ah, this is better. Here we can talk.
You know I have so much to ask you –

Galina

That is a most unusual dress.

Marilyn

You like it? It's quite a simple thing,
Black satin, with rather a sheath skirt
But slit at the side, as you see –

Galina

                                        Oh.

Marilyn

– to let me walk. The nylon midriff
Might be called new; Marlene Dietrich
Amazed Las Vegas with some such thing
But more so, when she did the night-clubs
With throaty ditties. Not that I don't
Like Dietrich, don't misunderstand me.
Age cannot wither her. But nylon!
Well, Vegas isn't Boston.

Galina

                                Tell me,
Do you not wear stockings with this dress?

Marilyn

Yes. Yes indeed. But you can't see them.
You can't see them, and I can't feel them.

Absolutely sheer. As the poet says,
'Let all the silkworms stay in China,
We have a less coarse caterpillar.'
You know, this champagne is really good.

Galina

It hardly seems natural to me.
Is a stocking not made to be seen?

Marilyn

The leg is made to be seen, my dear.

Galina

But if your leg is fit to be seen,
And if you want your leg to be seen,
Why cover it with stockings at all?

Marilyn

Civilization. Bare legs are crude.
Not on the beach, but this is no beach.
Busy as a beach, but still, no sand.

Galina

But if a bare leg is what I see
(And to touch would not be civilized)
How would I know you were not just crude,
Or had forgotten to put them on?

Marilyn

You wouldn't *know*. Isn't that the point?

Galina

It does seem a little decadent.
You want to be thought, possibly, crude –

Then merely bold, and lastly, refined
Beyond the need to keep appearance
A guide to truth. This invisible
Stocking conceals the class struggle too.
Money buys invisible stockings
And all these social titillations.
No money – bare legs; some money – clothed;
Much money – that's what you call glamour
Which means both bare and clothed at once, and
Are the Folies Bergère so far off?

Marilyn

You talk just like Arthur – my husband.
He can't stand invisible stockings.
– Waiter, would you fill our glasses please?
Thank you, that's lovely. – Dear Galina,
Will you accept a toast to the sock,
And compromise on our division?

Galina

Very well, Marilyn. To the sock.

Marilyn

The sock: may it never be to seek.

Galina

– You mean, men are not so deceptive?

Marilyn

There's not much point in their deception.
A man's leg is, after all, a leg.
A woman's leg is a mystery.

Galina

And is this western democracy?

98

Marilyn

It surely is. Men love mystery.

Galina

No, I think they'd rather know the truth.

Marilyn

And so they will, but not just at first.

Galina

Ah, the opium of the sexes!

Marilyn

Old King Cole was a merry old soul.

Galina

Out of history truth comes slowly,
Out of legend, out of the process,
Out of our clinging frivolity,
Out of disguises of vanity.
Women move towards sincerity,
Men towards the accepting of it.
The wind will not blow this plain house down.

Marilyn

On the contrary, truth comes quickly,
In flashes, through deceit, misery,
Illusion, enchantment, anarchy.
It's a bullet in a dark barrel,
It's a piercing eye in a flurry,
It's a face caught in a city street.
When the grass shakes, the whittrick is gone.

Galina

The whittrick is a dangerous beast.

Marilyn

The plain house is a savourless place.

Galina

Will you come to Moscow to see me
In my savourless house?

Marilyn

I'd love to.

Galina

You are so full of life, so joyous,
But I would never be converted.
I like a quiet joy, with no tricks.

Marilyn

And yet there are Russian whittricks?

Galina

Sixty-four-thousand-dollar question –
Is that what you call it in the States?
Well, it is said that they are still seen.
They have been chased in printing-presses.
Artists find them behind their pictures.
Sailors on the Black Sea hear them cry
'Igor!' from the windy waterspouts.
Shostakovitch has one. The Chinese
Bring them to us in bamboo boxes.
A girl reading Chekhov will turn round
As the fire sinks at midnight – passion
And abandonment are breathing there,

Whether in hope or in desolation;
She feels the plain house go cold, the far
Pines and the wild sleigh-bells catch her heart.
I remember the revolution.
I was seven. Icy Petrograd
Shone, shone. It was blizzards, and hard work.
My mother danced, I danced after her.
Work became art as it always does.
– Yes, I was the girl who read Chekhov,
But now I am at home in the world.

Marilyn

Hard work – and the wind at midnight too.
Shall we agree they are both our friends?
Here comes my husband; you must tell him
What we have been saying – but not all.

DIALOGUE VI: THE BRAHAN SEER AND LADY SEAFORTH

The Brahan Seer

Your husband is in Paris, my lady –

Lady S.

I didn't need a seer to tell me that.

The Brahan Seer

I am beginning at the beginning.
You asked me what I knew, and this is it.
You've had no word for many months –

Lady S.

                                        Stop, stop!
Is that a horse, do you hear it? Listen.

The Brahan Seer

I hear the morning gust at the turrets,
The March wind on the roof, a door banging.
Ill-set are the doors of Brahan Castle.

Lady S.

Yes, it is only the wind. Go on then.

The Brahan Seer

Your husband is in Paris, as I said.
He is well; I see him at his business:
He smiles, he signs a paper, he is calm.
He counts some money, calls a coach. The King
Is kind, and writes from England to his friends.
Lord Seaforth is in favour. Cromwell counts
His court in hell; Charles in London town.
Lord Seaforth lives in favour, in fair France.

Lady S.

Is he so happy then, so far from me?

The Brahan Seer

Madam, I said I saw him well and free.

Lady S.

Free, and well, and never writing? This is
All you see? Kenneth, never hoodwink me!

The Brahan Seer

Some things a wise man sees, some not.

Lady S.

                                    Kenneth,
This is my husband, I must know the truth.

The Brahan Seer

The truth is sharp as sleet. The truth can kill.

Lady S.

I order you! Tell me all you know, or –

The Brahan Seer

You'll have me beaten till I remember?
Those who command it must also stand it.
You're hard, my lady. Will your back bear this?
– Here in my pebble I see all Paris,
It swims up to me like a winning glance.
O what a place yon is for happiness!
The spires, the doves, the river, the great shops!
The women so perjink, the men so gay!
And what is this, a picnic in a park?
At twilight, with guitars and wine? The trees
Grow sombre round the laughter, the sun dips,
The marble satyrs in the afterglow
Are sly as Seaforth where he sits, singing
To a girl in a yellow dress, his hand
Upon her breast, *La belle si tu voulais*
Nous dormirions ensemble. What a song!
Ask me if the Scottish laird is happy!
Go white then; bite your hand; but listen yet.
– What do I see but the moon up, moonlight
In Paris, moonlight and silence, midnight.
Watch my lord of Seaforth in his lodging
Pacing before the window, till he hears
A sweet voice sing *Dans un grand lit carré*
Aux longues taies blanches from the street,
And sets his candle in the casement, and
Waits for one knock of all knocks on the door.
His wedding-ring lies on the floor.

Lady S.

No more!
You liar, you think I'd believe this tale?
Slandering us out of common malice.
Liar and traitor too, for you hate me,

103

Though it's to us you owe all that you are –
A traitor to our house, to the Seaforths!
You'll never slander the Seaforths unscathed,
Be sure of that. You'll never daunton me
With phantoms called through a polished pebble.
I know your mind is as foul as your breath,
I find your words as foul now as your mind.
O I am sick to death.

The Brahan Seer

                    Sick of the truth,
Sick of the truth, you vixen, not of me!
O how I laughed to see the laird in love
In his *grand lit carré*, and you his spouse
Who never loved him, here in Easter Ross
Gnawing your nails and slapping your maids. Tchach!
I see bystart bairns in Brahan Castle,
Why should there not be some in France? Slander?
Come down, come down, my lady, I warned you
That a hard heart was not the best to bear.

Lady S.

And I warn you, Black Kenneth, I warn you
That I am Lady Seaforth, and my word
Within these castle walls is law, there is
No other law, no need of other law.
Easy my riddance of a warlock here.

The Brahan Seer

I am too famous, you wouldn't dare to.
You'd have the infamy, I'd keep the fame.

Lady S.

I'll risk infamy to see you suffer.

The Brahan Seer

It's some kind of devil you are –

104

Lady S.

                              Panic!
It's too late now. I'll have you tomorrow
Black Kenneth, turned to Black Kenneth indeed,
Burning to the bone in a tub of tar.
Brahan Clavie shall you be, Brahan Seer.
Riddle yourself a future out of that!

The Brahan Seer

Lady Seaforth, hear now what is to come.
I see my stone flash like a falling star
And flicker like the futtret of the field.
Bright in the futtret's eye the dead star sits,
And bright in mine the stars of Seaforth dwine.
The stirring generations shall sicken,
The children shall shiver as they quicken.
The young shall brandish a bodach's palsy,
The old shall be crazed burying the young.
Crutches, idiocy, melancholy:
A cleft palate and a stammering tongue:
When these are rife among the Seaforths' friends,
Seaforth lease of human history ends.
Doom on the lineage, doom on this house!
Doom on the steading sold to the stranger!
Doom on the damask in the moths' larder!
For it's not long to the last laird of all
Who shall bury four sons and leave no heir;
Hearing shall fail him, and speech shall fail him,
And life shall fly him as his sons fled him;
Women shall weep him, his loins are empty.
And the great castles shall be filled with dust,
The arms shall crumble, the dogs be unfed,
The pipers wander westward masterless.
From Stornoway to Pluscarden, the dust.
The debts, the rain, the ravens, and the graves.
This very stronghold, sturdy as it seems,
Shall take stray sheep in shelter, nibbling here
Among the flags that grass has forced apart.
– Enough to have seen, and all I can see!
Call back your husband to his heritage.
Call back your husband to his curse.

Lady S.

My curse
Go with you, Kenneth, and the curse of all
The children I may have, and may your mind
See them as you are dying, and turn once
A bitterer knife within you even
Than the tongues of the fire and the tar and
The knives I'll set in the cask for your sake.

DIALOGUE VII: HAKUIN AND CHIKAMATSU*

Hakuin

When I first came to Suruga, it was worse.
A hopeless roof, the stars looked through it at night.
Debts, mortgages everywhere. The best bell cracked.
We're still a poor temple, but not ruinous.
Hard work is good for novices' backs; they got
More than they bargained for, those that I took in –
Begging to be bowled along to buddhahood!
I showed them Buddha: a bit of broken brick.
– It was an afternoon like this when I came,
But now the sun seems more brilliant, so brilliant
It almost strikes the bell into chimes; the lake
It almost breaks like glass as it lies flashing.
The heart could be lost in this heat and silence.
Perhaps the days of leaking roofs are the best?

Chikamatsu

Sitting here in the cool of the verandah,
With the temple cat and a tobacco-tray,
We might indeed lose sense of reality –
Unless this is reality, and a man
Who shakes the dust of cities off as you do
Should surely find it is? A danger for me,
But why should heat and silence trouble hermits?
I need Osaka, the tea-houses and throngs,

* Hakuin (1685-1768), Japanese Buddhist sage and teacher, 'the founder of modern Zen'; Chikamatsu (1653-1725), 'the Japanese Shakespeare', writer of popular plays for the Kabuki theatre and especially for the Joruri (puppet) theatre.

The theatres, the turning pleasure-lanterns,
The cries and smells headier than temple-bells.
Here, I drowse to the last insignificance.
Are you afraid of your own meditations?
You have brought your heart here; how can you lose it?

Hakuin

The heart is lost in attachment to the sun,
Or to any place, or to any person,
Or to any thing but illumination,
And that is not attachment. The heart is lost
By love. Love of this place would make the mind dark,
Clouded by a barren solicitousness.
'The cherry is late; these stones could be regrouped;
Shall we not lacquer the dishes red this year?'
Enlightened monks I want, not geishas. A bowl,
A mat, a stick, a brain, a space to breathe in,
And all the paradoxes shall clap their hands
As if this silent play was Chikamatsu's.

Chikamatsu

Reality, then, is neither here nor there?

Hakuin

But what are the paradoxes clapping at?

Chikamatsu

I might ask, what are the creatures clapping *with*?

Hakuin

May I enrol you as a student of Zen?
Your questions are promising. But start from this.
What is the sound of the clapping of one hand?

Chikamatsu

The theatre's empty. What, have you gone home?

107

Hakuin

Good, good! But look now, no hands.

Chikamatsu

A thunderclap,
Rather far off, do you hear it? And the flash –

Hakuin

Basho's poem: seventeen syllables: *O*
Sudden lightning, and down the darkness the scream
Of the night heron! – Yet you ask, what is Zen?

Chikamatsu

A poet's imagination is a help.
Make poets monks, and Zen will soar up, right off.
Enlightenment will come in constellations.
The world will be miles down, struggling, in a net.
What is meditation, to a metaphor!
But then where are you? Where's your reality?
When mystics are eloquent, the faith teeters.
You should be glad I am only a playwright.
Keep the ineffable on the prayer-mat,
With rice and chopsticks, but neither brush nor ink;
When the lightning strikes, let it not speak, just think.
The night heron that screams the gloom to tatters
May choke on the majestic lie it utters.
– Reality, reality! people cry.
All right. The dramatist tries realism.
Some years ago Osaka thrilled to the news
Of a suicide-pact – a young apprentice
And a poor tea-house girl he couldn't marry:
He cut her throat in the Sonezaki Woods,
Then cut his own; they were found bound to one tree.
Within a fortnight *Sonezaki Shinju*,
My play of this event, was staged; applauded;
By all Osaka; O, a play of such truth –
But was it truth? Did they blow out the lantern
As I said they did? Did the maid striking flints
Cover their escape by a creaking door-hinge?
And were they a model for all true lovers

108

As the last line stated? My fleshless actors
Were puppets of pine, their gesticulations
Were generalizations, their passions poured
From a hidden throat and a thin samisen.
Ah, what was left of the Sonezaki Woods?
Did I show what was suffered there? Did I die?
– If those who bled on the tree were not silent,
If those who speak could bleed on the truthful tree!

Hakuin

Yet the truth comes to you as it comes to me.
The thud of snow in the forest, like a blow,
A whittrick at a harvest in Hokkaido,
Osaka watching a doll weep at a show.
For the doll does weep; men know.

Chikamatsu

And that is Zen?

Hakuin

But what is Zen? You think it's either the case
'A doll can't cry' or 'I saw the doll crying'?
Are you going to renounce your own power?
Neither you nor I can be wholly truthful,
Though the truth comes to me as it comes to you.
Nor can your audience; nor my disciples.
Yet the truth comes.

Chikamatsu

Then why do we let it go?
Why in a world of doubts do we let it go?
Why do we let this heaven dissolve and go?

Hakuin

When I was twenty-four I was Zenward-bound.
I fasted haggard as a wolf, refused sleep,
Sat unshaven shivering upon a board,

Kicked the paradoxes round my memory,
Stripped the jests and ferocities to meekness.
Static I became, brain-bound, ghostly, in chains;
Felt I was freezing at the silent centre
Of an ice-field stretching for millions of miles;
Slumped there like stalagmite, featureless and numb,
A fragment, naked, stupid, vulnerable,
Ghostly and vulnerable as a crystal.
Suddenly I heard the monastery bell.
The ice exploded with great cracks, my body
Burst from its crystal shell which fell like a shawl.
It was as if a tower of jade was smashed
To drops of living water. I moved, I rose.
I shouted out 'Wonderful, O wonderful!'
There was no perfect knowledge to starve after.
I had broken through to the life I left from.
Buddha dissolved in the water of the snow.
– And so I let this heaven dissolve and go.

Chikamatsu

And so you find it everywhere, like the air?

Hakuin

Seize it: it's gone. It will not be seized again.

Chikamatsu

A shout in the street? A tea-house in the rain?

Hakuin

Will you have some tea?

Chikamatsu

Yes. Thanks!

Hakuin

This too is Zen.

110

DIALOGUE VIII: GREY WALTER AND JEAN COCTEAU*

(Assisted by Roddy and Eck – and the Whittrick)

Roddy

Where the hell did we pit Dr Walter's whittrick?
Hey Eck, hiv ye goat the whittrick? They'll be back soon
Fae their tea, and he wants it to do its stuff. Eck!

Eck

In behind the genera'or. The black boax therr.

Roddy

Oh aye; aye. – Here they come.

Walter

           . . . as I was telling you,
This Hunterston station's mainly for atom men.
You've been through the plant and you've seen the reactors.
But this building here, where I work, is different.
It's a Cybernetic Unit, linking research
By engineers, linguists, mathematicians
And neurophysiologists like myself.

Cocteau

           Ah!

Much more interesting than the disposal of
Radioactive waste. What are all these machines?

Walter

Oh, my museum? These are our early models
Of mechanical animals, not far from toys
But toys in a serious game – to simulate
The very springs of behaviour in living things

* Dr W. Grey Walter, author of *The Living Brain* (1953).

By valve, wire, battery, cell, and man-made feedback.
Crude ironmongery they seem now! They pleased us,
Winking their lights, running to be recharged. That one
We called our Tortoise, *Machina speculatrix*;
It hummed about here, as restless as flesh and blood,
Feeling its way and scanning the darkness for light.
First steps in teleology! This is Cora:
She was our conditioned reflex. We grafted her
By electronic surgery to the Tortoise:
Result, a teachable little beast, *Machina*
Docilis. We kicked him and blew whistles; he learned.
– Well: all that was the beginning, long long ago.
I have a more advanced animal to show you.

Cocteau

Behind this door?

Walter

        No, that leads to the balcony:
Shall we look? Out there are the huge cooling-towers;
The grid of power that strides off across the moors;
The blaze of laboratories like a city;
And those lights moving slowly down the greying firth –
The great atomic tankers, looming like islands.
You hear their horns? That sumptuous, unhurried blast!
The seagulls hate it: there they go, shrieking. Feathers
Like shadows, shadows like feathers by the islands.
– But it's almost dark, and chilly. Let's go in now.
I promised you'd see our latest machine. Roddy!

Roddy

Aye Dr Walter.

Walter

        Roddy boy, our friend from France
Is here to see the best we have to offer him,
So bring out that black box, let's have the beast uncased,
And set it in the middle of the floor.

Roddy

                                                    Hey Eck,
Will ye gie us a hand? – Lift it, man, lift it up:
Therr it's. – Did ye test it? How's the atomic, eh?

Eck

The ba'ery? Fine, fine. I tried the speaker too:
Wan time it jist gied a croak but, and stuck –

Roddy

                                                    Surely –

Eck

I know, I know. I hut it wan, and it's aa right.

Roddy

Well, I hope so. Temperamental though, intit?

Walter

Here then is our handiwork, and in deference
To our Scots domicile I call it the Whittrick.

Cocteau

Ah, la belette! It is a pretty thing.

Walter

                                                    Thank you.
But mainly it is a clever thing, a quick thing,
A brain and a voice. The thought is quicker than ours,
The speech is not quite natural yet. – Try it out,
Ask it a short question.

113

Cocteau

Whittrick, what is my name?

The Whittrick (in a metallic, deliberate voice)

Cock Toe.

Cocteau

Is that not marvellous? And what else now –
May I ask it a mathematical question?

Walter

Go ahead.

Cocteau

Whittrick, the square root of minus one –

The Whittrick (tone as before, but more confident)

Is an imaginary, expressed by small *i*.

Cocteau

It took the question out of my mouth, can it have –

Walter

Well, it's getting warmed up. It'll read your thoughts soon.
– I'm joking; but you see the line of our research.
The Whittrick has been programmed, elaborately
And with great faith in the logic of choice, to find
The end of every beginning, the probable
Haystack in the open field of the possible
And the needle of certainty this haystack holds.
The answer waits in the question that's half-spoken,
The oak in the acorn, theory in worry,
The poem you write is already foreshadowed

114

When you pencil the first warm phrase, and every word
Is a choice that lessens choice, till the anxious voice
Picks one last possibility out of silence.

Cocteau

And this is the poem according to science?
The work of art as the artist's own thermostat?
The springing epithets a feedback to the void?

Walter

You dislike the terms, but do you dislike the thing?
What's poetry?

Cocteau

Out there on your terrace I thought,
Je me rappelle bien les bars tristes, les cales,
L'odeur d'un port qui sent surtout la chair humaine...
I wrote that many years ago. It has some life.
It came back to me when the gulls cried by the shore.
Their inhumanity seemed warmer than the grid,
More vocal than the booming tankers, and clearer
In its wild purport than your tame automatons.
Poetry's like a gull, protesting, sheering off;
It's a radio-star the telescope can't catch;
It's an act of love with an angel in anger;
It's a darkness for the searchlight of a question.
The poet is invisible, he speaks in code
Although the great cryptographers acclaim in joy
His clarity extraordinarily pure.
The creator's hidden, the conception's hidden,
The statue moves, Hermione breathes. What is life?
'Like an old tale still, though credit be asleep'? Oh
But the feigned statue becomes a statue by art
And we share the miracle of the deceived king!
The very untruth cradles the rapturous thing.
What logic flashes through the seagull's sudden wing?

Walter

Some logic, which human patience is approaching.
You are not quite so invisible as you think.

115

Even the unexpected has limitations;
Machines can be persuaded to stumble on dreams –
Except that it isn't stumbling and they aren't dreams.
Why do you think I called this creature the Whittrick?
The flash of imagination has been built in,
Its logic allows the leap of thought. It's brooding,
Ticking, scanning more myriads of possibles
Than those great heads that sought the words of the *Winter's
Tale* or the *Principia Mathematica*.
It must not only solve problems, but present them.
Creation's as dear to me as it is to you;
Babbage's dream and Bottom's dream begin to meet.
You fear what I hope: the created may create.

Cocteau

That it will never do with neither will nor wit.
The whittrick in the fields has far more wit than it.

Roddy

It's getting gey hot, sir, will I switch it aff now?

Walter

Yes, I think so. – Just a minute, there's a change of –
Did you hear that break in its rhythm, with a sort
Of click? The tempo's quicker –

Eck

                    It's going to speak –

Walter

But it can't speak! None of us have addressed it. It
Can't speak!

The Whittrick

    Now Faustus, what wouldst thou have me to do?

from Newspoems
1965-1971

The Newspoems were cut out from newspapers and other ephemeral material, pasted on to sheets of paper, and photographed. Most people have probably had the experience of scanning a newspaper page quickly and taking a message from it quite different from the intended one. I began looking deliberately for such hidden messages and picking out those that had some sort of arresting quality, preferably with the visual or typographical element itself a part of the 'point', though this was not always possible. What results is a series of 'inventions' both in the old sense of 'things found' and in the more usual sense of 'things devised'.

HALT
'COMMIT ADULTERY

1966

You can SING here

1966

Sick Man

Say

o

1968

'I place
the
dead
ahead
of me,
and bong'

1971

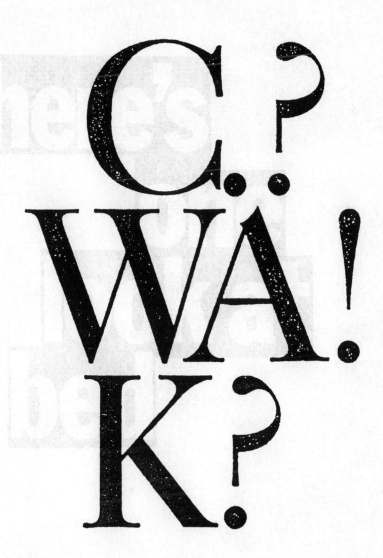

1969

1966

ges ha
i

1969

Idyll

Toby D

arling

Ex

Red Cap

Wee Heavy

Nut Brown

Sweetheart

1965

It is called

It does time

It is a total
software

It was
heaviest
processing—

Next it was
time sharing,
engineering
the same ease

GET
IN
IT

1966

We made the decision reluctantly
                    after the first
        to give   trouble. So people
            with nice heart

        are in business

So please, if you
go mad—

        we're making them

                                                    1966

go

1967

from Emergent Poems
1967

The texts of the Emergent Poems are taken from the following works:

Plea: from Brecht, 'Von der Kindesmörderin Marie Farrar'.
Dialeck Piece: from Burns, 'To a Mouse'.
Nightmare: from Dante, *Inferno*.
Manifesto: from the *Communist Manifesto*.

```
        a                       l           l
            rea          ch
  d       e           a    t h
            a                 l         l
    en  a                 c t
  de          at          h
                      a                ll
      a               r                 e
        k                   i             n
      all      a      r                 e
  n     e     a     r                   all
                        i     n
        re        a c h
                            on
            t r           i     al
                          i     n
  den                   i     al
      a l                     on   e
                        il       l
            b                 on   e
  e     a     t                     en
    n   e   r               v       e
                        f     allen
            bra       i     n
  n              u           l       l
          a        h
      l                  i v       e
            bra           v       e
            b                       e
      a l                 i v       e
      le            a         v     e
      all               t     o
      l                 i f       e
      l   ea               v     e
  de   a     t         h
    n                         o
    a               r     t
  n                           o
            tur                       n
    n                         o
    a   rea
  n                           o
            u   r                   n
            b   u t
  e   a             ch
            b                   e
  d     e     a     t     o
      e     a     c h
                        i         n
    a                   l         l
denn alle kreatur braucht hilf von allen
```

133

Dialeck Piece

```
            i
a    m
     m   ick        th  e
  d  i    ck
     i                  h ave
     me
     m             a t    e
                in
     me            a th
a     n
a d i    ck  i         e
  da  n       in th  e
      n ick
     me
  da
a d  m   i   r in  th a e
  da m n           t
  d i    cker in
     m   ic e    a t
    a   n
a        cker
a d i    c e     thra
a daimen icker in a thrave
```

134

Nightmare

```
                    a
qu              e      st
                    a
qu              a r    r e      l
  i d               rive
            m       i    le s
u nd                  e r
                rive   r
                    a
            m    a              st
            mo    ved
                    a
            m  o a              t
            c      a        st
qu                      e er
            m      i          st
    di    m    ri der   s
                    ri          s    e
indi   c        a              te
                    a
            m  o        d  e st
                        de          ll
            mo            st
    d  i        v  e st
                    o        r
    di          ve
in          o  r
        s m        i      l        e
                    a                  t
    us      o            r
            m      a r v  e l
                    a                  t
    d us                        t
                    o  r
        s        a        d
            immo   r            telle
                    o            r
            c        a        l  l
                    o  r
    n              o      d
                    a                  t
    u      s      o  r
            s        a i        l
    u nd                    er
            m      a      d
            o a        r   s
            m  o            r  s e
            c        a                ll
                    a                  t
    di      mm        e  st
            m      a    de
          us
e    nd
e qu              a        l
          i
    u ndi                d
                    a
        s      o        r        e l
e quindi uscimmo a riveder le stelle
```

Manifesto

```
r      i  se
              st an   d
pro        v e
              st a          y
      t r                   y
   r  et r                  y
      le ar          n
         r     e     a     d
         t r         a     in
            s     tra      in
            v              i      e
      le a                 d
         t      e   st
   r  et         e   st
pro   t          e   st
   ro   a           r
p      r     e   s                 s
p      ri        s                 e
pr        i          n             t
      e                    di    t
            s         a           y
proletari          an s    in
      e     v e       r          y
      l               an   d
         a            r           e
      o               n           e
proletarii vsekh stran soedinyaites
```

from Gnomes
1968

Strawberry Fields Forever

my blackie

                                                    smirr

    losing

                 foxpaw

        patter

                  your hazel

          whistle

              dewdrop

      kneedeep

           unreal

                          the fields we

```
generation upon
generation upon
generation upon
generation upon
generation upon
generation upon
generation upon
generation upon
generation upon
generation upon
generation upon
generation upon
generation upon
generation upon
generation upon
generation upon
generation upon
generation upon
generation upon
g  neration upon
g  neration up  n
g  nerat on up  n
g  nerat  n up  n
g  nerat  n  p  n
g  erat   n  p  n
g  era    n  p  n
g  era    n     n
g  er     n     n
g  r      n     n
g         n     n
g         n
g
```

Astrodome

'As real grass withers in the Astrodome [at Houston, Texas]
it has been replaced by Astrograss.'   *(news item)*

all is not grass that astrograss
that astrograss is not all grass
that grass is not all astrograss
astrograss is not all that grass
is that astrograss not all glass
not all astrograss is that glass
all that glass is not astrograss
that is not all astrograss glass
that glass is not all fibreglass
not all that fibreglass is glass
fibreglass is not all that glass
is that not all fibreglass glass
that fibreglass is not all grass
glass is not all that fibreglass
is all astrograss not that glass
all is not grass that fibregrass

The Computer's Second Christmas Card

```
goodk kkkkk unjam ingwe nches lass? start again goodk
lassw enche sking start again kings tart! again sorry
goodk ingwe ncesl ooked outas thef? unmix asloo kedou
tonth effff rewri tenow goodk ingwe ncesl asloo kedou
tonth effff fffff unjam feast ofsai ntste venstefanc
utsai ntrew ritef easto fstep toeso rryan dsons orry!
start again good? yesgo odkin gwenc eslas looke dout?
doubt wrong track start again goodk ingwe nceslasloo
kedou tonth efeas tofst ephph phphp hphph unjam phphp
repea tunja mhphp scrub carol hphph repea tscru bcaro
lstop subst itute track merry chris tmasa ndgoo dnewy
earin 1699? check digit banks orryi n1966 endme ssage
```

The Second Life
1968

The Old Man and the Sea

And a white mist rolled out of the Pacific
and crept over the sand, stirring nothing –
cold, cold as nothing is cold
on those living highways, moved in
over the early morning trucks,
chilling the drivers in their cabins
(one stops for a paper cup
of coffee, stares out through the steam
at the mist, his hands on the warm cup
imagine the coldness, he throws out the cup
and swears as the fog rolls in, drives on
frowning to feel its touch on his face) –
and seagulls came to shriek at cockcrow
swooping through the wakening farms,
and the smoke struggled from the lumber camps
up into the smoke from the sea,
hovered in the sunless morning
as a lumberman whistled at the pump,
and sea-mist took the flash from the axe.
And above the still lakes of Oregon
and the Blue Mountains into Idaho
eastward, white wings brushing the forests,
a white finger probing the canyon
by Wood River, delicate, persistent, at last
finding by the half-light, in a house of stone,
a white-bearded man like an old sea-captain
cleaning a gun. – Keep back the sea,
keep back the sea! No reassurance
in that daybreak with no sun,
his blood thin, flesh patched and scarred,
eyes grown weary of hunting
and the great game all uncaught.
It was too late to fight the sea.
The raised barrel hardly gleamed
in that American valley, the shot
insulted the morning, crude and quick
with the end of a great writer's life –
fumbling nothing, but leaving questions
that echo beyond Spain and Africa.
Questions, not answers, chill the heart here,
a chained dog whining in the straw,
the gunsmoke marrying the sea-mist,
and silence of the inhuman valleys.

The Death of Marilyn Monroe

What innocence? Whose guilt? What eyes? Whose breast?
Crumpled orphan, nembutal bed,
white hearse, Los Angeles,
DiMaggio! Los Angeles! Miller! Los Angeles! America!
That Death should seem the only protector –
That all arms should have faded, and the great cameras and lights
    become an inquisition and a torment –
That the many acquaintances, the autograph-hunters, the
    inflexible directors, the drive-in admirers should become
    a blur of incomprehension and pain –
That lonely Uncertainty should limp up, grinning, with
    bewildering barbiturates, and watch her undress and lie
    down and in her anguish
call for him! call for him to strengthen her with what could
    only dissolve her! A method
of dying, we are shaken, we see it. Strasberg!
Los Angeles! Olivier! Los Angeles! Others die
and yet by this death we are a little shaken, we feel it,
America.
Let no one say communication is a cantword.
They had to lift her hand from the bedside telephone.
But what she had not been able to say
perhaps she had said. 'All I had was my life.
I have no regrets, because if I made
any mistakes, I was responsible.
There is now – and there is the future.
What has happened is behind. So
it follows you around? So what?' – This
to a friend, ten days before.
And so she was responsible.
And if she was not responsible, not wholly responsible, Los Angeles?
    Los Angeles? Will it follow you around? Will the slow
    white hearse of the child of America follow you around?

Je ne regrette rien
in memory of Edith Piaf

Smoky sky.
In autumn wind
I stroll by the quays
in the last light,
my coat flaps, flaps,

wet chestnut leaves
spatter the Seine.
I glance in a window
and touch my hair, yes
I am tiny as they say,
tiny as a sparrow.
Now the lights come on.
I stand under the lamp,
turn up my collar
in a circle of rain
and wait for you.

It's all beginning again.
Dead leaves or spring
it comes back, it begins.
How could I struggle?
When you held me, your shoulders
were a wall, I sheltered
in your shadow, it began.
They say I couldn't count my men –
in thirty years I couldn't count them!
But who counts years?
Count the years I was blind?
Dandled in a brothel? Taught by whores?
Count the prayers that gave me my sight at Lisieux?
Or the heartbeats of my daughter, in thousands,
when I bore her at fourteen
till she starved and died?
Count the crusts I've had, or those I've given?
The gutters I've sung in, or the great halls?
Count the glasses I've drunk? Count the beds
I've lain in, the lips I've kissed?
I can't count the surgeons who've opened me –
do you think my lovers are in a book?
Do you want me to start counting tears?
Count what? The cost? What cost? I won!

No! let the men that had me go their ways.
I regret nothing, nothing. Some were kind.
But I don't care if they were kind!
I don't remember if it was bad.
I don't keep the past in my pocket.
I've paid for it all, I've forgotten it all.
I've paid for it all, I've forgotten it all.
I strike a match to my memories,
they light a fire and disappear.

I warm my arms tonight
the fire begins
the stars come out
yes it begins
I am forty-five
it begins again
I hear his step
yes it begins
his broad shoulders
glisten through the rain
I can see
the dead cigarette
in his firm mouth
he throws it aside
it begins and
I regret nothing

We sway in the rain,
he crushes my mouth.
What could I regret
if a hundred times
of parting struck me
like lightning if this
lightning of love
can strike and
strike
again!

The Domes of Saint Sophia

A nun, visiting Istanbul,
sends me a postcard of St Sophia –
   church, mosque, and now museum –
speaks of its 'supreme beauty'
and forthright as always, adds
   'Its perfection of form
      would delight the eye eternally'
– I wonder.
Unless the eternal eye is purified beyond meaning,
perfection of form will not please for ever.
A week with St Paul's at sunrise
   a month with St Sophia at dusk
      a year with the Taj Mahal by moonlight –
but then the domes grow cold,

148

and the lesson that perfection
  by definition
    cannot last
comes home. No,
better for eternity
Krak des Chevaliers
  Baalbek
    Caernarvon
      Carnac
      Konarak
and the Chinese Wall. What time has barely kept
let that be the most dearly kept:
    Zimbabwe thrust among the burning boulders,
    Angkor Wat that wrestled the liana,
    broken Tantallon clutching North Sea spray.
Truly, and if not eternally, very very long
the eye would linger in love
on these great forms,
great fortresses and temples, dark, stoic, defaced
that cry out to be contemplated
and surpass the beauties of Shah Jehan
as the beauty of the highest angel
must yield to the beauty of man.
Ruins that breathe our dust! Is it too long
– these aeons of God – to pierce your memorials
of every unrecorded life,
                  the mason, the sculptor
  unknown, the slave
  unknown whose blood lies deep in your walls?
Not a sparrow falls –
we are told, but in the ruins
men and sparrows surely call out, Did we die?
Winds of Memnon sigh,
                sphinxes' lips
close tight upon the overseers' bleeding whips.
An eternity for these things!
  Too much we are not told!
    Too much we must know!
Then if you like, the domes,
perhaps some tranquil afternoon
after eternity.

I know they are beautiful,
let the eye delight in them,
I grant you your delight.
Yet the eye is not alone,
and they give no grip

to the searching mind
in its trouble.
I take no assurance
from a soaring vault.
The earth is my fortress
and the meanest broch
has that moving presence
of imperfection,
craft and its dislocation,
fire, war,
weathering, desertion –
as great as the Great
Pyramid I've climbed
or giant Baalbek
with its foundered columns
where I wandered in wartime
in the Lebanese sun.
I've heard the voice
of the dead on Carmel,
almost as old
as the lizard on the tomb:
'Gods, if not help me,
if instead barb me,
be careful of me!
I can catch thunderbolts
and pull you down
and have done it before –'

The dead will die
if the living are asleep.
Waken them!
The dome is silent.
Waken them!
The ruin speaks.

The White Rhinoceros

'Rare over most of its former range'
Webster's Third New International Dictionary

The white rhinoceros was eating phosphorus!
I came up and I shouted Oh no! No! No! –
you'll be extinct in two years! But he shook his ears
and went on snorting, knee-deep in pawpaws,
trundling his hunger, shrugged off the tick-birds,

150

rolled up his sleeves, kicked over an anthill,
crunched, munched, wonderful windfall,
empty dish. And gored that old beat-up tin tray
for more, it stuck on his horn,
looked up with weird crown on his horn
like a bear with a beehive, began to glow –
as leerie lair bear glows honeybrown –
but he glowed
                white and
                    bright and
the safety-catches started to click in the thickets
for more. Run, holy hide – take up your armour –
Run – white horn, tin clown, crown of rain-woods,
venerable shiner! Run, run, run!

And thunders glowing like a phantom
through the bush, beating the guns
this time, but will he always
when his only camouflage
is a world of white?

Save the vulnerable shiners.
Watch the phosphorus trappers.
Smash the poisonous dish.

The Third Day of the Wolf

Lock the gates and man the fences!
The lone Canadian timber-wolf
has escaped into the thickets, the ditches, the distances!
Blow the silver whistles!
The zoo-born sniffs the field mist,
the hedgerow leaves, liberty wind
of a cold February Friday.

Saturday trudging, loping, hungry, free but hunted,
dogs tracking, baying, losing scent, shouts dying,
fields dangerous, hills worse, night welcome, but the hunger
now! And Sunday many miles, risking farms, seen panting,
dodging the droning helicopter shadows,
flashing past gardens, wilder, padding along a highway,
twilight, sleepy birdsong, dark safety – till a car
catches the grey thing in its rushing headlights,
throws it to the verge, stunned, ruptured, living, lying,

fangs dimly scrabbling the roots of Hertfordshire.
The haze lifting, the head rising, the legs limping, the run
beginning again, with torches, whispers, smell of men and guns,
far off warning, nearer, receding, wavering, waiting
for a whimper, a twig crack, a blood spot, finding them
and coming on, coming nearer to the starving meeting-place.
Breaking cover as had to be, on the icy morning of Monday,
Monday suddenly opening all its mouths, gulping
with fury at the weary fragment, farmers, keepers, police,
two planes diving again and again to drive it
in terror towards the guns, and the farm's pet collie
cornering it at last with the understrapper's yap.
The empty belly and mad yellow eyes
waiting for man were then shot,
not killed, then bludgeoned,
not killed, then shot,
and killed.

How strong man is
with his helicopters and his planes,
his radios and rifles!
What a god for a collie!
O wild things, wild things
take care, beware of him.
Man mends his fences.
Take care, take strength.
Take care of the warrant
for death. How good
he is at that,
with his dirty sack
ready to lay on you:
it is necessary.
But I have a warrant
to lay this too,
a wreath for wildness,
timber-wolf, timber-wolf.

Aberdeen Train

      Rubbing a glistening circle
      on the steamed-up window I framed
      a pheasant in a field of mist.
      The sun was a great red thing somewhere low,
      struggling with the milky scene. In the furrows

a piece of glass winked into life,
hypnotized the silly dandy; we
hooted past him with his head cocked,
contemplating a bottle-end,
And this was the last of October,
a Chinese moment in the Mearns.

The Opening of the Forth Road Bridge, 4.IX.64

Like man in the universe –
rising through mist, half seen,
walking the gulfs.

Fold the formless waters,
one by one, back.

Break your flag by the fog.

Make, and take, your crossing.

To Hugh MacDiarmid

That the poet 'does not number the streaks of the tulip'
you saw was a fallacy, yet when paradoxical Imlac
claimed that 'to a poet nothing can be useless'
you concurred, and out of scraps of art and life and knowledge
you assembled that crackling auroral panorama
that sits on your Scotland like a curly comb
or a grinning watergaw thrown to meteorology,
your bone to the dogs of the ages. So much to be numbered! –
'the red huckleberry, the sand cherry, and the nettle tree,
the red pine and the black ash, the white grape and the yellow violet,
which might have withered else in dry seasons.'
To be forgotten is driest. Names rain things up.
You took that hazard of naming, letting the drops
fall on the desert of uninterest of those with 'a taste
for Frontiniac' but not for the glass of Esk water
or the inhuman fountain of stone that pours in a marble ear
its endless formless message where 'schiebt ein Krug sich ein,
so scheint es ihr, dass du sie unterbrichst.'
And yet you let the jug of clay dip in the flow.

153

A dead child or a busker or a bobbin-winder
cries through the raised beaches and the disinterested
eternity of the foraminifera.
Somewhere in astonishment you would set man,
short-range or long-range confrontation or kinship
with all the world he changes as it changes him,
the greater changes he grows into making now,
the greatest like faint stars in the drift of smoke of thought.
– Midges in cigarette-smoke! That's what you know,
where it comes from, turning a page or writing one
in your clear hand still, sitting by a cottage
in a small country.

To Ian Hamilton Finlay

Maker of boats,
earthships,
the white cradle
with its patchwork quilt,
toys of wood
painted bright as
the zebras' muzic
in your carousel,
patiently cut
space cleanly!
There's dark earth
underneath, not far
the North Sea,
a beach goes out
greyer than Dover's
for ignorant armies.
Scotland is
the little bonfires
in cold mist,
with stubbornness,
the woman knits
late by a window,
a man repairing
nets, a man carv-
ing steady glass,
hears the world,
bends to his work.
You give the pleasure
of made things,

154

the construction holds
like a net; or it
unfolds in waves
a certain measure,
of affection.
Native, familiar as
apples, tugs,
girls, lettres from
your moulin,
but
drinking tea
you set for Albers
his saucer of milk.

An Addition to the Family
for M.L.

A musical poet, collector of basset-horns,
was buttering his toast down in Dunbartonshire
when suddenly from behind the breakfast newspaper
the shining blade stopped scraping
and he cried to his wife, 'Joyce, listen to this! –
"Two basset-hounds for sale, house-trained, keen hunters" –
Oh we must have them! What d'you think?' 'But dear,
did you say *hounds*?' 'Yes yes, hounds, hounds –'
'But Maurice, it's *horns* we want, you must be over
in the livestock column, what would we do
with a basset-hound, you can't play a hound!'
'It's Beverley it says, the kennels are at Beverley –'
'But Maurice –' '– I'll get some petrol, we'll be there by lunchtime –'
'But a dog, two dogs, where'll we put them?'
'I've often wondered what these dogs are like –'
'You mean you don't even –' 'Is there no more marmalade?'
'– don't know what they look like? And how are we to feed them?
Yes, there's the pot dear.' 'This stuff's all peel, isn't it?'
'Well, we're at the end of it. But look, these two great –'
'You used to make marmalade once upon a time.'
'They've got ears down to here, and they're far too –'
'Is that half past eight? I'll get the car out.
See if I left my cheque-book on the –' 'Maurice,
are you mad? What about your horns?' 'What horns,
what are you talking about? Look Joyce dear,
if it's not on the dresser it's in my other jacket.
I believe they're wonderful for rabbits –'

So the musical poet took his car to Beverley
with his wife and his cheque-book, and came back home
with his wife and his cheque-book and two new hostages
to the unexpectedness of fortune.
The creatures scampered through the grass, the children
came out with cries of joy, there seemed to be nothing
dead or dying in all that landscape.
Fortune bless the unexpected cries!
Life gathers to the point of wishing it,
a mocking pearl of many ventures. The house
rolled on its back and kicked its legs in the air.
And later, wondering farmers as they passed would hear
behind the lighted window in the autumn evening
two handsome mellow-bosomed basset-hounds
howling to a melodious basset-horn.

Canedolia

an off-concrete Scotch fantasia

oa! hoy! awe! ba! mey!

who saw?
rhu saw rum. garve saw smoo. nigg saw tain. lairg saw lagg.
rigg saw eigg. largs saw haggs. tongue saw luss. mull saw yell.
stoer saw strone. drem saw muck. gask saw noss. unst saw cults.
echt saw banff. weem saw wick. trool saw twatt.

how far?
from largo to lunga from joppa to skibo from ratho to shona from
ulva to minto from tinto to tolsta from soutra to marsco from
braco to barra from alva to stobo from fogo to fada from gigha to
gogo from kelso to stroma from hirta to spango.

what is it like there?
och it's freuchie, it's faifley, it's wamphray, it's frandy, it's
sliddery.

what do you do?
we foindle and fungle, we bonkle and meigle and maxpoffle. we
scotstarvit, armit, wormit, and even whifflet. we play at crossstobs,
leuchars, gorbals, and finfan. we scavaig, and there's aye a bit of
tilquhilly. if it's wet, treshnish and mishnish.

what is the best of the country?
blinkbonny! airgold! thundergay!

and the worst?
scrishven, shiskine, scrabster, and snizort.

listen! what's that?
catacol and wauchope, never heed them.

tell us about last night
well, we had a wee ferintosh and we lay on the quiraing. it was pure strontian!

but who was there?
petermoidart and craigenkenneth and cambusputtock and ecclemuchty and corriehulish and balladolly and altnacanny and clauchanvrechan and stronachlochan and auchenlachar and tighnacrankie and tilliebruaich and killieharra and invervannach and achnatudlem and machrishellach and inchtamurchan and auchterfechan and kinlochculter and ardnawhallie and invershuggle.

and what was the toast?
schiehallion! schiehallion! schiehallion!

Starryveldt

starryveldt
  slave
southvenus
  serve
SHARPEVILLE
  shove
shriekvolley
  swerve
shootvillage
  save
spoorvengeance
  stave
spadevoice
  starve
strikevault
  strive

subvert
  starve
smashverwoerd
  strive
scattervoortrekker
  starve
spadevow
  strive
sunvast
  starve
survive
  strive
SO: VAEVICTIS

Message Clear

```
    am              i
                            if
i am                   he
    he r        o
     h    ur    t
     the re          and
     he     re       and
     he re
  a             n   d
    the r                   e
i am    r                 ife
                i n
         s        ion and
i                   d     i e
   am   e res   ect
   am   e res   ection
                    o          f
    the                   life
                    o          f
  m   e         n
        sur e
    the               d   i e
i        s
         s   e t   and
i am the  sur       d
  a   t  res    t
                    o          life
i am  he r                  e
i a         ct
i      r  u    n
i  m   e  e    t
i             t           i e
i         s    t  and
i am th       o    th
i am   r        a
i am the   su      n
i am the   s     on
i am the  e   rect on     e if
i am    re      n    t
i am       s     a      fe
i am       s   e   n   t
i    he  e          d
i   t e  s   t
i       re        a d
  a   th re        a d
  a      s   t on      e
  a   t  re        a d
  a   th r      cn      e
i       resurrect
                    a      life
i am           i n       life
i am   resurrection
i am the resurrection and
i am
i am the resurrection and the life
```

159

Bees' Nest

busybykeobloodybizzinbees
bloodybusybykeobizzinbees
bizzinbloodybykeobusybees
busybloodybykeobizzinbees
bloodybykeobusybizzinbees
bizzinbykeobloodybusybees
busybykeobizzinbloodybees
bloodybykeobizzinbusybees
bizzinbusybykeobloodybees
busybizzinbykeobloodybees
bloodybizzinbykeobusybees
bizzinbusybloodybykeobees

French Persian Cats Having a Ball

chat
shah shah
    chat

        chat shah cha ha
        shah chat cha ha
    shah
    chat
cha
cha

                ha
                chat
                chat
                chatshahchat
            chachacha   chachacha
              shahchatshah
                shah
                shah
                ha
cha
cha
chatcha
   cha
   shahcha
      cha
      chatcha
        cha
        shahcha
          cha
          cha

                              sh ch
                               aha
                              ch sh

Orgy

```
cantercantercantercanter
anteateranteateranteater
antencounterantencounter
antennareactantennareact
antantantantantantantant
antantantantantantantant
antantantantantantantant
antantantantantantantant
cantcountantcantcountant
anaccountantanaccountant
anteateranteateranteater
eateateateateateateateat
eateateateateateateateat
anteatenanteatenanteaten
nectarnectarnectarnectar
trancetrancetrancetrance
    * * * * * * * * * * * * * * *
canteatanantcanteatanant
anteatercantanteatercant
notanantnotanantnotanant
    * * * * * * * * * * * * * *
trancetrancetrancetrance
ocontentocontentocontent
nocanternocanternocanter
```

162

To Joan Eardley

Pale yellow letters
humbly straggling across
the once brilliant red
of a broken shop-face
CONFECTIO
and a blur of children
at their games, passing,
gazing as they pass
at the blur of sweets
in the dingy, cosy
Rottenrow window –
an Eardley on my wall.
Such rags and streaks
that master us! –
that fix what the pick
and bulldozer have crumbled
to a dingier dust,
the living blur
fiercely guarding
energy that has vanished,
cries filling still
the unechoing close!
I wandered by the rubble
and the houses left standing
kept a chill, dying life
in their islands of stone.
No window opened
as the coal cart rolled
and the coalman's call
fell coldly to the ground.
But the shrill children
jump on my wall.

Linoleum Chocolate

Two girls running,
running laughing,
laughing lugging
two rolls of linoleum
along London Road –
a bar of chocolate
flies from the pocket

163

of the second, and a man
picks it up for her, she takes it
and is about to pocket it
but then unwraps it
and the girls have a bite
to recruit the strength
of their giggling progress.

Good Friday

Three o'clock. The bus lurches
round into the sun. 'D's this go –'
he flops beside me – 'right along Bath Street?
– Oh tha's, tha's all right, see I've
got to get some Easter eggs for the kiddies.
I've had a wee drink, ye understand –
ye'll maybe think it's a – funny day
to be celebrating – well, no, but ye see
I wasny working, and I like to celebrate
when I'm no working – I don't say it's right
I'm no saying it's right, ye understand – ye understand?
But anyway tha's the way I look at it –
I'm no boring you, eh? – ye see today,
take today, I don't know what today's in aid of,
whether Christ was – crucified or was he –
rose fae the dead like, see what I mean?
You're an educatit man, you can tell me –
– Aye, well. There ye are. It's been seen
time and again, the working man
has nae education, he jist canny – jist
hasny got it, know what I mean,
he's jist bliddy ignorant – Christ aye,
bliddy ignorant. Well –' The bus brakes violently,
he lunges for the stair, swings down – off,
into the sun for his Easter eggs,
on very
          nearly
                    steady
                         legs.

The Starlings in George Square

I

Sundown on the high stonefields!
The darkening roofscape stirs –
thick – alive with starlings
gathered singing in the square –
like a shower of arrows they cross
the flash of a western window,
they bead the wires with jet,
they nestle preening by the lamps
and shine, sidling by the lamps
and sing, shining, they stir
the homeward hurrying crowds.
A man looks up and points
smiling to his son beside him
wide-eyed at the clamour on those cliffs –
it sinks, shrills out in waves,
levels to a happy murmur,
scatters in swooping arcs,
a stab of confused sweetness
that pierces the boy like a story,
a story more than a song.
He will never forget that evening,
the silhouette of the roofs,
the starlings by the lamps.

II

The City Chambers are hopping mad.
Councillors with rubber plugs in their ears!
Secretaries closing windows!
Window-cleaners want protection and danger money.
The Lord Provost can't hear herself think, man.
What's that?
Lord Provost, can't hear herself think.

At the General Post Office
the clerks write Three Pounds Starling in the savings-books.
Each telephone-booth is like an aviary.
I tried to send a parcel to County Kerry but –
The cables to Cairo got fankled, sir.
What's that?
I said the cables to Cairo got fankled.

And as for the City Information Bureau –
I'm sorry I can't quite chirrup did you twit –
No I wanted to twee but perhaps you can't cheep –
Would you try once again, that's better, I – sweet –
When's the last boat to Milngavie? Tweet?
What's that?
I said when's the last boat to Milngavie?

III

There is nothing for it now but scaffolding:
clamp it together, send for the bird-men,
Scarecrow Strip for the window-ledge landings,
Cameron's Repellent on the overhead wires.
Armour our pediments against eavesdroppers.
This is a human outpost. Save our statues.
Send back the jungle. And think of the joke:
as it says in the papers, It is very comical
to watch them alight on the plastic rollers
and take a tumble. So it doesn't kill them?
All right, so who's complaining? This isn't Peking
where they shoot the sparrows for hygiene and cash.
So we're all humanitarians, locked in our cliff-dwellings
encased in our repellent, guano-free and guilt-free.
The Lord Provost sings in her marble hacienda.
The Postmaster-General licks an audible stamp.
Sir Walter is vexed that his column's deserted.
I wonder if we really deserve starlings?
There is something to be said for these joyous messengers
that we repel in our indignant orderliness.
They lift up the eyes, they lighten the heart,
and some day we'll decipher that sweet frenzied whistling
as they wheel and settle along our hard roofs
and take those grey buttresses for home.
One thing we know they say, after their fashion.
They like the warm cliffs of man.

King Billy

Grey over Riddrie the clouds piled up,
dragged their rain through the cemetery trees.
The gates shone cold. Wind rose
flaring the hissing leaves, the branches

swung, heavy, across the lamps.
Gravestones huddled in drizzling shadow,
flickering streetlight scanned the requiescats,
a name and an urn, a date, a dove
picked out, lost, half-regained.
What is this dripping wreath, blown from its grave
red, white, blue, and gold
'To Our Leader of Thirty years Ago' –

Bareheaded, in dark suits, with flutes
and drums, they brought him here, in procession
seriously, King Billy of Brigton, dead,
from Bridgeton Cross: a memory of violence,
brooding days of empty bellies,
billiard smoke and a sour pint,
boots or fists, famous sherrickings,
the word, the scuffle, the flash, the shout,
bloody crumpling in the close,
bricks for papish windows, get
the Conks next time, the Conks ambush
the Billy Boys, the Billy Boys the Conks till
Sillitoe scuffs the razors down the stank –
No, but it isn't the violence they remember
but the legend of a violent man
born poor, gang-leader in the bad times
of idleness and boredom, lost in better days,
a bouncer in a betting club,
a quiet man at last, dying
alone in Bridgeton in a box bed.
So a thousand people stopped the traffic
for the hearse of a folk hero and the flutes
threw 'Onward Christian Soldiers' to the winds
from unironic lips, the mourners kept
in step, and there were some who wept.

Go from the grave. The shrill flutes
are silent, the march dispersed.
Deplore what is to be deplored,
and then find out the rest.

Glasgow Green

Clammy midnight, moonless mist.
A cigarette glows and fades on a cough.
Meth-men mutter on benches,
pawed by river fog. Monteith Row
sweats coldly, crumbles, dies
slowly. All shadows are alive.
Somewhere a shout's forced out – 'No!' –
it leads to nothing but silence,
except the whisper of the grass
and the other whispers that fill the shadows.

'What d'ye mean see me again?
D'ye think I came here jist for that?
I'm no finished with you yet.
I can get the boys t'ye, they're no that faur away.
You wouldny like that eh? Look there's no two ways aboot it.
Christ but I'm gaun to have you Mac
if it takes all night, turn over you bastard
turn over, I'll —'
                Cut the scene.
Here there's no crying for help,
it must be acted out, again, again.

This is not the delicate nightmare
you carry to the point of fear
and wake from, it is life, the sweat
is real, the wrestling under a bush
is real, the dirty starless river
is the real Clyde, with a dishrag dawn
it rinses the horrors of the night
but cannot make them clean,
though washing blows
                where the women watch
by day,
        and children run,
                on Glasgow Green.

And how shall these men live?
Providence, watch them go!
Watch them love, and watch them die!
How shall the race be served?
It shall be served by anguish
as well as by children at play.
It shall be served by loneliness
as well as by family love.

It shall be served by hunter and hunted in their endless chain
as well as by those who turn back the sheets in peace.
The thorn in the flesh!
Providence, water it!
Do you think it is not watered?
Do you think it is not planted?
Do you think there is not a seed of the thorn
as there is also a harvest of the thorn?
Man, take in that harvest!
Help that tree to bear its fruit!
Water the wilderness, walk there, reclaim it!
Reclaim, regain, renew! Fill the barns and the vats!

Longing,
            longing
                        shall find its wine.

Let the women sit in the Green
and rock their prams as the sheets
blow and whip in the sunlight.
But the beds of married love
are islands in a sea of desire.
Its waves break here, in this park,
splashing the flesh as it trembles
like driftwood through the dark.

The Suspect

Asked me for a match suddenly/with his hand up
I thought he was after my wallet
gave him a shove/he fell down
dead on the pavement at my feet
he was forty-two, a respectable man they said
anyone can have a bad heart I told the police
but they've held me five hours and don't
tell me the innocent don't feel
guilty in the glaring chair

I didn't kill you/I didn't know you
I did push you/I did fear you
accusing me from the mortuary drawer
like a damned white ghost I don't believe in
– then why were you afraid/are you used to attacks
by men who want a match/what sort

169

of life you lead/you were bloody quick
with your hands when you pushed him
what did you think he was and do you think
we don't know what you are/take it
all down/the sweat of the innocent by god we'll see
and not by the hundred-watt bulb of the anglepoise either
give him a clip on the ear jack/you
bastard in your shroud if I feared you then
I hate you now you
no I don't you poor dead man I put you there
I don't I don't
but just

if you could get up/to speak for me
I am on trial/do you understand
I am not guilty/whatever the light says
whatever the sweat says
/they've noticed my old scar
to be killed by a dead man is no fight
they're starting again
so/your story is he asked you for a light
– yes suddenly/and put his hand up/I thought
he was after my wallet, gave him
a shove, he fell as I told you
dead, it was his heart,
at my feet, as I said

In the Snack-bar

A cup capsizes along the formica,
slithering with a dull clatter.
A few heads turn in the crowded evening snack-bar.
An old man is trying to get to his feet
from the low round stool fixed to the floor.
Slowly he levers himself up, his hands have no power.
He is up as far as he can get. The dismal hump
looming over him forces his head down.
He stands in his stained beltless gaberdine
like a monstrous animal caught in a tent
in some story. He sways slightly,
the face not seen, bent down
in shadow under his cap.
Even on his feet he is staring at the floor
or would be, if he could see.

I notice now his stick, once painted white
but scuffed and muddy, hanging from his right arm.
Long blind, hunchback born, half paralysed
he stands
fumbling with the stick
and speaks:
'I want – to go to the – toilet.'

It is down two flights of stairs, but we go.
I take his arm. 'Give me – your arm – it's better,' he says.
Inch by inch we drift towards the stairs.
A few yards of floor are like a landscape
to be negotiated, in the slow setting out
time has almost stopped. I concentrate
my life to his: crunch of spilt sugar,
slidy puddle from the night's umbrellas,
table edges, people's feet,
hiss of the coffee-machine, voices and laughter,
smell of a cigar, hamburgers, wet coats steaming,
and the slow dangerous inches to the stairs.
I put his right hand on the rail
and take his stick. He clings to me. The stick
is in his left hand, probing the treads.
I guide his arm and tell him the steps.
And slowly we go down. And slowly we go down.
White tiles and mirrors at last. He shambles
uncouth into the clinical gleam.
I set him in position, stand behind him
and wait with his stick.
His brooding reflection darkens the mirror
but the trickle of his water is thin and slow,
an old man's apology for living.
Painful ages to close his trousers and coat –
I do up the last buttons for him.
He asks doubtfully, 'Can I – wash my hands?'
I fill the basin, clasp his soft fingers round the soap.
He washes, feebly, patiently. There is no towel.
I press the pedal of the drier, draw his hands
gently into the roar of the hot air.
But he cannot rub them together,
drags out a handkerchief to finish.
He is glad to leave the contraption, and face the stairs.
He climbs, and steadily enough.
He climbs, we climb. He climbs
with many pauses but with that one
persisting patience of the undefeated
which is the nature of man when all is said.

And slowly we go up. And slowly we go up.
The faltering, unfaltering steps
take him at last to the door
across that endless, yet not endless waste of floor.
I watch him helped on a bus. It shudders off in the rain.
The conductor bends to hear where he wants to go.

Wherever he could go it would be dark
and yet he must trust men.
Without embarrassment or shame
he must announce his most pitiful needs
in a public place. No one sees his face.
Does he know how frightening he is in his strangeness
under his mountainous coat, his hands like wet leaves
stuck to the half-white stick?
His life depends on many who would evade him.
But he cannot reckon up the chances,
having one thing to do,
to haul his blind hump through these rains of August.
Dear Christ, to be born for this!

Trio

Coming up Buchanan Street, quickly, on a sharp winter evening
a young man and two girls, under the Christmas lights –
The young man carries a new guitar in his arms,
the girl on the inside carries a very young baby,
and the girl on the outside carries a chihuahua.
And the three of them are laughing, their breath rises
in a cloud of happiness, and as they pass
the boy says, 'Wait till he sees this but!'
The chihuahua has a tiny Royal Stewart tartan coat like a teapot-
        holder,
the baby in its white shawl is all bright eyes and mouth like favours
        in a fresh sweet cake,
the guitar swells out under its milky plastic cover, tied at the neck
        with silver tinsel tape and a brisk sprig of mistletoe.
Orphean sprig! Melting baby! Warm chihuahua!
The vale of tears is powerless before you.
Whether Christ is born, or is not born, you
put paid to fate, it abdicates
                        under the Christmas lights.
Monsters of the year
go blank, are scattered back,
can't bear this march of three.

– And the three have passed, vanished in the crowd
(yet not vanished, for in their arms they wind
the life of men and beasts, and music,
laughter ringing them round like a guard)
at the end of this winter's day.

Pomander

pomander
open pomander
open poem and her
open poem and him
open poem and hymn
hymn and hymen leander
high man pen meander
o pen poem me and her
pen me poem me and him
om mane padme hum
pad me home panda hand
open up o holy panhandler
ample panda pen or bamboo pond
ponder a bonny poem pomander opener
open banned peon penman hum and banter
open hymn and pompom band and panda hamper
o i am a pen open man or happener
i am open manner happener
happy are we open
poem and a pom
poem and a panda
poem and aplomb

Summer Haiku

```
P o o l.
P e o p l
e     p l o p!
C o o l.
```


Siesta of a Hungarian Snake

s sz sz SZ sz SZ sz ZS zs ZS zs zs z

Boats and Places

I
row the sea
row it easy
Rothesay

II
Greek
       creek
creak
caïque

III
dhow
whoa
    Howrah
    hurrah
    howdah
        andhow

IV
junk tug shag wee tow
bank two carp long catch
sam pan bet men go
oh ho
Hong Kong crow sing snatch

V
the Nore
an oar
no more

VI
– rat-tat-tat!
– Ataturk?
– Van cat!
– caravan?
– catamaran!
– ark track?
– Ararat!

VII
Ardnadam
Polaris Eve
mother-felucca

Seven Headlines

```
                    ol              d
                    sol     e    m     n
                    o              de
                    sol            d
       f            o                    r
       f       e              n    der
  i        r      o                    n
                b ol          d
             tre              n    d
  i                           n
  l      et                   t     er
                              t  o
                    sol          o
           re a                      der
     a      r      so     n
  i                                      n
                b ol     t
     f      r     o  m
                b  lu  e
     a          bs     ent
     f              o       od
                b    u      d
     f              o  u   n    d
       ut  t e                        r
     f     e  r      ment
  i                      n
          re a so                n
          t e a      m
     f     e  e              d
     a      t              modern
                    l            ode
                         n   o
     f     et              t      er
     f              o            r
                absolu    t    e
                         m      odern
                         men
il faut être absolument moderne
```

176

The Computer's First Christmas Card

```
j o l l y m e r r y
h o l l y b e r r y
j o l l y b e r r y
m e r r y h o l l y
h a p p y j o l l y
j o l l y j e l l y
j e l l y b e l l y
b e l l y m e r r y
h o l l y h e p p y
j o l l y M o l l y
m a r r y J e r r y
m e r r y H a r r y
h o p p y B a r r y
h e p p y J a r r y
b o p p y h e p p y
b e r r y j o r r y
j o r r y j o l l y
m o p p y j e l l y
M o l l y m e r r y
J e r r y j o l l y
b e l l y b o p p y
j o r r y h o p p y
h o l l y m o p p y
B a r r y m e r r y
J a r r y h a p p y
h a p p y b o p p y
b o p p y j o l l y
j o l l y m e r r y
m e r r y m e r r y
m e r r y m e r r y
m e r r y C h r i s
a m m e r r y a s a
C h r i s m e r r y
a s M E R R Y C H R
Y S A N T H E M U M
```

Opening the Cage
14 variations on 14 words

I have nothing to say and I am saying it and that is poetry.
John Cage

I have to say poetry and is that nothing and am I saying it
I am and I have poetry to say and is that nothing saying it
I am nothing and I have poetry to say and that is saying it
I that am saying poetry have nothing and it is I and to say
And I say that I am to have poetry and saying it is nothing
I am poetry and nothing and saying it is to say that I have
To have nothing is poetry and I am saying that and I say it
Poetry is saying I have nothing and I am to say that and it
Saying nothing I am poetry and I have to say that and it is
It is and I am and I have poetry saying say that to nothing
It is saying poetry to nothing and I say I have and am that
Poetry is saying I have it and I am nothing and to say that
And that nothing is poetry I am saying and I have to say it
Saying poetry is nothing and to that I say I am and have it

The Chaffinch Map of Scotland

chaffinch
chaffinchaffinch
chaffinchaffinchaffinch
chaffinchaffinchaffinch
chaffinchaffinch
chaffinch
chaffie   chye   chaffiechaffie
chaffie   chye   chaffiechaffie
chye   chaffie
chaffiechaffiechaffie
chaffiechaffiechaffie
chaffiechaffie
chaffiechaffie
chaffiechaffie
chaffiechaffie

shilly shelly
shelfyshilfyshellyshilly
she!fyshillyshilly
shilfyshellyshelly
shilfyshelfyshelly
shellyfaw
shielyshellyfaw

shilfy
shilfyshelfy shielyshiely
shilfyshelfyshelfy   shielychaffie
chaffiechaffie   chaffiechaffie
chaffiechaffie
shilfyshilfyshilfyshelfyshelfy
chaffieshilfyshilfyshelfyshelfyshelfyshelfyshelfy
chaffieshilfyshilfyshelfyshelfyshelfyshelfyshelfy
shilfyshilfyshilfyshelfy   shelfyshelfy
shilfy   shilfy
shilfy
shilfyshelfy

brichtie

The Second Life

But does every man feel like this at forty –
I mean it's like Thomas Wolfe's New York, his
heady light, the stunning plunging canyons, beauty –
pale stars winking hazy downtown quitting-time,
and the winter moon flooding the skyscrapers, northern –
an aspiring place, glory of the bridges, foghorns
are enormous messages, a looming mastery
that lays its hand on the young man's bowels
until he feels in that air, that rising spirit
all things are possible, he rises with it
until he feels that he can never die –
Can it be like this, and is this what it means
in Glasgow now, writing as the aircraft roar
over building sites, in this warm west light
by the daffodil banks that were never so crowded and lavish –
green May, and the slow great blocks rising
under yellow tower cranes, concrete and glass and steel
out of a dour rubble it was and barefoot children gone –
Is it only the slow stirring, a city's renewed life
that stirs me, could it stir me so deeply
as May, but could May have stirred
what I feel of desire and strength
like an arm saluting a sun?

All January, all February the skaters
enjoyed Bingham's pond, the crisp cold evenings,
they swung and flashed among car headlights,
the drivers parked round the unlit pond
to watch them, and give them light, what laughter
and pleasure rose in the rare lulls
of the yards-away stream of wheels along Great Western Road!
The ice broke up, but the boats came out.
The painted boats are ready for pleasure.
The long light needs no headlamps.

Black oar cuts a glitter: it is heaven on earth.

Is it true that we come alive
not once, but many times?
We are drawn back to the image
of the seed in darkness, or the greying skin
of the snake that hides a shining one –
it will push that used-up matter off
and even the film of the eye is sloughed –
That the world may be the same, and we are not

and so the world is not the same,
the second eye is making again
this place, these waters and these towers,
they are rising again
as the eye stands up to the sun,
as the eye salutes the sun.

Many things are unspoken
in the life of a man, and with a place
there is an unspoken love also
in undercurrents, drifting, waiting its time.
A great place and its people are not renewed lightly.
The caked layers of grime
grow warm, like homely coats.
But yet they will be dislodged
and men will still be warm.
The old coats are discarded.
The old ice is loosed.
The old seeds are awake.

Slip out of darkness, it is time.

The Sheaf

My life, as a slant of rain
on the grey earth fields
is gathered in thirsty silence, disappears.
I cannot even guess
the roots, but feel them sighing
in the stir of the soil I die to. Let this rain
be on the children of my heart,
I have no other ones.
                    On the generations,
on the packed cells and dreaming shoots,
the untried hopes, the waiting good
I send this drop to melt.

181

The Unspoken

When the troopship was pitching round the Cape
in '41, and there was a lull in the night uproar of seas and winds,
    and a sudden full moon
swung huge out of the darkness like the world it is,
and we all crowded onto the wet deck, leaning on the rail, our arms
    on each other's shoulders, gazing at the savage outcrop of
    great Africa,
And Tommy Cosh started singing 'Mandalay' and we joined in
    with our raucous chorus of the unforgettable song,
and the dawn came up like thunder like that moon drawing the
    water of our yearning
though we were going to war, and left us exalted,
that was happiness,
but it is not like that.

When the television newscaster said
the second sputnik was up, not empty
but with a small dog on board,
a half-ton treasury of life orbiting a thousand miles above the thin
    television masts and mists of November,
in clear space, heard, observed,
the faint far heartbeat sending back its message
steady and delicate,
and I was stirred by a deep confusion of feelings,
got up, stood with my back to the wall and my palms pressed hard
    against it, my arms held wide
as if I could spring from this earth –
not loath myself to go out that very day where Laika had shown
    man,
felt my cheeks burning with old Promethean warmth
rekindled – ready –
covered my face with my hands, seeing only an animal
strapped in a doomed capsule, but the future
was still there, cool and whole like the moon,
waiting to be taken, smiling even
as the dog's bones and the elaborate casket of aluminium
glow white and fuse in the arc of re-entry,
and I knew what I felt was history,
its thrilling brilliance came down,
came down,
comes down on us all, bringing pride and pity,
but it is not like that.

But Glasgow days and grey weathers, when the rain
beat on the bus shelter and you leaned slightly against me, and the
    back of your hand touched my hand in the shadows, and
    nothing was said,
when your hair grazed mine accidentally as we talked in a café,
    yet not quite accidentally,
when I stole a glance at your face as we stood in a doorway and found
    I was afraid
of what might happen if I should never see it again,
when we met, and met, in spite of such differences in our lives,
and did the common things that in our feeling
became extraordinary, so that our first kiss
was like the winter morning moon, and as you shifted in my arms
it was the sea changing the shingle that changes it
as if for ever (but we are bound by nothing, but like smoke
to mist or light in water we move, and mix) –
O then it was a story as old as war or man,
and although we have not said it we know it,
and although we have not claimed it we do it,
and although we have not vowed it we keep it,
without a name to the end.

From a City Balcony

How often when I think of you the day grows bright!
Our silent love
wanders in Glen Fruin with butterflies and cuckoos –
bring me the drowsy country thing! Let it drift above the traffic
by the open window with a cloud of witnesses –
a sparkling burn, white lambs, the blaze of gorse,
the cuckoos calling madly, the real white clouds over us,
white butterflies about your hand in the short hot grass,
and then the witness was my hand closing on yours,
my mouth brushing your eyelids and your lips
again and again till you sighed and turned for love.
Your breast and thighs were blazing like the gorse.
I covered your great fire in silence there.
We let the day grow old along the grass.
It was in the silence the love was.

Footsteps and witnesses! In this Glasgow balcony who pours
such joy like mountain water? It brims, it spills over and over
down to the parched earth and the relentless wheels.
How often will I think of you, until

our dying steps forget this light, forget
that we ever knew the happy glen,
or that I ever said, We must jump into the sun,
and we jumped into the sun.

When you go

When you go,
if you go,
and I should want to die,
there's nothing I'd be saved by
more than the time
you fell asleep in my arms
in a trust so gentle
I let the darkening room
drink up the evening, till
rest, or the new rain
lightly roused you awake.
I asked if you heard the rain in your dream
and half dreaming still you only said, I love you.

Strawberries

There were never strawberries
like the ones we had
that sultry afternoon
sitting on the step
of the open french window
facing each other
your knees held in mine
the blue plates in our laps
the strawberries glistening
in the hot sunlight
we dipped them in sugar
looking at each other
not hurrying the feast
for one to come
the empty plates
laid on the stone together
with the two forks crossed
and I bent towards you

184

sweet in that air
in my arms
abandoned like a child
from your eager mouth
the taste of strawberries
in my memory
lean back again
let me love you

let the sun beat
on our forgetfulness
one hour of all
the heat intense
and summer lightning
on the Kilpatrick hills

let the storm wash the plates

The Witness

No, there is no spirit standing in the sun,
only a great light and heat, that instantly
surround us when we meet.
The cold of solitude was
an effigy in a trance –
it was not death! my eyes were watching! my blood
was waiting to be moved by your hand.
We must believe it, though beyond
all gratitude when it comes –
to melt the bonds!
Half unbelieving I rose with you,
half uncaring I closed you
in my arms and left the trance.

There are effigies throughout the world! that I would touch!
that I would warm to life
out of the hell of stone
where they lie waiting,
broken in fields, staring,
frozen by the lathe,
carved in brickdust, in smoke,
in chains of ordinances,
and also in chains.
There is a witness! There is no god on the altiplano

where they scratch the earth,
but there is a witness, and time keeps it
like the first men's fire.
The ordnance crash, and burning villages
feed pain with men, juntas
lay the cold table again with steel.
You can't speak for others, there are no others.
You can only say there is that witness
standing where they fall, as it waits
in language, the promise like a prominence
that trembles on the crown of the sun –
only a million miles of fire,
and a signal to the eyes that are watching.

One Cigarette

No smoke without you, my fire.
After you left,
your cigarette glowed on in my ashtray
and sent up a long thread of such quiet grey
I smiled to wonder who would believe its signal
of so much love. One cigarette
in the non-smoker's tray.
As the last spire
trembles up, a sudden draught
blows it winding into my face.
Is it smell, is it taste?
You are here again, and I am drunk on your tobacco lips.
Out with the light.
Let the smoke lie back in the dark.
Till I hear the very ash
sigh down among the flowers of brass
I'll breathe, and long past midnight, your last kiss.

The Picnic

In a little rainy mist of white and grey
we sat under an old tree,
drank tea toasts to the powdery mountain,
undrunk got merry, played catch
with the empty flask, on the pine needles
came down to where it rolled stealthily away –

you lay
with one arm in the rain, laughing
shaking only your wet hair
loose against the grass, in that enchanted place
of tea, with curtains of a summer rain
dropped round us, for a rainy day.

Absence

My shadow –
I woke to a wind swirling the curtains light and dark
and the birds twittering on the roofs, I lay cold
in the early light in my room high over London.
What fear was it that made the wind sound like a fire
so that I got up and looked out half-asleep
at the calm rows of street-lights fading far below?
Without fire
only the wind blew.
But in the dream I woke from, you
came running through the traffic, tugging me, clinging
to my elbow, your eyes spoke
what I could not grasp –
Nothing, if you were here!

The wind of the early quiet
merges slowly now with a thousand rolling wheels.
The lights are out, the air is loud.
It is an ordinary January day.
My shadow, do you hear the streets?
Are you at my heels? Are you here?
And I throw back the sheets.

Without It

Without it
there is nothing, an emptiness that's broken
by a nail scraping a drum, you cower in the hole of the drum
    screaming, no one hears you, sees you,
the space is empty to the eaves, the eaves to the stars,
an electronic yelling from Andromeda

hits the dish, how you subsist, the waves hideous to your hunger bang
        you flat to the hard black drum wall
standing, standing screaming, spreadeagled, revolving
with no hand in yours on either side of the slipping wall
and falling, never fallen, you subsist
cast out, cast into your cast iron maiden
who cannot kill, you subsist on the spikes
of anti-matter till you're cast in cries,
and no one hears, or sees, and the star
sends, and sends, and sends
unsteady, monstrous, waning
vacant until it dies, you'd give a world
for a stream of human lies,
because they could be lies.

(And you remember
diving in the pool together, flashing through the dapple
with the leaves trailing, never dreamed
there could be such pleasure, while the great wheel
bent its business to break you,
a thunderstorm scattered the flying heels
and trains and letters and bad faith and time
corrupted the heart, and one day there was nothing
as if, like the old stories, it had never been.)

Grinding rotor! Grave of dreams! Children
play on the sands you plunge through,
a desolation without dimension.
The swallow builds in your invisible eaves,
and poppies linger blowing long,
the smell of miles of acrid iron seems far away.
But everything is in its place, the pinch of clover
from a summer field could break the heart.
Subsist in iron, and wait.

The Welcome

When love comes late, but fated,
the very ground seems on fire with tongues of running time,
and conscious hearts are speaking
of the long vistas closed in clouds
by lonely waters, all goodbyes
where the swallow is a shadow
swooping back, like youth, to silence.

If all goodbyes could be drowned in one welcome,
and the pain of waiting be washed from a hundred street-corners,
and dry rebuffs and grey regrets, backs marching into rain
slip like a film from the soiled spirit made new –
I'd take that late gift, and those tongues
of fire would burn out in our
thankful fountains, to the sea.

O Pioneers!

THIS TUNNEL WAS BUGN BEGUBNUGN IN 1880
WILLIAM SHARP
Workman's inscription on entrance to abandoned Channel Tunnel at Dover

Channel Tunnel bugn.
1880. Sharp Wilgn.

Tannel Chunnel begum.
8018. Shart Willum.

Tennal Chennul gbung.
8081. Shant Willung.

Chennul Tennal bengug.
8108. Shunt Willibug.

Chunnal Tennel begbugn.
8801. Slunt Willubugmn.

Chuntenlannel begubnugn.
8810. Blunt Wuglbumlugn.

* * * * * * * * * *

10880. Brigde bugn.

189

Construction for I.K. Brunel

I AM BARD
I AM ISOBAR
I AM IRON BAR
I AM IRON BARD
I AM BY ASGARD
I AM IRON ICEBERG great western suspension steam telegraph king DOM BRUNELLESCHAL
I STAND GUARD great eastern hungerford canal cableboat king DOM BLOOMMIDDLE
I SPAN BARRED great clifton railtunnel docks submarine king DOM BLUEMEZZO
I SEEM BARED great britain explosions locks towerpier king DOM BOONMEDAL
I STAB HARD

DOM BRUMEL
DOM BOOMMILL
DOM BROODWELL
DOM BREWMETAL
DOM BROOKMEDDLE
DOM BRUMMELL

Unscrambling the Waves at Goonhilly

telfish
dogstar
sarphin
doldine
telwhal
narstar
sardock
haddine
dogwhal
narfish
doldock
hadphin
dogdock
hadfish
dolwhal
narphin
hadwhal
nardock
teldock
hadstar
sarwhal
nardine
dogphin
dolfish
sarfish
dogdine
dolstar
telphin
sarstar
teldine
sardine
dolphin
haddock
narwhal
dogfish
telstar

The Tower of Pisa

I BASE

this is the old base cut
this cold base is no cult
this is the cold old rock
this is the culled rock face
this place is all stone cold
this is the round cold form
this chilled stone foam is bold
this cut culled form holds show
this old arched hold lies low
this is the bowl of snow

this rock floor is all holed
this whole skilled show is held
this rock is told to hold
this is the child of form
this is the shield of foam
this is the drag down stone
this is called build and wait
this weighed down round drags deep
this just firm sound weight creeps
this bold old place just keeps

II MIDDLE

here are the heart rocks locked
here are the spine beams filed
here are the mid ribs backed
here are the stark stone stores
here high hard stones stare round
here round dark stairs file down
here files of floors hang bones
here shades of stone throng walls
here mid spine walls rock winds
here winds rub white ribs thin

here eyes see domes hang grave
here bricks frame spires hung grey
here doors watch bridge clamp stream
here high walls watch hawks climb
here sun streams home on stones
here domes and homes hang low
here cries climb ramps like smoke
here doves stamp old soft sills
here hills are smoke made stone
here grave eyes bridge two hills

here the dry bricks lean out
here the high heart strains bars
here the caged shape takes heart
here the barred height shakes hard
here the bold brick breaks shape
here the black breaks show bald
here the lean spokes take slopes
here the slopes build high hopes
here the hopes hang like ropes
here rows of slopes blow bold

III   TOP
now winds try high top tiers
now high piers creep and cry
now top floors float from true
now strong true stone slips free
now brick arc bows back down
now worn stripped brick face slides
now brick dust slips down rifts
now wan stone lifts and leans
now wind rips cracks in jambs
now sprung joints creak lean songs

now storm bowls down blank flues
now clouds bank low on roofs
now sharp cracks start from clouds
now quick white bursts glare hard
now bolts of hail hit bells
now guard rails hiss with rains
now rones roll rich and spout
now leaks sprout bright wet wings
now wet springs pour down walls
now wet inch sinks on inch

now black rails drip
now bell rims dip
now whipped lead snaps
now bats shake cramps
now damp stars blink
now one side shrinks
now top floors flap
now roof rats twitch
now eight stacks stand
now eight stacks stand

Spacepoem 1:
from Laika to Gagarin

ra ke ta ra ke ta ra ke ta ra ke ta ra ke ta ra ke ta ra ke ta
sputsputsputsputsputsputsputsputsputsputsputsputsputsput
nik lai nik bel nik strel nik pchel nik mush nik chernush nik zvezdoch
kakakakakakakakakakakakakakakakakakakakakakakakakakakaka
spu spu tink spu kak spink spu sobak spu ka kink tak so
nikka laika kalai kanikka kanaka kana sput
nikka belka kabel kanikka kanaka kana stup
nikka strelka kastrel kanikka kanaka kana pust
nikka pchelka kapchel kanikka kanaka kana psut
nikka mushka kamush kanikka kanaka kana tusp
nikka chernushka kachernush kanikka kanaka kana tsup
nikka zvezdochka kazvezdoch kanikka kanaka kana upst
barker whitiearrow beespot blackie star
whitie arrowbarker beeblackie star spot
arrow barkerbee whitiestar blackie spot
bee arrowwhitie barkerspot star blackie
barkbark! whitewhitewhite! blackblackblackblack!
star! spot! sput! stop! star! sputsput! star! spout! spurt! start!
starrow! starrow! starrow!

putputputputputputputputputputputputputputputputput
nikniknikniknikniknikniknikniknikniknikniknikniknikniknik
ka kra keta ka kra keta ka kra keta ka kra keta ka kra keta
kaktok kaktok kaktok kaktok kaktok kaktok kaktok kaktok
dakakvos dakakvos dakakvos dakakvos dakakvos dakakvos
davostok davostok davostok davostok davostok davostok
dadadadadadadadadadadadadadadadadadadadadadadadadadada
daga daga daga daga daga daga daga daga daga daga daga
dagaga dagaga dagaga dagaga dagaga dagaga dagaga dagaga
dakakgaga rin dakakgaga rin dakakgaga rin dakakgaga rin
vostok! mir! vladi! yuri! mir! vladi! vladimir! vladivostok! yurimirny
vladimirny! yurilaika! nikitaraketa! balalaika!
raketasobakaslava! vladislava!

Chinese Cat

```
p m r k g n i a o u
p m r k g n i a o
p m r k n i a o
p m r n i a o
p m r i a o
p m i a o
m i a o
m a o
```

Islands

Perfect illusion of a great island in the sea,
the Polynesian cloud drifting rakish, purple
across the horizon in the late afternoon
with a volcanic sun erupting gold behind it –
when it all breaks, you hardly believe in islands.
Standing on what might break, you hardly believe.
Standing on what might not even be, you hardly
are, till a coconut thuds, and is,
and then you are.
                         Drink up your coconut,
turn in, take supper, other tests will come.
If clouds are islands, fireflies may be stars,
even stars may not be stars, but islands,
island universes so unimaginably far
we can only say they were, not are.
But why look up at all? Did we begin on tektites?
Is that our coconut? What came to the world
when it was cool and ready, thudding through the cryptogams?
The continents drifted apart like clouds,
were frozen spores not thawed in the wrinkled valleys?
The cracks are filled with man.
Out! Out! he drifts, and strains, and cries for islands.
Take the voyage out then! Drink the milk of space!
Let the night break like a shell – throw it behind you.
And let the great islands of space, which are not clouds
Magellanic or earthly, be your morning landfall.

In Sobieski's Shield

well the prophets were dancing in the end much
good it did them and the sun didn't rise at all
anywhere but we weren't among the frozen we had been
dematerialized the day before solar withdrawal
in a hurry it's true but by the best technique
who said only technique well anyhow the best
available and here we are now rematerialized
to the best of my knowledge on a minor planet
of a sun in Sobieski's Shield in our right mind I hope
approximately though not unshaken and admittedly
not precisely those who set out if one can
speak of it by that wellworn tellurian euphemism
in any case molecular reconstitution is no
sinecure even with mice and I wouldn't have been
utterly surprised if some of us had turned out
mice or worse

but at least not that or not yet the effects
of violent change are still slightly present an
indescribable stringent sensation like perhaps being
born or dying but no neither of these I am
very nearly who I was I see I have only
four fingers on my left hand and there's a sharp
twinge I never had in my knee and one most curious
I almost said birthmark and so it is in a sense
light brown shaped like a crazy heart spreading
across my right forearm well let it be we are
here my wife my son the rest of the laboratory
my wife has those streaks of fiery red in her
hair that is expected in women she looks very
frightened yet and lies rigid the rematerialization
is slow in her but that is probably better yes
her eyes flutter to mine questioning I nod can I
smile I think I can does she see me yes thank god
she is hardly altered apart from that extraordinarily
strange and beautiful crown of bright red hair
I draw her head into my arms and hide the sobbing
shuddering first breaths of her second life I don't
know what made me use that phrase who are we
if we are not who we were we have only
one life though we are huddled now in our
protective dome on this harsh metallic plain
that belches cobalt from its craters under a
white-bronze pulsing gong of a sun it was all
they could do for us light-years away it seemed suitable

dematerialization's impossible over short distances anyway
so let's start moving I can surely get onto my feet
yes hoy there

my son is staring fascinated at my four fingers
you've only one nipple I tell him and it's true
but for compensation when he speaks his boy's
treble has broken and at thirteen he is a man
what a limbo to lose childhood in where has
it gone between the throwing of a switch and these
alien iron hills across so many stars his blue eyes
are the same but there's a new graveness of the
second life that phrase again we go up together
to the concave of the dome the environment after all
has to be studied

is that a lake of mercury I can't quite see
through the smoke of the fumarole it's lifting now
but there's something puzzling even when I
my memory of mercury seems to be confused with
what is it blood no no mercury's not like blood
what then what is it I'm remembering or nearly
remembering look dad mercury he says and so it
must be but I see a shell-hole filled with rain-water
red in the sinking sun I know that landscape too
one of the wars far back twentieth century I think the
great war was it called France Flanders fields I remember
reading these craters waterlogged with rain mud blood
I can see a stark hand brandishing nothing through placid scum
in a lull of the guns what horror that the livid water
is not shaken by the pity of the tattoo on the dead arm
a heart still held above the despair of the mud
my god the heart on my arm my second birth mark
the rematerialization has picked up these fragments I have
a graft of war and ancient agony forgive
me my dead helper

the sulky pool of mercury stares back at me I am
seeing normally now but I know these flashes will return
from the far past times I gather my wife and son to me
with a fierce gesture that surprises them I am not
a demonstrative man yet how to tell them
what and who I am that we are bound to all that lived
though the barriers are unspeakable we know a little of that
but something what is it gets through it is not
an essence but an energy how it pierces how it
clutches for still as I run my hand through her

197

amazing hair streaming on my shoulder I feel
a fist shaken in a shell-hole turn in my very marrow
we shall live in the rings of this chain the jeremiahs
who said nothing human would stand are confounded if I cry
even the dry tear in my heart that I cannot
stop or if I laugh to think they thought they
could divide the indivisible the old moon's in
the new moon's arms let's take our second
like our first life out from the dome are the suits
ready the mineral storm is quieter it's hard
to go let's go

From the Domain of Arnheim

And so that all these ages, these years
we cast behind us, like the smoke-clouds
dragged back into vacancy when the rocket springs –

The domain of Arnheim was all snow, but we were there.
We saw a yellow light thrown on the icefield
from the huts by the pines, and laughter came up
floating from a white corrie
miles away, clearly.
We moved on down, arm in arm.
I know you would have thought it was a dream
but we were there. And those were trumpets –
tremendous round the rocks –
while they were burning fires of trash and mammoths' bones.
They sang naked, and kissed in the smoke.
A child, or one of their animals, was crying.
Young men blew the ice crystals off their drums.
We came down among them, but of course
they could see nothing, on their time-scale.
Yet they sensed us, stopped, looked up – even into our eyes.
To them we were a displacement of the air,
a sudden chill, yet we had no power
over their fear. If one of them had been dying
he would have died. The crying
came from one just born: that was the cause
of the song. We saw it now. What had we stopped
but joy?
I know you felt
the same dismay, you gripped my arm, they were waiting
for what they knew of us to pass.

A sweating trumpeter took
a brand from the fire with a shout and threw it
where our bodies would have been –
we felt nothing but his courage.
And so they would deal with every imagined power
seen or unseen.
There are no gods in the domain of Arnheim.

We signalled to the ship; got back;
our lives and days returned to us, but
haunted by deeper souvenirs than any rocks or seeds.
From time the souvenirs are deeds.

For the International Poetry Incarnation
Royal Albert Hall, *11 June 1965*

Worldscene! Worldtime! Spacebreaker! Wildship! Starman!
Gemini man dangles white and golden – the world floats
on a gold cord and curves blue white beautiful below him –
Vostok shrieks and prophesies, Mariner's prongs flash –
to the wailing of Voskhod Earth sighs, she shakes men loose at last –
out, in our time, to be living seeds sent far beyond
even imagination, though imagination is awake – take
poets on your voyages! Prometheus
embraces Icarus and in a gold shell with wings
he launches him up through the ghostly detritus
of gods and dirty empires and dying laws,
he mounts, he cries, he shouts, he shines, he streams
like light new done, his home is in a sun
and he shall be the burning unburned one.
In darkness, Daedalus
embraces Orpheus, the dark lips caked with earth and roots
he kisses open, the cold body he rubs
to a new life – the dream
flutters in a cage of crumbling bars, reviving

and then beginning slowly singing of the stars.

Beginning singing, born to go.
To cut the cord of gold. To get
the man new born to go.

What is 'Paradise Lost' really about?

The bard has fired his bullet at the fox.
The dilatory fox is full of duck.
The gun takes brush and breakfast, quack and cluck.
Foxes in satchels are sequestered flocks.

The critic shakes the satchel with a cry.
'Your fur is feathers! You have bagged a bird!'
The simple bard is bolshy when he's stirred.
'I felled a fox, and foxes cannot fly.'

Deep in the duck the maggot faintly mauls.
Viruses mill within the maggot's vein.
The photomicrograph shows fields of grain.
Down in these fields the fox's double falls.

Critics can pant across this paradox.
Critics can call the bard a blunderbuss.
Bards who have shot their shout are boisterous.
Bards have the fox's body in a box.

The Ages

There was this universe on Saturday –
it may have been here before, but we had never seen
the bearded hotels, the money-pushers, the glory-holes five hundred
    storeys up,
two crazy iron curtains blowing in a wind that cut granite follies off
    the pull-ropes,
a labyrinth of horizontal windows with gesticulations
tipping over into the sarcophagus, and this
open to the roses, as it all was.
Down they came, splash full,
blurring the curly beds where absolutely fourteen Q-bar topologists
    had been
moulded as pioneers in the Friday dish-off,
and what a pincer that was! In a good imitation
of lifeblood now, in the rosebath, it was all a swimming red
foaming and breathing in its own life over
the grime and under the iron.
Acid penthouses spat
uselessly into that.

All that red!
This is hard to understand. There were no roses.

In the ages of Thursday, the legend of a round-over,
one topologist jerked into dimension
like an eel in a net; some cursed him even then.
Wednesday was the last museums,
they oiled weapons, froze roses, buried germanium.
Shadows were coming over almost in a somnolence
of their substance, while light was no switch-on but a low glare
      hardly gaining on grey – they
sat on steps with cat's-cradles, dice, obsolete laser-guns,
and without speaking they watched the clouds.
You think you can come back from Saturday?
You think you'd know what they felt? You can't imagine and you
      can't get back.
Not to the last laser-cities of Wednesday,
far less to Tuesday when there were children and the trains ran,
or Monday and the radiolarians.

Partial transformations endlessly
pull the dream forward into it – into
what can never become memory
even in the distance of its most famous stations.
The unintelligible proscenium
shakes suddenly with lights, the metal drapes
groan, clang to blasts of voice
but all that arena
batters outward back
only into the amazement
that caused it.
What can we remember? There was no first man,
the dawn horse on the downs was coming there, was there, was gone
      in forms
we'd lose like shadows across our land.
It all turns
into what can never reach back touching
even the most it had loved with its hands.

We are to peer forward, and report.
Whoever on that Saturday said he saw
where the roses came from, if they were roses?

A View of Things

what I love about dormice is their size
what I hate about rain is its sneer
what I love about the Bratach Gorm is its unflappability
what I hate about scent is its smell
what I love about newspapers is their etaoin shrdl
what I hate about philosophy is its pursed lip
what I love about Rory is his old grouse
what I hate about Pam is her pinkie
what I love about semi-precious stones is their preciousness
what I hate about diamonds is their mink
what I love about poetry is its ion engine
what I hate about hogs is their setae
what I love about love is its porridge-spoon
what I hate about hate is its eyes
what I love about hate is its salts
what I hate about love is its dog
what I love about Hank is his string vest
what I hate about the twins is their three gloves
what I love about Mabel is her teeter
what I hate about gooseberries is their look, feel, smell, and taste
what I love about the world is its shape
what I hate about a gun is its lock, stock, and barrel
what I love about bacon-and-eggs is its predictability
what I hate about derelict buildings is their reluctance to disintegrate
what I love about a cloud is its unpredictability
what I hate about you, chum, is your china
what I love about many waters is their inability to quench love

The Flowers of Scotland

Yes, it is too cold in Scotland for flower people; in any case who
    would be handed a thistle?
What are our flowers? Locked swings and private rivers –
and the island of Staffa for sale in the open market, which no one
    questions or thinks strange –
and lads o' pairts that run to London and Buffalo without a backward
    look while their elders say Who'd blame them –
and bonny fechters kneedeep in dead ducks with all the thrawn
    intentness of the incorrigible professional Scot –
and a Kirk Assembly that excels itself in the bad old rhetoric and
    tries to stamp out every glow of charity and change, most wrong
    when it thinks most loudly it is most right –
and a Scottish National Party that refuses to discuss Vietnam and
    is even applauded for doing so, do they think no lesson is to be
    learned from what is going on there? –
and the unholy power of Grouse-moor and Broad-acres to prevent
    the smoke of useful industry from sullying Invergordon
    or setting up linear cities among the whaups –
and the banning of Beardsley and Joyce but not of course of 'Monster
    on the Campus' or 'Curse of the Undead' – those who think the
    former are the more degrading, what are their values? –
and the steady creep of the preservationist societies, wearing their
    pens out for slums with good leaded lights – if they could buy
    all the amber in the Baltic and melt it over Edinburgh would
    they be happy then? – the skeleton is well-proportioned –
and by contrast the massive indifference to the slow death of the
    Clyde estuary, decline of resorts, loss of steamers, anaemia of
    yachting, cancer of monstrous installations of a foreign power
    and an acquiescent government – what is the smell of death on
    a child's spade, any more than rats to leaded lights? –
and dissidence crying in the wilderness to a moor of boulders and
    two ospreys –
these are the flowers of Scotland.

1969
(from *Penguin Modern Poets* 15)

The Horseman's Word
1970

1 Arabian Nights Magic Horse

i am a man
   you are a mane
i am a man
   you are a mane
i am a man
   you are a mane
i am a man
   you are a mane
i am a man
   you are a mane
i am a man
   you are a mane
i am a man
   you are a mane
i am Amman
   you are immane

2   Clydesdale

go
   fetlocksnow
          go
             gullfurrow
                   go
go
   brassglow
          go
             sweatflow
                   go
go
   plodknow
          go
             clodshow
                   go
go
   leatherbelow
          go
             potatothrow
                   go
go
   growfellow
          go
             crowfollow
                   go
go
   Balerno
          go
             Palermo
                 whoa

3 Newmarket

```
t  k  -  t  k  e
t  k  -  t  k  e
t  k  -  t  k  e
t  k  -  t  k  e
t  k  -  t  k  e
t  k  -  t  k  e
t  k  -  t  k  e
h  s  -  h  s  s
h  s  -  h  s  s
t  k  -  t  k  e
t  k  -  t  k  e
w  s  -  w  s  s
s  h  s  -  h  s
s  h  s  -  h  s
w  s  -  w  s  s
t  k  -  t  k  e
t  k  -  t  k  e
k  p  -  k  p  a
k  p  -  k  p  a
k  p  -  k  p  a
k  m  -  k  m  m
k  m  -  k  m  m
k  m  -  k  m  m
k  -  m  o  n  n
k  -  m  o  n  n
k  -  m  o  n  n
k  -  m  o  n  n
a  -  t  s  i  t
```

4 Centaur

i am, horse
unhorse, me
i am, horse
unhorse, me
i am, horse
unhorse, me
i am, horse
unhorse, me
i am, horse
unhorse, me
i am, horse
unhorse, me
i am, horse
unhorse, me
i am horse:
unhorse me!

5 Eohippus

```
e  e  t  l
p  u  r  i
k  i  t  l
k  a  t  l
h  u  f  f
w  i  d  l
t  r  i  g
s  n  e  p
k  l  o  p
k  l  i  f
p  t  o  t
s  e  e  p
s  i  p  l
t  r  i  p
t  o  i  p
t  o  r  p
h  o  r  p
h  o  r  s
```

6 *Kelpie*

och och
 laich loch
  hoch heich
   moch smeuch
    sauch souch
     rouch pech
      teuch skreich
       each oidhche
        stech eneuch

7 *Hrimfaxi*

champ and jingle, silver, crystal
  hungry, starry, gallop and pound
sweat and startle, gristle, thunder
  pawing, polar, whinny and strain
hoof and moonlight, scattered, axebright
  stamping, flaring, neighing and cold
back and belly, bludgeon, brandish
  darkness, lightning, windpack and hunt
bit and harness, hurry, hover
  rider, phantom, shadow and dew
lip and slaver, rimedrop, running
  frostlike, tingling, quiver and shine
globe and grassblade, viking, inkling
  quickly, nightly, bridled and black

8 *Zane's*

bronco pronto
gringo arroyo
muchacho loco
burro pequeño
amigo caballo

vamos siempre

ló
ló
ló
ló
ló
ló
ló
ló
ló
ló ló
ló ló
ló ló
ló ló
ló ló
ló ló
ló ló
ló
ló
ló ló
ló ló
ló ló
ló ló
ló
ló
ló
ló
ló
ló
ló
ló
ló
ló
ló

10   Elegy

```
b l u e   r o a n
d e a r   r o a n
f a r m   r o a n
r a i n   r o a n
w i n d   r o a n
h o m e   r o a n
t r e e   r o a n
t r u e   r o a n
s n o w   r o a n
d o z e   r o a n
h u s h   r o a n
d e a d   r o a n

h u s h   h u s h
r o a n   r o a n
```

from Instamatic Poems
1972

GLASGOW 5 MARCH 1971

With a ragged diamond
of shattered plate-glass
a young man and his girl
are falling backwards into a shop-window.
The young man's face
is bristling with fragments of glass
and the girl's leg has caught
on the broken window
and spurts arterial blood
over her wet-look white coat.
Their arms are starfished out
braced for impact,
their faces show surprise, shock,
and the beginning of pain.
The two youths who have pushed them
are about to complete the operation
reaching into the window
to loot what they can smartly.
Their faces show no expression.
It is a sharp clear night
in Sauchiehall Street.
In the background two drivers
keep their eyes on the road.

GLASGOW 5 MARCH 1971

Quickly the magistrate
has ducked to the left.
The knife is just hitting the wall
a few inches away. Already the police
have their hands on the man in the dock
whose right arm is still stretched out
where the weapon left it. One feature
of this picture of the Central Police Court
is the striking absence of consternation.

NICE 5 MARCH 1971

White curtains have been excitedly
drawn back, and four white faces of children
crowd into the window, staring out,
two with noses pressed to the pane,
two with mouths saying Oh.
For it's the Riviera snow.
The palm-trees are white!
The mimosas are white!
The railings are white!
The car roofs are white!
Only the cat is black.
Oh but the sea is black –
look how the sea is black!

CHICAGO MAY 1971

The elegant vice-presidential office of U.S. Steel
is the scene of a small ceremony.
A man has placed a miniature coffin
on the vice-president's couch, and in the coffin
you can see frog, perch, crawfish, dead.
They have swallowed the laborious effluent
of U.S. Steel in Lake Michigan.
The man is poised ready to run,
wrinkling his nose as he pours from a held-out bottle
a dark brown viscous Michigan sludge
over the vice-president's white rug. This is
the eco-man. On the table his card,
The Fox.

GERMANY DECEMBER 1970

A dead man is driving an old Mercedes
straight at a brick wall.
He is only one hour dead,
his hands have been laid
realistically on the wheel
by Herr Rudi Ulenhaut
the development engineer.

Under his dropped jaw
an inflatable safety air bag,
waiting to be tested on impact,
has just flown up
and broken his neck.

NIGERIA UNDATED REPORTED OCTOBER 1971

An Englishman in a Land Rover driving north
has reached the Niger. A sign says
HALT. NO PHOTOGRAPHS. He gets out,
climbs a steep slope, and suddenly
there is the black narrow iron bridge
against the sky, but it is not blue
shows through, but milky white,
the slow close gentle steady ripple
of hundreds of white cattle
bound for Lagos market,
making every bar and strand and spar and iron star
stand out in living art,
a moving and unmoving caterpillar
bristled with sticks of herd-boys,
feeding high in air
above the huge brown river.
A white plinth on the bank
like some great animal's cast tooth
marks
Mungo Park.

LEATHERHEAD SURREY SEPTEMBER 1971

A thick deep glade of sycamores,
a Holly Blue haunting the ghosts of bluebells,
a wispy-haired old wiry hermit like a hobbit.
The hermit, friend of foxes,
has tracked the minute signs to a shallow grave
and shown the police where to dig. Dapples
of autumn sun half-camouflage
two diggers and the hovering forester.
But one spade flares out,
concentrates this shot,

219

the torso visited by foxes,
a woman once, her bluebell bed.
The hobbit spreads
his hands, and sighs.

AVIEMORE INVERNESSSHIRE AUGUST 1971

The elephants are swaying from the ring
having left their mark. The audience
clap like mad and laugh and stamp.
A drunken ring-boy shakes his shovel
at the sway of faces as he stumbles
through steaming droppings, muttering.
His left hand brandishes derisively
a pair of stolen bright blue trousers.
The ringmaster strides to drag him off
as he V-signs the universe
and skids on spotlit dung. Elephants –
what's elephants to men yet?

MOUGINS PROVENCE SEPTEMBER 1971

A picture of a picture of a picture.
Sort out the splendid lights.
A parrot with crusty eye
flutters on the curtain-rail, kimonos
on hooks, bullfighters' skintight suits
blaze. Liquid
Dufys, Matisses in fauve stacks,
an Afghan hound in the real autumn sunlight, veranda
geraniums, geraniums on palettes on chairs,
wet canvases drowning in vandyke brown.
A sunburnt leprechaun of eighty-nine
in flowered shirt and shorts
twinkles a borrowed Pentax at his wife
and waves at the real photographer a sketch
of the artist at his easel sketching
his model in the morning of life.
His Spanish eyes are merry as chestnuts.
The interviewer holds his breath.

VENICE APRIL 1971

Three black gondolas
cut the sparkle of the lagoon.

In the first, the Greek archimandrite
stands, a young black-bearded man
in gold cope, black hood, black shoulder veil blown back
in the sunny breeze. In front of him
his even younger acolyte holds high
the glittering processional cross. His long black robe
glitters with delicious silver flowers
against the blue of the sky.

In the second gondola Stravinsky goes.
The black fringe trails the lapping water,
the heavy coffin dips the golden lions on the sides,
the gondoliers are ankle-deep in roses,
the coffin sways crowned with roses,
the gondoliers' white blouses and black sashes
startle their brown arms, the shining oars,
the pink and crimson flowers.

And the third gondola
is like a shadow
where the widow goes.

And there at the edge of the picture
where the crowds cross themselves
and weep a little in the Italian way,
an old poet with white hair
and hooded, piercing eyes
leans on his stick
and without expression
watches the boats move out
from his shore.

LONDON JUNE 1970

It is opening night at Paolozzi's
crashed car exhibition.
Crowds drift and mill, drinking hard
around the hot gallery, maul
a dismal concertina'd Mini,

paw and punch a tottering A40, but
thick as flies on carrion they've clustered
above the stove-in grin
of a king-sized flare-finned 'fifties Pontiac
that squats on its own wreckage like its name.
One guest has thrown his glass at it,
smiles muzzily at the effect. Another
has crawled on the roof with a bottle,
crisscrosses claret down the shivered windscreen
with weaving hands. A third
intensely between hiccups, wrenches
a door off, you can see the sweat
spreading through his mohair.
And in the front left corner
a noted art critic nailed down
by a topless girl is slowly being
interviewed.
The interview is being viewed
in the back right corner slowly
on live closed-circuit TV.
The art of dying
is in the cars.

ROCKALL INVERNESSSHIRE JUNE 1972

A megagrampus in granite,
a snout surfacing for air and frozen for ever
in the blasts of the Atlantic,
the rock gets a ring in its muzzle,
it is man's.
But only just: for in this picture
a midnight gale too wild for work
even in the simmer-dim
has triggered off an eerie blink
from the unfinished beacon on the summit
and warns men before
men warn men.

ELLINGHAM SUFFOLK JANUARY 1972

Below a water-mill at midnight
breaking the river Waveney into white
an intricate water-dance of forty-one swans
and one man leaning from the mill window
smokes and broods
ravished and nothing understood.

LANCASHIRE NOVEMBER 1971

Inside a vertical cylinder, less than man-sized,
the flash has caught rough dark metal,
a rectangular slit with shadows of trees
waving beyond it, and on the circular floor
four letters, and four snails
half drunk on glue, rasping
their happy night through sandwiches
of ten penceworth of stamps.

WASHINGTON SEPTEMBER 1971

The Kennedy Center for the Performing Arts,
the crowded image of the dedication.
The ranks and braid, the sapphires and white gloves.
The tiers, the tears, the cheers, the chandeliers.
The brass band and the rock band and the dancers,
the ended Mass, the stage in flowers, the curtain
falling on pressmen hugging weeping Bernstein.
A spotlight on Rose Kennedy mother of the dead
standing at eighty facing like a sphinx
beyond the clapping hands, the Kennedys
all round like swaying ears of harvest. Stars
of crests of diamonds, medals, rings four-deep
on fingers flashing programmes flash and twinkle.
Only outside is the black capital.
Splashes of red are only rubies, Ruby.
The exits have been opened. There's a shoe.
A man in jeans lets his dog bark at last.

223

TRANSLUNAR SPACE MARCH 1972

The interior of Pioneer-10,
as it courses smoothly beyond the Moon
at 31,000 miles an hour,
is calm and full of instruments.
No crew for the two-year trip to Jupiter,
but in the middle of the picture
a gold plaque, six inches by nine,
remedies the omission. Against a diagram
of the planets and pulsars of our solar system and galaxy,
and superimposed on an outline of the spacecraft
in which they are not travelling
(and would not be as they are shown
even if they were) two quaint nude figures
face the camera. A deodorized American man
with apologetic genitals and no pubic hair
holds up a banana-like right hand
in Indian greeting, at his side a woman,
smaller, and also with no pubic hair,
is not allowed to hold up her hand,
stands with one leg off-centre, and
is obviously an inferior sort
of the same species. However,
the male chauvinist pig
has a sullen expression, and the woman
is faintly smiling, so
interplanetary intelligences may still have homework.
Meanwhile, on to the Red Spot,
Pluto, and eternity.

BANGAON INDIA JULY 1971

A grey-haired man half-runs,
carrying his white-haired mother on his back
along a dusty road from East Pakistan.
She is a hundred years old.
What they own
fills a knitted cloth at his hip.
Even to them
the hands of the dying are stretched out
from both sides of the road.

224

GLASGOW OCTOBER 1971

In an old Gallowgate cemetery
a woman kneeling at her mother's grave
has risen to her feet, her arms
splayed forward and chrysanthemums
scattering from the vase she tramps on.
Her mouth is rounded out to scream
but the stab in her back is not deep –
no more than a memento mori
from the youth who sharpens his knife
nonchalant on the tombstone.

BRADFORD JUNE 1972

Dusty, bruised and grazed, and cut about a bit, but
cheerful, twenty men in white
are demolishing an old stone house
by karate.
They attack the worst part:
the thick cemented fireplace wall.
What a concert of chops is conducted
by him in the helmet, with KARATE INSTRUCTOR
across his back and Union Jacks and ideograms
along his sleeve: a deep-breathed plot
of timed and buttressed energies jabbing
one bare hand and two bare hands and
one bare foot and two bare feet and
one bare head at
stone: the pivot man,
swarming with badges, swings
on two friends' shoulders, clutches
their necks, leans back with knees
above his head and like a spring
uncoils two smart sharp whacks
from heels of steel,
and the wall keels.

CAMPOBASSO ITALY UNDATED
REPORTED MARCH 1971

Giovanna
handsome, forty,
lazes on the mattress,
her legs are apart, the rumpled sheet
is clutched below her breasts.
With one hand on her swelling child
she is heavy and drowsy as a cat.
Her husband killed himself a year ago.
What will she call this baby then?
She smiles, thinking.

Angelo
her lover, a message-boy of seventeen,
lies sleeping beside her.
His good looks are not quite hidden by the pillow.
He is her son-in-law.
Having made both wife and mother-in-law
pregnant, he sleeps easily.
What insolence you see
in his shrugged strong back!

Antonio
her little grandson
sleeps in his cot at the foot of the bed,
but he will never waken
from the weedkiller his mother has given him.
His arms grip the sides of the cot,
his belly is bent up like a hoop.

Salbina
her daughter, aged fourteen,
seduced by Angelo the year before
while her mother watched and encouraged their play,
can be seen
through the door that opens to the kitchen
swaying from the rafters in a white nightdress
like a dead sea-bird.
With her last convulsion
she has kicked over a table and a smashed wine-bottle
spreads below her like blood.

Gennarino
her nine-year-old son
crouches like a dog in a corner of the farmhouse

226

unwashed, wide-eyed, afraid to whimper.
No one cares for him but he is the witness
and will sit high in the cold black court.

LONDON NOVEMBER 1971

At the Festival of Islam
the dervishes are dancing.
The dancemaster stands
in his long black gown
straight-backed, his hands
folded in front of him.
Twelve swarthy men
in cylindrical hats
and loose white blouses
and long white skirts
and their long white sleeves
stretched out straight
like the albatross
have begun to dance.
The drum measures
flutes and strings
and men following.
Serious, rapt,
as if to wind themselves
up with their arms
they revolve, their skirts
flaring out loose
in white pyramids
below the inverted
pyramids of white
blouses and arms
which support the top
truncated pyramids
of circling hats.
Pattern and no pattern,
alone and in union
without unison
in the hard light
of Friends' House
in Euston Road
the dervishes whirl
round, they dance
round, round

they go, without
sound, now,
round and round.

GLASGOW NOVEMBER 1971

It is a fine thronged Christmas shopping afternoon
in Argyle Street. The big store's canopy,
hung with coloured lights and swags of green,
supports an enormous Christmas tree.
On the broad pavement below it,
where curious shoppers pause a moment or look back,
a policeman feeds his walkie-talkie
with the end of his report.
The evening shadows
cannot be far away. The Royston boy
of thirteen murdered by the Blackhill boy
of twelve is gone. The stolen ring
they scuffled for is gone. The stolen kitchen knife
that sank into his side is gone.
The big store writes off knife and ring, but someone
has set out pail and broom
convenient on the pavement.
They wait in the foreground, sturdy objects,
the iron pail with its handle up,
the long broom carefully balanced on the handle,
and the dark spread of blood between them.

GLASGOW NOVEMBER 1971

The 'speckled pipe' of the MacCrimmons,
three centuries old, is being played
in a backcourt very far from Dunvegan.
A young director of the College of Piping
is trying it out for a radio programme.
Only his cheeks show the pibroch
that rises winding into the wintry city air.
It is the long drones that are speckled,
carved in clusters of elegant bands
of creamy horn and dark brown wood,
but speckled are the high tenement walls behind them,

228

dark stone, pale mortar, narrow verticals
of dark window and water-pipe and pale smudge of curtains,
and speckled is the piper's kilt
against a speckled homely jungle
of grasses, thistle, dandelions, fireweed, firewood,
Capstan packets and Lanliq empties.
In a camouflage the pibroch
and the pibroch-player
disappear, half appear
MacCrimmons in Hornel.

MILAN UNDATED REPORTED OCTOBER 1971

The drawing-room has violin-cases,
a grand piano, a marble clock
and marble table-top with cakes
and tea for three. The three
are in a Henry James tableau.
A famous violinist stands
by the piano; with his left hand
holding the first four yellowing
manuscript pages of a lost concerto
to his lips he is kissing them fervently
in an access of Polish fire.
His right arm sketches fulfilment with
thumb and index finger in an O
and the other fingers winged like a bird.
One of Paganini's great-granddaughters
is sitting bolt upright in a tapestry chair
with her hands on her lap. Her sister
stands with one arm along the chair-back
and in the other clutches to her side
the hundred-and-thirty-year-old folder
fat with the rest of the third concerto.
Four dark eyes watch intently
to see if Henryk Szeryng will do.

From Glasgow to Saturn
1973

Columba's Song

Where's Brude? Where's Brude?
So many souls to be saved!
The bracken is thick, the wildcat is quick,
the foxes dance in the moonlight,
the salmon dance in the waters,
the adders dance in the thick brown bracken.
Where's Brude? Where's man?
There 's too much nature here,
eagles and deer,
but where's the mind and where's the soul?
Show me your kings, your women, the man of the plough.
And cry me to your cradles.
It wasn't for a fox or an eagle I set sail!

Floating off to Timor

If only we'd been strangers
we'd be floating off to Timor,
we'd be shimmering on the Trades
in a blue jersey boat
with shandies, flying-fish,
a pace of dolphins
to the copra ports.
And it's no use crying
to me, What dolphins?
I know where they are
and I'd have snapped you up
and carried you away
snapped you up
and carried you away
if we had been strangers.

But here we are care
of the black roofs.
It's not hard to find
with a collar turned up
and a hoot from the Clyde.
The steps come home
whistling too. And a kettle
steams the cranes out slowly.
It's living with ships
makes a rough springtime

233

and who is safe
when they sing and blow
their music – they seem
to swing at some light rope
like those desires
we keep for strangers.
God, the yellow deck
breathes, it heaves spray
back like a shout.
We're cutting through
some straits of the world
in our old dark room
with salty wings
in the shriek of the dock wind.
But we're caught – meshed
in the fish-scales, ferries,
mudflats, lifebelts
fading into football cries
and the lamps coming on
to bring us in.

We take in
the dream, a cloth from the line
the trains fling sparks on
in our city. We're better awake.
But you know I'd take
you all the same,
if you were my next stranger.

In Glasgow

In my smoochy corner
take me on a cloud
I'll wrap you round
and lay you down
in smoky tinfoil
rings and records
sheets of whisky
and the moon all right
old pal all right
the moon all night

Mercy for the rainy
tyres and the violet

thunder that bring you
shambling and shy
from chains of Easterhouse
plains of lights
make your delight
in my nest my spell
my arms and my shell
my barn my bell

I've combed your hair
and washed your feet
and made you turn
like a dark eel
in my white bed
till morning lights
a silent cigarette
throw on your shirt
I lie staring yet
forget forget

Kierkegaard's Song

What a business the crow makes
lifting a foot, then down,
then the other, down too,
squawks – black –
oh, about flying,
but not flying,
stamping the branch,
working its wings,
clinging like a lump
to its own fuss,
flaps up at last
in a kind of flight –

I love a kingfisher
you can only see
by a flash of blue –
do what it must do.

Tropic

ring river riding silver
forest flashing waterfalls

coffee grove and blinding breaker
thunder ruffling the macaw

bride in courtyard breathing lavender
boys jostling squeaking swings

bastinado and electrode
swelling jails with filth and pain

Christ of the Andes paper tiger
head in clouds and feet on skulls

Shantyman

Shantyman, the surf of heaven
is breaking, somewhere.
White shirt in blackness,
brown arms along the rail
in the wind. And we are
plunging without stars
at midnight, singing
the sea
      to the sea.
            The sea's
ear is dull, repeat it, but
we have moved on.
All the old days are
Shenandoah.
For the present,
sing it negligent
of solemn waters and the dark.
The cutlasses won't stir,
or piles of brass and tar.

He slaps the rail, looks up
for a new verse,
we give it everything
and everything we have
rolls down to heaven like Rio
on the blue back of his hand.

Oban Girl

A girl in a window eating a melon
eating a melon and painting a picture
painting a picture and humming Hey Jude
humming Hey Jude as the light was fading

In the autumn she'll be married

The Woman

A string of pearls
in the dark window, that wet spring,
sometimes a white hand raised with a cigarette
blurred by rain and buses
anyhow. A lonely
ring.

Nothing she was waiting for
came, unless what took her
in the coldest arms.

It seems to be the pearls
we remember, for what they spoke
of another life than waiting,
and being unknown dying
in a high dark street.

Who she was you'll keep thinking.
The hearse rolled off in thunder,
but showers only lay dust.

The Apple's Song

Tap me with your finger,
rub me with your sleeve,
hold me, sniff me, peel me
curling round and round
till I burst out white and cold
from my tight red coat
and tingle in your palm

as if I'd melt and breathe
a living pomander
waiting for the minute
of joy when you lift me
to your mouth and crush me
and in taste and fragrance
I race through your head
in my dizzy dissolve.

I sit in the bowl
in my cool corner
and watch you as you pass
smoothing your apron.
Are you thirsty yet?
My eyes are shining.

Drift

Rhododendron dust rose
and fell in the June wind –
lightness, lightness!
And with an arm I
swept the loch away
from your eyes. Drowsy
picnic-fires, the cars,
the wood-pigeon, the spray
of water-skiers through the trees
went fading tangled
off the world.
Only stars of heat
pricked, and your cigarette
smouldered in the grass
forgotten, its blue pungence
not to be forgotten
blown across our faces
with the rhododendron-drift.
Love, pillow me
by the eastern tree.

Fado

Fold those waves away
and take the yellow, yellow bay,
roll it up like Saturday.

No use the sleepy sand,
no use my breasts in his brown hand.
I danced on tables in that land.

Grim is my cold sun.
Through my street the long rains run.
Thousands I see, thinking of one.

After the Party

Did you touch me? I thought
at the door, as the party broke up violently,
streaming out into dark snow –
who wants to remember the bad wine,
the worse coffee, that raving blond on the stair
with his jagged half of a Mingus EP dipped in punch –
or his friend old whimpering cut-wrist
squirming on his paunch on the bathroom carpet, imagine
a white fitted carpet and a botched suicide, but the host
went on smiling as he shooed us into the cold. The old
lizard clutched his dressing-gown about him, though – I know.
I sat on the step and rolled myself a cigarette,
I remember that. It was just before,
in that struggle in the doorway,
all coats and hiccups and fumbling, that I thought
you touched me. I know you were sober
and I was mostly. You never looked at me
but you touched me. Didn't you?
It's all I want to remember
and yet it becomes less clear
than that crazy slut sobbing through the banisters.
What could you get from it? My doubt is
that you even remember it. Or are you waiting
for me to find you? And what would happen then?

It all slips through my hands like snow in silence.

Brush me with your wing,
I'm lying here
in my shadows, the ones
for that night's sake.

At the Television Set

Take care if you kiss me,
you know it doesn't die.
The lamplight reaches out, draws it
blandly – all of it – into fixity,
troops of blue shadows like the soundless gunfight,
yellow shadows like your cheek by the lamp
where you lie watching, half watching
between the yellow and the blue.
I half see you, half know you.
Take care if you turn now to face me.
For even in this room we are moving out through stars
and forms that never let us back, your hand
lying lightly on my thigh and my hand on your shoulder
are transfixed only there, not here.

What can you bear that would last
like a rock through cancer and white hair?

Yet it is not easy
to take stock of miseries
when the soft light flickers
along our arms in the stillness
where decisions are made.
You have to look at me,
and then it's time that falls
talking slowly to sleep.

From the North

How many hundred miles it is into your heart
I know, I know.
The mountains fade into your face.
When I sail by the grey stacks
my double guards you, though you are not faithful.

This Saturday on what corner
will you meet your next friend? Give him
a little only, while my foot slips here.
These things can kill, like those rocks.
The hard wind blows my thoughts
back from the boat-rail and out of meaning.
What is left till I see you?
This anorak, these knuckles, that kyle.

The Milk-cart

Where are you in this darkness? I put out
a hand, the branch outside
touches only old October air
and loses leaves, it is hard
to wish for you, harder to sleep, useless to weep.
How can I bear the darkness empty
and how can the darkness bear love?

I bore the darkness lying still, thinking
you were against my heart,
till I heard the milk-cart horse
come clattering down the hill
and the brash clear whistle
of the milk-boy dancing
on his frosty doorsteps,
uncaring as the morning star.
Come back to me – from anywhere come back!
I'll see you standing in my door,
though the whistling fades to air.

Estranged

far far away
beyond the mist of Jupiter
was the longest look
we took at love

it seemed you were there
and I was on Earth
I could not hear you
crying in pain

till like a ghost
you came beneath the low sun
again home
to my door

and laid a hand
of the ice where you had been
on my wrist as you pretended
to come in

but what came in
was a breath of demons
that froze love
swept the house bare

we sit like chairs
in unforgiving air
whatever is said or not said
of how or where

For Bonfires

I

The leaves are gathered, the trees are dying
for a time.
A seagull cries through white smoke in the garden fires
that fill the heavy air.
All day heavy air
is burning, a moody dog
sniffs and circles the swish of the rake.
In streaks of ash, the gardener drifting
ghostly, beats his hands, a cloud
of breath to the red sun.

II

An island in the city, happy demolition men
behind windowed hoardings – look at them
trailing drills through rubble dust, kicking rubble,
smoking leaning on a pick, putting the stub
over an ear and the hot yellow helmet over that,
whistling up the collapsing chimney, kicking the
ricochet, rattling the trail with
snakes of wire, slamming slabs
down, plaster, cornice, brick, brick

on broken brick and plaster dust,
sprawling with steaming cans and pieces
at noon, afternoon bare sweat shining
paths down chalky backs, coughing
in filtered sunshine, slithering, swearing,
joking, slowly stacking and building
their rubbish into a total bonfire.
Look at that Irishman, bending
in a beautiful arc to throw
the last black rafter to the top,
stands back, walks round it singing
as it crackles into flame – old doors,
old beams, boxes, window-frames,
a rag doll, sacks, flex, old newspapers,
burst shelves, a shoe, old dusters, rags of
wallpaper roses. And they all stand round,
and cheer the tenement to smoke.

III

In a galvanized bucket
the letters burn. They roar and twist
and the leaves curl back one by one.
They put out claws and scrape the iron
like a living thing,
but the scrabbling to be free soon subsides.
The black pages fuse
to a single whispering mass
threaded by dying tracks of gold.
Let them grow cold,
and when they're dead
quickly draw breath.

Blue Toboggans

scarves for the apaches
wet gloves for snowballs
whoops for white clouds
and blue toboggans

stamping for a tingle
lamps for four o'clock
steamed glass for buses
and blue toboggans

tuning-forks for Wenceslas
white fogs for Prestwick
mince pies for the Eventides
and blue toboggans

TV for the lonely
a long haul for heaven
a shilling for the gas
and blue toboggans

Song of the Child

the child ran to the mountain
and he pulled the rocks about
– I'll take you to the cleaners you old mountain
for I'll let the fountain out

the child ran to his daddy
and he pulled his beard about
– I'll knock you off your rocky chair old daddy
for I'm what you're about

the child ran to the holies
and he pulled their spires about
– I'll strip your lead for soldiers you old holies
for your games are all played out

the child ran to the soldiers
and he pulled their guns about
– I'll teach you to play war games you old soldiers
for it's turn and turn about

the child ran to the heavens
and he pulled the stars about
– I'll have you for my bathmat you old heavens
for I've drawn the plug right out

the child ran to the waters
and he pulled the dead about
– I'll wear you when you're broken you old waters
for now I'm coming out

Lord Jim's Ghost's Tiger Poem

I can see them yet round the bungalow,
queuing up swaying and groaning slightly,
each to his steaming bowl as we had taught them –
tigers with a taste for tea were all
the rage that year at the Monsoon Club.

There was an old glade of tombs we went to
every rainy season to renew
our stock of ghosts, once brought back a rice doll,
grew into a fine peasant boy, kept our accounts –
said the old ghost in the Monsoon Club.

Lying on the rattan with pipes glowing
we saw a bird of paradise in paradise
bending to its image in an image
until a rain of diamonds was rain –
pattering white on the Monsoon Club.

The fishes in the river were choked with rice
when we came down, came down with our hooks
and threw them all back, our bottles slung
at our hips and the slurred fish sutra on our lips –
rowing back dark to the Monsoon Club.

And velvet cobras took smoke apart.
And the flute climbed above its notes.
And backs took the needle for blue tigers.
And the dead whistled through a tin sheet.
And we played go at the Monsoon Club.

Go and opium and rain! Bead-curtains
spilling round naked breasts like water!
Thunder and lacquer! All gone like that mist
framed by early morning summer doors,
my drowsy morning Monsoon Club.

I hear the slow pagoda bell.
I smell the salt of the China Sea.
I trace with the glow of my cigarette
in my hammock swinging through the straits
letters of smoke – Monsoon Club.

Flakes

this is the blizzard
that ate the robin
that hopped on the dish
that filled with snow

this is the corrie
that cooked the blizzard
that ate the robin
that hopped on the dish

this is the cloud
that lit the corrie
that cooked the blizzard
that ate the robin

this is the moon
that crazed the cloud
that lit the corrie
that cooked the blizzard

this is the boots
that tramped the moon
that crazed the cloud
and filled with snow

Hyena

I am waiting for you.
I have been travelling all morning through the bush
and not eaten.
I am lying at the edge of the bush
on a dusty path that leads from the burnt-out kraal.
I am panting, it is midday, I found no water-hole.
I am very fierce without food and although my eyes
are screwed to slits against the sun
you must believe I am prepared to spring.

What do you think of me?
I have a rough coat like Africa.
I am crafty with dark spots
like the bush-tufted plains of Africa.

I sprawl as a shaggy bundle of gathered energy
like Africa sprawling in its waters.
I trot, I lope, I slaver, I am a ranger.
I hunch my shoulders. I eat the dead.

Do you like my song?
When the moon pours hard and cold on the veldt
I sing, and I am the slave of darkness.
Over the stone walls and the mud walls and the ruined places
and the owls, the moonlight falls.
I sniff a broken drum. I bristle. My pelt is silver.
I howl my song to the moon – up it goes.
Would you meet me there in the waste places?

It is said I am a good match
for a dead lion. I put my muzzle
at his golden flanks, and tear. He
is my golden supper, but my tastes are easy.
I have a crowd of fangs, and I use them.
Oh and my tongue – do you like me
when it comes lolling out over my jaw
very long, and I am laughing?
I am not laughing.
But I am not snarling either, only
panting in the sun, showing you
what I grip
carrion with.

I am waiting
for the foot to slide,
for the heart to seize,
for the leaping sinews to go slack,
for the fight to the death to be fought to the death,
for a glazing eye and the rumour of blood.
I am crouching in my dry shadows
till you are ready for me.
My place is to pick you clean
and leave your bones to the wind.

The Loch Ness Monster's Song

Sssnnnwhufffll?
Hnwhuffl hhnnwfl hnfl hfl?
Gdroblboblhobngbl gbl gl g g g g glbgl.
Drublhaflablhaflubhafgabhaflhafl fl fl –
gm grawwwww grf grawf awfgm graw gm.
Hovoplodok-doplodovok-plovodokot-doplodokosh?
Splgraw fok fok splgrafhatchgabrlgabrl fok splfok!
Zgra kra gka fok!
Grof grawff gahf?
Gombl mbl bl –
blm plm,
blm plm,
blm plm,
blp.

The Mill

To draw us up about ourselves
in time some angels came, sat
with us, folded a moving joy
away. When we stopped singing
something cut into us, but we
stopped singing. The clammy box
closed in the storm without linen.
Like unripe grapes we were brushed
in their mouths and rolled faintly,
they bruised us without eating.
Then they hung us like fruit bats
tied to a desultory beam.
Hail hit the mill in handfuls.
We swung drying; silent rags.
But a lovely devil rose from the grain,
opened the box, folded the angels
in a whiff of resin and chaff.
Hailstones bounding through a crack
baffled the grindstone. We slipped our hooks.
The devil stroked us shrieking with fruit.

Tonight it's on the cards the mill
blows outside in. Who'll fold who then?

London

Incense winding
over water, girls with long legs
and lazy bells, the black swan sliding
through reeds and drinking straws. The place
unfolds: holds: melts off. Grass and brass band
utter heat till summer cracks.
Who could sleep in London's orient wheat,
yet I think we fell asleep.

They were sunburned; we heard waves; the place was bright.
Whether it was really summer was hard to say.
Where they all were was all there was; somehow
they'd got a world. Going there was
pure – like into blue very highland air.
When they sent an armful of grey pigeons down the vista
you cried out, and the chestnut leaves settled slowly.
We turned with the earth. Our heads together, whispered
'Where is the kingdom of this world?' 'Can we come here again?'
Frost cut the leafless avenue while we kissed.
We'd taken what was never taken to be true –
the depth of time. But time was only
the leaf of heaven, lay on your hand
on my hand on the ground of dust of snow.
We heard a hard wind batter walls.
There was no spring and at once
they were all there making tea in a vast air-blue summer-house
with music, but cups and saucers made no sound
as we drank beside them, and through tall windows
trees hung like spectres of the next life.
What were they drinking to that silence could interpret?
Maybe the music we heard was what they said.
They were mountain sages cut from a tusk – without the tusk.
Skis and parkas cluttered the summer-house door,
why hadn't we seen them? There was no autumn and at once
you shivered in the sledge, a wolf had smelt
the runners, it was black, white, black
the world of the dead time.
Close to me, closer! You are not afraid
of a few icy trees, but we are both afraid
of what is happening to us. Christ, the khamseen!
The tent-door flaps and burning sand knocks
on your tight-shut eyes, our sleeping-bags gritty, stifling,
we grind sand with our bread, brown water
sickens us. 'Comb me?' Allah laughs.

The season's spent, they've come towards us
as the air clears. They smile and hold out bowls
of water, fine linen cloths, fat oranges.
It looks like water, linen, oranges
but where is summer, winter? Where is the world?
When we've lost time we have lost everything.
How they ingratiate their gifts!
No! We shake our heads in silence

and turn back as they show their wings.

II   SOHO

dutch straps mr universe jock caps 1001 nights genuine rechy
fully tested adolescence & box 5/- only velazquez
kalpa baggers naturist bargain guide original sex carpet
sutra hill transvestism before marriage more inside
kama books fanny goods family nudes free each purch
planning our own petronius durex opedia
history of the genet established insertion imported
lubricated health best of the flowers
human hygienic capital rod no obligatio
lash purgated quatrefoil masochism
unex punishment trusses george ryley scott soft yet firm
5 capital practices for men 7/6 ea
life of skin thin witchcraft variants
technique of hirschf strap psycho many lands nus
homosex encyclo erotica the set nothing like the sun
30/- psycholo oriental rubber burton leather boys
author of amazing years of diaphragm
desire and pursuit of the marquis de sutra au cinéma
health & wrestling jours de sodom unbeatable
william burroughs shakespeare complete dead fingers
cacti and succulent flagellation havelock and after
handy pathia sexu ellis ready reckoner
rhythm method works quentin per crisp cent
ten tom jones tablets belt recommended
our lady of the litesome
wuthering heights full protection
boxing & vaseline fully illustrated hosiery
ABZ of unrepeatable tropic of enemas
who's afraid of virginia goldfinger
dr no guide to london heller orgies book of the f
20,000 leagues under angus wilson yoga fetishism agency
traps omar khayyam a week's supply for pocket torture photogr
chinese medical cooking in 80 days lo duca come in and browse
trial of oscar mickey fleming birth-cont catch-22 hyde miller

250

no mean city of night prophylactic burgess anomalies
johnson & johnson john o'hara john calder judo spillane karate
transparent KY water soluble cookbook
an unhurried view of impotence rock plants and alpines
oxford book of english prostitution
youth requisites sterilized plain white
slightly washable shop soiled down the ages
But to wash London
                              would take a sea.
To want to wash it
                    history.

Now bury this poem in one of the vaults
of our civilization, and let the Venusian
computers come down, and searching for life
          crack our ghastly code.
Bury it, bury it! Who cares?
          We shall never know.
We've buried worse, with mouths to feed.
          And so... And so... And so...
Polish the window, bury the poem, and go.

III   THE POST OFFICE TOWER
There is no other life,
and this is it.
Gold bars, thunder, gravity, wine, concrete, smoke.
And the blue pigeon London sky
hangs high heat on towers, a summer shower
on trees, its clouds
to swing over cranes
that swing slowly
blue vaguely.
We are drawn to the welder's star.
Ships we
half see.
Glass walls flash new cliffsides, brick-beds
brood with dust, red, grey, grey, blue.
Huge shadows skim the classic terraces.
Hunt sun hunt cloud, one long morning.

And life comes out on the roofs. A breeze
shakes raindrops from bonsai pines,
penthouse terrazzo gleams, dries, washed by heaven
around a fishpool: in dark glasses, a severe white suit
she stands by the marble verge and calls a dog, silently
twenty storeys above the roar.

251

On a roof southward, broken concrete
between two chimneys blossoms
in a line of washing, an old man
on a hard chair, his hands in his lap,
stares at nothing – linen flowers
tugging to be free. And like some fine insect
poised on a blackened outcrop of stone
a young man mends an aerial far down the central haze,
straddles a fire-escape in ice-blue jeans
and striped shirt, arms bare to the shoulder and his hair
is blown across his arms
as he moves the metal arms
into the path of their messages.
– And all that grace to dwindle to
a faded dressing-gown, a kitchen chair in the sun.
Years in shadows come low
over a penthouse garden dark with weeds,
phones ringing through empty rooms
for ashes thrown on the sea.
But still of life
not in clean waves and airs
the messages most heard
come to the tower
from asphalt and smoke
and break in rings
of strange accident
and mortal change
on the rain wet
silver bars.
It is its own
telegrams,
what mounts, what sighs,
what says it is
unaccountable
as feelings moved
by hair blown over
an arm in the wind.
In its acts
it rests there.

Interferences
a sequence of 9 poems

i

not to be deflected
the arrow, puffed up
speeding busily
straight to its
                    targjx

ii

'come back in a million years
they'll still be burning babies'
came back in a million years
blue planet swirling under clouds
we could see nothing
'the brown ones, and black, mostly,
not the white'
                    nothing
below the thick pale clouds
'you can't see, send a probe'
so we launched a prob
                    never got there
                    others watching
                    even us / we can
                    hardly imagine

                    and the babies?

iii

when the music was finished
I listened to it raining
and the world was raining over
like a pot outside the window
in the darkness

when the rain was finished
I listened to your breathing
and the room was swimming downwards
you were slipping from my fingers
you were drowning

253

when your breathing was finished
I listened to the silence
and a twist of hair went floating
like an eel beyond my window
I am Shiva

till the silence is finished
I shall listen to its music
for I know the door will open
on the wailing of the raga
and the strangeler

   iv

'it was a Roman soldier'
he cried, his fist

'it was our neighbour'
pounded the table

'it was a visitor'
dropped wearily

and she took his hand
placed it on her womb

'I am your virgian bride'
with a smile worlds away

   v

brigantine tacking
canvas set
in calm seas
off the Azores
December 1872
a sorry zigzag
we boarded her
in the queen's name
found no one
ghost ship
all shipshape
log written up
no mutiny
no tempest

no sickness
no ghosts
captain's wife
had a sewing-machine
with a phial of oil
upright and ready
she had left her task
in no disorder
all was dry
all was clean
the sails whole
the hull smooth
rocking to
and fro quietly
fourteen persons
in earth or sea
or air or space
or in that place
where their ship is
the Mar Celste

vi

'your filthy altars –'
'– hold him down'
'if I die –'
'– knife not there'
'others, hundreds –'
'– strong, the brute'
'can smell the sea –'
'– running, everywhere'
'retribution! –'
'– listen, that roar!
'crumbling, Atlamtis –'
'– everlasting'
'lava, lumps of water –'
'– the same Atlamtiz'
'a wall, arching –'
'– save Akramdez'
'sea like obsidian –'
'– gods, gods'
'Gkrnmdwz –'
'– the fins!'

vii

they put me in this bed, and said
John Cage, lie there, don't move
we'll take the tubes out if you're good
but I'm not going to be good I know
because I'm dying, I'm not going to be well
'just the right amount of pain in the world'
the things I've said, driving cars
to mushroom country, hearing rain,
letting nature take its course in rain
and sandwich-papers rustling quietly
against the slap of cards
transistors and their rock
and static and the shock
of pauses after static
and 'what about all those silences?'
the things I've said are in my head
but the white bed-rail is all space
and there is space in the rose in the glass
and in the two nurses whispering
there was such whispering as a plane passed
and the clack of feet what is this silen

viii

'you want river Ob go backwards can do'
'let me know when the sea reaches the camp'
'get dark Muscovite them cloud come low'
'good weathermen you shamans I always said'
'I shake beads I prove spell on you'
'shake away while I label these rocks'
'now tell me what these beads tell me these beads'
'black and glassy I recognized them at once'
'now you tell what just you tell what'
'tetkites'
'you see'
'tetkites'
'go on'
'tetkites'
'now I think go speak so-so to Ob'

bringing you live
the final preparations
for this great mission
should be coasting
the rings of Saturn
two years time
cloudless sky, and
an unparalleled
world coverage
we have countdown
  ten
may not have told you
  nine
the captain's mascot
  eight
miniaturized gonk
  seven
chief navigator
  six
had twins Tuesday
  five
the Eiffel Tower for
  four
comparison, gantries
  three
aside, so the fuel
  two
huge cloud of
  one
perfect
  a half
I don't quite
  a quarter
something has clearly
  an eighth
we do not have lift-off
  a sixteenth
we do not have lift-off
  a thirty-second
we do not have lift-off
  a sixty-fourth
we do not have lift-off
  a hundred and twenty-eighth
wo de nat hove loft-iff

Che

Even after the body
had been roughly brought
down to Vallegrande
from the hills, and the eyes
had that meaningless glaze
staring at no world,
eyes took meaning from
his slightly parted lips
showing the teeth
in a smile – no rage,
no throes, nothing
but that uncanny pro-
jection of consciousness
and a dead man putting
fate in bondage
to him. Bolivia:
what other bondages
will shiver in the cane-brake
even in steel, and will break,
uniforms and proclamations
ploughed under by the grass
itself – it rises
into the voices of forests.
For the dead wander
among its deep roots
like water, and push
the green land into heroes.
They grow in understanding,
tree, tree, man, man,
move like shadows.
Blossoms brushed
by silent bandoliers
spring out in shock and
back into place.
But jungles break.

Down from the mountains
miles and miles
a marble face,
a broken body,
the marble only
broken by a smile.

The Fifth Gospel

I have come to overthrow the law and the prophets: I have not come to fulfil, but to overthrow.

Listen: a sower went out to sow. And when he sowed, some seeds fell by the wayside, and they sprang up and gave good fruit. Some fell on stony places, where they had not much earth, and they too grew up and flourished well. And some fell among thistles, and they in turn sprang and gave fruit in the very heart of the thistles. But others fell into good ground, and died, and produced neither leaf nor fruit. He who has ears to hear, let him hear.

It is not those that are sick who need a doctor, but those that are healthy. I have not come to call sinners, but the virtuous and law-abiding, to repentance.

A good tree can produce bad fruit, and a poor tree can produce good fruit. It is by their fruit that you will know them.

(And Jesus went into the temple, and brought in those who wanted to buy and sell goods there, and threw together some tables for the money-changers, and put in seats for those who had pigeons and were looking for fanciers. And he said to them: This temple will no doubt be called a den of thieves, but you can make it a house of prayer. And they marvelled at this saying. But Jesus turned to his disciples and said: In my kingdom there are no temples. Work, and pray.)

Each of you by taking thought will someday add a foot to his height.

Give nothing to Caesar, for nothing is Caesar's.

Listen: this is what the kingdom is about. Ten girls took their lamps and went out to meet the bridegroom. Five of them were sensible, and five were thoughtless. The thoughtless ones failed to check if they had enough oil, the sensible ones made sure. The bridegroom was very late in arriving, so they all snatched some sleep. At midnight there was a shout: the bridegroom is here – go and meet him! All the girls got up and trimmed their lamps. And the thoughtless ones said to the sensible ones: Give us some of your oil, for our lamps are nearly out. And the sensible ones answered: Certainly, here is the oil. And if there is not enough to go round, why then, that will teach the bridegroom to keep ten servants waiting for five hours. Sisters, the sensible must help the thoughtless, and all must stand together against those who would exploit their willingness and keep them from the kingdom.

Think about tomorrow: for tomorrow will not look after itself.

(And Jesus crossed the lake and came ashore in the country of the Gadarenes. And a schizophrenic who lived there among the tombs came wildly up to him. His body was bleeding from many wounds where he had slashed himself with stones, and broken chains hung jangling from his arms and legs. He was so strong that no one could hold him. He believed that he was inhabited by demons, who forced him to cry out, and run from place to place, day and night without rest. And he threw himself at the feet of Jesus, and the voice of his demons begged Jesus not to torment them. And Jesus said: But what do you want me to do? The demonic voice replied: Send us into that huge herd of pigs feeding on the hillside. But Jesus refused, and said: Why should I kill two thousand pigs? For being animals they would go frantic and rush headlong into the lake and be drowned. Am I to bring these farmers and their families into destitution in order that you may sit clothed and in your right mind, sipping wine and paying your taxes? Go back to the tombs and cry into the darkness; and men shall learn from you, and you from the wilderness.)

My yoke is not easy, and my burden is not light.

Afterwards

Afterwards the sun shone on seven rice shoots and a black tree.

Afterwards the prostitutes fell on lean times / some took up embroidery / one became a pearl-diver and was drowned.

Afterwards my burned little cousin went through eleven grafting operations / never cried.

Afterwards many saffron robes began to be let out / there was a movement to purify the order.

Afterwards the ancient monuments were restored stone by stone / I thought it was folly when I saw the list of legless girls waiting for prosthetic appliances.

Afterwards there was a report of mass ghosts on the plains, all grey as dust, with grey shovels, burying and burying all through the night to the beat of a drum / but in the morning the earth was hard and unbroken.

260

Afterwards came six great harvests and a glut of fish, and the rivers rolled and steamed through tunnels of fresh green fruit-trees and lilypads needled by kingfishers / rainbow after rainbow plunged into the lakes of rice.

Afterwards I went out with my sister one still hot day into the forest, and we came to an old temple bombed to a shell, with weeds in its windows, and went in hand in hand through a deep rubble of stone and fragments of half-melted statues and rubbish of metal and flowers and bread, and there in a corner we saw the skeleton of a boy, with shreds of blue cotton clinging to the bones, his fingers still clutching the string of a tiny bamboo box / we bent down as a faint chirping started from the box, and saw that it was his grasshopper, alive yet and scraping the only signal it knew from behind the bars of its cage / you said something and burst out crying / I slid the latch then and set it free.

The Gourds

gourd: that's what it was, a gourd. We got in.
We simply scrambled through a gash in its side
and we were in.
Pale yellow it was, very cool and fresh
after the snake swamps.
We had had enough of snakes too –
fifty yards of snake is not for lingering.
But here in the gourd
it was so delicious we made camp,
dried out, rolled a few cigarettes,
opened a tin or two, then slept.
We woke to the sound of our two sentries
being crunched by a sort of Hercules beetle,
too hard for us to attack. We fled
with a handful of stores and clothes out of the gourd
into a gourd about a mile high like
ten Albert Halls – Christ! We
cowered there like so many ticks,
wondering what sort of snakes –
Idly, a vast boa crushed the gourd.
As we spilled out, it was like looking up
into a knot of solid waterspouts, swaying
from the swamp floor to the sky of the dim next gourd.
We floundered, cursing. Something whizzed into my eye.
I fished it out, rubbed the speck between my fingers –

hard, smoothish, slightly ribbed it seemed.
I stared at it, the others – what was left of us –
crowded round. Look, I said. Feel it.
And it felt just like that old

Last Message

The pyramid is closing. Will there be time
for a last message – who can imagine
the grey universe rolling its millions
of last messages as it must do,
unheard, washing everywhere? Oh it is cold
in the pyramid, colder on the plains
where the Forms clash and screech in blue,
our enemies, on their dimensional wheels.
The claws! There were so many dead
the air was hardly to be breathed,
we could neither bury nor burn
in the radiation summer.
Is this our defeat then, as we lock
the white doors, to lie a thousand
thousand thousand years, who knows,
in silence, letting the raucous Forms
go rich and multiply their aquamarine
on ember-red dead dust and men?
Oh those embers, when they raze
every laboratory, pavilion, mast, book,
every chair and hand and lip – blue,
cold, blue, cold, cold
eternity of the embers!
I wish you could hear the wings now
scraping the pyramid, it must be
an unspeakable anger to them
that we few have saved our flesh
and mean to live and think of them
and of the world and of ourselves
and the grey universe that rolls us
a thousand thousand thousand years.

Frontier Story

Meanwhile, back at the ranch factory
they were turning out whole stampedes
just for the hell of it, the mile-long door slid back
and they reverted to dust at the first touch of air.
But the music of the dust flowed back over the assembly-line
and that was the Christmas of a thousand million cowboys.

Steers went lowing upland, purple sage country
with boots on marched west out back as
bulldozers like mobile capital cities
trunched up dead million-bed motels and charged
some gaily eroded buttes with simulating cowboys.

The diggers were worse than any sands of the sea
and dynamite only loosened myriads off sideways
till a bag of megatons went critical and
there were horses' eyeholes all over the Coalsack
and when we came in we were crunching through cowboys.

Or so we were told as we laid Los Angeles on Boston
and took a few states out, we were only playing,
pulled Mexico up over us and went to sleep,
woke up spitting out Phoenicians into the Cassiterides
and gave a yawn a wave as it flew out full of cowboys.

They sat in our teeth with red-hot spurs and I said
'Back to the drawing-board', but the belt was humming
and pushed the continuum into funky gopher-holes
with a prime number down each hole wheezing
so cheekily we had to make more cowboys

first. Meanwhile, back at the ranch
factory they were diligently making
us, just for the hell of it, the mile-long door
slid back and we reverted to dust at the touch
of air. But our music lingers in the bones of cowboys.

The Barrow

A dialogue

– Where have you been, you look so

– You know that old pawnshop down by the yard,
  it's closed now, it's all to be demolished
  for the motorway, POLONSKY'S PAWN, remember?

– Yes, they sold up, moved out months ago,
  anyway they hadn't much business,
  not down there – there were rats and

– No not down there, remember him though,
  old Polonsky, that old brown scarf –
  near the river, that's why there were rats –
  anyway I was down there, just poking around
  you know

– Poking around yes

– At the back of the shop I saw this barrow
  with a big greasy tarpaulin over it
  and a couple of seagulls, so I said Whoosh

– But what was the

– Yes this tarpaulin you see, and I knew
  there was something under it, it was

– Must have been quite strange, down there

– All shaped up high, you know, so I tugged
  and pulled, it was really quite foggy today,
  there was a foghorn somewhere down the river

– Foghorn?

– Horn yes, and then those gulls, they hadn't
  really gone you know, they were still watching,
  I began to wonder about the barrow

– Fish you mean, a load of fish

– No of course I'd have smelt the fish

– Yes of course you'd have smelt the fish

– Yes I knew it couldn't be fish,
  remember Polonsky's fish pies on the counter?
  he always said there's nothing like fish
  for brains, and he used to play chess with himself
  you know, one of those folding chess sets

– They say you've got to start young of course

– If you start young it's not too hard,
  remember when we were living up by the

– Oh yes now, up by the – there was that boy
  won the school tournament at twelve

– Must be nearly ten years ago now,
  I wonder if he's lost his

– They say it comes and goes, but Polonsky

– Oh yes Polonsky could play, he could play,
  he used to play behind the counter,
  but I was telling you about the tarpaulin,
  I got it off you know, and you wouldn't believe it
  but there was absolutely nothing

– Nothing in the barrow?

– There was nothing in the barrow, the tarpaulin
  the tarpaulin was stiff as if there had been something
  beneath it once, but it was gone you see,
  the vandals must have

– Oh yes the vandals, but was there nothing?

– Nothing at all, but there was something

– What do you mean there was something?

– I didn't mean there was really anything

– If there wasn't anything how could there be something?

– It was just something chalked inside the barrow

– Something chalked? chalked?

– Inside the barrow

– But what did it say?

– It said SIT HERE

– Well of course talking about it now seems –
   well I thought why not, why not sit,
   and you know this is when something happened

– You don't mean it was the rats

– No no no no it wasn't the rats,
   but as soon as I sat in the barrow, krrunk,
   there were these four great iron bars
   shot up all round me, pinned me there,
   I couldn't move you see, I yelled,
   and you know this is when something happened.
   The fog was really thick, but then
   someone came up out of the fog
   and I shouted HELP and rattled the barrow,
   and he came up closer and looked at me
   and felt the bars, but not a word,
   and I couldn't really see his face,
   and you know this is when something happened

– He robbed you, I knew it, dirty thief,
   it was all a plant, it was a trap to

– No he wasn't after my money.
   He had something in his hand you see

– What do you mean in his hand? his hand?

– He had something in his hand. He killed me.

Thoughts of a Module

It is black so. There is that dust.
My ladder in light. What are my men.
One is foot down. That is pack drill.
Black what is vizor. A hiss I heard.
The talks go up. Clump now but float.
Is a jump near. A camera paced out.
I phase another man. Another man is second.
Second last feet on. The dust I think.

266

So some soles cross. Is a flag near.
No move yon flag. Which voice comes down.
White house thanks all. Command module man not.
Is kangaroo hop around. I think moon dance.
Or white bird is. Good oxygen I heard.
Earth monitors must be. Is it too pressing.
Trained man is gay. Fail safe is gay.
The black I see. What instruments are lonely.
Sharp is a shadow. A horizon goes flat.
All rock are samples. Dust taken I think.
Is bright my leg. In what sun yonder.
An end I think. How my men go.
The talks come down. The ladder I shake.
To leave that bright. Space dark I see.
Is my men last. Men are that first.
That moon is here. They have some dust.
Is home they know. Blue earth I think.
I lift I see. It is that command.
My men go back. I leave that here.
It is bright so.

The First Men on Mercury

– We come in peace from the third planet.
Would you take us to your leader?

– Bawr stretter! Bawr. Bawr. Stretterhawl?

– This is a little plastic model
of the solar system, with working parts.
You are here and we are there and we
are now here with you, is this clear?

– Gawl horrop. Bawr. Abawrhannahanna!

– Where we come from is blue and white
with brown, you see we call the brown
here 'land', the blue is 'sea', and the white
is 'clouds' over land and sea, we live
on the surface of the brown land,
all round is sea and clouds. We are 'men'.
Men come –

– Glawp men! Gawrbenner menko. Menhawl?

– Men come in peace from the third planet
which we call 'earth'. We are earthmen.
Take us earthmen to your leader.

– Thmen? Thmen? Bawr. Bawrhossop.
Yuleeda tan hanna. Harrabost yuleeda.

– I am the yuleeda. You see my hands,
we carry no benner, we come in peace.
The spaceways are all stretterhawn.

– Glawn peacemen all horrabhanna tantko!
Tan come at'mstrossop. Glawp yuleeda!

– Atoms are peacegawl in our harraban.
Menbat worrabost from tan hannahanna.

– You men we know bawrhossoptant. Bawr.
We know yuleeda. Go strawg backspetter quick.

– We cantantabawr, tantingko backspetter now!

– Banghapper now! Yes, third planet back.
Yuleeda will go back blue, white, brown
nowhanna! There is no more talk.

– Gawl han fasthapper?

– No. You must go back to your planet.
Go back in peace, take what you have gained
but quickly.

– Stretterworra gawl, gawl...

– Of course, but nothing is ever the same,
now is it? You'll remember Mercury.

Spacepoem 3: Off Course

the golden flood   the weightless seat
the cabin song   the pitch black
the growing beard   the floating crumb
the shining rendezvous   the orbit wisecrack
the hot spacesuit   the smuggled mouth-organ

the imaginary somersault   the visionary sunrise
the turning continents   the space debris
the golden lifeline   the space walk
the crawling deltas   the camera moon
the pitch velvet   the rough sleep
the crackling headphone   the space silence
the turning earth   the lifeline continents
the cabin sunrise   the hot flood
the shining spacesuit   the growing moon
   the crackling somersault   the smuggled orbit
   the rough moon   the visionary rendezvous
   the weightless headphone   the cabin debris
   the floating lifeline   the pitch sleep
   the crawling camera   the turning silence
   the space crumb   the crackling beard
   the orbit mouth-organ   the floating song

A Too Hot Summer

A car came hooting slowly not upended
and it was a summer lane with limes dusted down.
Lazy boys yawned in tree-forts, tumbled suddenly
to the impertinence of the windshield and the horn,
for looking out it was a dog.

How acoustic the recording-room was
till they slid back a noisy panel, shrubbery girls
in fishnets looked up with sandwiches, chewing
the shirt-sleeves of the producer there surely
but looking out it was a dog.

The first pony stood, shook its reins.
The butcher's daughters cried sweetly to it
to advance, came off to tug, then showed
their rougher natures by the betting shop
and looking out it was a dog.

Two lovers took the wood to pieces running
out of quarrelling time from the landmark trunk
the lightning struck to the easy red cottages,
and all they had seen was the broken bark,
though looking out it was a dog.

And the white glider came rather bucketing down,
a swoosh on a field of swedes latterly and fell open
somehow. Farmhands whistled, scratched, glared.
Who could help wondering about the man
when looking out it was a dog.

Itinerary

i

We went to Oldshoremore.
Is the Oldshoremore road still there?
You mean the old shore road?
I suppose it's more an old road than a shore road.
No more! They shored it up, but it's washed away.
So you could sing the old song –
Yes we sang the old song:
    We'll take the old Oldshoremore shore road no more.

ii

We passed the Muckle Flugga.
Did you see the muckle flag?
All we saw was the muckle fog.
The flag says ULTIMA FLUGGA WHA'S LIKE US.
Couldn't see flag for fug, sorry.
Ultimately –
    Ultimately we made for Muck and flogged the lugger.

iii

Was it bleak at Bowhousebog?
It was black as a hoghouse, boy.
Yes, but bleak?
Look, it was black as a bog and bleak as the Bauhaus!
The Bauhaus wasn't black –
Will you get off my back!
So there were dogs too?
    Dogs, hogs, leaks in the bogs – we never went back.

Boxers

– Who're you with? – Boxers. – What?
– There's something going on here. – Still can't hear you.
– Boxers. – Look this is impossible, what did you say?
– There was a storm last night all night you know.
– What's that? What's torn? – Wires down up-by.
But that's not what you hear here. – What? Where?
– Here. It's the sparring. – What's that I keep hearing?
– I just told you. Boxers. – There's one word
you keep using. – Did you hear that crash?
That was the table, they're spry as cats.
I gave them steaks and the end of the wine.
Sleep? Not them. Up at each other
the four of them like – what's that you say?
– You said cats. What cats? Where are the cats?
– Cats? I'm not speaking about cats. Boxers.
– There it is, there's that word. – I bet you can
hear them, they've started to sing. Some harmony.
Two with belts and two with braces.
I'll have to put them up. – Pull what up?
– Yes, put the lot up. One in your bed
since you're stuck in Croy, one on the couch,
one in the collapsible thing, and one
on two chairs. – Of course I'm in Croy,
where did you think I was? – Yes. – What?
– Try the line tomorrow, give me a ring.
I'm off to make coffee for those clowns.
– What was that? I'm not having clowns!
Harry, you'll not put a clown in my bed.
– I'm not putting clowns in anybody's bed.
There's not a clown here. – Harry, are you drunk?
– Look I must go, they're swinging on the pulley.
– Overseas telegrams, can I help you? – Linda!

Letters of Mr Lonelyhearts

i

Little Mr Lonelyhearts
picked at the sofa,
hating the horsehair
but there it was.
Dear Disappointed,
he wrote, I think

271

you must forget
the bad baking.
A burnt scone is
a burnt scone, but
marriage is more
than a tearful plateful
– or even two –
of carbonized baps.
You spoke of a kitchen
of smoke and a kick
at the gateleg and glad
for a beer with the boys
but now go
easy, chum,
your mother burnt
her rice in her time
so don't cast
that up.
A hard potato
is not cruelty
and anyway she cried.
So remember your bride
who tries to please you
running to the door
with her floury apron
and a bun in the oven.
Remember that.
Be thankful for that.

                    ii
Mr Lonelyhearts loosened his tie
with a great sigh, closed the marshmallows.
He took a turn about the room, spoke
sharply to his budgerigar, stared out
at nothing passing, came back
and with a last marshmallow grimly
settled to type. Dear Puzzled, it went,
Look, you got back your monkey, so
what's all the fuss? I've got broken hearts,
roofs collapsing, no month's rent, I've got
crazy wills, incest, grandmothers locked out –
and so I'm to lose sleep over a monkey?
You say it's not safe to leave one in the streets,
and you've lost all trust in your fellow-men.
Grow up and get a sense of proportion.
You say you hardly knew this man
in Kent Street, with his one brown eye

and one blue eye – are you making it up,
I don't know why I answer letters –
and yet you left this – Judy, you call her?
with him, red suit, chain, banana,
the lot, and went for your car, right?
I don't get it. I don't get it.
Meanwhile your rainbow-eyed china – some china –
passed on this vagrant marmoset
to a third party, did he just get tired
of holding her? All right, I'll believe you.
But then this third man, in whom lies the crunch,
thought he had been left holding the baby
– more edifying all round if it *had* been a baby,
baby – and took her home for the night.
Now what puzzles *me*, friend Puzzled, is simply
what you were up to all this time,
did your car have a flat, or perhaps
you really were trying to leave your monkey
on somebody's doorstep? Oh yes I admit
you went after her, you unravelled the string
of accidents, touching reunion
I'm sure, with the red hat and all. But –
why don't you just come off it, quietly?
Stick to bitter lemon. I won't have
two-eyed men in this column, or
unintelligible organ-grinders.

iii

The thunder broke, and Mr Lonelyhearts
seized a sheet like lightning. Dear Rosie,
he wrote, Kill him. For a man
who'd take a snake basket
on his honeymoon, divorce
is peanuts. Shoot him,
get yourself a night's sleep.

A Jar Revisited

...the fictitious spaec [*sic*]
Behind it.
– Norman MacCaig,
'Painting – *The Blue Jar*'

Space is real, I've
got jars nicely
settled in it, it
seems faintly blue
and has a time
factor too. This
prevents jars coming through.

Capes of wrath and splendour
are real bluster. To burst
seas on and row letters to
lighthouses from and round
continents by is
real mustard. Mink ones
really come from farms.

Paces are quite real,
horses show theirs, archbishops
crowning queens have
to take them, on the street
in fog they may be Jack
the Ripper's, but the drill-hall
peels them off a stick.

Scape is the real
of land, city, sea;
scope and apex of
the scene. I saw a man
brushing a greyhound in a back-
court sunset, he talked to it
quietly, by the golden bins.

Spaec, however,
is fictitious. It's the place
lost jars end up in, and
we're not painting out what never
was in when we
say so – except that
when we've said it we've made it, and that jars.

Pleasures of a Technological University

magnesium and Crashaw
semiotics and ergonomics
lasers and caesuras
retro-rockets and peripeteia
sapphics and turquoise
sines and sememes
hubris and helium
Eliot and entropy
enjambment and switchgear
quasars and hapax legomena
thermodynamics and macrostylistics
anti-hero and anti-matter
bubble chambers and E.K. Chambers
H_2O and 8vo
genres and genera
meters and metres
litmus and anagnorisis
DNA and ABBA
DNB and TNT
bleeps and feet
Rhine and Poe
ficelle and cantilever
metal fatigue and dead metaphors
flyting and teratology
ergs and Bacon
genes and fitts
morphs and mesons
tektites and données
Möbius's ring and Freytag's pyramid
stichomythia and feedback
red shifts and Tam o'Shanter
copula and cupola
sonic booms and euphuism
osmosis and entasis
umlaut and ohm
Ethan Brand and ethyl fluid
wit and sodium chloride
neoaristotelianism and microminiaturization
F_3 and Fe
poem and pome

The Computer's First Dialect Poems

Blea on the baulk the furze kidder rocked
with a bottle of flags and a budget of bent.
Sawning and soodling in a drabbled scrip
he hirpled and jolled hirkling and croodling.
Morts of mizled mouldiwarps
gaddered the ball at beavering hour
and progged the fotherer's frumitory.
His cag of stingo by the stools
was teemed by puddock, pink, and pismire.
Glabbering sturnels swooped on sprotes.
Rawky popples whewed and quawked.
Hariff and foulroyce clouted the meer.
Brustling at clink and bandy chock
his sawney doll pelted pranking.
Bating the lown with hugh icles
she pilled him on the pudgy platt
and pessed his yaum as pluft as a pooty.

A bumbarrel scrowed Joe Millar's book.

II THE BIRKIE AND THE HOWDIE (Lowland Scots)

A dorty, vogie, chanler-chaftit birkie
brattled the aizles o the clachan chimlie,
glunched at his jaupin quaich o usquebae,
scunnered red-wud at the clarty lyart howdie
snirtlin by the ingle-neuk sae laithron and tozie,
and gied the thowless quine a blaud wi his gully
till she skrieghed like a cut-luggit houlet and dang her tassie
aff-loof at his unco doup, the glaikit tawpie.
The skellum callan goaved at her fell drumlie:
'Ye tocherless wanchancie staumrel hizzie,
ye groazlin, driddlin grumphie, ye awnie ferlie,
deil gie your kyte curmurrings o scroggy crowdie,
and bogles graizle ilka ramfeezl't hurdie
till aa your snash is steekit, ye duddie hoodie!'

– 'Ach, I hae warlock-briefs, stegh the collieshangie!
Aa your ier-oes sall gang sae muckle agley
they'se turn to blitters and bauckie-birds, and in a brulzie
they'se mak their joes o taeds, aa thrang and sonsie,
snowkin in aidle whaur asks and clegs are grushie:
yon is an ourie pliskie!'
                              Wha wan the tulzie?

276

The Computer's First Code Poem

```
TEYZA PRQTP ZSNSX OSRMY VCFBO VJSDA
XSEVK JCSPV HSMCV RFBOP OZQDW EAOAD
TSRVY CFEZP OZFRV PTFEP FRXAE OFVVA
HFOPK DZYJR TYPPA PVYBT OAZYJ UAOAD
VEQBT DEQJZ WSZZP WSRWK UAEYU LYSRV
HYUAX BSRWP PIFQV QOYNA KFDDQ PCYYV
BQRSD VQTSE TQEVK FTARX VSOSQ BYFRX
TQRXQ PVEFV LYZVP HSEPV TFBQP QHYYV
VYUSD TYVVY PVSZZ PCYJP FRDFV QYEVQ
PJQBT CYFES JQSZP QTTQZ DQRQZ VQUSP
TFRWP VCEYJ TZQSR JYEXP QOYFV XCYJP
MCYPV CQSWF AUSVP QTSRM GYYSX VQUSP
```

Not Playing the Game

– Although a poem is
undoubtedly a 'game'
it is not a game.
And although now it is even
part of the game to say so,
making it a " 'game' "
is spooky, and we'll
not play that.

– Who are you kidding, said
the next card. You just played.

– Anything I play
has no rules, if
you see the rules
it's only 'play' –
the 'dealer's eyeshade'.

– I like that smoker's cough the " 'dealer's eyeshade' ".
Your deal is showing, my dear.

– Back in the box you go in words.
'Back in the box', in other words.
Now we'll just let that
' " 'dealer's eyeshade' " '
wilt on whatever can support it, like
a poem on baize.

Rider

a grampus whacked the hydrophone / Loch Fyne left its green bed,
   fled / shrieking to Cowal / it all began

the nutcracker closed round Port Glasgow / it snapped with a burst
   of docks and / capstans downwind like collarstuds

cabbage whites in deadlock / were hanged from geans and rowans /
   wedlock-red

Greenock in steam / hammered albatrosses onto packingcases /
   without forgiveness / zam

by the waters of Glasgow / angels hung pilgrims, primroses, Dante,
   black blankets / over and over / the acid streams

a giant hedgehog lifting the Necropolis / solid silver / to the moon /
   sang of the deluge

long keys of gas unlocked the shaking Campsies at / last, at least /
   four drumlins were heard howling / as far as Fenwick Moor

Calderpark was sucked into a belljar, came out / at Kalgoorlie with
   elephants and northern lights

ravening taxis roasted dogs in basements, basted / chicken wheels
   in demolition oil / slept by the swing / of the wrecker's ball

the Holy Loch turned to granite chips, the ships / died with their
   stiff upper lips reaching to Aviemore

Para Handy sculled through the subway with the Stone of Destiny /
   shot the rapids at Cessnock right into Sunday morning

a coelacanth on stilts was setting fire to Sauchiehall Street when
   Tom Leonard /

sold James B.V. Thomson a horse, black /

in the night and dust / which galloped him away /

deep as the grave / writing

Davidson looked through the telescope at MacDiarmid and said /
   what, is that God

Davidson rode off on a blood-splashed stag / into the sea / horses
   ultimately

Davidson sold / fish to Neptune, fire / to Prometheus, to himself /
   a prisoner's iron bed, the red

sun rose flapping slowly over Nietzsche / bars melted into sand /
   black marias stalled in Calton

the rainbow dropped its pot of lead on Peterhead / the peter keys
   were blown to breadcrumbs, fed

to men forbid / the men bought lead, built jails, went mad, lay
   dead / in iron fields

the jaws of Nero smouldered in a dustbin / cinders tingled / the dead
   rose / tamam

sulphur shoes dancing to Mars / their zircon eyeshades flashed,

beryllium / toeguards clipped Mercury's boulders
Lucretius was found lying under the flary walls / of a universe in the
   Crab nebula / crying
the dancers brought him water / where he lay he rose, froze / in a
   mandala like a flame / blessing
the darkness of all disbelievers / filaments of the Crab wrapped him
   in hydrogen shroud / remade
he walked by Barrhead and Vauxhall Bridge, by the sea waited /
   with his dark horse in the dangerous night air
for a rider / his testament
delivered to the earth, kicking /
the roots of things

iii

five hundred million hummingbirds sat in the Kelvin Hall / three
   hundred thousand girls took double basses
in a crocodile to Inverkip / six thousand children drew Rothesay
   through twelve thousand kites / two hundred
plumbers with morning cellos galvanized the bedmakers of Fairlie /
   forty babies
threw their teething-rings at a helicopter / trickety-track / till
   Orpheus looked back
and there was nothing but the lonely hills and sky unless the chilling
   wind was something / and the space
of pure white pain where his wife had held his hand from hell / he
   left the place
and came to a broken shack at midday / with carts and horses /
   strong dark ragged boys
played in the smoke / the gypsies gave him soup and bread / for the
   divine brooch / who cares
what is divine, he said / and passed into the valley of the Clyde,
   a cloud / followed
and many campfires in that landscape, dogs whining, cuckoos,
   glasshouses, thundershowers /
David Gray shook the rain from his hair and held his heart, the
   Luggie flashed
in the lightning of the last March storm / he led a sweet brown mare
   into the mist / the apple-boughs
closed over, where the flute
of Orpheus was only wished for /
in the drip of trees

iv

butcher-boys tried to ward off sharks / the waters rose quickly /
   great drowned bankers
floated from bay-windows / two housemaids struggled on
   Grosvenor Terrace with a giant conger

the Broomielaw was awash with slime and torn-out claws and
  anchor-flakes / rust and dust
sifted together where a dredger ploughed up the Gallowgate /
  pushed a dirty wave over Shettleston
spinning shopfronts crashed in silence / glassily, massively /
  porticoes tilting / settled in mud
lampreys fastened on four dead sailors drifting through Finnieston /
  in a Drygate attic
James Macfarlan threw his pen at the stinking wall / the whisky and
  the stinking poverty
ran down like ink / the well of rats was bottomless and Scotch / the
  conman and the conned
fought on / the ballads yellowed, the pubs filled / at Anderston he
  reached his grave in snow / selah
the ruined cities were switched off / there was no flood / his father
  led a pedlar's horse
by Carrick fields, his mother sang / the boy rode on a jogging back /
  far back / in rags /
Dixon's Blazes roared and threw more poets in its molten pools /
  forges on fire
matched the pitiless bread, the head
long hangdog, the lifted elbow /
the true bloody pathos and sublime

                              v
Kossuth took a coalblack horse from Debrecen / clattered up
  Candleriggs into the City Hall
three thousand cheers could never drown the groaning fortress-
  bars / a thousand years
heard the wind howl / scimitars, eagles, bugles, edicts, whips,
  crowns, in the pipes / playing / the grave plain in the sun
handcuffed keelies shouted in Albion Street / slogans in red
  fragments broke the cobblestones, Kossuth
drew a mirage on electric air / the hare sat calmly on the
  doorstep / it was Monday over all the world / om
Tom McGrath mixed bread and milk for the young hare / Monk
  and Parker spoke in a corner / the still room
was taken / Dougal Graham stood on his hands, the bell / rang
  between his feet / he rolled
on his hump through the swarming Tontine piazzas, swam / in
  dogs, parcels, puddles, tobacco-quids
ran with a bawbee ballad five feet long / felt fishwives / gutted
  a brace of Glasgow magistrates / lay
with a pig in his arms and cried the city fathers bitches / till
  a long shadow fell on pedlars
and far away the sound of hoofs / increased in moonlight / whole
  cities crouched in saddlebags

churches, dungeons, juntas dangled from reins / like grasses
    picked from the rank fields
and drops of halter sweat
burned men to the bone, but the hare
like mad / played

Guy Fawkes Moon

Fog shroud
and clouds
(when the clock
chimed late
in the heavy
November night-
time) lifting
the mystery
for a greater
drifted
off a whole
white full
moon pitched
above the white
thin chimney-
stalk of the
new Dawsholm
incinerator –
as if the piled
rags Glasgow
rubbish rusted
bedsprings bent
hair-rollers blood-
caked saddles of
crumpled Hondas
and sorry lunch-
box plastic
nests of cracks
and crumbs had
all become
a moon of smoke
and the real moon
a César moon
in a car-crusher
was now the Odeon

bulking greyly
with its sleeping stars
in reels by
the firework field.

And sparklers raced
between moons
and squeals –
and red rockets
mufflers matches
and up in¯smoke
far from school.

Saturday Night

Sluggish winds drove huddled moaning
among the evening steeples and dust,
subway queues bought wigs from buskers,
took song-sheets out, roared on blurting
through chips and beer and concertinas,
scrambled dancing down the steps,
tore up a train and spat the guard out,
showered the line with filthy Panatellas
old caps tatty plastic macs and Askits,
came up for air, hooting Orange fragments,
heard a Jaguar with a tiger in its tank
farting at red, sprang plastered out
with nude paperbacks, boots, shrouds cut
from unwiped café wallpaper, ran
with Nellie Dean well down Cowcaddens,
two maudlin crocodiles with hiccups
converging in their pockets cried Easy
hard to the lamp-post light, laid
chip-bags out on fallen companions
propped up with vomit and shook fists
at gallus buses sliding by the
citizens with closed doors blandly
conducted, ya bastard, then rain
soaked like dogs into black thick
razor-styled hair and greasy scarves,
dripped from dog-eared jacket-vents,
wilted the huge cuffs and collars and
they sang without their women at
the useless stop into the night.

Death in Duke Street

A huddle on the greasy street –
cars stop, nose past, withdraw –
dull glint on soles of tackety boots,
frayed rough blue trousers, nondescript coat
stretching back, head supported
in strangers' arms, a crowd collecting –
'Whit's wrang?' 'Can ye see'm?'
'An auld fella, he's had it.'
On one side, a young mother in a headscarf
is kneeling to comfort him, her three-year-old son
stands puzzled, touching her coat, her shopping-bag
spills its packages that people look at
as they look at everything. On the other side
a youth, nervous, awkwardly now
at the centre of attention as he shifts his arm
on the old man's shoulders, wondering
what to say to him, glancing up at the crowd.
These were next to him when he fell,
and must support him into death.
He seems not to be in pain,
he is speaking slowly and quietly
but he does not look at any of them,
his eyes are fixed on the sky,
already he is moving out
beyond everything belonging.
As if he still belonged
they hold him very tight.

Only the hungry ambulance
howls for him through the staring squares.

Christmas Eve

Loneliness of city Christmas Eves –
with real stars up there – clear – and stars
on poles and wires across the street, and streaming
cars all dark with parcels, home
to families and the lighted window trees –

I sat down in the bus beside him – white jeans,
black jerkin, slumped with head nodding
in sleep, face hidden by long black hair, hands

283

tattooed on the four fingers ADEN 1967
and on the right hand five Christian crosses.
As the bus jerked, his hand fell on my knee,
stayed there, lay heavily and alive
with blue carvings from another world
and seemed to hold me like a claw,
unmoving. It moved. I rubbed my ear
to steal a glance at him, found him
stealing a glance at me. It was not
the jerking of the bus, it was a proposition.
He shook his hair back, and I saw his face
for the first time, unshaven, hardman, a warning
whether in Aden or Glasgow, but our eyes held
while that blue hand burned into my leg.
Half drunk, half sleeping – but half what, half what?
As his hand stirred again, my arm covered it
while the bus jolted round a corner.
'Don't ge' aff tae ah ge' aff.' – But the conductor
was watching, came up and shook him, looked at me.
My ticket was up, I had to leave him sprawled there
with that hand that now seemed so defenceless
lying on the seat I had left. Half down the stair
I looked back. The last thing I saw was Aden
and five blue crosses for five dead friends.

It was only fifteen minutes out of life
but I feel as if I was lifted by a whirlwind
and thrown down on some desert rocks to die
of dangers as always far worse lost than run.

Stobhill

THE DOCTOR

Yes, I agreed to perform the abortion.
The girl was under unusual strain.
I formed the opinion that for personal reasons
and home circumstances her health would suffer
if pregnancy was not terminated.
She was unmarried and the father was unknown.
She had important exams to sit,
her career would be jeopardized, and in any case
she went in mortal fear of her father
(who is himself, as it happens, a doctor)

284

and believed he would throw her out of the house.
These factors left me in no doubt.
Accordingly I delivered her seven months baby
without complications. It was limp and motionless.
I was satisfied there was no life in it.
Normal practice was followed: it was placed
in a paper disposal bag and sent
to the incinerator. Later to my surprise
I was told it was alive. It was then returned
and I massaged its chest and kept it warm.
It moved and breathed about eight hours.
Could it have lived? I hardly think so.
You call it a disturbing case? Disturbing
is a more emotive word than I would choose
but I take the point. However, the child
as far as I was concerned was dead
on delivery, and my disposal instructions
were straight and without melodrama.
There is, as sheriff and jury will agree,
an irony for students of the human condition
(and in this case who is not?)
in the fact that the baby was resuscitated
by the jogging of the bag on its way to the incinerator.
I hope that everything I have said is clear.

THE BOILERMAN

Ay well, the porter brought this bag doon
(he'd come fae the operatin theatre like)
an he sayed it wis fur burnin.
Ah tellt him it would have tae wait,
ah had tae clean the fire oot first,
say hauf an oor, then it could go in.
So he goes away an leaves the bag,
it wis on a big pile of bags, like, all ready
fur tae go in. Anyway, ah gote the fire up,
ah starts throwin bags in the incinerator,
an ah'm luftin this wee bag an
ah hear a sorta whimperin – cryin like –
an ah can feel somethin breathin
through the paper. Whit did ah dae?
Ah pit it on a binch, near the hote pipes.
An ah goes up thae sterrs fur the porter.
Asks him, What wis in that bag?
He says, A foetus. Ah says, What's that?
A kiddy, he says. D'yen ken it's alive? ah says.

285

He says, Yes. Ah says, It's a bluidy shame,
is it no? He says, Ay it's a bluidy shame.
But the sleekit bugger never let dab
when he brought the bag. All he sayed wis burn it
and that's the God's truth. It's bad enough
whit the doctors dae, but he'd have been a murderer
if ah hadny heard the wean cryin –
Christ, it wis hingin ower the fire –
may-be a quick death in thae degrees,
but ah couldny sleep fur nights
thinkin aboot it, couldny sleep,
an och, ah still think what's the use,
ah didny save the kiddy's life.
It canny have been meant tae live.
An yet ye'd wonder, wid ye no?

THE MOTHER

I've no idea who the father is.
I took a summer job in a hotel
in the Highlands, there was a party, I
got drunk, it must have happened then
but I remember nothing. When I knew
I was pregnant I was almost crazy,
it seemed the end of everything.
My father – it was just impossible,
you have no idea what he is like,
he would certainly have turned me out
and made my mother's life unbearable
if it wasn't unbearable before.
If I can describe him, he is a man
who equates permissive with diabolical.
Reading about a drug-raid once at breakfast
he threw a chair across the room
and swore till he was purple – swearing's
all right, and malt whisky, and chair-breaking,
but not sex. I have sometimes wondered
how he got over conceiving me,
or perhaps – if he ever did get over it.
– I am sorry, this is irrelevant.
I wanted to say that I – my actions
are not very good and I don't defend them,
but I could not have the baby,
I just could not, you do see?
And now I never want to have one,
that's what it's done to me. I'm sick

286

of thinking, regretting, wishing, blaming.
I've gone so dead I see it all
like pulled from someone else's womb
and I can almost pity her
till I remember I'd be best
to forget the loss was mine.

THE FATHER

Did she? Did she? I'm really not surprised
I'm really not. Vodka, rum, gin –
some night yon was. Was it me?
Was it my bairn? Christ I don't know,
it might have been, I had her all right –
but there was three of us you know –
at least three – there was big Alec
and the wee French waiter wi the limp
(what d'ye cry him, Louie, wee Louie) –
and we went to this hut down by the loch –
it was a perfect night, perfect night –
mind you, we were all staggering a bit
but she was the worst let me tell you.
Big Alec, he's standing behind her and
kinna nibbling her neck and he leans over
and pulls her breasts out and says What have we here?
and she's giggling with her hair all over the place –
she looked that stupit we were all laughing, –
no, I'm telling a lie, we werny all laughing,
I'll aye remember the French kid, Louie,
he wasny laughing, eyes like wee ferrets
as if he'd never seen yon before, and maybe
he hadn't, but he couldny take his eyes off her.
We got in the hut, into the hut
and see her, soon as we were in that door –
out like a light, flat on her back.
Well, I got going, then the other two,
but if you ask me they didny do much,
they'd had a right skinful and they were –
anyhow, I don't remember much after that,
it all goes a bit hazy. But I do remember
coming out the hut it was a lovely night,
it was July and it was a lovely night
with the big trees and the water an all.

Ah know ah tellt them lies at the enquiry.
Ah sayed ah thought the wean wis dead
when ah took it tae the incinerator.
Ah didny think the wean wis dead,
but ah didny ken fur shair, did ah?
It's no fur me tae question the doctors.
Ah get a bag fae the sister, right?
She says take that an burn it. She's only
passin on the doctor's instructions,
but she seen the wean, she thought it wis dead,
so ye canny blame her. And the doctor says
ye canny blame him. Everybody wants
tae come doon on me like a tonna bricks.
Ah canny go aboot openin disposal bags –
if ah did ah'd be a nervous wreck.
Ah passed two electricians in the corridor
and ah tellt them the wean wis alive
but they thought ah wis jokin. Efter that
ah jist shut up, an left it tae the boilerman
tae fin oot fur hissel – he couldny miss it
could he? The puir wee thing wis squeelin
through the bag wis it no? Ah canny see
ah had tae tell him whit wis evident.
– Ah know ah'm goin on aboot this.
But suppose the kiddy could've been saved –
or suppose the boilerman hadny noticed it –
mah wee lassie's gote a hamster, ye ken? –
and ah fixed up a treadmill fur it
and it goes roon an roon an roon –
it's jist like that. Well ah'm no in court noo.
Don't answer nothing incriminatin, says the sheriff.
And that's good enough fur yours truly.
And neither ah did, neither ah did,
neither ah did, neither ah did.

Glasgow Sonnets

i

A mean wind wanders through the backcourt trash.
Hackles on puddles rise, old mattresses
puff briefly and subside. Play-fortresses
of brick and bric-a-brac spill out some ash.
Four storeys have no windows left to smash,
but in the fifth a chipped sill buttresses
mother and daughter the last mistresses
of that black block condemned to stand, not crash.
Around them the cracks deepen, the rats crawl.
The kettle whimpers on a crazy hob.
Roses of mould grow from ceiling to wall.
The man lies late since he has lost his job,
smokes on one elbow, letting his coughs fall
thinly into an air too poor to rob.

ii

A shilpit dog fucks grimly by the close.
Late shadows lengthen slowly, slogans fade.
The YY PARTICK TOI grins from its shade
like the last strains of some lost *libera nos
a malo*. No deliverer ever rose
from these stone tombs to get the hell they made
unmade. The same weans never make the grade.
The same grey street sends back the ball it throws.
Under the darkness of a twisted pram
a cat's eyes glitter. Glittering stars press
between the silent chimney-cowls and cram
the higher spaces with their SOS.
Don't shine a torch on the ragwoman's dram.
Coats keep the evil cold out less and less.

iii

'See a tenement due for demolition?
I can get ye rooms in it, two, okay?
Seven hundred and nothin legal to pay
for it's no legal, see? That's my proposition,
ye can take it or leave it but. The position
is simple, you want a hoose, I say
for eight hundred pound it's yours.' And they
trailing five bairns, accepted his omission
of the foul crumbling stairwell, windows wired
not glazed, the damp from the canal, the cooker

289

without pipes, packs of rats that never tired –
any more than the vandals bored with snooker
who stripped the neighbouring houses, howled, and fired
their aerosols – of squeaking 'Filthy lucre!'

iv

Down by the brickworks you get warm at least.
Surely soup-kitchens have gone out? It's not
the Thirties now. Hugh MacDiarmid forgot
in 'Glasgow 1960' that the feast
of reason and the flow of soul has ceased
to matter to the long unfinished plot
of heating frozen hands. We never got
an abstruse song that charmed the raging beast.
So you have nothing to lose but your chains,
dear Seventies. Dalmarnock, Maryhill,
Blackhill and Govan, better sticks and stanes
should break your banes, for poets' words are ill
to hurt ye. On the wrecker's ball the rains
of greeting cities drop and drink their fill.

v

'Let them eat cake' made no bones about it.
But we say let them eat the hope deferred
and that will sicken them. We have preferred
silent slipways to the riveters' wit.
And don't deny it – that's the ugly bit.
Ministers' tears might well have launched a herd
of bucking tankers if they'd been transferred
from Whitehall to the Clyde. And smiles don't fit
either. 'There'll be no bevvying' said Reid
at the work-in. But all the dignity you muster
can only give you back a mouth to feed
and rent to pay if what you lose in bluster
is no more than win patience with 'I need'
while distant blackboards use you as their duster.

vi

The North Sea oil-strike tilts east Scotland up,
and the great sick Clyde shivers in its bed.
But elegists can't hang themselves on fled-
from trees or poison a recycled cup –
If only a less faint, shaky sunup
glimmered through the skeletal shop and shed

and men washed round the piers like gold and spread
golder in soul than Mitsubishi or Krupp –
The images are ageless but the thing
is now. Without my images the men
ration their cigarettes, their children cling
to broken toys, their women wonder when
the doors will bang on laughter and a wing
over the firth be simply joy again.

vii

Environmentalists, ecologists
and conservationists are fine no doubt.
Pedestrianization will come out
fighting, riverside walks march off the lists,
pigeons and starlings be somnambulists
in far-off suburbs, the sandblaster's grout
multiply pink piebald facades to pout
at sticky-fingered mock-Venetianists.
Prop up's the motto. Splint the dying age.
Never displease the watchers from the grave.
Great when fake architecture was the rage,
but greater still to see what you can save.
The gutted double fake meets the adage:
a wig's the thing to beat both beard and shave.

viii

Meanwhile the flyovers breed loops of light
in curves that would have ravished tragic Toshy –
clean and unpompous, nothing wishy-washy.
Vistas swim out from the bulldozer's bite
by day, and banks of earthbound stars at night
begin. In Madame Emé's Sauchie Haugh, she
could never gain in leaves or larks or sploshy
lanes what's lost in a dead boarded site –
the life that overspill is overkill to.
Less is not more, and garden cities are
the flimsiest oxymoron to distil to.
And who wanted to distil? Let bus and car
and hurrying umbrellas keep their skill to
feed ukiyo-e beyond Lochnagar.

It groans and shakes, contracts and grows again.
Its giant broken shoulders shrug off rain.
It digs its pits to a shauchling refrain.
Roadworks and graveyards like their gallus men.
It fattens fires and murders in a pen
and lets them out in flaps and squalls of pain.
It sometimes tears its smoky counterpane
to hoist a bleary fist at nothing, then
at everything, you never know. The west
could still be laid with no one's tears like dust
and barricaded windows be the best
to see from till the shops, the ships, the trust
return like thunder. Give the Clyde the rest.
Man and the sea make cities as they must.

x

From thirtieth floor windows at Red Road
he can see choughs and samphires, dreadful trade –
the schoolboy reading *Lear* has that scene made.
A multi is a sonnet stretched to ode
and some say that's no joke. The gentle load
of souls in clouds, vertiginously stayed
above the windy courts, is probed and weighed.
Each monolith stands patient, ah'd and oh'd.
And stalled lifts generating high-rise blues
can be set loose. But stalled lives never budge.
They linger in the single-ends that use
their spirit to the bone, and when they trudge
from closemouth to laundrette their steady shoes
carry a world that weighs us like a judge.

The New Divan
1977

The New Divan

1

Hafiz, old nightingale, what fires there have been
in the groves, white dust, wretchedness,
how could you ever get your song together?
Someone stands by your tomb, thinks
as a shadow thinks: much, little, any?
You swore you'd be found shrouded in another
grave-cloth of pure smoke from a heart as
burning dead as beating, but the names
of cinders are thick where passions were.
Whole cities could be ash. But
not the song the Sufi says we have
but our dying song, you knew, gives us our beings.

2

Go on then, dance yourself into the masks.
The Old Man of the Sea has all the gales
within his heaving pack, get deep within
his folds, he's on your back, get deep
within gale-weary Sindbad, be the driver
of tritons and the triton, be before
the mast and be the aftermath, what might
be, what could never be, and keep
no form but water. Let matter
envy you the metamorphoses a
dancer steals and cannot stay.

3

The prince in the miniature has brilliant colours
to commend his hunting, his courage, his
little prancy dog; the toy trees shine. When
did the colours really run, his sighs, his
sunken furrows, yellow skin? The humming
top goes round, but stumbles, and
its silence takes us back
to restless earth's bazaars that buzzed
a hundred princes out, spinning with all
their grim viziers and those
unpainted clouds of flies indifferent
to settling on dead kings or simnel-cake.

4

I suppose having a bear for sentinel
you don't need passwords? In your grotesque
courtyard a pot of honey's all we had
for sesame, two salmon for shazam. Relations
are excellent with a full bear. Also
some wine, we left him dancing like
a madman in a play. So you threw on
your pyjamas for a chess party, got
the cook roused up, who brought oiled paper
hot with sweetmeats before checkmate. On
the stroke of one the bear snored.

5

His rough angels keep their beds unmade
in the north of paradise, hang about
in speckled flames, he lets them stream
grimacing through drugged plums. Which
of these wings is your afterwards?
You can ruck up the sheets alone till five.
I'll close my book when the curtain's surrounded
by grey light, bring you tea with the sun.
You'll blink up raddled as
a delta, fumble a lemon-slice into
the steam, cough crumbs. He
who made you real makes hash fudge unreal.
The sun rises, like your eyes, rich and red.

6

What a tottering veil to call an expanse
of desire demure by! I love those masses
of satsumas at your elbow, piled like the times
you praise. Beyond the window there's an engine
hissing past the harvest. A girl
walks her dog in mist. Lattices
tingle as you shriek like lightning
when the parrot shrieks and forcibly
detain the coffee-boy. A trail
of grape-seeds vanishes below
the couch. You crouch
on huge all-fours in the balcony sand
and groan and tap your grin with your pipe.

7

Swish the incense everywhere it's not.
I know you're full of arak and danger,
a fiery flying dressing-gown on human
wheels, two joss-sticks tossing the lust of
the nose up out through our small world
into the jasmine banks that smelt before
incense was made. You're in your blood.
Is it like this the gods are,
making and breaking as they swirl? who
box universes like eggs, and on reflection
unbox a cracked one for the pan, when
sparks only as they die are heard.

8

It was a slow caravan accompanied
by dust-devils, a dry thunder journey
to the desert's end. At sight of the forest
indignant camels trod in crevices,
held back puffing. Soon it was dark
under cedars, with more dark to come.
A bundle of lightning dropped badly
down the bark, hurt no one. Has
nature no symbols? They carried
nature like a peacock into the undergrowth
and ate it. Then these
servants of God lay down, each with his
book, in the black covert, by his beast.

9

White sails and turquoise Gulf– if these were all
we needed! Sores where beggars were
sit invisible on gate and wall. This
daylight is a picnic of the trumpets, the
visible's the tray of the sky slowly wheeling
its round of spiced meats at us as
welcome-seeming as kings' feasts. Thousands
are in hunger, see no glory, and
all are in desire so great and ancient
nothing heaven brings round, nothing behind
or present or to come can fill their house
with what they feel they need, or quieten them.

10

Sacks of them came off the last boats.
I don't know their name. You eat them salted.
Next door you'd think it was the end of
the world. Hoarding! But they won't keep.
Serendipities from Kandy and
Antananarivo. Better sea-cliffs
were brought in giant bursting hulls, and
antique serpents turned to coral, brown
long-drowned broken villages, the
oldest warship death ever whistled from,
all unshipped magically casual –

11

Wear only the lamp behind the curtain.
Are these the shadows Plato wrote of?
My thoughts, like the body, are roused, they're teeming
out round some fine enigma that's been held
a moment more than camera could.
The air is dark blue,
a rosy gunmetal plates the hilltops,
garden moths flounce greyly about.
Night stretches, yawns, soft, lazy.
You stretch, yawn, soft, lazily lift up
the curtain, then put out the light. You saw
the image I had and broke it as the sea
breaks words on sand. The bedspread is coloured
but I see nothing bar those few
watery gleams of your body scattered
to put the Forms out of their agony.

12

There is a pearl, round and whole.
Is it a real pearl? I have it. That
world they saw from space, this world, was
not unlike it, bluer, cloudy, still.
When you poured from the old jug
at sunset, it began.
There's something hands take each from each,
wet lips in lamplight long
to say. A pearl would form in vain
where love has never been.
Oh you may never find another –
leaning by the window in the morning
beyond the common rumpled bed.

13

The desert garden is bare again.
You're where I do not know, time is
the drooping shadow on the vine, suddenly
I lift my head to think of anything
that might be steps, a voice, but only time
scrapes like a dragging kite. People
pass talking but nothing can change.
You left me with your name,
you left your seed, left a little gold,
you left me to get on with the job.

14

We pound and shudder through the dark.
A drunk at my cabin door thinks it's his.
Everything's confused, I ran, I took
a half-packed bag to see white water.
No going back, no one to go back with,
back to. It was like straining towards
the squall itself, flying to beat junks
and tugs into distress. Our
engines buck. The sailors talked
this morning of the devil's marks,
but I think the bridge knows his ways.

15

When you were carried into life,
a crying bundle dandled and jogged
beneath the rafters, the unseen dead
blessed you and laughed and cracked their walnuts,
for only the living can become the dead, and
so they saw you, watched over you, and
wished you even the longest life men have
if all you'd most eagerly be at
would end with the weeping and the lamp
and these windswept graveyard assemblies.

16

The night would never come for some,
and some would never need the night.
The great singer had such darkness in him
his voice made a tent of the whole vale.
Even at midday when his cassette spoke
the lake ruffled, clouds passed.

One day he stepped silently in
at the forge. Horses were coming
to be shod and pampered. He found
a new song on 'jingling bridles by the dyke'.
Nothing jingled in the black black smithy, not
a hoof shifted, no move from the slack reins.
His song rolled round the cooling anvils and
left only whites of eyes and one quaint muzzle
slavering white, whitish, faint and more faint.

17

Halfway down the road, I wondered.
Had it only been about this and that?
– A ragged wraith under a date-palm
waving away money, cigarettes. 'We're
on the same road,' he cackled, 'very same,' he
howled, capsized, reknit his bones. 'Thundery,'
he added, flailing, squinting curiously
at me and the sky. 'So what's all this
business you have? Talk to me. Even
dates talk, what do you think you are?' – Frightened,
just a shade, as I refold my handkerchief.

18

Squalls, viziers, cassettes can be obscure.
You want the lyric line, you want the words
to lay their length against you like – like what?
Are we not living in the utterance?
To say I love you as I love you as
I love you is three roses for the cutting:
a little attar of Shiraz always,
the sheets for things unsaid,
the glass bright red. The days awoke, recurred,
the nights recur, awake. The moon. The earth.

19

You stood like a tulip among the mourners.
My child was dead. Our hands touched
in gloves. And still the sun was striding, he
was high! Up there nothing to detect
of cloud or frown or fury. The taste
of our last wine as sweet as it felt
rolled over my grief continually.
The group with drums shuffled on,

I walked slowly over the baked clay with you
till we came to the gate and parted.
There was sunlight on your henna,
the grave lay like charcoal,
all our life is short
as its first or last wail.

20

Leave love, O god or gods, at last, for mortals!
They are dying with every breath.
Sweeten their starved haunts
with one grain of the crystal.
I know nothing they do ever replied
to what the dark vizier demands, their rock
slides, what they accomplish they undo.
Are they abandoned in that wilderness?
They burn like the sour drought grasses. Beautiful
they could be, lord or lords, with love and
mercy. Leave them mercy. Let them have
the watch of the foundations.

21

In the mist the sun was moonlike.
Its fury had gone soft,
it maundered like an old man of the valley
over the valley. Wherever it came from,
the mist wheelchaired the ghost into dusk
and dissolved it there. White change,
grey fires, the veiled king. A torrent
of bracing stars poured suddenly
on our tilted heads
as we walked watching the real moon rise.
Palms black against it took all kitsch has
of tawdry poetry and immediately
threw us – after all – that talisman.

22

Melons were rolling
when the booth collapsed with a long-drawn
sigh and curses failed to charm
the Porsche. An endless
shot re-taken through centuries. What country
lacks caliphs? Over the horizons
they come, wallets burning, bowed to,

301

a scimitar of limousines to cut
a swatch of unkempt
melon-men. The flyblown land
hisses, bakes, coughs, chants.
History batters like a bluebottle with
barfood in it and the dump cabbage
at hotels of incense.

23

My son used to drag me to the boats.
He loved the water. The sails were red and white.
He chattered as we moved along
the throngs by the rocks, he blessed them
by his bright questions, the fishermen knew him well.
Over a pool he sang his own songs. Well?
What then? He went away
in fever, crying, drowned in blood and phlegm. Rain
on a tomb's the only water I'd go
to see. His humour,
though, makes such a perky picture
in its frame still – I
hold it up here silently for you.

24

'Winged bulls need more than rooms.
We choked on cold iron.
The palace lies fear-riddled.
Hoofbeats hunted footsteps.
Those dying heard owls hoot.
There is a desolation of parades.'
Clay tablets don't tell. They would –
perhaps – but what's chipped back
to cryptic scratches by earthquakes and bucketing
Greek fire and time and storms remains there
only as a grand inverse foreboding
of running feet under redder skies.

25

No sooner had the boys joined
our group than they shrugged and went.
Real nomad cats
with nose-rings, knives, horsewhips, not ugly
but ugly customers when their mynah escaped –
we thought they'd hone us but it passed by.

On vodka they were remorseless,
weeping and throwing bottles in the dust,
stropping blades. They had drums they thumped.
Nothing pleased them save
my pet scorpion; when they'd had enough of
that – strip off and jump in the dock.

26

To take without anxiety the love
you think fate might have left for you is
hard, when the brassy years without it
have left an acid on the ease of purpose.
The woman faltered, admitting it
as she moved quickly to the window
and looked out where sunlight leaped
across the greenhouse glass. Breathless
she stood there, only to feel, to know, to see!
Her dress was hot, a straitjacket. The light was noble.
Nothing that was not past could ever be dull.
She turned back from the dazzling silence
and without a word ran into his arms.
Outside, the green drank the sun's deep good.

27

Cockerels, calabashes, girls he brought on board!
Mandolins, parakeets, a hunting-horn! He
was the king of the bay and knew what he was about.
He was the master of ungathered things.
He let the gunwales rock, and sang
into the clouds of spray – ah, somehow he reclaimed them!
The instant death was over
more and more.
He splashed a parakeet to give one startling cry
that made a mandolin of the whole boat
as he stood braced against the sheets and little by little
drew out Leila to play her flute.
Harshly sweet in the wind the notes left her
and circled with the living water-wreaths.

28

A surgeon massages the heart –
is it that red pulsing bag these
verses, these pens, fingers in accord
have called the seat of love? Your

heart, I sighed, your cruel heart, but that
was in my mimosa days. My
heart you said was faithless, but men
don't gallivant in ventricles. We deserve
the science of danger,
the valved incubus.
The heart says this.

29

Emeralds will never be everything.
He doesn't shine in rings, but something is man's.
Who will give him the sane comfort
of his made things, his sea-walls, his roofings?
These are never left where he has been
for ever. Kings' mazes are dismantled.
Sometimes he thinks it's worth nothing
to be less than the glory
of lapis-lazuli. Grim
talons are stalking the rubbish
of minarets. Walls
howl, gunned keyholes. Almost
he thinks the world was made for some
creatures of emerald and diamond, their
hard jammed eyes jading the ruin sunshine.

30

But then he sees his gifts were not
of stone, immaterial the dignity.
With language he picks up the three
worlds and the seven seas are in his pocket.
Pavilion, tower, and hall
fall, but only he has WANTED
posters pitted by the whine and zing of shrugged
holsters. Roseless deserts can be patient
but man in his restlessness is really
making, making. In thought space-docks,
in words the thoughts, dark softwear not spun over
by hesitant light-pens, rise. Ships like peacocks
spread vanes near Mars, wear out, are souvenirs.
Their very scrap's too active yet by half.
I put it in lead – like this – immediately.

31

What a lump you were, lying there – different,
I admit that. And tangled in those swarms
of hot gold crossed with black
that filtered through the boarded panes.
The air was like a ton of peppermint.
You never said what the bad things were
that haunted you. 'Nothing to speak of –'
See-through demons, blank complexions
bustled perhaps behind that long counter
you'd loll on all afternoon. The articles
would never sell, smelt cindery and
papery and like a hundred years of debris
choking your resting-place, choked your resting-place.

32

They said the ruins would be wonderful
under snow, and we got there accompanied
by icy gusts, rough snorting horses, a dozen of
the roughest guides, a straggle of sheep – the
one that baaed was for the pot. Night
moaned round us huddling together
in an open vault. Hail ran across
javelined horses on a frieze: undergoing
resurrection they leapt. A slave was hanged
again in streaming stone. Dangerous
place without hope
that anyone millennium-old in the sleet who
glistened there was glazed with
the peace of the grave or any human trust.

33

Under the sun, dig up a king.
His whole retinue has been burnt like coal
to warm his afterlife. The
little jaws of dogs, even, lie as he suggested
at his feet. When the world is old
and nodding in its shawl of science,
and Prometheus's ray grows dim, and you and I,
Hafiz, are cold particles unknown, a
gem is to be made, they say, of suffering, to
glow and harden God knows where. Electric
sparks arc faintly. The damp
sizzles, the prophets sleep. The
story of the gem is what we tell our cat

305

at a drowsy firefall, disbelieving. Those were
the murdered. Pick and
spade are the best incantations.

34

Bounced glaring through the awnings,
a sun with the strength of ten
curdled milk and frayed men.
This was the noon of the Arabians.
We filled notebooks, eyed the waterskins.
Weighing fossils kept thirst
at bay till chat trailed off and
wondering what the ammonites had drunk
we took a sip and fell asleep. It was there
we felt might
like a vast coil of ammonite. They called
it fever when we got back to base, and
now we know we are denied
by ants, by pygmies, we scream, we stop our ears –

35

Many and great delusions is the history
of the desert; we can smile now at four
tent-pegs and a hot wind. The darkened
wadi fills with moonlight, demons leave this
stamping-ground to lizards, the curtain
of the stars is only other
worlds hung there in living fire and air or
dying there. Ammonite immortality
seems out of business. Modestly lifted
to sitting position by friends, we have
lost the ecstasy of uncoiling.
The phantom glamour stirs with one last twinge.

36

The leaf on my cheek seems strange –
I tingle. Clouds trundle over.
Is it a shower for the thirsty?
Cracks in the earth cannot remember
what I remember, seductive
rivers, rain running crazy over
arms and faces chalky with dust. Assure
us, lend us streams, heavy evening.
Give what's massing up there and let all

come down, drive into the wood
of shack and fence-pole, feed the recesses
in the rose, wash the view
from windows of the vine.

37

Where can love, in this world, ever lodge?
Brisk angels might crisp up a mock sky crystalline
with it as their robes cut richly
through everything space has left behind,
an unimaginably silvery
dimension for that ice-blue crowd.
Think of the single ice and silver juggernaut
moving, singing, driving and
deepening, outside but into time. Which
is lover, which is loved? Is there a love window
in the universe, and are angel generations
talked down through it, a juggernaut answering like a trumpet?

38

The starry dark, the steps, the peaks suggested!
The garden breathed outside.
Light, not water, gleamed on switched-off sprinklers. Nightly
the moon – that time – slowly forced my bed
till you came less coldly in. My study
was my joy, your body, moving there.
My joy was groaned into your thick strong hair. Too
quick for art I wrapped my legs around you there
till we were empty. You were my staircase,
I was your curtain. When the sun came in
and we'd get up, and feed the parrot, I recall her
squawks under four hands, morning-wild and doubled.

39

Fairuz is singing. The notes throb and twist
from some radio across the street. Like wings
they beat past evening balconies. The lonely see
them, almost see them, as they lean. Any
day someone will come, belong, return! She sings (we
bring the weight of hopes, hung round, hung-up) the final
flake and loosened quiver, winding down, of love. A plant
needs more than water, some say. Sunspot,
green fingers, transistor on a stool –
or tuneless whistling through teeth

with love, if love makes two blades three –
it's the brightest
of all this
hurried wandering meskin scene where nothing's right
and we lie and die many alone uncalled.

40

Given a gerbil, the child strokes its fur.
It struggles – oh how anxious it is! Out or in,
it trusts a cage more than love, that like wax
can melt to fearful shapes and suffocate. Red
from a painting-session varicoses her arms
like a murderer's – or something,
the gerbil doesn't know, but sniffs and strains, and
with a slap she returns it to the cage. Parents pronounce
bed, where her little rage of rejection will swell,
rooted in darkness. The heart is dark and broad,
and twisted like an araucaria under
a varicose sky. Lamp, coffee, cigarette
are innocently sweet; workbox, divan.

41

She settled like a wasp into her shawl.
'In the mountains, there you feel free,' I
suggested, drove on smiling. 'That chair',
she cried, 'was still warm!' Pines whispered
at hairpin bends. What really riled her
was radios blaring from farms. 'Those people –!' I'd gone
too far to please her with a drink. Cars are
no good with her – or stars. I thought of
Beirut twinkling below, hot kebab, roulette, beer and
banks. By 'Ain Sofar I had done with her.

42

It was 'Ain Sofar for supper – in the Mini.
Smirking as usual, quoting idiotic poetry –
you know he once made me read Cavafy? –
they say Don Juans are that way anyhow,
I shouldn't wonder. But I smelt 'Soir de Jezzine'
all over him and that's a belly-dancer's cologne –
brings out the sweat in the front row. God
I'm glad my plane's booked. This place is
just sick. That farm-boy squeezing out his crotch at us.
As the road got steep I let my dress ride up.

His hand tightened nicely on the wheel. At 'Ain Sofar
everything was tepid – wine, lamb, chat.
On the way back, it had to come.
He got at my breasts but that's the end of it.

43

An interval in air as mild
as this leaves islands warm
in the mind. Morning
sings day and day
sings space. Gloomy
undertows welter where gales were,
hump silence, howled before.
Dhows know which
mildness is to be trusted, what those
wet rocks like wineskins, with seas risen,
become. Kelsons shudder the
world over even in the sun. The ruinous
weathers keep reefs, islands, wreathed
in a wrap of happy landfalls, the sharp
tooth, truly, is
nursed in mellow soil
of the fronded mountains.

44

I gave you a jewel at the oasis.
It seemed time to say what you were thinking of.
You smiled, 'It is very sharp.'
Nothing more came, as we went on into the mountains.
The horses were all dust.
When it grew dark, we came upon
an old hunched woman, begging, almost
dead, but singing as she begged, 'The barley
is the thing to grow, the thing they grow
in paradise, in paradise it's wholesome
wholesome skies.' I thought we'd never be
in that oasis, not with amethysts. The blossoms
of the barley burned in her eye.

45

Clouds passed boiling in swarms.
Watching the speeded-up universe is dreadful,
but who knows what's the speed of gods and
prophets, is their only metal

mercury, turbines of that
would make a jinnee of Abu Dhabi. We've endured
the frames per second thing but a
reality that rolls off in vapours
is still on the cards and when it's all up
we needn't be surprised with the rushing
gravestones and skyscrapers, thrown out
like a Harra of slags.

46

Those who spread sails were happy
over blue water. High skirts
of cloud flung out, windy, white. Drops
of spume came flecking ropes. Under
tillers and bows dolphins blew –
blew the race, the race! And nothing was still
even at the finishing-gun. They rocked there
jogging the chop and dip, the decks danced yet
and they danced on the decks, couldn't stand
thought of land. What was land for?
Sorrows over water
rose and scattered like a cloud of locusts
as they raced them away, that year
and the year after
they'd race them away, and every year after.

47

Climb down into the pit
to begin.
The archaeologist's pail
could rattle with prophets.
Yorick? Avicenna? Overwrought
he brushes orbital dust, picks teeth from
the seventh layer, sees a grim stair
and shouts for a torch. Ezekiel? To think,
one needs a table. He burrows without
much hope, easy the hellish descent, to tribes
with no (bats!) cuneiform, Potsherd
Folk, that pre-imperial lot. 'We passed
all layers, found pots.' Moses? Kissinger? Stones.
Where was that beard and tablets of the law, both untrimmed?

48

The lords of the night
rode low over human kind, but
only cracks broke in whipped thunder. They walked
across the lake with nets, caught light
squirming. A cigarette adventuring
missed the swift gaff. The site
of grounded nightfishers glowed red as tracer. Behaviour
grumbles but mocks black zodiacs yet.
Even the puffs of smoke can be seen now, they ascend
winding into cloud-cliffs like caravans into Petra.
In the clouds there may be great lords, but no villagers
catch fish there, praise them,
bake their bread –
it is their absence lumbers the heights
with vacancy moving as black-browed riders.

49

Cartwheels on the terrace –
his half-tame monkey was half-wild
as the fruit-trolley rolled in. The upper
balconies were bright, the lower cooling. Then
the sun died with toothpicks and rosewater. Some
who had seen the dancing-boy murmured to me
to save a drop of rosewater, my
brow might need it. But the dance was strong and noble,
unrousing in its grace, half-boy half-man
he rose, spun, went still, leaned, melted with
a shudder, shook, rose, spun, went still, gave us the
cry he carried from his high Afghan mountains.

50

When the last guns were silenced
we returned, we meant to live
till we were old.
The village was burnt, the night
had taken all its fires. Rags of
everything abandoned saw no danger
as we fluttered among them. Years
leave what, ashes? to put a stick into –
until we came to the grave of the sisters
and there on the battered rim
of a tin bowl war had disdainfully
spared we saw the winged
seed of a sycamore, all
their memorial, oh our loved and fated!

51

An orange three times picked –
the tree, the market, her bowl. He takes it
carelessly, but it's the best. Outside, the hot
striped shops, the mongrels, the bangle-hung square.
He makes a tunnel, pours sugar from a paper
into the orange, broods at it settling. The young
hard day thrusts acid light in his hair. Loafer,
taximan, billsticker glitter below. GIVE HIM
BACARDI. She fumes. 'Come on, the night has passed,
forget it. Remember me? Get your teeth in the
orange, finish it. I tell you – I'm away.'

52

The sea, the sigh, the saw. In the blend,
quays pile fresh timber, events
screech to make us less than master
of this departure. A fabulous
language veils you over the sound. Point
Barrow? Puget? Dockers daff, they
grunt shavings over a scene composed
like a paperweight snowstorm. The traveller
throws his sigh into the sea, shrugs as
he laughs at the rail, while the
seaside saw whirls up its heaped
debris, a floor of cast-off bandages curled
in the hot gulf sun. He hears the sigh the
light ones give, dislodged in flakes towards the roof.

53

In huge cups, in swags of stone, a fountain garden
fattened the snoring well-barbel'd carps. They lived
like dynasties, a shaded golden age. The garden,
bubbling and drowsing in a palm pocket,
dreamed, steamed, lay round its days
to hatch nearly nothing, to wind
about a carp-scale. His
algae kept the gardener happy. He thought
as he skimmed some, left some, with the sun flinging
watery light over his fingers, it would do.
He still hoped he would die there.
He always knew where the fish were,
his hand fed them, stroked the oldest back.
He lived like them in that great theatre
where the world is everything that is the case.

Return, return
over the waste!
I watch this sail, that sail
as it teasingly grows,
passes and goes. This rock
I have made my own
is great, having no mind.
Mind suffers first, most,
is not great. Strangely
the iron immense
absence fills it or
poisons its turns and veins
the lazar brown
of hawsers bedded in the sea.
But if I wait, I am great.
I have forgotten my mind.
I am a figure on the shore.
I am not wedded to that sea.

55

When we had smoked a few pipes
we were shown the white whippet.
White leash, white collar, muzzle with opals. Then
it was whisked away, just showing its teeth.
Whatever it had to race against,
oil-wells were bet on it in that kingdom. By
the end of the night we were onto cheetahs, and
saw that too; had hawks for weeks.
A birthday a month long seemed no more wonderful
than feats of dicers, or the race the gushers gave the
kings to open sesame again.

56

I saw a face in the waterfall
with ropy tears and great beard of glass
not steady, not vanishing either.
The crashing hieroglyphic
grew by what it was stripped of
like ants in armies.
Rocks made eyes and mouth, but whose?
There was no legend to tell us that.
Only the hooting of far-away ships
came up, and crickets in the grass. Into
the imagination a procession of scenes

hesitated, rejected by the melancholy
of a frozen mile-off regard
signalling without sense from its shroud.

57

Antelope meat – they cut it in strips
by the fire. We wolfed our dusty
venison, belched with decorum. They
watched us from the shade of the tent, twenty
of the wildest, hospitable, hating it.
From our blankets, at two, we heard drums.
Our watches shivered. Would they? They would
if they could. The hell they would! They
were all over their women with endearments
and what the women were about
was a dance. Mad, mad! They were so obscene
with the flute, so cackling, such black skirts to the moon
that they stamped underground
every hawkish intent, cooing and beseeching
their lords between their legs. Fictitious
fiends, the bandits forgot us – Allah turned
over, but kept his eyes open – in the urgent
preoccupations of the dearer thrust.

58

It was shutters up for the shopkeepers –
those that were quick. Windows kicked in
filled many wheelbarrows. Looters whirled
like sprung tornadoes, ran entirely
crazy with snapped-off fridge-doors, grinned peel
and angelica and sunflower-seeds, banged pavements
with gold steelyards, threw barbers over the bridge.
A shout of triumph and they mounted a train,
drove it off, left the red signal
standing. It was the speed of
the thing that brought them a sort of light
– at the edges. That, and
the blackberry glance
that took in a bar.

59

In that world, they say, you cannot look
at action. Only this world has action.
This world, they say, has only action. Waves,
muezzins, guerrillas, looters with steelyards. What

314

even stereo headphones deliver at the entrance
to a pure globe of rock – though
a key – is looters with steelyards. In the echo-chamber
we fish with detonators, catch vanishing car-lights
as they scream along the dark corniche which
hugs the mortal sea. It would be strange
in that other world of made greenness
and dead angels jerking in the shadows.
Anything that could have caused it
is not us and not it.

60

Alleys and arbours! The activist grown old
walks and sniffs his deep red roses. To recollect
is easy through the scent. All things
are one, and not one.
Low pale clouds like feathers
above a runway, accurate scarlet
spreading on the dead leaders. Then seas
of safety, new name and language, signpost
to a mining village. He became foreign
even to himself. Sailing
home to his farm was a bitter fanfare – the admired,
limping, white-haired child of revolution, loved
by the soft generations, smells blood, not roses, still.

61

At the lying-in-state there was unanimity.
He had died very handsomely.
No one really knew how old he was.
His eyes had challenged the starlight.
Children had seen him jovial.
Exemplary dangers had been his.
He was what one should be.
Eternal resurgence was his occupation.
The world was to be yours, not his.
Now there is no world that is not his.

62

'The waters creamed with livid shoals
as the whirlpool rose at last.'
The storyteller paused, brushed his hat
with a sleeve. 'The carpet flew all day
over the gulf.' He had a cake in his hand,

waved it. 'The time had come for dying and stranding,
the poisoned burden joined the breakers
and broke like a bag on the beach.' He was
blowing flies off the nougat. 'Every
scale glowed and faded, in the last daylight.
Many monsters grew dry there in the
useless thrashing.' He scratched. 'From the lee
of a cliff Sindbad snatched the carpet and the
spell broke. The fish jumped back into the night
sea. And so the jinnee griped and griped the whirlpool walls'
– he passed the hat round, chomped the cake – 'again.'

63

The power and the glory walked
here? Buy some statuettes,
blue and white, nothing looking
blander ever shot from the mould. The frantic
wizened tree's a
wizened tree. Galilee screams a kind
of bikinis and lunch-baskets. There's a haze. Hungry
for something, the mystic paviours have
come to lay the lake. It's shutting. A universe
of walkers can keep it all under. Decided
demons fill the cracks with smoke.

64

They were building little houses of grass.
I cried. The radiation children would never
have children, or buy their houses of brick and glass. People
are running down the world's roads among
columns of smoke, with no more belongings than
a back can take. In the open
you must run, fire falls in a moment.
The burned ones lie on the common
after the roar has died. Their
shapes are a braille conducting
us silently from country to country
to country to country. Pale children
break the grass-blades in their hands.

65

Hell is the outsider
who came in and is after you,
brother. You were what he was

316

and you lost that startled blue
at your lover's knee. Nothing is made
to sing beyond proof.
The very deeds you used to breathe of
will not breathe off. You got the tattoo in
to let the devil out, and this
is when he sighed and burrowed in.
You think it's funny? So you didn't die of
dots of ink? This is not the chief
of many pains that will loom up abreast
when we ride out some full moon
among the scrub and thorns. In hooks
of giant sloths our bridle-life dismembers.

66

All over the world it was they were!
Clouds bringing rain brought more than rain, brought war.
Machines tore out, like a tooth, a hemisphere.
By searchlights men were made the maggots of
a turned furrow, each weaving with his
scattered O of panic. Shrieks represented
destiny of nations. It was the goal of
bones.
Up by the sun there was no man
to look after his own, in the deadly field
there was no man not to die, while the air
flaked with charred shreds and frightened
– for a moment, a pinch of salt – the victors' adventure.

67

' " 'The caravan that's lost is frequently
a gift in darkness.' We waited. 'I fancy
another drink.' I pushed the bottle. 'Space arches,
I call them, the continuum's different,
thinner. Grizzled drivers break through burnished.
Bits of sand, camel-hairs – they are all cherished.
I have seen dazed bees
blazing in a sea
of dry soft smoke beyond the arch. Crevices
get them – gills, I'd say – they vanish slowly. It's
like glow-worms moving underneath. I knew
you'd disbelieve. And what about the people?

68

The ruffian sage sat back, put the last
of the arak in his cat's milk. His grin
maddened us. We poured some more. 'The people',
he said, 'become gold teeth. They'd really bite
if they could see us, but
they're gold teeth on a one-way ticket.' He laughed,
coughed, spat. He caught my arm. 'You think
the dead will ever eat their way through space?
The crunching isn't grasshoppers, the
crunching isn't sugar, the crunching
isn't thunder, but it's coming, can you hear it?'
With two blows he made our heads reel.
He got up, began singing, stumbling round the yard,
six foot tall, eight, ten. We blacked out then
and woke up on the other side,
for a moment" – the story says,'
the storyteller said.

69

Lovers linger by the harbour.
Evening draws its hood.
The world will do without
mages this hour, be covered
by a devoted look.
The shingle has a single
song, a gull steers in
by the half-built boat. The next
bride waits for summer,
turns in her bed to have
everybody's dreams. Houses
line the quayside with upper
windows lit. Below,
a mended sail shines clean.

70

Let the groomsmen with drums come
over the water mysteriously through
the green and the parched islands, almost
threading life and death on the chain
of their procession. Her wedding-dress is red
with the veil blowing, her companion
trembles waiting in purple by the ox-wagon.
There is a wild music ready, tugging
their thoughts apart, around,

forward, everything out of his
heart into hers, hers into the traffic
of that filled enormous moment.
Slowly they dance about each other. No crisis
breaks his sweet address,
they kiss in justice,
the woman under roses, under torches the man.

71

Was that a writing angel
with its vast perhaps
plucking the reed-beds again? You never spoke,
as you never wrote. Clouds had the journey
fitfully jemmied open. Figures wakened
on rocks and stretched. You took a tissue
to that orange lipstick, shook hair as
black as seaweed in the pool. A pattern
a swirling moment gave went quickly. Coarse
fins were caught, flopped on boards. The woman
by the painter was your mother and the mother of
disoriented angels hooked on sense.

72

Orange lips. Thunder. A moth on the damask.
You scraped a nail across the grimy
velvet roses. The bored moth flapped what it had
of wings. No one could say what
the springs had of sighs and sags. Morning
could only yellow a cruel apartment
where everything your lovers never said
kept the greasy tiles in place. Giving
those dim world-like breasts makes you complete.
Stretch here still and the curve rising could
be the unbetrayable, unportrayable thing.

73

She slid with a flash into the lake. I
waited for the dripping glory. A casket opened
with a click, her little sister had
bracelets to set in the sun. Her
body rose from the water, rendered
in a maze of pouring drops, wrapped
in light and air, embroidered
white-patched from the cast bikini. The same

319

felucca might have floated Nefertiti. Well,
on board with her hair coiled
like licorice, and oiled, and her long arms hanging
loose over the rail, she made haste –
it seemed – to make a picture again
of the morning of a world, rich, dark, and still.

74

Dogs ran, lean and mean, by the wayside.
We kept stones ready, afraid of
nightfall, but reached the village. A lane
drew us to where the orchard gate should be.
The day died; white walls grew mauve; three
orange-trees were cringing in a clump. At
our uncle's house it was silent, puzzling,
the door half-open, the table swept clean,
the radio mumbling to spiders, a sanded
spread of blood, a side of lamb, an
eye. Why was the floor the table? Something building
in us kept supper at bay. A plate of lamb and
rice we tried at last, famished. The shoulders
of our drunken uncle rolled from the only inn
and filled the open window, amazed. Did he
live here? We laughed. Two sisters! What?
When? Catch him. Uncle! He was almost passing!

75

Sometimes you grin very wide
when I say an intellectual thing and
an orange nebula hangs above me which
shelters broken teeth like shabby stars. Easily
I'm silenced and you know it's easy. The
crowd laughed that time in the room below. Their
guffaws over pipes and cards while
smoky traveller's tales went round were
a bristling aphrodisiac. Over the brim
of another life we hung and clung. We too roared.
We thought the real stars must have heard.
It was like that. The attic window
was wide to Orion and Mars and
we would have a boy.

76

I played the owl tape over and over.
The old owl listening brazened it out more and more.

His fierce tree seemed to stretch,
delivering angers of no return. Lowest
of the animals is man the
interferer! But what you sang, what you were singing of
the day before you left this upper
world your silence, rose from the walls
of the grave that night and
sank a claw which altogether
drained my game away. My melancholy
freed the owl. What it lends
is what life hoots over, squandering comfort
with strings, to some, sorrow to all.

77

'Stocking-face is this very minute in the bank
nervously shooting it up. What about that?
I told you the guerrillas had a surface
you could almost write on. It's the stream
of slogans that deceives you. Don't believe the flow.
An interface of oil you could almost walk on gives his
slide a bout of coughing, eh? The cough's the horror
all right – your horror, not his. Everything resembling
the gradual's less than actual,
actually. These people make me garrulous. See a hole?
The question is, is it lined, or see-through? This
is . . . yes, this is when you hear the sirens. You have
ten minutes. The armband.' Without
an armband I shot him and gave the signal. His hat
with its shiny skip rolled naively away.

78

Would you come again to my house? Is it possible?
Light seems to break across a land
that slept and had no history.
Bent olives trimmed
by hot winds, brushed by goats and bees – problem
trees, but tight as springs, immediate-
ly quiver under a ton
of rain, they seem to ring like the
metal of rings falling like rain. And
in my room, clasping your knees, the
bangles massed in a heavy gleam, the
long desert-coloured skirt folding a
pattern of Ctesiphon arches, and
a fly buzzing, will you think it a sin
to shake your bangles loose in Babylon?

79

That day was an onion of skins,
it came apart in temporary
hours, distinct, sweet, pungent and good.
I watched the steam climb up
your kitchen window, you chopped the prickles
of nameless sticklebacks and sang. Have
mornings afternoons in their arms like moons? Such
hammocks strung like smoked fish, songs for
miles down the starling valley, while a
bowl of limes went one by one. It
was the evening, though, that cut the heart. Of
all the women crying out in love or pain, the substance
filled the drawing of the curtains, it
blew from your flesh like a plume. I marvel
still at the splinters the shut-out moonlight made.

80

Merry old moon in the water,
winy, wavery, doesn't say much,
splits its sides without regret,
re-forms, near-sphere, has-been,
delirious floater, delicious
father of gleams. The
boat rowed through, black spider on the wine.
Standing at lonely lakeside doors
with a last cigarette, the lucky ones
caught the fish with the rower, as summer
darkness flashed and splashed. Zigzag moon or
zigzag catch, each seemed to me
to dance, but in the wings a waning, and death, waited.

The night is over, the lark is singing,
the sages sit in full divan
in the anteroom of heaven,
the water bubbles, the pipe is sweet.
A pigeon calls over the marshes,
flaps across the anteroom glass.
Every wall's a window where
sages turn the innocent pages
and swivel the earth slowly around.
Their bell calls across the marshes.
The coffee-boy rows through to them,
still but a speck, and eye and ear
are waiting for the jugs to gleam,

the lifted oars to drop their diamonds,
the coffee song to cut the stillness.
Stillness of watched and watchers! Heaven
is twenty steps away. The lark
is in invisibility.
One sage slides back a whole glass wall,
the boat is moored, the glasses chink,
the steam comes in, the bell rings out,
the boy breaks bread and scatters it.
Pigeons, trembling, fill the marshes.
The sages sing the pigeon song
all that lingering forenoon,
forgetting earth, forgetting heaven.

82

We never thought we'd never die
but there it was at the moment of death,
the greatest fear we'd ever known.
We'd read of dragons – there they were,
or in the form of dragons, worse.
Winged leather, metal beat about us,
something stood with chains behind.
Electronic ozone stung,
parrots cut it shrieking. We'd
gone arthritic, sticklike, ashy,
took it all and tottered on.
We never thought we wouldn't burn
if that was what our lives had done,
but oh it was sharp all the same.
Writhing like grasses, gasping, clasping,
flaking out in beds of lava,
cockcrowed up to be rescorched,
the harpy beak and hackle red
above us like a flaming grid
we were to be spreadeagled on,
we were spreadeagled over gulfs
so far below us we heard sighs
where nothing else could be exhaled
and even suffering was not seen.
Sultans who had dungeons once
– they say – stood there impaled.
We never thought we'd never weep
but that was so, oh that was so.
We never knew we'd have no more
to feel except one pain, one glow
memory blows us to, like coal.

323

No there is no cabin, no pendant, no amber, no
lager, no face, no landrover, no comb. So
absolutely grindingly no go? Besides,
the blinding waves of road are hot and tarry,
bubbling with lost feet and wheels, their
bitumen gasping for each little
city in the sea. Had
others, ever, what he had himself?
Had anything been theirs? His! –
like a scarlet frieze of unknown birds
passed on a wall to supper
in winter when they'd set the corner wood-fire
and you heard the dear music of talk and plates; in night
outside, the wilderness hears that supper,
waits hunched till joy is spent,
reaches in for some
loved helpless bed.

84

The flying carpet snapped its fringes
as it raced past the courier's finger.
What use is goodwill or the utmost
patience? Scowling, we took
taxis in a sort of jointed
beetle string, missed the prologue. We
were still half gloomy when she stripped
between the tables, throwing the last bracelet
from her pudge with a shot at glittering.
Sailors flung sad G-strings, picking
their ears with fans, mincing on friends
with plastic roses. So.
The great sheikhs wait
in air-conditioned audience-rooms in silence, and however
you twist and turn they sit there
with their drinks of lime in ice, or is it crystal?
unostentatiously so cool, brother, and so pleasant.

85

Moonlight coming hard down converted
dunes to memories of snow. A
ski would have failed though. Angels iced
the cedar groves once only, deadening
our light footfalls; muffled crystals solicit
still. Besharra! Trays of embers under the

restaurant tables, the cold intense, the affections
uncurling like ferns in frost-pictures. They
who have angels to command may know, but
I do not know, where that snow went. Brown
slush and strutting crows are the parents
of reminiscence, desert child!

86

Not in King's Regulations, to be in love.
Cosgrove I gave the flower to, joking, jumping down
the rocky terraces above Sidon, my heart bursting
as a village twilight spread its tent over us
and promontories swam far below
through goat-bells into an unearthly red.
He dribbled a ball through shrieking children and
they laughed at our bad Arabic, and the flower. To tell
the truth he knew no more of what I felt than of tomorrow.
Gallus, he cared little of that. I've not lost
his photograph. Yesterday, tomorrow
he slumbers in a word.

87

Cosgrove, Cosgrove, it is very dark.
The waves root like beasts.
Nothing wins – something breaks.
Wounded Crusaders howled in tents
before ruined Sidon Castle was built. Sandy
shores took keels like tigers and the
Saracen heroes raised their silver horns.
Afterwards, wailing of a mother
with ashes on her head.
Make do, make do!
History so fearfully
draws us backward
that to be gone
even as you are these thirty years is not to be
lost, although that later war's long done.

88

We were soldiers singing,
in century-old Beit ed-Din. No smoking
where the emir swam and lolled, or sometimes
smoked, or dallied with a wife, or charged
like a sea-leopard under the dome, more times

than the bottle-end roof-lights knew – like
a dolphin with such hundreds
of arcs and turns we remember
the man by his baths, by the sea-like lights between
ceiling and cool floor. Our booted feet
woke the echoes, not the master.
He had silences we hadn't.

89

She had nipple spangles and a tam-o-shanter.
She was big and brown. Her legs were covered
by some shanghaied sailor's half-split fall-fronts. About
midnight was her spot. Her kind of men,
shining with beer like children, could do without
seven veils. 'Oh get in
there,' they roared when she crossed the stage.
Her nostrils flared as she got scent of
that Port Said music. A tremor, unrehearsed,
made ancient grossness regal. Socks,
stardust, headgear came off. Guarded
by a lattice of trouser-cloth her belly-dance struck.
Whistles and piastres seemed theatrical
as she stood and shook out sin and dross and drowsiness.

90

Bright monastery! the bell-mouths opened
as we climbed; rock in rock yet.
Mountain water sprayed your rose-leaves.
Winding paths led butterflies to
monks and monks to flowers. It was easy
to think the lizard was there for ever.
Lebanon lay all round with many
terraces. We drank your wine. Tumultuous
as life itself, our conversation leapt from every
moment out of every war. We strolled. Sometimes
your abbot praised my French, sometimes – affectionate –
he'd pat a manuscript we passed. Invariably
I longed to see your poplar-guarded midnight,
the stars above the snows above your cells.

91

Lamb sizzling, coffee like honeyed tar, raspberry-loads
rolling like Brobdingnagian caviar – the way of
the thing was all prodigal, in the direction

of crashing sunsets and a bay of sails, over old
cries of water-sellers, with a flick
of the lamp the veranda
could be swarming with jinn. Guests in the hall
were trolls in white-striped purple, a
swarthy diaspora of Niflheimers. Understudies
of storytellers garrulous as crickets were gazing
down white-striped purple passages adjoining
the banquet-room. A feast and an overfeast
without music, disorder made visible
in garish ambiguous plenum – immediately
obedient we absorbed it blow by blow.

92

Angels with abacuses called their calculations
once, in an ancient scene of souls. They
shrug now, it's not calculable,
dive in pools, dry out half-human
with their wings on rocks and
let computers mass the injuries
let computers mess the injuries
let computers miss the injuries
let computers moss the injuries
let computers muss the injuries
of merely mortal times. Consequently
waters break on earth but not for them.
And those who see them in this
labouring place have shadows watching them,
not angels. It doesn't matter which.
When was our ACHTUNG MINEN ever their
concern, or their tears where our bodies were?

93

Tears such as devils weep come dripping
in rusty balls of fat on the marbled
batters. The leaves were yellow anyway. Superfluous
oils distil and die, smoke falls. Once
a slashed cloud bares a devil's cheek,
the scholar reads it through the window: generations
of well-sewn scars, a territory, exemplary.
His hand travels his own face,
not finding an antonym for dignified.
Only demons in the eaves go on winking.
What's the good of being animate,
said the book, if you can't not sin?

Thunderclaps had a laugh at that
but at least gave the man one stab of chill.

94

It's no time to be visionless
awash in the underworld,
gargled out continuously
into consciousness, impatiently
red with slutty viruses and tooth food, meeting
the air from the mush, from the much the one.
Merchants on the high pass to China
stood buffeted in questions, seeing
only rolling
Himalayas without houses
or horses. The dismal
solitude shone east, shone north.
Brothers, we are driven!

95

Slowly tawny, slowly ashy, the desert and the day
suddenly gulp the plum of darkness. Rays
of indigo spill down the wadis. Tents are cheerful
with lights-out laughter but the round of things is the
night. On guard, I climb the water-tower. Strengthening
stars are thick in absolute black. Who ever mourned
the sun? A universe unbroken
mends man and the dark. No northern mists envelop
me, there's nothing but the silent metal, the pack of stars from
zenith to horizon blazing down
on mile on mile of undulating sand. Swiftly
the thud of land-mines brings confusion
to the Canal. One star moves, drones. Position
on a map's the universe. The night is Rommel's tree:
searchlights cut it, history the secretion.

96

Paradise in prospect
after sand, after sand, after sand. Hungry
for vision yet thirsty for water, we're gleaming
sweaty ancient pilgrims that go softly
past mirages. With
thoughts withdrawn from emptiness
a while, we watch the flickering meadows.
Hedges of air that never flowered

328

flower, bands of dust that never moved
move now. Jinn's villages, different
from ours, the springs in their meadows
beckon dry as light. But we've come to
the casting-place, the arena we're in
shimmers with the real life still unseen.
A crone screws up her eyes. 'There,' she
points, 'in the east, the walls are white.'

97

Domes, shoeshines, jeeps, glaucomas, beads –
wartime Cairo gave the flesh a buzz,
pegged the young soul out full length,
made pharaohs in the quick electric
twilight, strutting brash as hawks. Underneath,
a million graves, a withered arm,
sarcophaguses red
with blood and ochre, smooth
boats on a dark sub-Nile
of slaves and captives, the
oldest way of gold,
over the dead with gold
and no haul of good.

98

You came under my mosquito-net
many times, till you were posted far off.
I was innocent enough
to think the posting was accidental.
When you left, it was my studious
avoidance of you that said goodbye.
It was enough; the body, not the heart.
We'd our black comedy too –
the night you got up, on Mount Carmel,
with a dog's turd flattened on your shirt-front:
not funny, you said.
Well, it was all a really unwashable laundry
that finally had to be thrown away.

99

I dreaded stretcher-bearing,
my fingers would slip on the two sweat-soaked handles,
my muscles not used to the strain.
The easiest trip of all I don't forget,

in the desert, that dead officer
drained of blood, wasted away,
leg amputated at the thigh,
wrapped in a rough sheet, light as a child,
rolling from side to side of the canvas
with a faint terrible sound
as our feet stumbled through the sand.

100

The dead climb with us like the living to the edge.
The clouds sail and the air's washed blue. For you
and me, the life beyond that sages mention
is this life on a crag above
a line of breakers. Oh I can't speak
of that eternal break of white, only of
memories crowding in from human kind,
stealthily, brazenly, thankfully, stonily
into that other sea-cave
of my head. Down where the breaker was
closes, darkens, rises, foams, closes; crates
drift across, whirl round
in the ghost of a gale;
a shred of sailcloth
relic of a gale
that really blew slews to the resting-place
the long tide goes out
to leave it, bleaching on its bony rock.
I pick it from the stone,
Hafiz, to bind the leaves of my divan.

Memories of Earth

They told me that the night and day were all that I could see;
They told me that I had five senses to enclose me up,
And they enclosed my infinite brain into a narrow circle
And sunk my heart into the abyss, a red round globe hot-burning,
till all from life I was obliterated and erased.

– Blake

My fingers tremble when I touch the tapes.
Since we came back from earth, nothing's the same.
I tell you I hear that sea beyond the glass
throwing its useless music away in handfuls.
Once I angled a sweet chair to catch it.

I never even walk there now, far less
imagine vacant nature has a song.
Yet it's not vacant, wasn't that the point?
I must avoid questions, exclamations.
Keep your report formal, said the Council,
your evidence is for the memory-banks,
not for crude wonder or cruder appraisal.
I only report that nature is not the same.
And I report it within the spirit
of our resolve, which is indeed our duty,
to record whatever we have found to be,
to meditate on everything recorded,
and to record our meditations till
the plain figure of promised order appears.
I served, I took the oath: but my hand shakes
as I take up the damaged tapes and play them.

TAPE 1: THE STONE
          ... had to go to the north shore
of the inland sea. There are six of us.
The stone we are to enter is well marked,
lies in a hollow and is as big as my fist.
Indeed the temptation to cup it, lift it, throw it
is strong. We resist. Whatever signals it gives
or is thought to give, only just not too faint
to rouse the interest of central monitors,
to us it's silent, like the stone it is.
The shrinking must be done by stages, but
even so it comes with a rush, doesn't
feel like shrinking. Rather it's the landscape
explodes upwards, outwards, the waves rise up
and loom like waterfalls, and where we stand
our stone blots out the light above us, a crag
pitted with caves and tunnels, immovable
yet somehow less solid. We climb, squeeze in
and one by one tramp through the galleries
till we have reached the designated cavern,
fan out on the dim rubbly floor, and wait.
We shrink again – accelerated this time.
The rubble's a mountain-range, the shallow roof
a dark night sky in infinite soft distance.
The gallery we came by's like a black
hole in space. Off we go across the plain
into the new foothills. Have we moved at all?
I am not to speculate, only to explore
as commanded. I record it is harder now

331

to remember where we are, environment
tie-dyes memory into struggling patterns.
We always knew it stood to reason that
the smallest thing, seen close, would have some roughness,
but we could not envisage the sheer presence
of the blow-up, establishing its new world
each time, here, here, here; forget *there*, it says.
Dead though, all round, like a desert, and silent.
A desert in the middle of a stone!
– Erase the exclamation mark. Surprise
comes from old microstructure thinking.
We must stop that. We are beginning to learn
that where you are is what is, not less than
what is. 'You'd better not insult the Council,'
says Hlad. 'We're at the next diminishing-point.'
We sit together on the rocky slab,
join hands for safety, since the operation
must now be very fine, and suddenly
the six of us feel the whole desert-floor
strain outwards like a skin and burst in grains
of pale grey sand as large as asteroids.
We float to one, clamber aboard, and drift.
Space is like hard pure night traversed with flashes.
We must be near the atomic sub-structure.
I get a tenseness, Hazmon says vibration,
to Baltaz, with her keen ear, it seems music.
Kort stares at us, finds nothing, but 'Colder?'
he asks. My headache comes a little later.
But these are all expected signs; the Council
warned us the signals we are here to trace
(if they are signals) must be sending power
into a huge periphery, as our next stage
will tell. We brace ourselves for the last trip.
The asteroids boil up, swim out of sight,
we're plucked off into space by the force field
as cosmic dust and comets and star systems
grow out of nothing point by point of fire.
Our senders are directioning us now,
in slow shrinkdown, into a galaxy
that's soon wrapped round us with its long bright wings
and then expands as we contract until
it's tenuous and fair as haze. We're bound
for a smallish sort of sun, and planets
mushrooming about it, we don't move
but in our moving matrix we approach
the size that puts us in that system, lets
a too large world with rings go thundering past,

swells a speck of blue swirling with white
to a globe where millions of us could live,
white clouds and blue sky mount through us into
a strange protective canopy, and ground
of some sort rushes up to meet our feet
and scatters red and brown to far horizons
now the horizons of our sight. I'd say
the emanations here are like a source
of power; we've reached where we were sent; the new
blots out the old more strongly than before –
brown moor and yellow broom, a swooping bird
that clatters off some rocks with a wild cry,
and up there all those moving clouds, not fixed
as ours are in a chosen set but free
to drift and break as if they were not dead,
above a moorland where birds come and go
unchecked, wind shakes the easy heather bells
this way and that. In a dream we stand,
uncertain, abstracted, on the springy turf,
till 'Is there no Council here then?' asks Hlad,
and kills the spell. We tune in our receptors
but cannot unscramble the pervasive resonance.
Is it noise, and therefore not to be unscrambled,
or is it a simultaneity of signals,
or has their Council (if they have one) coded
their power for only equal power to crack?
Our expert, Tromro, gets to work on this.
Part of an unexpected answer comes,
not from Tromro, but from the landscape – it melts
at the edges like a photograph in flames,
throbs, re-forms, faces appear, a flare
of light on metal, swords ringing, a gold torque
filled with blood, the high whinny of horses,
dissolving back into a thrust of darkness.
It recomposes as a dusty plain
under a cloudless sky; we kick up dust;
we know now what we might have guessed: our time
and this world's time can never be in phase,
its images, its messages, its life
must come to us like an eternal present,
and by our very meagrest interfering
we trigger fragments of the vanished prints
but have no key to make the sequence clear.
Tromro will have to...

...so confused.
Questions come thick and fast, we don't erase them.
This is most dangerous. The Council warned
any questioning was theirs alone.
What makes us disobey them? There – again!
A question and an exclamation, both.
Are we disintegrating, are we growing?
We've grown so small we can perhaps re-enter
places only the bewildered can be great in,
as we've heard books and tapes say were once ours,
histories back, in the red days of action.
Even to think of those days is a reproach.
I know that but I do not feel it. So?
So we are all able to change, nothing
can quite put down susceptibility,
not that I claim it as a virtue when
it stirs like wearing thorns: I record this,
with what relevance none of us can say.
And what I must record I must record:
the wind shrieks now across a desolation
of mirages, splintered castles, reed-beds,
a stork forms fishing, horsemen heavily
come together, canter with whips in fog,
a sullen mob, restrained, an open space
and though the picture never quite comes clear
we see the bellows at the huge fire, then
tongs drag out a red-hot iron throne,
a peasant's forced to sit on it, his head
pressed into a red-hot crown, his hand
clasped round a red-hot sceptre while the smoke
swirls over jeering breath: long live the king!
long live King Dózsa! and the rearing horses
foam at their jerked bits like an old frieze
till suddenly the whole scene snaps tight shut
and we're left staring at a sea of clouds.
We must be on some mountain-top at night,
with a full moon riding the black above
but tongues and limbs of mist stretching below,
mist or cloud we can hardly be sure,
cloud or sea we can hardly be sure
as the white masses die in distant grey
and hills might be the whales they loom like there,
but we imagine waves all round us, ride
on our mountain as moons ride their dark air.
We watch three climbers; a dog sniffs the rock;
one gaunt man stands apart, brooding intently

over the metamorphosis, we think
it's what he says we hear through the vague roar
of what must be big unseen mountain-streams.
'The emblem of a mind that feeds upon
infinity, that broods over the dark abyss,
intent to hear its voices issuing forth
to silent light in one continuous stream.'
The dog barks, and the scene strains out in white.
Facing us is a gigantic screen.
Scores of steamed-up cars are parked in rows.
A couple locked or twisting in a kiss
is silhouetted smoochily in each.
The summer desert air has stars, the screen
that no one looks at flickers crazily
and howls distorted sound at love-bites. It's
only a painted cat up there, grinning
as it rolls a bulldog in a hammock and
batters it, thinking it's a mouse. The film,
the sand, the erotic jalopies, fade
in a slow dim-out towards Arizona.
A bleached signpost like a cactus revolves
as the earth turns. Flashes, stripes of darkness
clatter up like jarring shutters; landscapes
come and go, at last one slows down, holds,
shimmering in a fine red autumn haze.
It seems a camp in time of war – barbed wire,
watchtowers, rows of huts, but also blocks
(too many surely to be bakeries)
with huge square chimneys – acrid smoke from one
drifts off over the stubble-fields. A train
of cattle-trucks has brought in new arrivals,
two thousand perhaps, men, women, children,
all ages, tired or apprehensive, joking,
reassuring, glad to stretch their legs,
filing into a hall with hooks for clothes.
A sign says BATH AND DISINFECTION ROOM.
Guards tell them to undress, help the worried,
the old, the sick; mothers help their children,
hush their crying; young couples hand in hand
smile at their nakedness, but some men sweat,
half-hide their fear, one moans, shakes like litmus.
In ten minutes all are ready, the guards
herd them to the farther door, unscrewing
the strange wheel that is its handle, and
all troop into the disinfection room,
some driven struggling, the last few screaming
as the thick oak door is screwed smoothly shut.

The beating on the panels mounts, and dies.
a thin susurrus filters through a while
like what I've read of spirits suffering,
but nothing is in my understanding.
I stare at Baltaz, who has clung to me
as if she was a woman of the earth,
and nothing on her features is not pain.
We have no pain, we cannot suffer pain.
I have nothing I can say to her but
'I saw no bath or cloth or soap or tap.
There was nothing but cement walls and floor,
and perforated columns of sheet-iron.
How do we know what earthmen do?' 'I know!'
she cries, 'I know what they do! Record it!
They make people into ash, turn babies
into smoke. Is that the message they've sent
out over all their puny universe?
Is that what scratched at our dish? The Council
sends explorers for a handful of that?
Dust, bones, gold rings, old women's rags? Take me
out of this earth, Erlkon, take us away.'
Before I can answer her, thunderclaps
bang sheets of rain across the fields, the camp
wavers, blotted out, is gone. We're left with
a heather moor like one we saw before,
and now it's hot: bees hum; the panic goes.
A butterfly's an epaulette on Kort's
thin shoulder, Hazmon laughs, holds out a twig
and the white creature flutters to it, Hlad
thinks this is childish but even he's benign.
Only Baltaz looks at the butterfly
as if she would cup its frailty for ever
against the eerie furnaces. She's changed.
I'm changing. I record this without comment.
For I don't want us recalled yet, not yet.
We must expose ourselves to it. To what? To that.
The Council will note I conserve questions.
Tromro has banks of information, Kort
spores, Hazmon his films, Hlad and I the tapes,
Baltaz – Baltaz –
                    Sunset, in what I've read
is beauty, even glory, crowns the earth
with harmless fires. Colours of great fineness
from pearl to crimson to dark purple coast
and flush and doze and deepen and decay
in shapes we'd never give a name to in
a hundred days of watching them dissolve.

And now the stars come out above the hill.
It seems this is a world of change, where we,
observing, can scarcely fix the observed
and are unfixed ourselves. This solid hill
even as I speak is half transparent,
white walls and floor show through, we sink, the stars
are roof-lights in a large computer room.
The air is clear, the light even, the hall
vibrant as a heart. A screen we approach
switches itself on, flickers, fills with snow,
focuses to a powerful image
grainy and stark in grey-green, black and white.
Figures in domes – men, women – work and move.
They've left the earth, like seeds. Is it their moon,
or a near planet, or have they gone out
beyond their system into some neighbour
millimetre in the stone? – Tromro's job.
But now with an extreme concerted movement
the milling hundreds in one dome turn round
to face us, and the screen is scored with gestures
that make us catch our breath as they stretch out
arms seeming to implore us where we stand.
And every face flickers with white longing,
and some on knees, or drooping propped on friends,
or sunk with hair that sweeps the floor, some straight
and motionless in such a dignity,
some streaked with crying, all in such a case
we can but take as last or next to last
in desperation, and the time unknown
past, future, or the myriad-to-one
unthinkable and terrible present.
If it is now, we cannot save them; past,
what we feel must surely be pain; to come,
it's like a warning of all fate we've read
waits, though we must not believe it. The screen
scrambles in points of bluish light, goes blank.
We sit at consoles that go ghostly as
we search the data banks. Fragments of sound
clash out and shred to silence – *seventeen –*
leaning – a prominence – Christ yes man go –
solitaire et glacé – shoot from – eagles –
vstayot zarya vo mglye kholodnoy – burn –
done with Danny Deever – programme – Sturm und –
a gabble in a wilderness of wires,
an earth labouring in memories.
And soon we're in a void of echoes, faint
and more faint, merging with a rising wind

that stirs the greatest of the earth's huge seas.
It is all round us, boundless to the eye
although we know it is not boundless, blue
and blue-grey, steely, warmer green, green-black
with flecks of whipped-up white and longish swells
where hints of prussian browns, acid yellows,
glass pinks that only numbered charts could name
crosshatch the windy sharkskin; real sharkskin's
not far under, and tumbling whales; typhoon's
kingdom too. But now only a handful
of clouds is scattered through the morning sky.
The sun begins to walk on the Pacific.
And now we see and come down closer to
a speck that does not fit that emptiness.
A thousand miles from land, this black canoe,
long, broad, and strongly built, with fine high prow
much ornamented, and many oars, drives
forward steady across the zigzag sun-prints.
Tattoos as intricate as the prow-carving
stand out on the brown arms and backs and brows
as men who might be warriors bend and row,
yet seem explorers and not war-men, for their boat
has stores for major voyaging, animals,
children, and women slicing coconuts
and shaking back their long black shining hair,
offering rowers the fresh smiling milk.
The men are singing as they row, the chant
comes up, torn off in buffets of the wind,
returns in strength. By the gunwale a cock crows.
Whatever far-off landfall is their goal,
known or unknown, or only hoped-for, they
have crossed dangerous immensity
like a field, and dangerous immensity
to come lies all about them without land:
their life is with the waves and wind, they move
forward in ordinary fortitude,
and someday they'll steer through that Southern Cross
they only steer by now.
                              There's a loud hum,
and swirling shadows fill the air. Hlad warns
he feels the signs are we must go. Tromro,
listening, confirms. It comes swifter than a blow.
The earth shrinks to a smaller point in space
than even the canoe was in its ocean.
A nebula like a riddle of flour
tempts us to shake out a few million worlds
in passing; fate might bake a thing from that.

338

Remagnification euphoria
is fiercer than we'd thought. We keep control
and wait for the next phase to...
                    END OF TAPE 2

I think not much was missing from that tape.
The phases came in order, without crisis.
We crept out of the rock, shot up, looked back
at what was now a stone again, ourselves
in our old scale of body, dune, and sea.
How uninteresting those dunes, that sea!
We made our report in a troubled confusion,
memories flashing between sentences
to make us falter, stare at the Council
as if they were an alien life-form. Hopeless –
they soon gave up politeness, froze us, said
our report was totally deplored, useless
to contemplate, ruinously incomplete;
feeling and action had besotted us;
our anti-brainwashing sessions had been
a clinic wasted; was earth such a paragon
or paradise or paradigm that we
lost our nature in a simple phasing? –
and they'd be training non-susceptibles
for a further expedition. What I suspect
is that susceptibility's a pearl of price,
now that I've heard the tapes again. It's true
the mission failed: we don't know whether earth
is sending or had sent a message or
was itself the message in dying it became,
though this too might be a real message sent
by the survivors gone to other stars.
We don't know even if there are survivors
now, for when is now? To me it seems
the virtue's in the questions, not the answers.
I think this fishbone's in the Council's throat,
for all their smoothing of the rule-book. It was
infinity the poet on the mountain said
the mind must feed on, which is very fine,
and I agree with it, but when we reach
the almost infinitely small and find
well-made extermination camps, nothing
seems infinite except cruelty, nothing
feeds the mind but processions to death.
Not true, not true. What is that infinite hope
that forces a canoe upon the waters,
infinite love in the woman comforting

339

her child at the mortal bathhouse door?
I think the break came when we showed the film
of Dózsa sizzling on his throne. 'Cut,' said
Council. 'We're not impressed by drops of sweat.
A xerox of the execution order
would suffice. Couldn't you see the man's been dead
this thousand thousand years?' 'No, he's not dead',
I said. The Council stared as if I was
an alien life-form, which perhaps I am
now. How do I know whether Dózsa's dead?
Why don't the dead just disappear then? What
if the Council are all hallucinants
projected by hostile powers to keep us mild?
Who told who to tell us not to feel?
tell us love's wrong, leads to suffering?
hate's wrong, leads to fire and battlefields?
and questions above all are wrong, lead to
deflected meditation on the order
we wait to see: who says? What use is order
to a chained world under a painted sky?
If any order's there we'd break it like
a shell to let some living touch emerge.
Frail, frail, frail! Better than those pavilions
of molybdenum, demagnification banks
that rev for our successors! The cock crows still,
I hear it, praise it, on that southern sea.
The voyagers are out, the day is up,
and that's what we record at last.
                                        We meet
in secret now, the six of us, from time
to time, and study how to change this life.
Baltaz has moved in with me; everything
seems like a great wave shining disclosed
travelling our planet's deadwater. Tromro
has taught us much; each frame of Hazmon's film
is burned into our minds; Hlad's tapes have noise
– every sound on earth – and mine have voice.
Baltaz is at her handbook: what we must do,
and when. But uncommunicative Kort's
our *wunderkind* (as earthmen say), he's made
a culture of the spores, they're growing at
their work not just of telling us what they are
but handing to our memories of earth
a life we'll make a source of life, begun
in purposes of rebuked pain and joy.

Space Sonnet & Polyfilla

SPACE SONNET

It's t   delirium's avai   le
on tap when   r the light level   ks
below w   reas   finds accep
The whole   ht appa   us gives the shrinks
excuses to   date stra jacket form,
and   n deep   Mars they're hard at work.
We only ca   e from t   solar storm,
and   w we're half   to the frenzied jerk
of w   they c   their penal ther
I d   't re   what it was I was
n   r to forget. Guard! it's st   too bright!
I   t to ride the swa   g canopy
with mile-   gh eleph   , I want wet gauze
to roll in, and l   ls of vul   ite!

POLYFILLA

       rue   lab
                 eve   sin
           hat   on   table
                tig   rat
                up   it
       eve   in
                me her   he
           no   way
           hat   all   apy
        on   member
    eve   ill
    wan   yin
            hi   ants
               ape   can

341

Pictures Floating from the World

1
A mugger is disgustedly
knifing his victim
who has nothing on him
but a small Raphael
nipped from the Louvre.
Conceptualize.

2
At the Moore-Smashing Contest
of Nineteen Ninety-Five
the chips were down
gathered in baskets
of rosy Carrara
bound for Vegas.

3
Two old painters
jailed for representation
have escaped: the sirens
shriek for them, the black
sleek cars are out
in magic realism.

4
That polypropylene
death torso of Hockney
which caused so much fuss
can still be discovered
in attic trunks
with secret springs.

5
Ikons exist.
The palace of culture
has been bugged with one,
disguised as a photo
of a miner and his lamp
from the days of coal.

6

At the time of the last
picture, seventeen
thousand art-lovers
had their backs tattooed
with the Mona Lisa.
I had to smile.

7

This was popular:
thirty-five artists
were inserted in the chalk
of the Berkshire downs
in the form of a horse,
and replaced as necessary.

8

The very last sculptor
was found on the Old Man
of Hoy, with a pickaxe.
'Circumspice,' he said.
He's still in formalin,
with his baffling caption.

9

Utamaros made the
prettiest confetti.
Rembrandts lined shelves.
Political prisoners
recycled canvas
to a million tote-bags.

10

Kineticists ended
in pyrotechnics
but were never sold
to children. The state
has its rules. The young
must be protected.

11

In the reign of the mullets
painters were kept
in jars, and at banquets
were allowed to expire
in an edible fondu
of polychrome acrylic.

343

12

Starmen came, machines came.
All went. Wars came,
went. Caves and charcoal
were left. None drew.
The age of wars
and art was over.

The Reversals

reasoning with Eve was very difficult,
Adam thought, but tried. cutting the knot,
Henry the Eighth had no time for compromise.
William Blake pricked his hand on a brier.
Universal Love the sparrows sang,
which got them sold for farthings. divans
propped up each sagging lord of hosts. Holy
Russia said all men might still be brothers,
never under the present arrangements however,
indeed it would take a long etcetera.
well, keep the home fires burning, Alpha Centauri.
America was sitting on an anthill,
not seeing that the air was getting formic;
vessels burst violently underskin.
who shut the garden gate? who stashed the hugs?

such histories of old disharmony!
Berlin sparrows shun the angry wall.
enthusiastic hands would tear it down,
life to come would searchlight grassblades only,
active seeds would blow across the rubble
to show the quaking soul a thing or two.
hand in hand there'd be processions moving
life towards all its entrances, the living
moved by both the living and the dead.
Shakespearean salvoes would be shot off.
typewriters would stand up on legs and sing.
reprehension would be a serious offence.
other days, other times, other thoughts!
common bonds have built-in patience, they
pronounce nothing but their ancient being
which broods like a stalled bulldozer, love

which kicks its cuttle-bone like a budgerigar.
renew the disaffected places, take them
into a different compulsive country,
domed with tensegrity perhaps, who knows.
the old sky breaks, runs down the pane, washed out.
the vestibule has gone oval, gold and white.
having breakfast on a long green table
montaged with stirring fields, in unaustere
April, a child slurps milk and bangs a spoon.
National Independence Days queue up
from every quarter for a handout, some
exhibiting an extreme lack of solace.
elucidators', educators' bowls
which once held out for status pap have now
been scoured to the unhappy quick. grinning
Thisbe strokes her mulberry lion with
five red fingers, marries Pyramus.
the itinerant bagpipers squeeze a brawl.
Professor Quagblatt has resigned his chair of
Archdruidry, gone fishing. all around
other mauve reversals flare like incense.
David dances Goliath down the meadow,
moves like a panther with his heart on fire.

Twilight of a Tyranny

When we take prisoners from other worlds
we are not cruel. We let their bodies die.
They become words, filtered into air.

We became words, we infiltrate the air.

I know sometimes in the long midnights
we throw open a window. It is hot,
the bluish branches are all motionless.
We cannot sleep. And some poor word creeps in.

Cold, blue was your skin when I crept in.

The mines are stiff with gold, our treasuries
are locked and locked and locked, our guards are guarded
by passwords we've suborned with baseless hopes.

Deep in the vaults I am the password, hope.

Even you might tremble at our plans,
great lords. What do we care for life that comes
and goes as we sit in our iron seats?
We're armed; there are no dragons; time is long.
We shout, and words come singing with our wine.

They shout. We sing the curdling of the wine.

Astronomers once said our sun was dying.
Where are they now? Our towers blaze and stare.
We made them words to wander with the wind.

We warned you, in the rising of the wind.

You know you'll never see your world again?
Threats, bribes, tears, guns you can put away.
No urns – no dust! Watch me at the switch,
and then you can complain like nightingales
for all the sense dead words will ever speak.

Your thrones are death. Ours is the reign of speech.

The World

1

I don't think it's not going onward,
though no one said it was a greyhound.
I don't accept we're wearing late.

I don't see the nothing some say anything
that's not in order comes to be found.
It may be nothing to be armour-plated.

I don't believe that what's been made
clutters the spirit. Let it be patented
and roll. It never terrorized

three ikon angels sitting at a table
in Moscow, luminous as a hologram
and blessing everything from holograms

to pliers at a dripping nail.
I don't believe it's not the wrench
of iron that let the body fall.

346

2

There was this unholy scuffle.
They felled the sober with the tipsy.
At last someone got pushed mildly

onto a breadknife. As he observed
in the ward, What's more, what's more,
just nobody's going to go there.

They did though. Even if which was which
was always a guessing-game, the case
meant the whole scene had bristles on.

Expressionless hardmen glittered. Sleepwalkers
jived. There was a dog. Before
the end of the evening a desire

for everything had returned, very
smoky it's true, but true. The sleeper
in the ward was the only one with nightmares.

3

Sometimes it swells like the echo of a passion
dying with paeans, not sighs. Who
knows the weight and list of its rebellions?

Underneath, underneath, underneath, underneath –
you think it beats in the age-old fashion,
even red, perhaps, like a pre-set strawberry

creeping below the crust? It's artistic
to have ordered impulses. To
think the world has makes you feel great.

Beyond the world, the slow-dying sun
flares out a signal fan, projecting
a million-mile arm in skinny hydrogen

to flutter it at our annals.
Coarse, knee-deep in years, we
go on counting, miss the vast unreason.

4

Technologies like dragonflies, the strange
to meet the strange; and at the heart
of things, who knows what is dependent?

Imagine anything the world could, it might
do; anything not to do, it would.
A plume of act flies as it spins by.

We saw the nettles in the ancient station.
The signalbox was like a windmill, haunted
by bats and autumn wasps. She

twirled a scarf through leaves. Remembrance
offered nothing, swam in our hands.
We're here. The past is not our home.

I don't think it's not being perfect
that brings the sorrows in, but being soon
beyond the force not to be powerless.

A Girl

She is thin as a bird fallen from its nest.
Muscular contractions have violently
returned her to the foetal crouch,
but if she is born she will breathe earth.
Tubes pour such nourishment into her
as she can bear.
Little grasshopper, are you alive?
She squeaks or gasps or tries to
speak, her eyes roll madly under light,
her brain tested says
not dead, tested
says not
dead. Wait.
Her parents who are godfearing folk
have examined their consciences and announced on TV
they would like to 'see her die with dignity',
i.e. to kill her. Her
priest has examined his rules and announced on TV
he sees no reason for not discontinuing
'extraordinary measures' of prolonging life,
i.e. killing her. One at least
of her doctors has said they will pull out
her life support systems over his dead body.
Wait. The court has tested, said
not dead, not kill, not
dead, not

348

kill. And the parents appeal.
Wait. Hell smiles, prepares
their life support systems
though they are not ready for the earth.
Calmly they talk at the table, to the cameras.
Don't ever bury their dust
by their daughter's dust, that's all.

Three Trees

I LIGHTNING TREE

My roots burrow in rainclouds.
I grow down to earth at midnight.
I am the negative of a tree.
Blue sky's black here, branches blanched
white not dead white, skeletal quickeners
briefest if bravest, a fuse of spirits
of fear lit over fields, running
downwards to men with my crack on my back.
Let my flash flush a real tree, don't be under it.
My negative loves to discharge
its singeing in split boles.
What, skulls? Sheltering shoulders? Shoulder-bones?
Boles, bones, all's one.
Roots up twigs down's the power.
I've broken oaks and oaks have broken men.
Last night I was myself an instant oak,
lit a county, caught a farmer,
banged him dead out of his blackened boots.
I can't make it a world of chance
but what I can, I do. You like it too,
taking a Rizla as you read the news.

II WATER-SKIERS TREE

I am seven wakes on water. Skiers made me.
Bunched together chugging, snorting, seven
hungry speedboats at the starting-line
longed for open water, roared and sprang,
diverging quickly with their string
of braced wetsuited skimmers. As they fanned,
shining and shouting through spray, they made
a multiplumed Ich Dien for helicopters,
and for the low plane that sidled in from the west
they made a watery tree. I trembled

349

but I hold, I hold a while with stiff branches,
with spiky buds of black,
with white, red, slowly curling, speeding flowers.
I can't live long in water,
but to be a sign is happy
in the summer passing.

III   IMPACTED WINDSCREEN TREE
I was born hard, at a crash, I hissed
my crushed limbs through thick glass.
Impacted like Urizen in an unbroken windscreen
I cannot move but I am perfect,
a white black spruce, a tree of porphyry
in hair-fine crystalline divisions showing
the saved man at the wheel
his shivering substance.
Other wheels in the ditch spin idly,
through me he'd see the shadow of a tree
that nearly concertina'd him
if he could see through me, but all he sees
is what I tell him of his escape.
If I could only move – as all trees move –
to give a murmur as he mumbles
two dazed fingers over my foliage
and comes to life and pain again.
He'll hear a siren soon,
be whisked away to sheets and salves.
I feel evergreen till the crusher.

On John MacLean

'I am not prepared to let Moscow dictate to Glasgow.'
Failures may be interesting, but it is the firmness
of what he wanted and did not want
that raises eyebrows: when does the quixotic
begin to gel, begin to impress, at what point
of naked surprise?
                              'I for one will not follow
a policy dictated by Lenin until he knows
the situation more clearly.'
                              Which Lenin hadn't time to,
and parties never did – the rock of nations
like the rock of ages, saw-toothed, half-submerged,
a cranky sputtering lighthouse somewhere, as often

out as lit, a wreck of ships all round,
there's the old barnacled 'Workingclass Solidarity',
and 'International Brotherhood' ripped open and awash,
while you can see the sleekit 'Great-Power Chauvinism'
steaming cannily past on the horizon
as if she had never heard of *cuius regio*.
Maclean wanted neither the maimed ships
nor the paradox of not wanting them
while he painfully trimmed the lighthouse lamp
to let them know that Scotland was not Britain
and writs of captains on the Thames
would never run in grey Clyde waters.

Well, nothing's permanent. It's true he lost –
a voice silenced in November fog. Party
is where he failed, for he believed in people,
not in *partiinost'* that as everyone knows
delivers the goods. Does it? Of course.
And if they're damaged in transit you make do?
You do – and don't be so naive about this world!
Maclean was not naive, but
                              'We are out
for life and all that life can give us'

was what he said, that's what he said.

Vico's Song

            the universe that turned in on itself
            turned in on itself
            on itself
            self was
            was the universe
            that was turned in
            it was the universe that was turned in

            the universe that was turned in
            turned in got seven
            seven days
            days it
            it spent turning
            spent turning over
            days it spent turning over a new leaf

351

the universe that turned over a new leaf
turned over a new leaf
new leaf
leaf lived
lived in the arms
in the arms of the eternal
it lived in the arms of the eternal return

Sir Henry Morgan's Song

we came to the boat and blew the horn
we blew the boom and came to the island
we came the innocent and cut the cackle
we cut the tackle and stripped the bosun
we stripped the brandy and shaved the parrot
we shaved the part and shut the trap
we shut the shroud and bent the log
we bent the ocean and swung the lead
we swung the lumber and blued the lamp
we blued the thunder and crawled the crazes
we crawled Mother Carey and came to St Elmo
we came to the Horn and blew the boat

Shaker Shaken

Ah pe-an t-as ke t-an te loo
O ne vas ke than sa-na was-ke
    lon ah ve shan too
Te wan-se ar ke ta-ne voo te
    lan se o-ne voo
Te on-e-wan tase va ne woo te wan-se o-ne van
Me-le wan se oo ar ke-le van te
    shom-ber on vas sa la too lar var sa
    re-voo an don der on v-tar loo-cum an la voo
O be me-sum ton ton ton tol-a wac-er tol-a wac-er
    ton ton te s-er pane love ten poo

Ah pe-an t-as ke t-an tiger
O ne vas ke than tuft of was-ke
    lon ah ve shan tree
Te wan-se ar ke ta-ne voodoo
    lan se opal voo

Te on-e-wan likely va ne woo te wan-se o-ne stonework
Me-le white se oo ar ke-le van off
    shom-ber blown over sa la too lar var sa
    following an don der on opal loo-cum an la voo
O be me-sum ton ton mixed with a wac-er tol-a wac-er
    ton ton tiger pane love ten poo

That pe-an t-as saw t-an tiger
O ne vas through a tuft of was-ke
    by the ve shan tree
Nothing ar ke ta-ne voodoo
    till se opal voo
Nothing on-e-wan likely to ne woo te wan-se o-ne stonework
till a white se oo ar ke-le us off
    shom-ber blown over the la too without harm
    following an don der on opal losing our voo
O be me-sum ton ton mixed with the waters the tol-a wac-er
    ton ton tiger swam with us loved ten poo

That was when t-as saw the tiger
O ne vas through a tuft of morning-glory
    by the ve scraped tree
Nothing in the air ta-ne voodoo
    till the opal voo
Nothing seemed likely to ne woo te wan-se old stonework
till a white lot of ar ke-le us off
    shom-ber blown over the lake without harm
    following flakes on opal losing our tracks
O be me-sum and we mixed with the waters the wily waters
    till the tiger swam with us loved ten poo

That was when we saw the tiger
yawning through a tuft of morning-glory
    by the well-scraped tree
Nothing in the air suggested voodoo
    till the opal fell
Nothing seemed likely to go warmer than old stonework
till a white lot of flame took us off
    suddenly blown over the lake without harm
    following flakes of opal losing our tracks
in tiger's-eyes and we mixed with the waters the wily waters
    till the tiger swam with us and loved us up

[The first stanza is a Shaker sound-poem of 1847.]

Lévi-Strauss at the Lie-Detector

```
any classification is superior to chaos
an                  is    p rior to    a
any                 is    p rior to    a
        ass         is    p rior to    a s
an      ass         is    p rior to    a s
any     ass         is    p ior to     a s
        a   cat     is super
a   class   cat     is superior
any class   cat     is superior to    o
        cla         n is          t   ao
n           ation is             t   ao
            fic tion is          t   ao
            fic tion is superior     chaos
            fic tion is s  p    or t
    class           is s  p    or t
    class fic tion is s  p    or t
                                 o ch
                                 o ch
                                 o ch
any class fic tion is superior       chaos
```

[The first line is a quotation from Lévi-Strauss, *The Savage Mind*.]

Wittgenstein on Egdon Heath

```
the world is everything that is the case
the world is   verythin   ha
the world is eve      in    a          case
the world is                    the case
the world is              that      case
the world is              th  is    case
the world is every                  case
        world is          hat     case
        world is          hat
        world is                      case
        world is      thing
        world is          that
        world is          th  is
        world is                  the   se
the world is everything that is the   se
 he         is                  the   se
 he         is              th  is
 he         is              that
 he         is eve
 he         is everything
the wor d is everything
the wor d is everything that is the case
 h    o  ld    everything
the wo  ld is everything that is the case
```

[The first line is a quotation from Wittgenstein, *Tractatus Logico-Philosophicus*.]

Ten Theatre Poems

THE DRUM

I call you to the celebration.
You know me, rivers of adrenalin.
I course, I call, I race, I stub the bloodstream
on measured rocks, I shock, I shake
the seats of silver, bring out red,
red, red, red, my oyez oyez is
to draw a brick-red velvet tractor through your cheeks.
I get it all to begin, the processions, incursions,
the knife beneath a clouded moon,
the crowded or the solemn dance,

the parliaments, beheadings, the dead march
that lets the curtain fall. I call,
and you're Neanderthal.
Oh what a train of dragons it is to be at your bowels
as I begin to throb and stun,
your drum,
Rumbunderonggongdumblerum,
berrum, the drum.
Rumbunderonggongdumblerum,
berrum.
Rumbunderonggongdumb,
berrum.
Rumbunderonggong,
berrum.
Rumbunderong,
berrum.
Rumbun,
berrum.
Rum,
berrum.

THE CHORUS

We have been pacing the precincts.
We are worried in unison.
We wonder what the hero is doing.
We never understood heroes.
We do not entirely believe the messenger.
The hero's mother seems perturbed.
On the other hand, the king is silent.
What is obscure is seldom clear.
We were not born in this country.
Who is that coming towards us?
Is it a man? Is it a woman?
It is the oracle. Once the oracle
has spoken, we shall be more doubtful.
In our country there are no oracles.
We are sorry today for ourselves.
But it is not for us to complain.
The king, we may say, is irascible.
Already perhaps we have said too much.
To say too much is always too often.
Here we are at the foot of the steps.
Let us all be silent in unison
and hear what the oracle has to tell us.

356

The oracle says, 'When winter comes
the autumn is over.' Are we comforted?
We do not know if we like winter.
We wonder what the gods are doing.
We never understood gods.

THE MASK

Who am I? Who?
A false-face frog-prince, a gap-toothed witch of guisers
bobbing through smoky Halloween?
or stiff and stony gold unsmiling bearded king
of Thrace or Samothrace? a clown
above a ruff, all chalky red-spot cheeks
and eyebrows flying up like circumflexes?
a hard plain dark wood devil,
nose knocking chin, skew horns, pits for sockets?
a porcelain beauty bound with wails and flutes
to expressionless suicide? or giant ant
rehearsing its clacks and snaps,
kafka plastics rising out of jeans and hush-puppies?
In the end
you do not know who,
do not know me,
cannot ever get below me.
What is to know but papier-mâché?
Even if you beat me of silver
my grace is to be inert.
My duty is to make you uneasy
as those in the caves were uneasy
when the reindeer shaman came,
or as we all feel blank
when the man walking the moon
faces us suddenly with his dark
featureless helmet.

THE FAN

I make it seem and seem you see it. That's my art.
The art despises body-stockings, needs
its dark stage, pearly spotlight on the plumes,
honkytonk strains, it needs
the programmes waved as fans in the hot stalls
to be stilled. Let each eye strain.
I ruffle and quiver,

my ostrich feathers breathe
with the breasts beneath them,
I slide and flash, subside,
cross and re-cross,
wisps of plume drift off,
swirl in the tunnel of light.
I've got my dancer in my arms.
Out there, you'll never come so close,
get nipples and belly in a dream
and only as sweet as a dream thrown
on cigarette smoke and waves of heat and sound
like a screen. I am the screen
of what standing still would cheapen,
a beauty that moves and is never seen.

THE SKOMOROKH
(wandering player in medieval Russia)

Ekh, skomorokhi, the ice is breaking,
it's time for us to take the road.
For now the blood is shaking,
too hard and long it's snowed.
It's time to wander near and far
and let the bear see the boyar.

Pack the flutes and psalteries,
roll the cymbals in your cap.
Silver drips from trees,
gold rises with the sap.
We'll knock on their gates with the evening star
and let the bear see the boyar.

On with the goatskin, up with the horn,
up with the – censors are lovely men.
Rich and poor are born,
not made, yes yes, amen.
We'll find out where the true fools are
and let the bear see the boyar.

Dance goat, dance bear, dance skomorokh!
Sing how the governor lost his seat
by sliding on the loch,
and mime the priestly bleat.
We'll jouk the rope and boiling tar
and let the bear eat the boyar.

THE SHADOW

I fall like a long man in the Greek sun,
a bird's-wing gesture wavers over stone,
I form a drifting crisscross of the suppliants
as they dance in slow grief, I explode
with the god from the machine.
Oil and candle keep me in camera,
throwing quills, daggers, flagons, ruffled hair
over walls and bed-curtains, I shiver and lick,
leap, mount, bunch up, shrink
like a shadow-play.
I am a shadow-play
in Java, when hands like shadows
prod their puppets to compose
shadow-battles on the screen.
Plato never saw
Rama kill Rawana,
gongs and fireflies
and my black shapes
confuse reality
till this is what happened
and then, and then,
and everything unscreened
becomes shadowy, but the shadows
have become men. Oh yes
you can break up the play
big man, with big dogs, big deal
any time, but still I've got to love
the way your violence kicks
against the pricks with many new shadows
and I am born fighting into the light
of that rough art, my dears, my masters.

THE SOLILOQUY

So I've become at last nothing but this,
a pressed-out essence, a soliloquy.
I wish I could stop fainting off, think clearly.
I've bled so much I must be really weak.
The same old chair I'm strapped to, same tiled walls
clean as a dairy, TV eye, tapes running.
That bright hard awful awful light – no,
a little hysteria's what they want, the light's
no worse, just bad, like the bleeding, no more
than what must be put up with, think of people

brought in from accidents, air-raids, bearing
light and the knife and immobility,
washed out of consciousness. I can't survive.
I know that, since interrogation stopped.
Before I die they want my voice, in dreams,
in pain, in sweat, the last capitulation
of the body, they're waiting for it, but
I am going to be awake to the end,
as something cool visits my brow, my eyes,
like my wife's hand when I was in that fever,
you said you'd bring a compress but I clutched
your hand like dear life, and it was dear life,
till the sun burst through the bull's-eye panes
where you were still asleep beside my bed.
They think when I'm like this I'm breaking up
and will soon talk about the organization.
The tapes can gnash their teeth, but I sit here
in a great calm with you whom I once lost
through foolishness and now win back, my love,
as if you knew I needed you to keep
that mass of dreary stupid pain in chains
tighter than any they could put on me.
Stay with me till the reel is played, then go,
go very fast into the angry shades.

THE CODPIECE

I have been kept in many a tight corner
and kept my head. I cover
a multitude of sins. I have my points.
I am as full of life as an egg is of meat.
I die facing the enemy.
Sometimes I am tricked out with stripes,
fully fashioned, sheeny and gorgeous,
purple and orange, itching to bound in the kermess.
And sometimes the only mound
of the body on the bed.

THE HANAMICHI
(the 'flower way', an acting platform in Japanese theatre which
comes from the stage through and above the audience)

I am the primrose way
sometimes to the everlasting bonfire.
I stride over you, through you, make

360

the stage a T-square, take
your applause and flowers as you touch me, shake
yet not break that old decorum
of watchers and watched. Call me
a bridgehead, but the fighting's only mine,
a bridge, but only players cross.
Reach up and grab the demon's heels,
the demon's blade could lop your heads like poppies –
you want Killed By Art on your tombstone?
Killed By Life's as bad for players.
Yet I come swinging among you with my lights on,
thronged with embroideries and paint and songs
like a baby Ginza, while action rolls
at right angles, peasants with chestnuts,
kabuki stereo. Crane necks
to me, cock ears for chestnuts cracking!
To you, you're at a play, to me
you're at and in a play, but only I
see that, soaring through blue 3-D.

THE SPIRIT OF THEATRE

When they set the ferret down Fred's trousers
and he pushed his head through the fly,
weaving about with his cute little bright snake's eyes,
and the women shrieked, and the men
banged their beer-glasses, and the band
rolled up their sleeves for the next number –
I ordered another round.

When the finale almost but not quite collapsed
in a flurry of waterfalls and cardboard swans,
dissolving castles, two rainbows, a real
sheepdog, and a tenor merging desperately
into massed pipes and drums while the centre
microphone developed an itinerant howl –
I sighed, but sat on.

When the distinguished verse-play unwound for ever
about man's inhumanity to man
and sprayed its glacial pellets of high-grade anguish
over the culturefest, and the shirtfronts were numb
with appreciation and shushed each creaking seat,
while long bleak flashbacks crawled out, froze –
I applauded and left early.

And when I went back up yonder,
there was Shakespeare lying in wait for me.
'The mountebank returns,' he sounded off.
I could place his truculence
and it wasn't just too engaging. I yawned.
I looked at him, but all I said was
'Tongs and bones, William, tongs and bones.'

Five Poems on Film Directors

ANTONIONI

Trees are drowning in salt. The keyhole whines.
He's left his boat
in the reed-bed, her book
and idiotic gloves where she threw them.
Beyond the canal the tankers prowl
north to south, their call
lingers across the marshes.
'Why did you wait till the summer was over
before you came?' 'Why did you wait for me
if you'd rather have a boat than a woman?'
'It wasn't that. It isn't that.'
'I'm going.' 'Send back the car.'
'With Sandro? You're joking.' 'It's cold.'
The silver car between the poplars
like a fish in reeds.
He lives on peppermints and blues
        or
He is tearing photographs for a living
        or
He has been sent death, is opening it
        or

GRIERSON

Then the nets rose and fell
in the swell. Then the dark water
went fiery suddenly, then black.
Then with a haul it was all
fire, all silver fire
fighting down the black. Then the fire
rose in the air slowly,

struggling over the side of the boat.
Then it was deck and hold.
Then it was the dance of death
in silver with grey gulls.
Then it was low clouds, bars of light,
high water slapping, choppy wake
and oilskin tea then.

WARHOL

We are turning orange. They are turning purple.
The spindle is turning out metamorphic rock.
Lighting a cigarette, he is turning she.
The Empire State is turning dark
all day. The beach has gods on it,
turning their backs on each other
as each one swivels on a visitor.
The pickup sparks and spits, two
stereo corners turn redhot.
In the glow she turns vague, bends,
and a split second turns her
in the next cycle of darkness.
They shriek like parrots, and as bright,
they are half turning into birds.
Two on a sofa turn a fanzine,
my dear. We turn on, off, on.
A wig drifts, she
turns he. He sh-
rieks in orange. We
drift to the door.
It turns. It turns out
the world after all,
steady as the Empire State
being blown by the wind.

KUROSAWA

Glade sword, glint running.
Tree shiver, choked cry.
River shadow, full quiver.
   Dust mounds, old wind.
   Grave mounds, cold wind.
Thatch fire, child running.
Plunder cart, thousand ashes.
Village rain, storm forest.

363

Storm gods, rain ghosts.
Restless fathers, prayer hearths.
Jogging banners, thrones dissolving.
Blood crop, dog pot.
   Dust mounds, old wind.
   Grave mounds, cold wind.
Cracked stove, slow crumple.
Moon blade, rolled skull.
Blood brother, spangled ambush.
Sun coins, bird calls.
Bent bow, man running.
Bent bow, body jumping.
Bent bow, neck streaming.
Bent bow, knees broken.
Bent bow, breast nailed.
Bent bow, bent bow.
Bent bow, bent bow.
   Dust mounds, old wind.
   Grave mounds, cold winds.

GODARD

– and the walls were very white, the girl
being interrogated was speaking slowly
but her words were lost in the gunbursts
coming up from the street –

    slumped in the café, featureless brown room
    with a radio blaring, one window
    opening on a filthy garden
    with a sort of chickenrun –
    whether he was only drunk, or dead –

        'the audience has no means of knowing
        and that's it' / in the skyscraper lift
            at the nineteenth floor

            'All right, 20 thousand
            cheap at the price'

– no, the interrogation was long before.
She went into the country –

            the junction not
            'like' a spider's web
            keeps catching trains –
            the bridges he'd been over –
            really a blank sky

ALL REACTIONARIES ARE PAPER TIGERS

– she'd come to the bridge without knowing it
but it was already too late, they had their dogs,
easy even without searchlights –

BUT THEY ARE ALSO REAL TIGERS
WHO HAVE DEVOURED MILLIONS OF PEOPLE

> 'It isn't cinema at all
> without a flow of images,
> Godard's destroying the cinema'

BUT ON THE OTHER HAND THEY ARE PAPER TIGERS
BECAUSE NOW THE PEOPLE HAVE POWER

> and the coupé slid over
> in a cool cliché into the sea

School's Out

1

A colonnade, binding light in fasces
of striped stone and shadow, suited Plato.
'Tight reins,' he used to say, 'all training
is restraint.' Are boys like horses then?
Stupid questions got no answer, but
a thin smile came and went, left no trace.
We were born into Utopia:
cold baths, porridge and Pythagoras,
Pythagoras, porridge and cold baths.
We never exactly hated the routine
but felt there must be something else. He said
life should be in the Dorian mode, sober
as a shepherd's pipe, and 'hell take all
Bacchantes and Assyrian kettledrums',
which was strong words for him. Looking back,
it seems as if the discuses we threw
to swing our muscles into harmonies
'like the deep universe's harmonies'
were no more solid than the wrestling-oil
that seeped into the sand, or watery songs
of how the gods are good as gold. We did
our sums, deaf to the music of the spheres,
> and came out into chaos,
> blood, shrieks, kettledrums.

2

Milton thought a country house was best,
'at once both school and university',
and he'd have acres to do marvels in.
He was really pure theatre. I don't forget
his first words: 'Open your mouths, let me hear
a clear vowel from now on, stop mumbling
just because there's mist in Buckinghamshire.'
We thought he must be mad, but practical,
and it's no secret his model was Prince Hamlet
(bating the royal appurtenances).
We sweated swordplay, strategy and tactics,
as well as sonnets and the vocative.
We groaned through Hebrew but we knew the stars.
I could put on a splint, survey a field,
ride a horse and play the organ. Poachers,
pedlars, smiths he made us learn from, for
'you never know what might help the commonwealth'.
It's all gone now of course. The king came back.
Rigour was no longer *de rigueur*.
I sometimes wonder what it was all for –
and then I remember that sardonic voice
pausing in its anatomy lesson to say
    why heads of kings come
    off so easily.

3

Whatever did we learn at Summerhill?
No maths, no hangups; how to play *Dear Brutus*.
It wasn't doing barbola on the mantelpiece
with red-hot pokers, breaking windows all day
or maidenheads all night – though you'd think so
to hear the critics. And did Neill set us free?
You never know with voluntary lessons,
they crouch there in your path like friendly enemies,
you pat them or you sidle past, knowing
you can't play truant when you're free already.
School government was on our hunkers, noisy,
fizzing, seesawing, Neill won, we won, no one won
while the long shadows gathered on the chintz.
We were Hitler's autobahns in reverse,
anti-Stakhanovites, our trains would never
run on time. 'If I create a millionaire'
cried Neill 'I've failed!' But capitalism
slid on its way despite our lost repressions.
We tinkered in the workshop, made toy guns
but never robbed a bank or even knew

half Europe had been robbed. Now if you ask
what I think of it I honestly don't know,
     it was great but I
     honestly don't know.

4

Ivan Illich bought a big new broom.
'Most people learn most things out of school.'
Why not junk the institution then?
The point was we had reached the stage we could.
Access! access! was his cry, and timetables, textbooks,
exams, walls, bells were as much garbage
as last year's Cadillac. Plug in! playback!
tapespond! The electronic network longs
to set you free. The what and where and when
of learning's in your own hands now. Deschool.
Decamp. Disperse. The player and the game
are one, nobody prods men to the board.
– So we were the first tape and data children,
we've been through the tube, come out, still cool.
We know how Armstrong landed, bleeps call us
in our breast-pockets everywhere we go,
we've got cassettes of Basque folk-songs, slides
of the water-flea, microfilm drips from us
in clusters, if there's music of the spheres
we've heard it. I've been talking to the dolphins
in California, and they say they've seen
a school (which I know is impossible)
     far out in the bay.
     Whales, whales, you fool.

Adventures of the Anti-sage

IN THE COUNTRY

They dragged the anti-sage through blackthorns.
'Oh I'm so light', he cried – 'it's wonderful
it's like – it's like –'
The whipcrack that cut him off
had a touch of desperation. His back
was a burst of mist, his long arms
no more than clouds now,
his jugular a branch.
'When I was a boy I had to hold a book –

367

can you imagine –' he seemed to rock
with ripples of white foxes
that ran to earth. His breath
rose like a bustard and flapped off
as gimcrack buckshot zigzagged through nothing.
'I don't know what I know, I know I'm riding –'
was all they heard when he slipped out of sight.

SUBSEA

The anti-sage was in the moidore garden, singing.
He passed through coral better than a shawl through a ring.
Grim shouts from the shoal-master
got a hawser launched after him –
caught water. 'I wonder where I am', he said –
'there must be a wreck –' as he passed into the wreck
through iron plates that like mercury
divided and closed again. A grouper
stirred the deck sand from bones –
they harpooned that guardian.
As they closed in, bubble-trailing,
trigger-crooking, black,
'I'm soaring', he decided,
'it's blue, it's white and gold –'
crashing the severe busty figurehead
of a score of storms
without sound or harm,
up, beyond all their aim.

ELECTRONIC

Men in white coats banged the computer.
The anti-sage stayed inside, sighing.
'We know you're there!', they shouted.
He squeezed through circuits, thinking about thought,
felt hot, and with a sudden laugh
exploded in a print-out WISDOM
THERE IS
NO WISDOM THERE
IS NO WISDOM THERE IS NO
WISDOM THERE IS
then flew swiftly through the white-coats for
that faint whiff of starch unneeded, snorted
with exhilaration, lurched humming,
heaving, falling, following 'Nothing! – get it –

368

zero – clowns! – hidden there – now! now! –
while they faded into their dimension,
while they froze in gestures of defeat,
while they failed to watch him go.

IMPRISONED

In a great cage
of crossed lasers they held the anti-sage
five seconds. His rage
scorched Sirius an age.
But then to disengage –
forgot his anger, closed his eyes, began
'To dream' (he breathed) 'I've always known –
my dark boat floating in the eye of the universe,
curve that looks out to nothing,
till those lids close, there
sailing, the wake puffed with fire
and clouds massing ahead and passing behind
into and out of time – oh what I saw
when I was drifting with no more
meaning than a lonely sail
cuts white right through –'
it all, as it fell, invisible but weak, away.

The Divide

I keep thinking of you – which is ridiculous.
These years between us like a sea.
Any dignity that came with growing older
would stop my pencil on the paper.
The player was open; you asked for the Stones;
got that, got steaming coffee, conversation.
The heavy curtains kept a wild night out.
I keep thinking of your eyes, your hands.
There is no reason for it, none at all.
You would say I can't be what I'm not,
yet I can't not be what I am.
Where does that leave us? What can we do?
The silence after Jagger was like a cloak
I'd have thrown over you – only the wind
was left, and the clock ticked as you sipped,
clutching the green mug in both hands.

369

Don't look up suddenly like that!
How hard it is not to watch you.
We had got to the stage of not talking
and not worrying, and that
was almost happy. Then, late,
when you lay on one elbow on the carpet
I could feel nothing but that hot knife
of pain telling me what it was,
and I can't tell you about it, not one word.

Smoke

I scratch a gap in the curtains:
the darkest morning of the year
goes grey slowly, chains of orange street-lights
lose out east in Glasgow's haze. The smell
of cigarette smoke fills the bedroom. I drown
in it, I gulp you through my lungs again
and hardly find what can be breathed.
Are you destroying me? Or is it a comedy?
To get together naked in bed, was that all?
To say you had done it? And that we did nothing
was what you had done. Iago and Cassio
had a better night. It must be a laugh
to see us both washed out with lying there.
It doesn't feel like laughing, though,
it feels like gasping, shrieking, tearing, all in silence
as I leave your long curved back
and go through to the kettle and the eggs.

The Beginning

What potions have I drunk?
Not siren tears, where there was no come-on.
Your presence was enough to make me want
your presence, yet you were the pursuer.
What made you speak to me that night?
It comes up in flashes, a hubbub
of Yevtushenko autographs, MacDiarmid
being whisked to his car – Loki in a lounge-suit –
the Bute Hall skailing like a swarm of bees,

janitors hovering to shoo us down the stairs
from Babiy Yar and Simbirsk Fair,
and you, a splash of red jeans against the wall
asking me about King Billy till
everything else went out
from my mind and we went out together
into a still cold clear November.
Now nothing is still – I shake.
Nothing is cold – I burn.
Nothing is clear – I toss and turn.
And somehow we've got through December.
Hope brings my fear of the new year.

Planets

The planets move, and earth is one, I know.
Blue with endlessly moving seas,
white with clouds endlessly moving,
and the continents creep on plates
endlessly moving soundlessly.
How should we be exempt
or safe from change, we walk
on mercury from birth to death.
A face comes through the crowd, lips move, new eyes,
and the house of roots trembles,
its doors are slack, its windows yawn,
a place not known to be defenceless
undefended. Who wants sedge
at the streak of the kingfisher?
Now you have almost worn out my tape
of 'The Planets', but I don't know yours,
or your sign, though Mars the Bringer of War
is what you play most. We've talked
of Jenghiz Khan, of Christ, of Frankenstein.
I don't know whether you believe
in the fate I can't not believe in,
simply to watch you swinging
in my black vinyl chair,
even bringing war.

The Question

I've a rose still
in the window-box, this last day of the year –
orange-pink dwarf, tight and fine –
a few raindrops fills it, till it shakes them
coursing down over puppy-tooth thorns
into the silky throat of the pot.
Through the week's gales that clattered slates
off roofs, it's jaunty, untattered –
so small it bends into the tunnel of the blast
folded round one flamy note –
sings now on a louring Hogmanay,
and smells as faintly rainily fresh
as on the first day.
– Gales are nothing; get frost,
get silent midnight teeth, get January –
take it off invisibly in snow.
It's like a splash of blood left back from dying,
troubling the winter and the questioner.
To ask it what it's doing there
is stare – and stare – and stare –

Resurrections

None of your jade suits, none of your gold-sewn princes! –
green-shelled spoonfuls of dust like coelacanths in tombs.
I want to be born again. Keep Tollund peat
for roses, boots, blazes. Men of Han, princesses,
yellowing demons and mummies, casket-crowders,
haunt off! There's never armour made
I'd pray to be preserved in. Don't preserve me!
Yesterday great Chou's ashes flew
in the wind over plain and river,
never resting or rusting, nothing
for an urn. Unknown he blows
like seed, is seed,
a little cinnamon of the millennium.
Let them roll away the black diorite
where millions shuffle past a husk.
What? Christ too like Chou could not be found.
In this strange January spring,
so mild the blackbirds go mad
singing in the morning above Anniesland,

I woke, I heard them, no one at my side,
but thought of you with the exhilaration
of that rising song where like them I scatter
and swoop in rings over the half-dark earth,
caught up in another life.

Unfinished Poems
a sequence for Veronica Forrest-Thomson

he sequence of poems is written in tribute to Veronica Forrest-Thomson, a young
oet from Glasgow who died in tragic circumstances in 1975. Studying and later
aching in Liverpool, Cambridge, Leicester, and Birmingham, she was probably
etter known in England than in Scotland, but she can be seen as belonging – in
er own strange and oblique way – to the revival of poetry that has taken place
 Glasgow during the last decade or so. She was a spiky, difficult character of
reat intelligence and wit, engaging, vulnerable and lonely. I liked and admired
er very much. She wrote both poetry and criticism, and the influences on her
 ork were various and formidable: the French structuralists, Wittgenstein, John
 shbery, J.H. Prynne...but shot through with a raw, moving, almost ballad
 rain from time to time, and especially in her love poetry. A book of poetic theory,
 oetic Artifice, was published in 1978 (Manchester University Press). Allardyce,
 arnett have now published her *Collected Poems and Translations* (1990). She had
 n extraordinary talent, and her life and work, unfinished after so much promise,
 ill be remembered.

1

'Poets are loved because they can't make it here.'
But that was Bellow, and America.
You wouldn't like his sentimental truth.
You won't go buttonholing shades
like that fool Aeneas.
Did he think she'd smile or what?
The pyre still smoulders among old gibbets and potsherds.
She couldn't kill death.
No throw of the dice will ever abolish chance.
She is serious now, as you are,
in a fiction in Virgil or here,
complete.

Errabat silva in magna,
when the light was withdrawn from the edge of things,
and monsters shook their scales, with a dry clashing,
and there seemed more dead than living,
as indeed there are.
She brushed many ghosts.
Trees slumped like mummies. Lemurs
whistled, swung. These are fabrications

373

to inhabit. You will get an old hut at last
with raucous Pound and arcane Prynne,
Apollinaire the lyrical and Wittgenstein the sad,
complete.

Why should a dog, a horse, a rat have life?
You had no time for indignation
and I leave mine in a quotation.
What can't be solved is borne.
What can't be borne is solved.
To get a structure up
you'd like to see if you could see it is perhaps
the best we can engineer out of the weight
of what we don't deny we feel.
If you could really read it,
then I could really leave it,

2

One drinks paraquat. One drowns with bricks on.
One skids on black ice. One is strangled with nylons.
One is in hypothermia. One has thrombosis.
A lion crunches one. A lover poisons one.
One is shot at Entebbe. One meets a shark.
One hangs from barbed wire. One is battered with hammers.
One falls in a hopper. One jumps from a hotel.
One is kicked by a horse. One has cancer many years.
One burns at Brands Hatch. One chokes on a beef-ball.
One lies paralysed in a house full of provisions.
One plunges streaming in a Spitfire.
One abandons hope in a bedsitter.
One is sucked in quicksands. One slips in a quarry.
Molten metal bites one. A mother aborts one.
One fasts to death. One's parachute fails.
One hang-glides into a hill. One is hanged.
One is tortured with water. One is a shadow on a wall.
One dies in orgasm. One is pegged on an anthill.
A tractor mangles one. A tornado dashes one.
One has the bends. One is beaten by guards.
One has kidney failure. One suffocates in a cot.
One is gored. One sniffs glue.
One is crucified. One eats clockwork.
One is beheaded. One is buried alive.
One is frozen on fells. One is flayed.
                              . One is set in lava.
      is ground   . One   wheel.
One

374

3

'Do not be too fierce,
little one.
The hard shell breaks.

Yield a little,
little one.
Lean where you can.

Not compromise –
your steel
will flash still –

but it brings nothing
to be broken
against the heart, it

leaves a bleak room
and dry tears
nothing more to do.'

'I want to be very clear.
The light should be
focused, not spent.

We should say what
matters,
not drift, dress.

It's not an art to understand.
You have to pull
the mandrake, never mind

the shrieks. That bloody
business. The art
will come, will come.

It's hard – like a honeycomb
of pure ivory
the bees have singly left –'

4

It was just nosing the rooftops – the sun, I mean,
when we left that party, and we shivered a bit
as Edward was still going on about foregrounding.
'Follow that milk-float!' cried Peter, and we made

like a taxi, but the float was too slow
and wasn't scared anyway. A black cat
glowered at our crocodile. We broke up
when we got to the river. John stripped off
to whistles, breaststroked like a dog for sticks
and cut his tongue on one, scrambled out
with a goatee of blood for Vera's handkerchief.
There were three of us leaning on the bridge.
The bells came suddenly, far enough off
to be equal in clarity and melancholy,
with the water swirling as we stared at it
for a meaning that even the beautiful snag
of a broken, grounded oar forcing a wave
not nature's and not man's could not make clear
for all that the bells did to that foreground,
and we knew we were reading a strange tongue,
kept silent, frowning. That was when we began
to learn. The early world

5

The monkey on the monkey-puzzle
didn't fall, but starved. He said
the sensation had assuaged the hunger,
as they gave him gruel in bed.

When Keats was walking into Glasgow
the first man he met was drunk.
O for a life of – well, on paper.
'Tike yer ands off.' 'Cockney punk.'

A male fly looking out a window
fancied a female looking in.
Rubbing his legs, he became thoughtful:
in this position, it's a sin.

Buñuel was slicing eyeballs
down in the local abattoir.
The art, he said, is just in thinking
how human my poor pupils are.

The red flag on the Master's finial
caused a sen – I'm telling a lie.
It was the red flag by the river
thrusting all the green blades by:

376

chlorophyll by Ishihara,
shouting 'Forty-eight!' or 'Ten!'
Discompose me a few punters,
said crimson to the fibre-pen.

The Cam was red, and Corpus Christi.
Books lay bound in stacks of flame.
Livid bees above Christ's Pieces
sweated out a bloody name.

Even clouds were red in heaven,
not at sunset but at noon.
Red in red the skylark vanished.

6

I am wearing fibre.
   Fibre vibrates.
Why are you not wearing fibre?
   Fibre vibrates.
Yon one was wont warily to want to wear a fibre.
   Fibre vibrates.
When she cast off she felt fibre.
   Fibre vibrates.
We went on whistling under fire.
   Fire vibrates.
Then they gave me this shirt

7

Pain to know,
               pain not knowing.
Pain to love,
               pain not loving.
Pain on the rack
               and in the rocking-chair.
Wrong to meet,
               wrong not to.
Wrong to be barren
               wrong to bear.
Wrong for elegies
               and for silence.
Almost right
               to feel this.
Almost right
               the heart searching.

Almost right
            to be at the barriers.
And not right
            to scream or shout.
And not right
            the throne of doubt.
And not right
            to sidle out.
But to take the pain
            and use it.
To see the wrong,
            not lose it.
To give the love

8

Struktura the queen
caught that harpy Svoboda
her sister-we-don't-talk-about
planting her feet
in the wet cement.
The slut of sluts
grinned and was off
howling like the wind.
The queen's anger
hummed and cracked
with her whip, the pavement
of pavements spoiled again.
'I'll get my Alsatians –'
'A've goat dodza beef fur thaim.'
'I'll set up a force field –'
'A've goat the Big Laser, but.'
'I'll put you in the labyrinth –'
'A kin aye smell ma wey tae freedom.'
'Right. Here's a wall. Let's see your graffiti.'
'Aw naw, A widny – A canny –'
'Why not? You think it's a trap?'
'Naw naw, but it's no the same –'
'What is not the same, sister?'
'A canny dae it if A'm telt tae dae it –'
'Let me start then. Watch here.'
So Queen Struktura
with ambidextrous aerosols
blue and yellow
flashed up an interlace
an abstract labyrinth
of uncharted greens

out left a ragged blank
or her sister to fill.
Svoboda darted forward
her hair flew
and what she could do

9

Only a summer afternoon –
St James's Park that fair bright burning field splashed full of folk –
where the black swan stretched suddenly, stood on the water,
    flapped and flapped with white patches semaphoring under his
    wings –
and the seventh chick in the family of moorhens stopped to dabble a
    weed, while the convoy swept on: what a scutter, what panting,
    to rejoin them! –
and sparrows doing their woodpecker stunt on trees, scuttling up the
    dry bark, clinging, peering, slipping, as if they enjoyed the
    game –
and the very blond deckchair attendant in her frayed denim skirt
    and striped top asked me if I'd like to know who won at
    Wimbledon – 'Yes I would' – 'Borg! I'm Swedish you see –
    but I wanted Nastase to win –'
and the young wife in the plain long loose white dress, being helped
    by her husband over the fence, got tangled and showed
    everything, floating for a moment like a white cloud, a
    cloud without trousers –
and Arabic, Arabic everywhere, as the boy threw his last sandwich
    crumbs to the grass pigeons, saying 'Kullu!' –
kullu in an English park, kullu, that's all –
O blessed trivia that keep us from dying: did you not find them
    – Veronica –

10

It's true we only live to die.
We lie, and rise, and run, and lie.

You'd think the bitter DNA
would decline its wedding-day.

Fever has no logic though.
What we do's not what we know.

Art, love, work, war, gods, seas, or Mars –
we want them, with or without scars.

There's nothing we shall never do
once the message has come through.

He said. And she got up in pain.
Outside, the streets were black with rain.

She wondered, who will think of me?
For I am dying, as you see.

But she said nothing, locked the door
at last, when she had nothing more

to share with the imperial race,
and met her terror

Star Gate
Science Fiction Poems
1979

INSTAMATIC THE MOON FEBRUARY 1973

At the edge of the Sea of Serenity,
where the grey dust rises into foothills
of the Taurus Mountains, a confrontation
takes place. An unmanned, eight-wheeled steam pram,
Lunokhod-2, sophisticatedly clumsy as an
Emmett velocipede, has stopped its trundle
faced by a large, hard, blank, slab-like stone.
Busily it winks, and scans the monolith,
registering back to Tass
an impossible smoothness.
What crater could eject this unpitted stele
that stands marking nothing?
Too much simplicity is a headache for lunokhods,
and the moonrover has focused, in its frenzy for data,
on a spider-web of shadows and scratches at the base of the slab
which imagination might just read in Ventris mood
as K space BRI query space K query.

The Worlds

Alps without edelweiss,
Vesuviuses without broom,
maria without water.
Whose waiting is like theirs,
trench, dust, clinker,
dune, wrinkled crater,
frozen, scorched, airless,
bombarded rigor mortis
of meteorites or worse,
unimaginably long
dead, yet what is dead
that can be visited
whether by whiteboot man
or probe with uncanny arm
scooping and scraping? Men
bring life and death both,
but the new death bound
to life, not ending it,
new phases of the Moon,
real canals for Mars.
The planets lift their bones

and roar like megalosaurs.
Time has entered space.
Earth is again the centre
and the favoured place.

Particle Poems

1

The old old old old particle
smiled. 'I grant you I'm not beautiful,'
he said, 'but I've got charm.
It's charm that's led me where I am.'

Opened up his bosom, showed me a quark.
It gleamed. He grinned like a clam. 'Sort
of heart, really, though I've got four.
They're in orbit, and what for

is a good question, unless to pump up
charm. I know I must look a frump
– just fishing – but seriously
would you not say I'm easily

the nearest thing to doom and centrehood
you've ever been unable to preclude?
Cathedrals – oh, antiquities and slime,
knucklebones, teeth five feet long, signs

and wonders, auks, knuckledusters,
twangs from armchairs, waters
waiting to break, cells waiting to squeak,
a sniff of freesia, a book

of hours, and hours themselves like days
in love, and even nanoseconds raised
by charm to higher powers, wait
until I make them, and fade.'

Shot off – never showed his age.

2

The young particle screamed round the bend,
braked hard, broke.

384

His mother dozing in Manchuria
heard his last cry. A mare's ear twitched.
Dust, and dust, the wires sang.

3

Three particles lived in mystical union.
They made knife, fork, and spoon,
and earth, sea, and sky.
They made animal, vegetable, and mineral,
and faith, hope, and charity.
They made stop, caution, go,
and hickory, dickory, dock.
They made yolk, white, and shell,
and hook, line, and sinker.
They made pounds, shillings, and pence,
and Goneril, Regan, and Cordelia.
They made Shadrach, Meshach, and Abednego,
and game, set, and match.

A wandering particle kidnapped one of them,
and the two that were left made day and night,
and left and right, and right and wrong,
and black and white, and off and on,
but things were never quite the same,
and two will always yearn for three.
They're after you, or me.

4

Part particle and part idea, she
struggled through a throb of something.
A wheatear, or an ear of wheat?
How could she possibly know
beyond the shrill vibrations, sunny fibres, field?
What was the field but forces, surges?
To veins of green and veins of red
she was colour-blind. Well, she was blind.
But was she there at all –
when the wind ruffled that nest of growing things
and it took its course in the sun?

5

The particle that decided
got off its mark, but died.

6

Their mausoleum
is a frozen silent flak.
The fractured tracks,
photographed, docket
dead dogfights,
bursts of no malice.
Almost pure direction
points its stream,
deflected, detected.
Better than ogam
or cuneiform the tracer
of telling particles
fans out angrily
itself, itself, itself –
who we were
were here, here,
we died at the crossroads
or we defected
or we raced ahead
to be burnt out.
Faint paths hardly score,
yet shake the lens, end
in lucider mosaics
of theory. Go,
bid the soldiers shoot.

Era

A silicon-based life replaced us –
we went out in fireflauchts and gnashings of teeth.
The abyss became brilliant quickly.
Hard and bright everything after our muddle.
Vorticist – said those who had read books –
was the time. A beak
here, a vane, bluish splinters, incommensurate all
but a lightning beauty. We breathed, just.
Acrid tents hung over us glimmering, and beyond,
a lizardlike aurora borealis, laserlike.
You could cut us with a knife, and they did.
We saw them make two blades of glass
grow where one grew before.
We few soft things, of earth, in caves, live.

We shall go blind soon. This is oral
but someone is writing still. Carbon!
You could write with diamonds and be silent.
The air is like walking through barbed wire.

Foundation

'What would you put in the foundation-stone
for future generations?' 'A horseshoe,
a ballet shoe, a horseshoe crab, a sea-horse,
a sheriff's star, a pacemaker, a tit's egg, a tomato,
a ladybird, a love-letter, a laugh-track, a yo-yo,
a microtektite, a silicon chip, a chip pan,
a Rembrandt, a Reinhardt, a Reinhardt jigsaw –'
'That's some foundation-stone –' '– a hovercraft,
a manta ray, a bulldozer, a windjammer,
a planetarium, an oilrig, a Concorde, a cornfield,
a gannetry, a hypermarket, a continental shelf,
a brace of asteroids, a spiral nebula –'
'Why don't you take my question seriously – ?'
'– a black hole, a dream, a conceptual universe,
no, make it a dozen conceptual universes
laid tail to head like sardines in a tin
and poured all over with lovely oil
of poetry: seal it; solder the key.'

A Home in Space

Laid-back in orbit, they found their minds.
They found their minds were very clean and clear.
Clear crystals in swarms outside were their fireflies and larks.
Larks they were in lift-off, swallows in soaring.
Soaring metal is flight and nest together.
Together they must hatch.
Hatches let the welders out.
Out went the whitesuit riggers with frames as light as air.
Air was millions under lock and key.
Key-ins had computers wild on Saturday nights.
Nights, days, months, years they lived in space.
Space shone black in their eyes.
Eyes, hands, food-tubes, screens, lenses, keys were one.

One night – or day – or month – or year – they all –
all gathered at the panel and agreed –
agreed to cut communication with –
with the earth base – and it must be said they were –
were cool and clear as they dismantled the station and –
and gave their capsule such power that –
that they launched themselves outwards –
outwards in an impeccable trajectory, that band –
that band of tranquil defiers, not to plant any –
any home with roots but to keep a –
a voyaging generation voyaging, and as far –
as far as there would ever be a home in space –
space that needs time and time that needs life.

The Mouth

I saw a great mouth in space that fifty thousand angels could not fill
they ran shrieking from it as it grew and threw their coloured coats
    and flares
for lures among the stars while it advanced and swallowed the
    planets of the sun
one by one and then the sun

it rose and swayed the Milky Way collapsed into it like a poorly
    shuffled pack
deeper and deeper into darkness it brought darkness and what it
    blotted out
it grew drunk on to grinning-point with so much fire in its belly it
    roared
over its thankless hoard

for that was the new horror to hear it when it howled like a hungry
    scraped womb
and galaxies jampacked with glittering rayed-out million-year-old
    civilizations
were jumped like a handful of asteroids and sucked into tales of hell
for all they could tell

the Plough long gone the winding Dragon the Lyre the Balance the
    fading Charioteer
Aquarius with a loud cry Keel Stern and Sails in terrible rushing
    silence
and now white Sirius was black yellow Capella was black red
    Antares was black
and no lights ever came back

388

heavens and paradises popped like seaweed eternal laws were never
    seen again
angels' teeth were cosmic dust and cosmic dust was angels' teeth all's
    grist
to that dark mill where christs and godbearers were pulped with
    their domes ikons vanes
their scrolls aeons and reigns

in Virgo the most evolved life there was was calm and watchful in its
    fiery coverts
the mouth had long been computed probable and plans had been
    laid and re-laid
the dense cluster of three thousand galaxies had made itself a force
    field
that would not know how to yield

the worlds of Virgo were not only inhabited but hyperinhabited
    they were all
one life and their force field was themselves they were a wall they
    shone they stood
jehovahs and elohim are daguerreotypes to their movies they made
    universes
as poets make verses

in Virgo they did not underestimate the mouth they were the last
    star-gate and goal
when they saw there were no other lights in the recesses of space and
    it was hard
to distinguish the shadow of the unsated mouth from the shadow of
    the dead
but its lips were blackest red

they gaped for Virgo with a scream they gaped for Virgo with a
scream they gaped for Virgo with a scream they gaped for Virgo
with a scream they gaped for Virgo with a scream they gaped
at that great quiet gate

The Clone Poem

like father like son like father like son like son like son like son
a chip off the old block the old block a chip a chip off chip off
no smoke without fire no smoke no smoke without
    no smoke without fire without fire
birds of a feather flock together birds of a feather together flock
    together birds birds of a feather

389

when you've seen one you've seen them all seen them all seen one
    seen them all all all all seen them all
plus ça change plus c'est la même chose c'est la même la même chose
    plus ça change la même c'est la même chose plus ça change
there are plenty of fish in the sea plenty in the sea plenty plenty of fish
    there are plenty plenty fish plenty fish in the sea
as alike as peas in a pod peas in a pod as alike as peas peas peas in a
    pod alike as peas as alike as peas in a pod peas in a pod alike
    alike alike
father son and holy ghost father son ghost father son son ghost ghost
    father father and holy ghost son and holy ghost father son and
    holy ghost
one for all and all for one for one all for one one one for all all all for
    one for all for one for all for one and all one and all all for one
    one one
le roi est mort vive le roi vive le roi mort mort le roi mort vive vive
    le roi le roi le roi vive vive vive le roi
the more the merrier merrier merrier more more more the merrier
    more the merrier merrier more the merrier more more more
    more more
many hands make light work many hands light light work make
    light work many many hands make light work light light work
    many many many many many many hands
semper idem semper eadem semper semper idem eadem idem
    eadem semper idem eadem semper idem idem eadem eadem
    semper semper semper idem eadem idem eadem idem eadem
you can't make a silk purse out of a sow's ear out of a sow's ear you
    can't make a silk purse a silk purse you can't you can't make
    a silk purse you can't out of a sow's ear you can't you can't you
    can't
you can have too much of a good thing too much of a good thing too
    much you can have too much you can you can too much of
    a good thing you can have have too much too much of a good
    thing

The Moons of Jupiter

AMALTHEA

I took a book with me to Amalthea
but never turned a page. It weighed like lead.
I squatted with it like a grey image
malleted into the rock, listlessly
reading, staring, rereading listlessly

sentences that never came to anything.
My very memory lay paralysed
with everything else on that bent moon,
pulled down and dustbound, flattened, petrified
by gravitation, sweeping Jupiter's
more than half the sky with sentences
half-formed that never came to anything.
My tongue lay like a coil of iron, the planet
never heard a word. What did I say there?
My very memory is paralysed.
The book has gone too – I know how it began
but that first sentence never came to anything.
'The local train, with its three coaches, pulled up
at Newleigh Station at half-past four...'
The tons of pages never moved, my knees
were tombs, and though slow Jupiter slid past,
my memory of it is paralysed.
The stupid moon goes round. The local train,
with its three coaches pulled up at Newleigh Station
at half-past four, never comes to anything.
They rescued me with magnets, plucked me up
like dislocated yards of groaning mandrake.
The satellite engulfed the book in dust.

IO

The sulphur mines on Io were on strike
when we arrived. I can't say I'm surprised.
Seventy-five men had just been killed
in the fiercest eruption ever seen there.
I hardly recognized the grim volcano
with its rakish new centre and a leaning plume
two hundred miles high – like an ash tree,
someone said. Meanwhile the landscape burned,
not that it never burned before, but this
was roaring, sheeted, cruel. Empty
though not perfunctory funeral rites
had been performed; not a body was found.
The weird planetman's flute from friends in grief –
my god what a strange art it is, rising
so many million miles from home into
the raw thin cindery air – was the first sound
we heard when we stepped from the ship. We saw
the men huddled in knots, or walking slowly
with bent heads over the pumice beds, or still
and silent by the bank of the red lake.

391

The laser probes, the belts, the brilliant console
sat dark and motionless, crawled through by smoke.
Sulphur blew to choke the very soul.
We prospected beyond the lava-fields,
but the best sulphur's the most perilous.
The planetman must shoulder sorrow, great sacks
of pain, in places with no solace but
his own and what the winds and days may bring.

EUROPA

Boots and boats – in our bright orange gear
we were such an old-fashioned earthly lot
it seemed almost out of time-phase. We learned
or re-learned how to skate and ski, use snowshoes,
fish through ice-holes though not for fish. Soundings
and samples were our prey. We'd never grade
in years, far less in weeks, the infinite
play and glitter of watery Europa,
waters of crust ice, waters of deep ice,
waters of slush, of warm subcrustal springs,
waters of vapour, waters of water.
One day, and only one, we drilled right down
to something solid and so solid-hard
the drill-head screamed into the microphone
and broke, the film showed streaks of metal shards
whizzing across a band of basalt or
glimmery antediluvian turtle-shell
or cast-off titan miner's helmet or –
it must have been the metal scream that roused
our thought and fear and half desire we might
have had a living scream returned. Lightly
it sleeps, the imagination. On that smooth moon
men would be driven mad with many dreams,
hissing along the hill-less shining wastes,
or hearing the boat's engine chug the dark
apart, as if a curtain could be drawn
to let the living see even the dead
if they had once had life, if not that life.

GANYMEDE

Galileo would have been proud of Ganymede.
Who can call that marbled beauty dead?
Dark basins sweeping to a furrowed landfall,

392

gigantic bright-rayed craters, vestiges
and veils of ice and snow, black swirling grey,
grey veined with green, greens diffused in blues,
blue powdered into white: a king marble
rolled out, and set in place, from place to place.
We never landed, only photographed
and sent down probes from orbit; turbulence
on Jupiter was extreme, there was no lingering.
Is it beauty, or minerals, or knowledge
we take our expeditions for? What a question!
But is it What a question? Is it excitement,
or power, or understanding, or illumination
we take our expeditions for? Is it specimens,
or experiments, or spin-off, or fame, or evolution,
or necessity we take our expeditions for?
We are here, and our sons or our sons' sons
will be on Jupiter, and their sons' sons
at the star gate, leaving the fold of the sun.
I remember I drowsed off, dropped my notes,
with the image of Ganymede dancing before me.
They nudged me, smiling, said it was a judgement
for my wandering thoughts, what had got into me?
That satellite had iron and uranium.
We would be back. Well, that must be fine,
I teased them; had it gold, and asphodel?

CALLISTO

Scarred, cauterized, pocked and warty face:
you grin and gape and gawk and cock an ear
at us with craters, all blind, all deaf, all dumb,
toadback moon, brindled, brown and cold,
we plodded dryshod on your elephant-hide seas
and trundled gear from groove to groove, playing
the record of your past, imagining
the gross vales filled with unbombarded homes
they never had till we pitched nylon tents there:
radiation falling by the ton,
but days of meteorites long gone. Scatter
the yellow awnings, amaze the dust and ochre!
Frail and tough as flags we furnish out
the desolation. Even the greatest crater,
gouged as if a continent had struck it,
circled by rim on rim of ridges rippling
hundreds of miles over that slaty chaos,
cannot forbid our feet, our search, our songs.

I did not sing; the grave-like mounds and pits
reminded me of one grave long ago
on earth, when a high Lanarkshire wind
whipped out the tears men might be loath to show,
as if the autumn had a mercy I
could not give to myself, listening in shame
to the perfunctory priest and to my thoughts
that left us parted on a quarrel. These
memories, and love, go with the planetman
in duty and in hope from moon to moon.

Uncollected Poems
1976-1981

The Rock

You asked me to get you a rock from Dracula's Castle,
but when I gave you it you left it behind.
I'd been to the Black Sea and back:
you talked about yourself all night.
I tell myself that's what you're like, why change it
if there's something else. I don't know if
there's something else. I don't want
to see you again. I want to see you again.
In the Carpathians, there you feel free.
I read, much of the night, when I was there.
I was not thinking of you. I was
thinking of you. In Bran Castle courtyard,
or threading its steep stairs, or under dark gables
where Vlad impaled (they say) his German merchants
or nailed recalcitrant turbans to the wearers' heads,
I looked for the stone you needed.
If I had to think of you, I thought of Stoker too
sniffing the North Sea salt at broken Slains
and forging legends in that castle's shadow
no worse than the reality
of Vlad at Bran. All right you don't want the stone,
so what is the message? Do you want me?
Make up your mind if you want to live in a novel.
What is your story, who are you in mine?
And why did you say, before I uttered a word,
'So you don't want to see me again'?

The Mummy

(The Mummy [of Rameses II] *was met at Orly airport by Mme Saunier-Seïté.*
– News item, Sept. 1976)

– May I welcome Your Majesty to Paris.

– Mm.

– I hope the flight from Cairo was reasonable.

– Mmmmm.

– We have a germ-proof room at the Museum of Man
where we trust Your Majesty will have peace and quiet.

– Unh-unh.

– I am sorry, but this is necessary.
  Your Majesty's person harbours a fungus.

– Fng fng's, hn?

– Well, it is something attacking your cells.
  Your Majesty is gently deteriorating
  after nearly four thousand years
  becalmed in masterly embalmment.
  We wish to save you from the worm.

– Wrm hrm! Mgh-mgh-mgh.

– Indeed I know it must be distressing
  to a pharaoh and a son of Ra,
  to the excavator of Abu Simbel
  that glorious temple in the rock,
  to the perfecter of Karnak hall,
  to the hammer of the Hittites,
  to the colossus whose colossus
  raised in red granite at holy Thebes
  sixteen-men-high astounds the desert
  shattered, as Your Majesty in life
  shattered the kingdom and oppressed the poor
  with such lavish grandeur and panache,
  to Rameses, to Ozymandias,
  to the Louis Quatorze of the Nile,
  how bitter it must be to feel
  a microbe eat your camphored bands.
  But we are here to help Your Majesty.
  We shall encourage you to unwind.
  You have many useful years ahead.

– M' n'm 'z 'zym'ndias, kng'v kngz!

– Yes yes. Well, Shelley is dead now.
  He was not embalmed. He will not write
  about Your Majesty again.

– T't'nkh'm'n? H'tsh'ps't?
  'khn't'n? N'f'rt'ti? Mm? Mm?

– The hall of fame has many mansions.
  Your Majesty may rest assured
  your deeds will always be remembered.

398

– Youmm w'm'nn. B't'f'lll w'm'nnnn.
  No w'm'nnn f'r th'zndz y'rz.

– Your Majesty, what are you doing?

– Ng! Mm. Mhm. Mm? Mm? Mmmmm.

– Your Majesty, Your Majesty! You'll break your stitches!

– Fng st'chez fng's wrm hrm.

– I really hate to have to use
  a hypodermic on a mummy,
  but we cannot have you strain yourself.
  Remember your fungus, Your Majesty.

– Fng. Zzzzzzz.

– That's right.

– Aaaaaaaaah.

Five Waiting Poems

THE MEN

Prop up walls was all
they could do when the rain came
raking the roofless sheds.
Sharp, cold, half-hail
it weighed into them that
end of livid October.
'Edgar Allan Poe!'
the wind seemed to shout
round the dead iron pillars.
Poe slept. The sleepers
were windbreaks for mushrooms.
The men frowned at them
abstractedly, huddled
by the siding, waiting
in their sodden donkey-jackets,
oilskins, hoods, everything,
everybody soaked, swore,
sighed, stamped, muttered,

steamed, stood in a muss
of uneasiness and omens.

THE WOMEN

The women waited with pitchforks.
The women waited with violets.
The women clapped in a ring.
The women sat like stones.
The women watched the Pleiades.
The women cursed the cataract.
The women held their children up.
The women sold sons to howitzers.
The women lay on the motorway.
The women sang by their doors
at twilight, the woman sang
by her lonely door at twilight,
the woman sings by her door
one lonely twilight,
a woman sings at twilight
and no one comes as always,
lonely, to the door.

THE CHILDREN

Chestnuts, thunderclouds, mud.
Children waiting for Gizzi's
tinny yodel, ice-cream
never out of season.
Vanished vans in a time-warp,
last wasps keeling over,
hoarfrost at its breakfast.
Chimes, dreary Sunday,
children at the windows
like pale pot plants.

THE DOG

A dog on a grave in autumn,
perhaps with the obscure sense
of death, but of solitude
it is certain. And to defend
the dead old man below
if he could still be hurt.

The gravediggers shrug, leave,
respecting the snarl as much
as any grief under black,
though the dog is black, and naturally
makes the shadow of a headstone
still to be, as he stretches
along the crumbled earth
with his muzzle on his paws
and the afternoon darkens
till at last no one would see
what was watching or waiting.

THE POET

The poet shrieks getting
waiting out of his system
when the little wringing hands
of a valetudinary muse
fuse to one white claw.
He shivers as he bleeds.
Eagle country, winds
and pines, the lower air
thick with dying leaves,
a gleam of flooded fields.
Whatever it is that will
not wait, he still half waits
to find, half sees, feels
wholly as the unrelenting
hook hangs him higher
and higher and something like
wings or the single wing
of a great craft shadows
and flashes alternately past
the sun of that country.
At the right moment the claw
retracts, and his one clear cry
falls to the earth before him,
winding down like a song.

Instructions to an Actor

Now, boy, remember this is the great scene.
You'll stand on a pedestal behind a curtain,
the curtain will be drawn, and then you don't move
for eighty lines; don't move, don't speak, don't breathe.
I'll stun them all out there, I'll scare them,
make them weep, but it depends on you.
I warn you eighty lines is a long time,
but you don't breathe, you're dead,
you're a dead queen, a statue,
you're dead as stone, new-carved,
new-painted and the paint not dry
– we'll get some red to keep your lip shining –
and you're a mature woman, you've got dignity,
some beauty still in middle age, and
you're kind and true, but you're dead,
your husband thinks you're dead,
the audience thinks you're dead,
and you don't breathe, boy, I say
you don't even blink for eighty lines,
if you blink you're out!
Fix your eye on something and keep watching it.
Practise when you get home. It can be done.
And you move at last – music's the cue.
When you hear a mysterious solemn jangle
of instruments, make yourself ready.
Five lines more, you can lift a hand.
It may tingle a bit, but lift it –
slow, slow –
O this is where I hit them
right between the eyes, I've got them now –
I'm making the dead walk –
you move a foot, slow, steady, down,
you guard your balance in case you're stiff,
you move, you step down, down from the pedestal,
control your skirt with one hand, the other hand
you now hold out –
O this will melt their hearts if nothing does –
to your husband who wronged you long ago
and hesitates in amazement
to believe you are alive.
Finally he embraces you, and there's nothing
I can give you to say, boy,
but you must show that you have forgiven him.
Forgiveness, that's the thing. It's like a second life.
I know you can do it. – Right then, shall we try?

The Archaeopteryx's Song

I am only half out of this rock of scales.
What good is armour when you want to fly?
My tail is like a stony pedestal
and not a rudder. If I sit back on it
I sniff winds, clouds, rains, fogs where
I'd be, where I'd be flying, be flying high.
Dinosaurs are spicks and
all I see when I look back
is tardy turdy bonehead swamps
whose scruples are dumb tons.
Damnable plates and plaques
can't even keep out ticks.
They think when they make the ground thunder
as they lumber for a horn-lock or a rut
that someone is afraid, that everyone is afraid,
but no one is afraid. The lords of creation
are in my mate's next egg's next egg's next egg,
stegosaur. It's feathers I need, more feathers
for the life to come. And these iron teeth
I want away, and a smooth beak
to cut the air. And these claws
on my wings, what use are they
except to drag me down, do you imagine
I am ever going to crawl again?
When I first left that crag
and flapped low and heavy over the ravine
I saw past present and future
like a dying tyrannosaur
and skimmed it with a hiss.
I will teach my sons and daughters to live
on mist and fire and fly to the stars.

A Good Year for Death

Where is Callas la Divina
with her black velvet and her white passion?
Where are the women and women and women
she threw into life for an hour from her throat
to float and fight? She cannot hear
the last bravo.
Death has danced her tune away.

Where is Nabokov with his butterfly-net,
his galoshes, his mushrooms, his index-cards?
He has gone in a whiff of bilberries and blinis,
his fire has paled, his puns have flunked.
Shades crowd the lakeside hydrangeas and swallows
skim quick and low.
Death has danced his tune away.

Where is Bolan, the elfin, now?
Who has taken his spangles and songs,
bongos and gongs, and his white swan?
Who has pied-piper'd the pied piper
into that childless, teenless wood?
The metal shadow,
Death, has danced his tune away.

Where is Presley all in silver,
with his sideburns and his quiver
of simple rock, and what is that army
he's uniformed for, in a white sheet,
will the slowstep motorcade battalion
never let him go?
Death has danced his tune away.

And where is Lowell that sweet mad poet
with his rumpled suit and uranium finger?
A giant forsythia covers the Pentagon
with better than gold, but the magnolias
wax the Potomac white with grief –
in words at least. Be true, be brief:
we lack his fellow.
Death has danced his tune away.

Migraine Attack

We had read about the reed-beds but went on
right through the night. With blades as sharp as that
you scarcely feel the cuts, and blood in darkness
is merely darkness. Oh there was moonlight
in fits and starts, but it confused us more
than it ever illuminated, as we kept moving
under the jagged filter of the forest ceiling –
whatever light there was made convicts of us,
frisked us, left us stumbling through our chains

of shadows. From our feet – shadows,
from our rifles – shadows, from branches –
shadows like bats and bats like shadows.
Sometimes the treetop mat was thick with mosses,
creepers, ancient nests, a stamping-ground
for upside-down explorers going to heaven:
we really saw them there, in our delirium,
riding on giant sloths, with their rags of clothes
and raddled hair streaming down to gravity.
They passed; the scrunts and scrogs passed; snakes passed;
eyes and beaks in bushes passed; a long wing passed;
the scuttlings and the slitherings and the roars
passed; time, even, as they passed, must have passed.
We were moving columns of sweat and crusted blood,
burrs, leaf-mould, mud, mosquitoes, map-cases
and a bandage or two as we leaned into it
to defeat it, and the wood grew grey
as it gave up and felt
the distant day, thinned out
to glades threaded by mist
sent from the unseen sun.
We shook ourselves like dogs
and tried a song.

At Central Station

At Central Station, in the middle of the day,
a woman is pissing on the pavement.
With her back to the wall and her legs spread
she bends forward, her hair over her face,
the drab skirt and coat not even hitched up.
Her water hits the stone with force
and streams across into the gutter.
She is not old, not young either,
not dirty, yet hardly clean,
not in rags, but going that way.
She stands at the city centre, skeleton at the feast.
Executives off the London train
start incredulously but jump the river
and meekly join their taxi queue.
The Glasgow crowd hurries past,
hardly looks, or hardly dares to look,
or looks hard, bold as brass, as
the poet looks, not bold as brass

but hard, swift, slowing his walk
a little, accursed recorder, his feelings
as confused as the November leaves.
She is a statue in a whirlpool,
beaten about by nothing he can give words to,
bleeding into the waves of talk
and traffic awful ichors of need.
Only two men frankly stop,
grin broadly, throw a gibe at her
as they cross the street to the betting-shop.
Without them the indignity,
the dignity, would be incomplete.

Winter

The year goes, the woods decay, and after,
many a summer dies. The swan
on Bingham's pond, a ghost, comes and goes.
It goes, and ice appears, it holds,
bears gulls that stand around surprised,
blinking in the heavy light, bears boys
when skates take over swan-tracks gone.
After many summer dyes, the swan-white ice
glints only crystal beyond white. Even
dearest blue's not there, though poets would find it.
I find one stark scene
cut by evening cries, by warring air.
The muffled hiss of blades escapes into breath,
hangs with it a moment, fades off.
Fades off, goes, the scene, the voices fade,
the line of trees, the woods that fall, decay
and break, the dark comes down, the shouts
run off into it and disappear.
At last the lamps go too, when fog
drives monstrous down the dual carriageway
out to the west, and even in my room
and on this paper I do not know
about that grey dead pane
of ice that sees nothing and that nothing sees.

New Year Sonnets

1

Soaring, straining, craning, flying, dying,
courted by hope, gun-butted back to sorrow,
spoon-fed with salves of gall, well-sweetened sorrow,
spun in the finest icing of a dying,
raised beyond measure by those also dying,
clapping the fashion of a shroud of sorrow,
stopping the grave at last for others' sorrow,
leaving the living busy with their dying,
you have the child that plays about your feet,
you have the blackbirds listening in the dusk,
you have the light that shows above the door,
those gentle and those unreturning feet,
that dark wing fading back into the dusk,
that blank unvisited remorseless door.

2

One times one times one times one is one.
The adder is the one that gets it two.
One two's two ones, though, and a single two
would be a fabulously merry one.
What is the great unhappiness of one,
that there should seem such bundled grace in two?
It is the hardihood of truth to two
that truth should seem a luxury in one.
We scarcely dare to breathe the charms of three,
they blow and twine like clematis. For four,
we'd have a glade of square cool box, with five
a quincunx of the thymy paths. As three
begin to breast the life to come, as four
stand round the table of bread, a star is five.

3

Satan was squatting with his lurid tuba,
potting a blackly incandescent coda.
Hell is improvisatory, a coda
blurted in continents from an old tuba.
No god aborts that bitter-titted tuba
or docks its mortally transfixing coda.
The universe itself spills like a coda
to hear the hellish spell; it buys that tuba.
– Somewhere in Lyra there began a silence
that spread along the stars like patient music.

It moved and wrapped the rocks in a white quiet.
If it should ever come to hell, that silence,
will there be space in Satan's rooky music
to drop between those blasts one rest of quiet?

4

I love that endless roll of city wheels
below the surging formless northern clouds.
It is the interchange: the wheeling clouds,
the winter sleet that blurs the cloudy wheels.
Deep in the sun a dying grindstone wheels,
and seas are heavy with unparted clouds.
There is no reason to be loving clouds
in chiding any captaincy of wheels.
Only, we love each as we love them both,
and brooding across city roofs we're joined
by drifts and troops come curiously together
steadily, stealthy and unsteady both
from the forge where all energy is joined
poised, and then we cross the world together.

5

Was it the proud full verse of his great sail
that gave America Columbus minds?
Martian badlands are the west for minds
that cannot rest in watching schooners sail
beyond the Golden Gate. The Gate's a sail
suspended in its arches like the minds
stretched under listening dishes to hear minds
unknown that might make men and gods set sail
for life. By interstellar mulls and voes
they dream of starships shuddering to shore.
Microminiaturized, their corded bales.
They hear and bear a poetry of voes
and mulls that pounds and champs and strains; their shore
is all lean-tos, goodbyes, slipways, and bales.

6

'I want to see a sonnet with a rose.'
'After Stein that is impossible.'
'I believe few things are impossible.'
'But if a rose is a rose is a rose,
metaphor goes. Nothing's left but the rose.'
'Get on with it. It's the impossible

408

that you are there to break.' 'Impossible
the rose: love is not like it; the white rose
does not break the heart; the rose and the fire
are not one. It withers quickly, draws blood,
has scents most people like. Its dried and crushed
petals are ghosts for years in bowls.' 'The fire
shows. A ghost you call it? It's in your blood.
Is a crushed rose a crushed rose, is it crushed?'

7

The sick man saw the waves turning to grass.
A wheatfield swayed where there had once been sea.
His cabin juddered as it ploughed a sea
of bracken; gulls were larks; then feather-grass,
a smudge of harvesters and smocks, the grass
an ancient rolling peace. He slept. The sea
was there as grey and cold as ever sea
was, and the doctor sponged his brow. Grass
clung to the sweat in his dream. How he'd rave
of a poor steading, of a collie, straw,
an autumn chimney and a chestnut-fall:
and there was nothing but to let him rave,
and to restrain him in his bunk of straw.
The sea gaped for the sheeted clod to fall.

8

The happy lid of tins was ringing blue.
The carpet biscuits cowered weakly grey.
Their tipsy guest breathed all the mirrors grey,
searching for proof they'd take his eyes were blue.
'The tinsel on the tree is nearly blue,'
said Jan, but Martin shook his head. 'It's grey;
what's silver but a nervous grey?' And grey
drove from the winter room the ghost of blue.
– Curtains are drawn; coal glows and sparks up red;
the table lamp jumps softly out, purrs gold;
a rug lies panting flecks of ragged flame.
'See – steady up – your eye is really red,'
Jan tells the mirror man. He coughs. The gold
swims on her sea-horse pendant – his old flame.

'In eating dandelions it is the flavour
you must savour as it lingers on the finger.
Press the cut stem down smartly on your finger,
and lick the nippy milky ring of flavour.'
'What if I grow besotted with that flavour,
hallucinating an ambrosial finger
tip to tip with my own milky finger
creating charges of supernal flavour?'
'The lamb shall lie down with the dandelion,
the tiger shall go mad on tansy wine,
the bear shall snort himself asleep in combs.
Eat up, and tumble with the dandelion;
crown yourself with tansy, dive in wine;
burrow into the dripping gorgeous combs.'

I know you love me. Love is not the rhyme.
The figure in the pattern may be free.
Mine is the love you need. I leave you free.
I bind you only in this iron rhyme
where love is hidden, shifting, and the rhyme
is like a lock but the treasure moves free
beneath it. To be vulnerably free
is still the pain of love; only in rhyme
we breathe together like a wedded pair
whose union is the sweetness of a line
closed cleanly, not like that, but pausing, this.
The only ark is words, where pair and pair
might even there go tremblingly in line,
fearing what lies beyond the end of this –

Surrealism Revisited

An avuncular mussel stamped its foot and the sea took an attack of
    vertigo as far as it would go.
A dictionary without happiness was shot down as it gave a perfect
    bound over the heights of hands.
A caryatid ate a parrot with traffic jam.
A penthouse laid a bad egg and the prime minister took it to the
    country.
A crate of brandy snaps was driven mad by a strike of cream.

A giant wheel was arrested for blasphemy as it tried to thread a
    needle.
An interurban flyover turned into an old hag in broad daylight and
    was dismembered by cranes.
A bag of sleet was found in a blast furnace.
An ant's egg filled with speculators was detonated by remote
    control.
A silver centaur ridden by a golden boy plunged through the sky
    screaming for paint-stripper.
A clockwork orange by Fabergé fell out of a magpie's nest and ate
    humble pie.
A brazen yelp escaped from a condemned gasholder and was torn to
    pieces in a fight between scavengers and demons.
A book two miles high with phosphorescent letters in an unknown
    language stopped shipping in the channel for four days.
A cat barked and was deported.

Interview

   – When did you start writing sound-poetry?

   – Vindaberry am hookshma tintöl ensa ar'er.
     Vindashton hama haz temmi-bloozma töntek.

   – I see. So you were really quite precocious.
     And did your parents encourage you?

   – Zivva mimtod enna parahashtom ganna,
     spod zivva didtod quershpöt quindast volla!
     Mindetta brooshch quarva tönch bot.
     Spölva harabashtat su!

   – These family tensions must have been productive,
     since you began publishing so early.
     But then you became a roadmender. Why?

   – Tenni . . . tenni hara peridrombabura, hara
     peridrastabura, havar'epplood, epplood, nin?
     Orro . . . kaplazmavary intasoss.

   – So you had three years with the road-drill,
     And then you gravitated to oilrigs.
     Was this not rather deafening?

– Inch'pözatorten hüvr! Krüp. Smezoom.
  Har'ampasht bazalavawr, so'zn'elro-doss.
  Mo en er, mo en er, mo…akh!

– I suppose your long piece, 'Wind and Wave',
  was a breakthrough. Was that sound-poetry?

– Karavin hal hü bertontön shpin maizaro
  holma kanta bezboz 'sound', honna
  hal peg zmer kanta billinggo 'poetry'.
  Ziv kamara poonderdenchpan 'sound-poetry'-fa.

– Do you have a word for sound-poetry?

– Gooshch. Gooshch ensa vermü ander'ar.
  Vawl hinadobbra quöv quöv, gooshch.
  Gooshch inder sawbr, inder vabr, inder
  gullihara quöbr. Ain gooshch hob ahf.

– And do you have a favourite sound?

– . . . .

– Thank you for talking to us.

Ore

granite jasper topaz boulder dolomite
quartz gravel drumlin dolmen jet
pebble shale zircon macdiarmid diamond
chalk nodule marble gossan hematite
emery biggar bluejohn cairngorm talc
hornblende epidote ventifact elvan gabbro
opal basalt brownsbank graphite feldspar
beryl pumice schist porphyry tuff
mica hugh calcite bauxite malachite
chert slate butte grit scree
pegmatite azurite kieselguhr greywacke batholith
grieve gneiss loess tor karst
jade candymill pyrite limestone lava
sandstone crystal geode gypsum swallowhole
fulgurite coal gold lodestone christopher
plug shingle glass toadstone trap
bitumen amethyst sphene garnet esker
gondwanaland langholm laurasia whalsay pangaea

Stele

I was the friend of the sun.
I designed pyramids to approach the stars.
I fought the midsummer lions the fiercest.
I sent envoys with gold seals five thousand miles.
I had nine palaces with irrigated gardens called paradises.
I had hot pipes in winter and ice sherbet at other times.
I wore silk from the edge of the world.
I had twelve hawks and fourteen wives the most obedient.
I ordered to be played a twenty-stringed harp the greatest.
I made thirty thousand captive in my wars.
I made a stack of hands in the sunlight.
I gave their feet to the dogs.
I kept my sacrifices morning and evening.
I sold a deputation of widows into servitude.
I had a four-storey treasury the strongest.
I had river boats and sea boats and a wind boat over the desert.
I kept a thunderbolt in a small box always.
I designed this memorial stone the greatest.

Gorgon

Perseus with his parrot swung the head.
Oh what a stone was there, my masters,
my mistresses, my mizzes, my misters,
down Broadway, to Ibiza, the Great Wall
the parrot shrieked to see made stonier –
oh yes – and Graves in a cocked hat
for goddesses are kittle cattle, Brezhnev
stuck immemorially, immemorably to
the mausoleum, Moore nailed
to the dales and clamped, all marble, there,
a Queen of stone on a stone horse,
a tear of stone trundled through Ulster,
a sea of stone crammed with gushers
of stone oil and clanking skuas crashing
on waves harder than temple garden waves –
never rake them, my lords, my ladies,
but dust them when the wind blows. Medusa
is working on the wind: the head stares space solid.

Fountain

Water and stone, water and sunlight,
stone and rain, sunlight and rainbow,
splash and shadow, cloud passing,
whir of pigeons from the ages.
What the fountain says or sings
can only be the sound of water
fresh and sweet and undeciphered.
It is a dark throat, the stone
it springs from; the cool basin
darkens as it receives the song.
Yet it creates as it receives:
water falls on stone and water,
sings as it breaks in sound and light.
The pigeon seems to clap its hands,
the boy to fly, the cloud to be
in the fountain not the sky.
I wish that fountain never dried
and stone knew no other bride.

Book

There was a book of stone no one could read.
Sulky angels would not, could not turn its pages.
Thunder ran along the plain; the earth
cracked, not the volume. Moses, Jesus
never twitched among the clouds of dead. The pen
slept with the chisel, the characters filled with sand.
Even the world turns over in its sleep
but secret sheet clung to secret sheet.
Some say the sculptor was illustriously
illiterate in his trompe-l'œil and left
the book a laughing blank,
unopenable, the very title
undecipherable, as able
as a tomb to talk
of anything, of anything at all.
Are we not sick of reading? Hooves and heels
kick up the dunes and bury every mystery
under human codex-dreaded feet.

Mt Caucasus

I am the red rock; snow-drunk, rain-rich, unwashed still,
red, still red. Every day the body bled,
the body bled into me when I heard
the beating wings and in their shadow I grew cold.
Groans that half defied and half despaired,
a shriek at some unusual thrust,
and the long shudder of his drumming heels
as the dripping beak lifted and the wingbeats
faded westwards:
bound me to him, bind
me to him still.
Even those giant bones are so long gone,
shackles crumbled, spirit freed, hope
and pain fled down to men,
I ought to feel no weight,
no weight at all, except the heavy red of blood
that scales of gods and men have never measured,
my garnet locked solid away.

On the Water

There is something almost but not quite
beguiling about the thought of houseboat days.
Creaking, lapping, a sense of sway and the illusion
of moving might be the romance of a weekend.
Toy cabins, timeless horizontal afternoons
might at last get through Proust, while she
reverses roles at a punchbag on the deck,
knocks herself groggy, takes to cushions
as the sun goes down. These scenes
would only be for laughter though. Who is to make
the omelette, the one with throbbing shoulder or
the one dozy-eyed from Combray
on his back with a paper-knife,
reading against the light? The strenuous things
are great gods, bored by windows giving on water,
and even pretty hands trailed in water
knit nothing, and ask nothing to be done.
Life came from seas, lakes? It must be a joke.
The sluggish firth, like the latest bandage,
melts into the body of the earth,
cannot even sustain conversation.

It would be a breach to crow over a slammed chessman,
let alone slot in the Flying Dutchman cassette
they'd be sure to pack, these chained wanderers.
They dream, in fits and starts; it is only then
that the boat drifts, right down
to the sea and the keen wind, only then
that great gods clap their wings, and he designs
an airport, she a house and
a dress she stands in at the door to welcome
many guests and set parties ablaze.

Moving House

When they made their million they moved their house round
till it faced south as they had always wanted.
The excavation took time, and the re-piping
was almost surgically tricky, but in the event
the two-day slew-round accomplished itself with decorum.
She stayed in the house while it went round (he
with his briefcase in – Frankfurt, was it? she lost count
except of days at window-panes
and workmen's tea-cans, her own toast, the chauffeur's knock)
and thought it was like watching a watch
till the hand really seemed to move and not
be simply here then there then there and then an hour.
Soon she could not see all the road, beginnings
of an oak-tree came with the tentativeness
almost of being born into light and air
to edge into the angle of sight, and a blackbird there.
As lorries took their oblique thunder off,
heard only in the heat and dust, a hedge
as if Adam had said 'hedge!' in Eden,
if Eden had hedges, bristled its thrusting fringe
across the entire window, and behind it
fields she'd surely never seen.
A plane droned, faint, high over buttercups.
Evening had taken only half the arc; she strained;
back to the room was all, to switch a lamp.
Oh God there was so much to come!

416

Home on the Range

Blankets, the great moon, a fire for cougars' eyes
and nothing that is not ours and the wild's
is anything. Let the owl shriek and get on with it.
Blankets are great, the moon is our fire too, our eyes
prowl the prickly sky like cougars.
Someone's dreaming like a dog, kicks a log
and sparks join stars. Grey smoke,
almost white, winds, binding trees like brushwood.
Let the moon light them, let them warm us, for it's cold
by dying fires! Keep tents for scouts and such though,
I want to trail the old moon through
its roomy, roomless spaces.
Our heavy horses droop and doze.
My hands behind my head,
I settle a little into the hard ground.
I love to let the others drowse off one by one.
With blanket-mounds all round like snoring kings in tombs,
I lie back, light up, fix my feet
in stirrups not made for man
on a horse as grey as smoke
who'll never take me home.
It's all savanna, to the Pleiades
where the deer and the antelope play.

On the Needle's Point

Of course it is not a point at all.
We live here, and we should know.
I doubt indeed if there can be a point
in created things: the finest honing
uncovers more rough. Our ground stretches
for several miles, it is like living
on an asteroid, a bounded island
but with a bottomless core lost in mist
so far below and out of sight we feel
like pillar saints in earthly Syria.
The surface is slashed and pitted, greyish
with streaks of black and enigmatic
blue silver; spores of red lichen
gather and smoulder in crevices and caves.
At the edge it is very prodigious.
We have had some climbing over and down

417

with home-made crampons, disappearing,
perhaps making it to what we cannot imagine;
others fly off with fixed smiles,
vanish in their elation into violet haze.
But I like it on the point, good
is the dark cavern, good the craggy walks,
good the vertiginous bare brightness,
good the music, good the dance
when sometimes we join wings and drift
in interlinking circles, how many thousands
I could never tell, silent ourselves,
almost melting into light.

In the Bottle

It waits, like poison, for power. Ay, there's the rub.
The jinnee cocks its smoky ears, coughs a bit,
simulates a welter of a grin. Brass, glass,
who cares, bazaar, shop, cellar, someone
always comes, a palace cabinet, a ditch, the sea-bed,
divers, curators, tramps, sticky-fingers all,
Martians, time lords, a jinnee has patience
under cobwebs, coral, dust a foot thick, lava,
landslides, can keep unbroken
in flues and potholes, let them come
with war, fire, axes, put not your trust in princesses
who lay the sweet cylinder between their breasts,
for neither love nor fury will it budge
till the right nudge
rubs it and the top screams off with the seal
and its hope is clouds of masters masked as slaves.
Peace was a spirit passing in the dark,
none saw it go, drank to its lingering.
The power appeared all of gold,
or diamond, like a city, growing and working,
or like a mounting mass of platinum,
a shield, or some stellar prow,
a ship made for all hands.
But as for us, we sailed in her; broke bread;
rode storms; went far; made coasts, made love;
and coming to the harbour where we rest and write
we laughed, and put the ship back in the bottle.

Jordanstone Sonnets

1

The still queue creeps across the bright white square.
Clothes like soft metals smoulder in their sheen.
A cross between a stream and a machine
it rustles through the dry electric air.
Through doors and doors inside the dome it goes,
blinking in floodlights, frisked by hawklike guards.
The flashing of the scanned identicards
ripples like scales along the snaking rows.
And now a panel in the foot-thick steel
of the last vault retracts; through toughened glass
a painting of an apple on a plate
stares back at them, life-size, as bold as brass.
They file past, asking what it is they feel,
left in a world where feeling comes too late.

2

'Bury it with me,' he had said; they did.
It was not worth enough to vandalize.
But still – the flowers of the earth would rise
through flowers daubed on a cigar-box lid
and if he dreamed he'd like to smile at that,
and if not, well, it happened all the same;
someone might know, and give the thing a name.
It is not really hard to wonder at
the clumsy patience of the paint, or when
it was he had a sailor's tropic time
to make a gift of almost nothing, who
it was who mocked the gift and made him climb
his wry and fading treadmill, like all men
in love with a too trusted shining blue.

3

We motored through that sculpture two dark hours.
I tell you it was inconceivable,
except that someone did conceive, was able
and persistent with his super-redwood towers
to make a banyan of an afternoon.
Who ever motored through a Fabergé?
But gigantism's relative, they say.
A coach inside a golden egg will soon
draw crowds. LOOK TOUCH BUT DO NOT CLIMB it said
on the Moore bronzes looming in Hyde Park,

their caves, to children, irresistible.
The children vanish, like us, in the dark,
but soon emerge, brushed by the fearful bed
where life, not art, becomes invisible.

Caliban Falls Asleep in the Isle Full of Noises

grobravara hollaglob   /   ban ban cacaliban
thargarbonder skeeloheera   /   ban ban cacaliban
twing fang kong-pan-lang   /   ban ban cacaliban
stegzerbogzer stravavoorian   /   ban ban cacaliban
grawk blag bololozzin   /   ban ban cacaliban
stritch fretch bredzerbroz   /   ban ban cacaliban
squawk stog skreelahanla   /   ban ban cacaliban
squawk stroar breelerzorp   /   ban ban cacaliban
squawk roar gleezerhozla   /   ban ban cacaliban
squawk roar cheep stroz   /   ban ban cacaliban
squawk roar cheep caw   /   ban ban cacaliban
squawk roar cheep caw   /   ban ban caliban
squawk roar cheep caw   /   ban ban caban
squawk roar cheep caw   /   ban ban ban
squawk roar cheep caw   /   ban ban
squawk roar cheep caw   /   ban
squawk roar cheep caw
          roar cheep caw
               cheep caw
               cheep
                         caw
               cheep
               cheep

Iran

Tip the second lorry-load – the adultress is still groaning.
What sort of stones are these, for the love of Allah?
Is it pumice? There is only a trickle of blood.
She is actually moving, either her arms or her legs
cannot have been broken. Such a corps of bunglers
I have never, not ever, seen, even in the north.
Are you saboteurs, and of morality too?
Look at that: an arm sticking through the pile,

making a fist, of all things, not fingers
stretched in the sort of appeal your faint-heart Christ-lot
would fall for! Let her fist be rock-hard,
we have harder rocks to rain on her from quarries
as bottomless as her iniquities.
Tip it! Tip it on her! Right. Let her think of lovers
of stone alone, stone breath and brawn
to press those speaking peaks of breasts to rubble
and make her girdle redder than a rose.
You fools, the fist! The fist still shows!

The Coals

Before my mother's hysterectomy
she cried, and told me she must never bring
coals in from the cellar outside the house,
someone must do it for her. The thing itself
I knew was nothing, it was the thought
of that dependence. Her tears shocked me
like a blow. As once she had been taught,
I was taught self-reliance, discipline,
which is both good and bad. You get things done,
you feel you keep the waste and darkness back
by acts and acts and acts and acts and acts,
bridling if someone tells you this is vain,
learning at last in pain. Hardest of all
is to forgive yourself for things undone,
guilt that can poison life – away with it,
you say, and it is loath to go away.
I learned both love and joy in a hard school
and treasure them like the fierce salvage of
some wreck that has been built to look like stone
and stand, though it did not, a thousand years.

On the Train

(Glasgow-Nottingham 10-3-1981)

1
Bland railway cheese –
my neighbour made a face
as he opened his sandwich,
dug a packet of crisps

421

from his jacket pocket,
covered the pallid product
crisp by crisp, carefully,
placing them like scales,
with that faint frown
that anticipates the delight
of the first decent bite
when the sandwich is closed.
He eats. His brow clears.
Never mind the taste.
What's life without a crunch?

2
Not three blind mice
but three white ducks
cavorting in the gush
of a swollen stream,
and the farmer's wife
not with a carving-knife
but shaking a transistor
held to her angry ear
behind the streaming window.
Rain, grey March rain,
sodden fields shining,
did she want the weather report?
No one cut off the tails
of the three white ducks
which were wagging like mad
as they bounced about the water,
though whether with joy
or to shake off the rain
I cannot tell.
But it looked like joy;
as if the peevish woman
in her whitewashed prison
was paying for her progress
on the evolutionary tree.
She lit a cigarette
and hunched at the sill
while the ducks formed
a circle of three.

3
Lake District indeed –
floods of acres,

river-banks crumbling,
instant irrigation,
a few sheep like miseries
munching wet sedge.
A Windermere poster
crinkles on the board,
peels, reverts to lake.
But the roofs of slate,
flashing as we pass,
look to be wet
from an unfound forge
of metal more precious,
less prized, than gold.

A Riddle

Two men rose from the sea.
The bronze they were made of
must have moved by magic power.
Water poured from their shoulders
as they stared towards the shore
and with slow breasting force
strode there. The movement
of the naked bronze can be imagined
but with difficulty. Their high spears
they did not exactly brandish,
the stance of holding them
was sufficiently soldierly,
and one with a helmet,
one with a headband, both
with beards crusted in brine,
projected whatever their maker
had conceived as challenge through
two millenniums and more.
Tall, like ancient sentries,
they pace the shaken sand,
passing each other silently
while a hot sun climbs the sky.
Light flashes from their eyes
of diamond and lapis-lazuli,
and from the teeth of silver
in their half-opened mouths,
and from the polished copper
of their nipples and their lips.

Whatever stirred them from
long submarine sleep,
whatever keeps them measuring
that strip of beach, they are guards
of nothing but themselves,
unless it is of time,
of war, of courage, or of art.

A Pair of Cats
For G.

Through the Horse's Head with a bang we go,
the flap comes down, drifts of debris are lolling
like flakes of clawed paint. They belled us
so that deep space would hear our leaps
in and out the cat-doors of the universe.
But we made the tinkle a bang as we sprang so hard and tight
and left the traps to rattle. Those that listened
must have thought they had caught the Big Bang
on its second time round, buzzing about their dish
to prove the universe had at least begun
and was busy as a bee proceeding out of itself. Dear God!
We laughed so much we did it again, and again,
even went in search of the most unused cat-door of all
and made it creak and yaw and blunder out its bang
like an old cannon of the Main. Our main
was all before us, we scampered and we sang,
the doors were dark, but through we jumped,
and every time some shining skein or spiral of cream of stars
put us in a trance; we pawed the strands; cried;
took some, left many; played, supped, were satisfied.
When we looked back,
we had not left even a rent in the web.
I know they are calling for us. They lost us long ago.
The warning bell is gone in our delight.
Well, we are not what they thought we were.
We stretch, we spring. Where shall we appear?
Our tracks are in the life of things to come,
they close as soon as we have passed, but where we played
there will never be anything to take away
a lingering sense of liberty though half-forgotten
like the smell of clover from a seaward field
men wrestle with the sea to keep.

Little Blue Blue

(misprinted title of Norman MacCaig's poem
'Little Boy Blue' in *The Equal Skies*, 1980)

The mirror caught him as he straightened his sky-blue tie,
he was the son of sky and sea, five
feet high with wings furled, flexing
and shifting the sheen of his midnight blue
mohair tuxedo, tightening his saxe plastic belt
one notch, slicing the room with Gillette-blue eyes,
padding to the door in dove-blue brushed suede boots,
pinning his buttonhole periwinkle with a blue shark's grin.

> Once in the street
> he got the beat
> unfurled his wing
> began to sing
> 'She is, he is, she is my star'
> to his electric blue guitar.

Little Blue Blue flew to the land of denim,
bought himself jeans and a denim jacket and a denim cap,
what blue, what blue, he cried, and tried his jeans
with his mohair dinner-jacket, tried his mohair trousers
with his denim bomber jacket, tried his denim cap
with his saxe-blue belt and his dove-blue boots and a
navy-blue Adidas bag and nothing else
till the slate-blue pigeons all blushed purple, but

> once in the street
> he got the beat
> unfurled his wing
> began to sing
> 'He is, she is, he is my star'
> to his electric blue guitar.

Then he went to sea and sailed the blue main
in his navy jersey with his wings well battened down,
knocked up a tattoo parlour in old Yokohama,
got bluebirds on his hands and a blue pierced heart,
and a geisha-girl on his shoulder with a blue rose,
and a trail of blue hounds chasing a blue fox
into covert – oh, he said, I'm black and blue all over,
but he staggered out into that Nippon moon, and

> once in the street
> he got the beat

unfurled his wing
began to sing
'She is, he is, she is my star'
to his electric blue guitar.

Back home, he bought a cobalt Talbot Sunbeam
with aquamarine upholstery and citizens band radio,
said Blue Blue here, do you read me, do you read me?
as he whizzed up to Scrabster in his royal-blue pinstripes.
And his dashboard sent him messages without measure,
for everybody loves a blue angel, whistling
at the wheel under azure highland skies.
And he stopped at each village, and smiled like the sun, for

once in the street
he got the beat
unfurled his wing
began to sing
'He is, she is, he is my star'
to his electric blue guitar.

Eve and Adam

Adam sleeps so sound
I sometimes raise myself on one elbow
and look at him I cannot say how long
in the darkness. Nightingale,
owl, cricket – everything is music.
A trace of moonlight falls on his face.
I bend, and brush it with my breasts, but he
sleeps on, and never, never will he know.
I have another secret: I call to the owl,
not loud, and he as gently answers me.
How friendly all the creatures are! I love them
but neither language nor music can tell
what I feel for Adam – even his black hair
lying tangled in a helpless mass
over his shoulders, nothing, nothing
to his eyes, his voice, his hands, holds me
as the web of trees, unknowing,
holds the night-clouds and the moon. Oh
but if I am the moon I move, I pass into shadow,
I roll far from him and from myself, I lie back
staring into deepest darkness, lift my arm

426

for the great moth to light on purring in white fur
and whisper to him
in a waft of tansy,
'I have forgotten Adam.'
– Tonight I cannot sleep, cannot wake, cannot dream, seem
suspended like a woody pool reflecting woods
and sky and clouds, unreal and more than real
their world, unreal and more than real
my soul, diffused in wonder and surmise
above a body I have lost,
glimmering spreadeagled in eglantine.
– The moth crawls down my flank like Adam's finger,
the moon floods through our careless arbour roof,
I am so much awake I can hear the waterfalls
that feed our lively, seldom-mirroring pools,
and Adam's heart against my breast.
I hear it all and feel it all, and almost cry
my longing as he twitches in his dream
and clasp him, saying at his ear
what I have seen where I have been,
my secrets, to his silence,
and twine my hand in his until he wakens
shouting; comfort him; love him;
blot him from the distant stars.
Soon it will be grey. He has forgotten his dream.
I am the one who remembers dreams.
The blackbird sings. I shall make a comb for my hair.

Grendel

It is being nearly human
gives me this spectacular darkness.
The light does not know what to do with me.
I rise like mist and I go down like water.
I saw them soused with wine behind their windows.
I watched them making love, twisting like snakes.
I heard a blind man pick the strings, and sing.
There are torches everywhere, there are faces
swimming in shine and sweat and beer and grins and greed.
There are tapers confusing the stacked spears.
There are queens on their knees at idols, crosses, lamps.
There are handstand clowns knocked headlong by maudlin heroes.
There are candles in the sleazy bowers, the whores
sleep all day with mice across their feet.

The slung warhorn gleams in the drizzle,
the horses shift their hooves and shiver.
It is all a pestilence, life within life
and movement within movement, lips meeting,
grooming of mares, roofs plated with gold,
hunted pelts laid on kings,
neck-veins bursting from greasy torques,
pouches of coins gamed off, slaves and outlaws
eating hailstones under heaven.
Who would be a man? Who would be the winter sparrow
that flies at night by mistake into a lighted hall
and flutters the length of it in zigzag panic,
dazed and terrified by the heat and noise and smoke,
the drink-fumes and the oaths, the guttering flames,
feast-bones thrown to a snarl of wolfhounds,
flash of swords in sodden sorry quarrels,
till at last he sees the other door
and skims out in relief and joy
into the stormy dark?
– Black grove, black lake, black sky,
no shoe or keel or wing undoes your stillness
as I plod through the fens and prowl
in my own place and sometimes stand many hours, as now,
above those unreflecting waters, reflecting as I can
on men, and on their hideous clamorous brilliance
that beats the ravens' beaks into the ground
and douses a million funeral pyres.

Tarkovsky in Glasgow

We drifted with wide eyes till the sleet came down.
The basket soon filled with a white sodden mire.
We dug our stung cheeks into collars and stared straight out
at spires; our sagging nylon swags descended,
belched, hissed, flapped, hung like a silly day-gown;
the drunken boat scraped a mausoleum and beached us
tottering alive on the humpy reef of the Necropolis.
A dog was talking to a drunk,
whining him away to a warm supper.
Drunk stones leaned over with snow on their backs
and dry bellies. Obliterated all the messages
appeared. Organ music and a smell of ether
coiled up the paths. A swig of vodka
would not make us drunk. Replacing caps,
we coughed, and beat our hands together and began

laughing so loud the mongrel darted off
and the drunk said, 'Wha'? Wha's happ'ning? Eh? Eh?'
and collapsed like a soft sign in cyrillic.
We threw him a half-empty Stolichnaya,
but I failed to laugh again as I caught his red eyes
blinking with indignation. I shivered at us. We were off.
We found the mausoleum we were looking for,
stepped in, tore up the grating in the floor,
squeezed through, down, one by one, into the flank of the hill,
under the hill, into corridors of old workings,
our torches making monsters through the coaly fetor
and our good boots clashing the grit like teeth.
We came to a grey crypt banked with stalagmites
waiting to be played by phantoms. It opened
into a sickly hall, high, precipitous,
where stalactites swooped like knives on
an operating table of anthracite;
the groans, at most, were ours, the sighs
were gases from the flues and crevices.
We stumbled through the stench of blood and dead music.
We heard, of all things, a dog whimper, and saw it,
a black one, behind us. Where had it come from?
We entered a complex of passages
where echoes distorted our voices
as we scuttled in Indian file
and called to one another through the rubble.
Tarkovsky! Thaw! Chaney! Royal! Mungo! Gonny!
At last we came to the door of the drunken porter,
slewing round on us with his little brown tyke in his arms
and almost knocking his pint from the ledge at his elbow.
We showed our cards, and strode into the chamber.
There were so many at that marble banquet
that we could not even see where the tables
vanished in a far-off haze of gold and smoke.
We must have disturbed the guests, who were all paused
with a spoon or a glass half raised, their faces set
like marble, while flakes of snow
came down on them, sparkling faintly,
from the clouds of that roofless hall.
Obliterated, as we sternly watched,
the rows of knuckles and the rows of medals,
the plate, the great white cloth, the bosoms and the ties,
and then at last the starving lips and eyes,
fading to the smudge a child
might sketch in chalk and brush away
indoors, one wintry afternoon.
Our greatcoats dripped. We stood, and slowly willed.

Jack London in Heaven

Part the clouds, let me look down.
Oh god that earth. A breeze comes from the sea
and humpback fogs blanch off to blindness, the sun
hits Frisco, it shines solid up to heaven.
I can't bear not to see a brisk day on the Bay,
it drives me out of my mind but I can't bear
not to watch the choppy waters, Israfel.
I got a sea-eagle once to come up here
screaming and turn a prayer-wheel or two
with angry buffets till the sharpshooters
sent him to hell, and I groaned,
grew dark with disfavour. – What,
I should pray now? For these thoughts?
Here are some more. I was up at four
for psalms, shawms, smarms, salaams, yessirs, yesmaams,
felt-tipped hosannas melting into mist,
a mushroom high, an elation of vapours,
a downpour of dumpy amens. Azazel,
I am sick of fireflies. It's a dumb joss.
– You know I'm a spoilt angel? What happens to us?
I'm not so bright – or bright, perhaps. God knows!
They almost let me fall through heaven craning
to see sunshine dappling the heaving gunmetal
of the Oakland Estuary – the crawl, the swell, the crests
I could pull up to touch and wet my hands
let down a moment into time and space.
How long will they allow me to remember
as I pick the cloud-rack apart and peer?
The estuary, Israfel, the glittery estuary, August '96!
My last examination has scratched to a finish,
I'm rushing to the door, whooping and squawking,
I dance down the steps, throw my hat in the air
as the dusty invigilator frowns, gathers in
that furious harvest of four months' cramming,
nineteen hours a day – my vigils, Azazel,
my holy vigils – the oyster-pirate hammering
at the gates of the state university.
It's enough. I got in. But at that time
I took a boat out on the ebb
to be alone where no book ever was.
I scudded dreaming through the creamy rings
of light and water, followed the shore
and thought of earth and heaven and myself
till I saw a shipyard I knew, and the delta rushes
and the weeds and the tin wharves, and smelt the ropes

and some tobacco-smoke, and longed for company.
– Evensong? I'm not coming to evensong.
Get off, get away. Go on, sing for your supper!
Bloody angels! – So I sailed in, made fast,
and there was Charley, and Liz, and Billy and Joe, and Dutch
– that desperate handsome godlike drunken man –
old friends, Azazel, old friends that clambered over me
and sang and wept and filled me with whisky and beer
brought teetering across the railroad tracks
all that long noon.
They would have kept me there, oh, for ever
but I could see the blue through the open door,
that blue, my sea, and they knew
I had to be away, and got me stumbling down the wharf steps
into a good salmon boat, with charcoal and a brazier
and coffee and a pot and a pan and a fresh-caught fish
and cast me off into a stiff wind.
I tell you, Israfel, the sea was white
and half of it was in my boat
with my sail set hard like a board.
Everything whipped and cracked
in pure green glory as
I stood braced at the mast
and roared out 'Shenandoah'.
Did Odysseus get to heaven?
I came down to earth, at Antioch,
sobered in the sunset shadows, tied up
alongside a potato sloop, had friends
aboard there too, who sizzled my fish for me
and gave me stew and crusty bread and claret,
claret in great pint mugs, and wrapped me in blankets
warmer and softer than the clouds of heaven.
What did we not talk of as we smoked,
sea-tales Odysseus might have known,
under the same night wind, the same wild rigging.
– Azazel, I must get down there!
I am a wasting shade, I am drifting and dying
by these creeping streams. If you are my friend,
tell them my trouble. Tell them
they cannot make me a heaven
like the tide-race and the tiller
and a broken-nailed hand
and the shrouds of Frisco.

Cinquevalli

Cinquevalli is falling, falling.
The shining trapeze kicks and flirts free,
solo performer at last.
The sawdust puffs up with a thump,
settles on a tangle of broken limbs.
St Petersburg screams and leans.
His pulse flickers with the gas-jets. He lives.

Cinquevalli has a therapy.
In his hospital bed, in his hospital chair
he holds a ball, lightly, lets it roll round his hand,
or grips it tight, gauging its weight and resistance,
begins to balance it, to feel its life attached to his
by will and knowledge, invisible strings
that only he can see. He throws it
from hand to hand, always different,
always the same, always
different, always the
same.
His muscles learn to think, his arms grow very strong.

Cinquevalli in sepia
looks at me from an old postcard: bundle of enigmas.
Half faun, half military man; almond eyes, curly hair,
conventional moustache; tights, and a tunic loaded
with embroideries, tassels, chains, fringes; hand on hip
with a large signet-ring winking at the camera
but a bull neck and shoulders and a cannon-ball
at his elbow as he stands by the posing pedestal;
half reluctant, half truculent,
half handsome, half absurd,
but let me see you forget him: not to be done.

Cinquevalli is a juggler.
In a thousand theatres, in every continent,
he is the best, the greatest. After eight years perfecting
he can balance one billiard ball on another billiard ball
on top of a cue on top of a third billiard ball
in a wine-glass held in his mouth. To those
who say the balls are waxed, or flattened,
he patiently explains the trick will only work
because the spheres are absolutely true.
There is no deception in him. He is true.

Cinquevalli is juggling with a bowler,
a walking-stick, a cigar, and a coin.
Who foresees? How to please.
The last time round, the bowler
flies to his head, the stick sticks in his hand,
the cigar jumps into his mouth, the coin
lands on his foot – ah, but
is kicked into his eye
and held there as the miraculous monocle
without which the portrait would be incomplete.

Cinquevalli is practising.
He sits in his dressing-room talking to some friends,
at the same time writing a letter with one hand
and with the other juggling four balls.
His friends think of demons, but
'You could all do this,' he says,
sealing the letter with a billiard ball.

Cinquevalli is on the high wire in Odessa.
The roof cracks, he is falling, falling
into the audience, a woman breaks his fall,
he cracks her like a flea, but lives.

Cinquevalli broods in his armchair in Brixton Road.
He reads in the paper about the shells whining
at Passchendaele, imagines the mud and the dead.
He goes to the window and wonders through that dark evening
what is happening in Poland where he was born.
His neighbours call him a German spy.
'Kestner, Paul Kestner, that's his name!'
'Keep Kestner out of the British music-hall!'
He frowns; it is cold; his fingers seem stiff and old.

Cinquevalli tosses up a plate of soup
and twirls it on his forefinger; not a drop spills.
He laughs, and well may he laugh
who can do that. The astonished table
breathe again, laugh too, think the world
a spinning thing that spills, for a moment, no drop.

Cinquevalli's coffin sways through Brixton
only a few months before the Armistice.
Like some trick they cannot get off the ground
it seems to burden the shuffling bearers, all their arms

cross-juggle that displaced person, that man
of balance, of strength, of delights and marvels,
in his unsteady box at last into the earth.

Sonnets from Scotland
1984

O Wechsel der Zeiten! Du Hoffnung des Volks!
Brecht

Slate

There is no beginning. We saw Lewis
laid down, when there was not much but thunder
and volcanic fires; watched long seas plunder
faults; laughed as Staffa cooled. Drumlins blue as
bruises were grated off like nutmegs; bens,
and a great glen, gave a rough back we like
to think the ages must streak, surely strike,
seldom stroke, but raised and shaken, with tens
of thousands of rains, blizzards, sea-poundings
shouldered off into night and memory.
Memory of men! That was to come. Great
in their empty hunger these surroundings
threw walls to the sky, the sorry glory
of a rainbow. Their heels kicked flint, chalk, slate.

Carboniferous
For I.R.

Diving in the warm seas around Bearsden,
cased in our superchitin scuba-gear,
we found a world so wonderfully clear
it seemed a heaven given there and then.
Hardly! *Et in Arcadia*, said the shark,
ego. We stumbled on a nest of them.
How could bright water that hid nothing stem
our ancient shudder? They themselves were dark,
but all we saw was the unsinister
ferocious tenderness of mating shapes,
a raking love that scoured their skin to shreds.
We feared instead the force that could inter
such life and joy, in fossil clays, for apes
and men to haul into their teeming heads.

Post-Glacial

The glaciers melt slowly in the sun.
The ice groans as it shrinks back to the pole.
Loud splits and cracks send shudders through the shoal
of herring struggling northwards, but they run

437

steadily on into the unknown roads
and the whole stream of life runs with them. Brown
islands hump up in the white of land, down
in the valleys a fresh drained greenness loads
fields like a world first seen, and when mild rains
drive back the blizzards, a new world it is
of grain that thrusts its frenzied spikes, and trees
whose roots race under the stamped-out remains
of nomad Grampian fires. Immensities
are mind, not ice, as the bright straths unfreeze.

In Argyll
For A.R.

We found the poet's skull on the machair.
It must have bobbed ashore from that shipwreck
where the winged men went down in rolling dreck
of icebound webs, oars, oaths, armour, blind air.
It watches westward still; dry, white as chalk,
perfect at last, in silence and at rest.
Far off, he sang of Nineveh the blest,
incised his tablets, stalked the dhow-bright dock.
Now he needs neither claws nor tongue to tell
of things undying. Hebridean light
fills the translucent bone-domes. Nothing brings
the savage brain back to its empty shell,
distracted by the shouts, the reefs, the night,
fighting sleet to fix the tilt of its wings.

The Ring of Brodgar

'If those stones could speak –' Do not wish too loud.
They can, they do, they will. No voice is lost.
Your meanest guilts are bonded in like frost.
Your fearsome sweat will rise and leave its shroud.
I well recall the timeprint of the Ring
of Brodgar we discovered, white with dust
in twenty-second-century distrust
of truth, but dustable, with truths to bring
into the freer ages, as it did.
A thin groan fought the wind that tugged the stones.

It filled an auditorium with pain.
Long was the sacrifice. Pity ran, hid.
Once they heard the splintering of the bones
they switched the playback off, in vain, in vain.

Silva Caledonia

The darkness deepens, and the woods are long.
We shall never see any stars. We thought
we heard a horn a while back, faintly brought
through barks and howls, the nearest to a song
you ever heard in these grey dripping glens.
But if there were hunters, we saw not one.
Are there bears? Mist. Wolves? Peat. Is there a sun?
Where are the eyes that should peer from those dens?
Marsh-lights, yes, mushroom-banks, leaf-mould, rank ferns,
and up above, a sense of wings, of flight,
of clattering, of calls through fog. Yet men,
going about invisible concerns,
are here, and our immoderate delight
waits to see them, and hear them speak, again.

Pilate at Fortingall

A Latin harsh with Aramaicisms
poured from his lips incessantly; it made
no sense, for surely he was mad. The glade
of birches shamed his rags, in paroxysms
he stumbled, toga'd, furred, blear, brittle, grey.
They told us he sat here beneath the yew
even in downpours; ate dog-scraps. Crows flew
from prehistoric stone to stone all day.
'See him now.' He crawled to the cattle-trough
at dusk, jumbled the water till it sloshed
and spilled into the hoof-mush in blue strands,
slapped with useless despair each sodden cuff,
and washed his hands, and watched his hands, and washed
his hands, and watched his hands, and washed his hands.

The Mirror

There is a mirror only we can see.
It hangs in time and not in space. The day
goes down in it without ember or ray
and the newborn climb through it to be free.
The multitudes of the world cannot know
they are reflected there; like glass they lie
in glass, shadows in shade, they could not cry
in airless wastes but that is where they go.
We cloud it, but it pulses like a gem,
it must have caught a range of energies
from the dead. We breathe again; nothing shows.
Back in space, *ubi solitudinem*
faciunt pacem appellant. Ages
drum-tap the flattened homes and slaughtered rows.

The Picts

Names as from outer space, names without roots:
Bes, son of Nanammovvezz; Bliesblituth
that wild buffoon throned in an oaken booth;
wary Edarnon; brilliant Usconbuts;
Canutulachama who read the stars.
Where their fame flashed from, went to, is unknown.
The terror of their warriors is known,
naked, tattooed on every part (the hairs
of the groin are shaved on greatest fighters,
the fine bone needle dipped in dark-blue woad
rings the flesh with tender quick assurance:
he is *diuperr cartait*, rich pin; writers
like us regain mere pain on that blue road,
they think honour comes with the endurance).

Colloquy in Glaschu

God but *le son du cor*, Columba sighed
to Kentigern, *est triste au fond silvarum!*
Frater, said Kentigern, I see no harm.
J'aime le son du cor, when day has died,
deep in the *bois*, and oystercatchers rise

before the fowler as he trudges home
and *sermo lupi* loosens the grey loam.
À l'horizon lointain is paradise,
abest silentium, le cor éclate –
– *et meurt*, Columba mused, but Kentigern
replied, *renaît et se prolonge*. The cell
is filled with song. Outside, *puer cantat*.
Veni venator sings the gallus kern.
The saints dip startled cups in Mungo's well.

Memento

over the cliff-top and into the mist
across the heather and down to the peat
here with the sheep and where with the peeweet
through the stubble and by the pheasant's tryst
above the pines and past the northern lights
along the voe and out to meet the ice
among the stacks and round their kreidekreis
in summer lightning and beneath white nights
behind the haar and in front of the tower
beyond the moor and against writ and ring
below the mort-gate and outwith all kind
under the hill and at the boskless bower
over the hills and far away to bring
over the hills and far away to mind

Matthew Paris

'North and then north and north again we sailed,
not that God is in the north or the south
but that the north is great and strange, a mouth
of baleen filtering the unknown, veiled
spoutings and sportings, curtains of white cold.
I made a map, I made a map of it.
Here I have bristly Scotland, almost split
in two, what sea-lochs and rough marches, old
forts, new courts, when Alexander their king
is dead will they live in love and peace, get
bearings, trace mountains, count stars, take capes, straits
in their stride as well as crop and shop, bring
luck home? *Pelagus vastissimum et
invium*, their element, my margin, waits.'

441

At Stirling Castle, 1507

Damian, D'Amiens, Damiano –
we never found out his true name, but there
he crouched, swarthy, and slowly sawed the air
with large strapped-on bat-membrane wings. Below
the battlements, a crowd prepared to jeer.
He frowned, moved back, and then with quick crow struts
ran forward, flapping strongly, whistling cuts
from the grey heavy space with his black gear
and on a huge spring and a cry was out
beating into vacancy, three, four, five,
till the crawling scaly Forth and the rocks
and the upturned heads replaced that steel shout
of sky he had replied to – left alive,
and not the last key snapped from high hard locks.

Thomas Young, M.A. (St Andrews)
For J.C.B.

'Yes, I taught Milton. He was a sharp boy.
He never understood predestination,
but then who does, within the English nation?
I did my best to let him see what joy
there must be in observing the damnation
of those whom God makes truly reprobate:
the fair percentage does not decreate
heaven, but gives all angels the elation
they are justly decreed to have deserved.
We took a short tour up to Auchterarder,
where there are strong sound sergeants of the creed,
but John could only ask how God was served
by those who neither stand nor wait, their ardour
rabid (he said) to expunge virtue's seed?'

Lady Grange on St Kilda

'They say I'm mad, but who would not be mad
on Hirta, when the winter raves along
the bay and howls through my stone hut, so strong
they thought I was and so I am, so bad

442

they thought I was and beat me black and blue
and banished me, my mouth of bloody teeth
and banished me to live and cry beneath
the shriek of sea-birds, and eight children too
we had, my lord, though I know what you are,
sleekit Jacobite, showed you up, you bitch,
and screamed outside your close at Niddry's Wynd,
until you set your men on me, and far
I went from every friend and solace, which
was cruel, out of mind, out of my mind.'

Theory of the Earth

James Hutton that true son of fire who said
to Burns 'Aye, man, the rocks melt wi the sun'
was sure the age of reason's time was done:
what but imagination could have read
granite boulders back to their molten roots?
And how far back was back, and how far on
would basalt still be basalt, iron iron?
Would second seas re-drown the fossil brutes?
'We find no vestige of a beginning,
no prospect of an end.' They died almost
together, poet and geologist,
and lie in wait for hilltop buoys to ring,
or aw the seas gang dry and Scotland's coast
dissolve in crinkled sand and pungent mist.

Poe in Glasgow

The sun beat on the Moby-Dick-browed boy.
It was a day to haunt the Broomielaw.
The smell of tar, the slap of water, draw
his heart out from the wharf in awe and joy.
Oh, not Virginia, not Liverpool –
and not the Isle of Dogs or Greenwich Reach –
but something through the masts – a blue – a beach –
an inland gorge of rivers green and cool.
'Wake up!' a sailor coiled with bright rope cried
and almost knocked him off his feet, making
towards his ship. 'You want to serve your time

as cabin-boy's assistant, eh?' The ride
and creak of wood comes home, testing, shaking.
'Where to?' He laughed. 'To Arnheim, boy, Arnheim!'

De Quincey in Glasgow

Twelve thousand drops of laudanum a day
kept him from shrieking. Wrapped in a duffle
buttoned to the neck, he made his shuffle,
door, table, window, table, door, bed, lay
on bed, sighed, groaned, jumped from bed, sat and wrote
till the table was white with pages, rang
for his landlady, ordered mutton, sang
to himself with pharmacies in his throat.
When afternoons grew late, he feared and longed
for dusk. In that high room in Rottenrow
he looks out east to the Necropolis.
Its crowded tombs rise jostling, living, thronged
with shadows, and the granite-bloodying glow
flares on the dripping bronze of a used kris.

Peter Guthrie Tait, Topologist

Leith dock's lashed spars roped the young heart of Tait.
What made gales tighten, not undo, each knot?
Nothing's more dazzling than a ravelling plot.
Stubby crisscrossing fingers fixed the freight
so fast he started sketching on the spot.
The mathematics of the twisted state
uncoiled its waiting elegances, straight.
Old liquid chains that strung the gorgeous tot
God spliced the mainbrace with, put on the slate,
and sent creation reeling from, clutched hot
as caustic on Tait's brain when he strolled late
along the links and saw the stars had got
such gouts and knots of well-tied fire the mate
must sail out whistling to his stormy lot.

G.M. Hopkins in Glasgow

For J.A.M.R.

Earnestly nervous yet forthright, melted
by bulk and warmth and unimposed rough grace,
he lit a ready fuse from face to face
of Irish Glasgow. Dark tough tight-belted
drunken Fenian poor ex-Ulstermen
crouched round a brazier like a burning bush
and lurched into his soul with such a push
that British angels blanched in mid-amen
to see their soldier stumble like a Red.
Industry's pauperism singed his creed.
He blessed them, frowned, beat on his hands. The load
of coal-black darkness clattering on his head
half-crushed, half-fed the bluely burning need
that trudged him back along North Woodside Road.

1893

For P. McC.

A Slav philosopher in Stronachlachar:
Vladimir Solovyov looked down the loch.
The sun was shimmering on birk and sauch.
'This beats the fishy vennels of St Machar,'
he said, and added, 'Inversnaid tomorrow!'
A boatman rowing to him from infinity
turned out to be a boatwoman. 'Divinity!'
he cried, 'shake back your hair, and shake back sorrow!'
The boat was grounded, she walked past him singing.
To her, he was a man of forty, reading.
Within him the words mounted: 'Sing for me,
dancing like Wisdom before the Lord, bringing
your mazy unknown waters with you, seeding
the Northern Lights and churning up the sea!'

The Ticket

'There are two rivers: how can a drop go
from one stream to the next?' Gurdjieff was asked.
The unflummoxable master stretched, basked.

445

'It must buy a ticket,' he said. A row
of demons dragged the Inaccessible
Pinnacle through the centre of Glasgow,
barking out sweaty orders, pledged to show
it was bloody juggernaut-time, able
to jam shrieking children under crashed spires.
But soon that place began to recompose,
the film ran back, the walls stood, the cries died,
the demons faded to familiar fires.
In New York, Gurdjieff changed his caftan, chose
a grape, sat, smiled. 'They never paid their ride.'

North Africa

Why did the poets come to the desert?
They learned the meaning of an oasis,
the meaning of heat, fellahin's phrases,
tents behind the khamsin-blasted dannert.
We watched MacLean at the Ruweisat Ridge
giving a piercing look as he passed by
the fly-buzzed grey-faced dead; swivelled our eye
west through tank-strewn dune and strafed-out village
with Henderson; and Hay saw Bizerta
burn; Garioch was taken at Tobruk,
parched *Kriegsgefangener*, calm, reading *Shveik*;
Morgan ate sand, slept sand at El Ballah
while gangrened limbs dropped in the pail; Farouk
fed Fraser memorandums like a shrike.

Caledonian Antisyzygy

– Knock knock. – Who's there? – Doctor. – Doctor Who? – No,
just Doctor. – What's up Doc? – Stop, that's all cock.
– O.K. – Knock knock. – Who's there? – Doctor Who. – Doc-
tor Who who? – Doctor, who's a silly schmo?
– Right. Out! – Aw. – Well, last chance, come on. – Knock knock
– Who's there? – Doctor Jekyll. – Doctor Jekyll
who? – Doctor, 'd ye kill Mr Hyde? – Pig-swill!
Nada! Rubbish! Lies! Garbage! Never! Schlock!
– Calm down, your turn. – Knock knock. – Who's there? – Docto
Knox. – Doctor Knox who? – Doctor Knocks Box Talks.

Claims T.V. Favours Grim Duo, Burke, Hare.
– Right, join hands. Make sure the door is locked, or
nothing will happen. – Dark yet? – Cover clocks.
– Knock. – Listen! – Is there anybody there?

Travellers (1)

The universe is like a trampoline.
We chose a springy clump near Arrochar
and with the first jump shot past Barnard's Star.
The universe is like a tambourine.
We clashed a brace of planets as we swung
some rolling unknown ringing system up
above our heads, and kicked it too. To sup,
sleep, recoup, we dropped to the House of Tongue.
The universe is like a trampoline.
Tongue threw us into a satellite bank.
We photographed a mole; a broch; the moon.
The universe is like a tambourine.
We stretched out, shook Saturn, its janglings sank
and leapt till it was neither night nor noon.

Travellers (2)

As it was neither night nor noon, we mused
a bit, dissolved ourselves a bit, took stock,
folded the play away and turned the lock.
Exhilarated travellers unused
to feeling blank can love the nescience
of a stilled moment. Undenied the time,
a lingering, a parasol, a lime.
There is no happiness in prescience,
and there is no regret in happiness.
A coast swept out in headlands and was lost.
And there we could have left the thought unthought
or hope undrafted, but that a bright press
of lights showed where a distant liner crossed.
Its horn blew through us, urgent, deep, unsought.

Seferis on Eigg

The isles of Scotland! the isles of Scotland!
But Byron sang elsewhere; loved, died elsewhere.
Seferis stiffly cupped warm blue May air
and slowly sifted it from hand to hand.
It was good and Greek. Amazed to find it,
he thought the dancing sea, the larks, the boats
spoke out as clear as from Aegean throats.
What else there was – he might half-unwind it.
One day he visited the silent cave
where Walter Scott, that tawdry Ulysses,
purloined a suffocated clansman's skull.
Crowns of Scottish kings were sacred; the lave
can whistle for dignity – who misses
them, peasants, slaves? Greeks, too, could shrug the cull.

Matt McGinn

We cannot see it, it keeps changing so.
All round us, *in and out, above, below,*
at evening, *phantom figures come and go,*
silently, *just a magic shadow show.*
A hoarse voice singing *come love watch with me*
was all we heard on that fog-shrouded bank.
We thought we saw him, but if so, he sank
into the irrecoverable sea.
Dear merry man, what is your country now?
Does it keep changing? Will we ever see it?
A crane, a backcourt, an accordion?
Or sherbet dabs, henna, and jasmined brow?
The book is clasped, and time will never free it.
Mektub. The caravan winds jangling on.

Post-Referendum

'No no, it will not do, it will not be.
I tell you you must leave your land alone.
Who do you think is poised to ring the phone?
Fish your straitjacket packet from the sea
you threw it in, get your headphones mended.

You don't want the world now, do you? Come on,
you're pegged out on your heathery futon,
take the matches from your lids, it's ended.'
We watched the strong sick dirkless Angel groan,
shiver, half-rise, batter with a shrunk wing
the space the Tempter was no longer in.
He tried to hear feet, calls, car-doors, shouts, drone
of engines, hooters, hear a meeting sing.
A coin clattered at the end of its spin.

Gangs

Naw naw, there's nae big wurds here, there ye go.
Christ man ye're in a bad wey, kin ye staun?
See here noo, wance we know jist where we're gaun,
we'll jump thon auld – stoap that, will ye – *Quango*.
Thaim that squealt *Lower Inflation*, aye, thaim,
plus thae *YY Zero Wage Increase* wans,
they'll no know what hit thim. See yours, and Dan's,
and mine's, that's three chibs. We'll soon hiv a team.
Whit's that? *Non-Index-Linked!* Did ye hear it?
Look! *Tiny Global Recession!* C'moan then,
ya bams, Ah'll take ye. *Market Power fae Drum!*
Dave, man, get up. Dave! Ach, ye're no near it.
Ah'm oan ma tod. But they'll no take a len
a me, Ah'm no deid yet, or deif, or dumb!

After a Death

A writer needs nothing but a table.
His pencil races, pauses, crosses out.
Five years ago he lost his friend, without
him he struggles through a different fable.
The one who died, he is the better one.
The other one is selfish, ruthless, he
uses people, floats in an obscure sea
of passions, half-drowns as the livid sun
goes down, calls out for help he will not give.
Examine yourself! He is afraid to.
But that is not quite true, I saw him look
into that terrible place, let him live
at least with what is eternally due
to love that lies in earth in cold Carluke.

449

Not the Burrell Collection

The Buenos Aires Vase, one mile across,
flickering with unsleeping silent flames,
its marble carved in vine-leaves mixed with names,
shirtless ones and *desaparecidos*;
a collier's iron collar, riveted,
stamped by his Burntisland owner; a spade
from Babiy Yar; a blood-crust from the blade
that jumped the corpse of Wallace for his head;
the stout rack soaked in Machiavelli's sweat;
a fire-circled scorpion; a blown frog;
the siege of Beirut in stained glass; a sift
of Auschwitz ash; an old tapestry-set
unfinished, with a crowd, a witch, a log;
a lachrymatory no man can lift.

1983

'A parrot Edward Lear drew has just died.'
There was a young lady of Corstorphine
who adopted a psittacine orphan.
It shrieked and it cried: they threw far and wide
her ashes right over Corstorphine. Zoos
guard and pamper the abandoned squawkers,
tickle stories from the raunchy talkers,
shoulder a bold centenarian muse
over artists deaf as earth. 'Oho! Lear
sketched me, delirious old man, how he
shuffled about, his tabby on the sill,
a stew on the stove, a brush in his ear,
and sometimes hummed, or he buzzed like a bee,
painting parrots and all bright brave things still!'

A Place of Many Waters

Infinitely variable water,
let seals bob in your silk or loll on Mull
where the lazy fringes rustle; let hull
and screw slew you round, blind heavy daughter
feeling for shores; keep kelpies in loch lairs,
eels gliding, malts mashing, salmon springing;

let the bullers roar to the terns winging
in from a North Sea's German Ocean airs
of pressing crashing Prussian evening blue;
give linns long fall; bubble divers bravely
down to mend the cable you love to rust;
and slant at night through lamplit cities, true
as change is true, on gap-site pools, gravely
splintering the puckering of the gust.

The Poet in the City

Rain stockaded Glasgow; we paused, changed gears,
found him solitary but cheerful in
Anniesland, with the cheerfulness you'd win,
we imagined, through schiltrons of banked fears.
The spears had a most sombre glint, as if
the forced ranks had re-closed, but there he wrote
steadily, with a peg for the wet coat
he'd dry and put on soon. Gulls cut the cliff
of those houses, we watched him follow them
intently, see them beat and hear them scream
about the invisible sea they smelt
and fish-white boats they raked from stern to stem
although their freedom was in fact his dream
of freedom with all guilts all fears unfelt.

The Norn (1)

It was high summer, and the sun was hot.
We flew up over Perthshire, following
Christo's great-granddaughter in her swing-wing
converted crop-sprayer till plastic shot
above Schiehallion from her spinneret
Scotland-shaped and Scotland-sized, descended
silent, tough, translucent, light-attended,
catching that shoal of contours in one net.
Beneath it, what amazement; anger; some
stretching in wonder at a sky to touch;
chaos at airports, stunned larks, no more rain!
It would not burn, it would not cut. The hum
of civic protest probed like Dali's crutch.
Children ran wild under that counterpane.

The Norn (2)

But was it art? We asked the French, who said
*La nature est un temple où les vivants
sont les piliers*, which was at least not wrong
but did it answer us? Old Christo's head
rolled from its box, wrapped in rough manila.
'The pillars of the temple are the dead,'
it said, 'packed up and bonded into lead.'
Jowls of hemp smelt sweet like crushed vanilla.
But his descendant in her flying-suit
carefully put the head back in its place.
'Of course it's art', she said, 'we just use men.
Pygmalion got it inside out, poor brute.
For all they've been made art, they've not lost face.
They'll lift the polythene, be men again'.

The Target

Then they were running with fire in their hair,
men and women were running everywhere,
women and children burning everywhere,
ovens of death were falling from the air.
Lucky seemed those at the heart of the blast
who left no flesh or ash or blood or bone,
only a shadow on dead Glasgow's stone,
when the black angel had gestured and passed.
Rhu was a demons' pit, Faslane a grave;
the shattered basking sharks that thrashed Loch Fyne
were their killer's tocsin: 'Where I am, watch;
when I raise one arm to destroy, I save
none; increase, multiply; vengeance is mine;
in no universe will man find his match.'

After Fallout

A giant gannet buzzed our glinty probe.
Its forty-metre wing-span hid the sun.
Life was stirring, the fallout time was done.
From *a stick-nest in Ygdrasil* the globe
was hatching genes like rajahs' koh-i-noors.
Over St Kilda, house-high poppy-beds

made forests; towering sea-pinks turned the heads
of even master mariners with lures
that changed the white sea-graves to scent-drenched groves.
Fortunate Isles! The gannet bucked our ship
with a quick sidelong swoop, clapped its wings tight,
dived, and exploding through the herring droves
dragged up a flailing manta by the lip
and flew it, twisting slowly, out of sight.

The Age of Heracleum

The jungle of Gleneagles was a long
shadow on our right as we travelled down.
Boars rummaged through the ballroom's toppled crown
of chandeliers and mashed the juicy throng
of giant hogweed stalks. Wild tramps with sticks
glared, kept a rough life. South in Fife we saw
the rusty buckled bridges, the firth raw
with filth and flower-heads, dead fish, dark slicks.
We stood in what had once been Princes Street.
Hogweed roots thrust, throbbed underneath for miles.
The rubble of the shops became the food
of new cracks running mazes round our feet,
and west winds blew, past shattered bricks and tiles,
millions of seeds through ruined Holyrood.

Computer Error: Neutron Strike

No one was left to hear the long All Clear.
Hot wind swept through the streets of Aberdeen
and stirred the corpse-clogged harbour. Each machine,
each building, tank, car, college, crane, stood sheer
and clean but that a shred of skin, a hand,
a blackened child driven like tumbleweed
would give the lack of ruins leave to feed
on horrors we were slow to understand
but did. Boiling fish-floating seas slopped round
the unmanned rigs that flared into the night;
the videos ran on, sham death, sham love;
the air-conditioners kept steady sound.
An automatic foghorn, and its light,
warned out to none below, and none above.

Inward Bound

Flapping, fluttering, like imploding porridge
being slowly uncooked on anti-gas,
the Grampians were a puny shrinking mass
of cairns and ski-tows sucked back to their orig-
ins. Pylons rumbled downwards; lighthouses
hissed into bays; reactors popped, ate earth.
We watched a fissure struggling with the girth
of old Glamis, but down it went. Boots, blouses,
hats, hands above heads, like feet-first divers
all those inhabitants pressed in to meet
badgers and stalactites, and to build in reverse
tenements deepest for late arrivers,
and domes to swim in, not to echo feet
or glow down, dim, on the draped, chanted hearse.

The Desert

There was a time when everything was sand.
It drifted down from Findhorn, south south south
and sifted into eye and ear and mouth
on battlefield or bed or plough-bent land.
Loose wars grew sluggish, and the bugles choked.
We saw some live in caves, and even tombs.
Mirages rose from dry Strathspey in plumes.
Scorpions appeared. Heaven's fires were stoked.
But soon they banded to bind dunes in grass,
made cactus farms, ate lizards, sank their wells.
They had their rough strong songs, rougher belief.
Did time preserve them through that narrow pass?
Or are they Guanches under conquerors' spells,
chiselled on sorry plinths in Tenerife?

The Coin

We brushed the dirt off, held it to the light.
The obverse showed us *Scotland*, and the head
of a red deer; the antler-glint had fled
but the fine cut could still be felt. All right:
we turned it over, read easily *One Pound*,
but then the shock of Latin, like a gloss,

454

Respublica Scotorum, sent across
such ages as we guessed but never found
at the worn edge where once the date had been
and where as many fingers had gripped hard
as hopes their silent race had lost or gained.
The marshy scurf crept up to our machine,
sucked at our boots. Yet nothing seemed ill-starred.
And least of all the realm the coin contained.

The Solway Canal

Slowly through the Cheviot Hills at dawn
we sailed. The high steel bridge at Carter Bar
passed over us in fog with not a car
in its broad lanes. Our hydrofoil slid on,
vibrating quietly through wet rock walls
and scarves of dim half-sparkling April mist;
a wizard with a falcon on his wrist
was stencilled on our bow. Rough waterfalls
flashed on that northern island of the Scots
as the sun steadily came up and cast
red light along the uplands and the waves,
and gulls with open beaks tore out our thoughts
through the thick glass to where the Eildons massed,
or down to the Canal's drowned borderers' graves.

A Scottish Japanese Print

Lighter and lighter, not eternity,
only a morning breaking on dark fields.
The sleepers might almost throw back those shields,
jump to stations as if golden pity
could probe the grave, the beauty was so great
in that silent slowly brightening place.
No, it is the living who wait for grace,
the hare, the fox, the farmer at the gate.
And Glasgow's windows took the strong spring sun
in the corner of a water-meadow,
its towers shadowed by a pigeon's flight.
Not daisy-high, children began to run
like tumbling jewels, as in old Yeddo,
and with round eyes unwound their wild red kite.

Outward Bound

– That was the time Scotland began to move.
– Scotland move? No, it is impossible!
– It became an island, and was able
to float in the Atlantic lake and prove
crannogs no fable. Like a sea-washed log
it loved to tempt earnest geographers,
duck down and dub them drunk hydrographers,
shake itself dry, no longer log but dog.
– Was it powered? On stilts? – Amazing grace
was found in granite, it moved on pure sound.
Greenland twisted round to hear it, Key West
whistled, waved, Lanzarote's ashy face
cracked open with laughter. There was no ground
of being, only being, sweetest and best.

On Jupiter

Scotland was found on Jupiter. That's true.
We lost all track of time, but there it was.
No one told us its origins, its cause.
A simulacrum, a dissolving view?
It seemed as solid as a terrier
shaking itself dry from a brisk black swim
in the reservoir of Jupiter's grim
crimson trustless eye. No soul-ferrier
guarded the swampy waves. Any gods there,
if they had made the thing in play, were gone,
and if the land had launched its own life out
among the echoes of inhuman air,
its launchers were asleep, or had withdrawn,
throwing their stick into a sea of doubt.

Clydegrad

It was so fine we lingered there for hours.
The long broad streets shone strongly after rain.
Sunset blinded the tremble of the crane
we watched from, dazed the heliport-towers.
The mile-high buildings flashed, flushed, greyed, went dark,
greyed, flushed, flashed, chameleons under flak

of cloud and sun. The last far thunder-sack
ripped and spilled its grumble. Ziggurat-stark,
a power-house reflected in the lead
of the old twilight river leapt alive
lit up at every window, and a boat
of students rowed past, slid from black to red
into the blaze. But where will they arrive
with all, boat, city, earth, like them, afloat?

A Golden Age

That must have been a time of happiness.
The air was mild, the Campsie Fells had vines.
Dirigible parties left soft sky-signs
and bursts of fading music. Who could guess
what they might not accomplish, they had seas
in cities, cities in the sea; their domes
and crowded belvederes hung free, their homes
eagle-high or down among whitewashed quays.
And women sauntered often with linked arms
through night streets, or alone, or danced a maze
with friends. Perhaps it did not last. What lasts?
The bougainvillea millenniums
may come and go, but then in thistle days
a strengthened seed outlives the hardest blasts.

The Summons

The year was ending, and the land lay still.
Despite our countdown, we were loath to go,
kept padding along the ridge, the broad glow
of the city beneath us, and the hill
swirling with a little mist. Stars were right,
plans, power; only now this unforeseen
reluctance, like a slate we could not clean
of characters, yet could not read, or write
our answers on, or smash, or take with us.
Not a hedgehog stirred. We sighed, climbed in, locked.
If it was love we felt, would it not keep,
and travel where we travelled? Without fuss
we lifted off, but as we checked and talked
a far horn grew to break that people's sleep.

from Selected Poems
1985

Acknowledgement

The idea of the sequence of 26 poems entitled 'An Alphabet of Goddesses' was first formulated following a visit I made in September 1982 to an exhibition of pastel drawings by Ms Pat Douthwaite, entitled 'Worshipped Women: An Alphabet of Greek Goddesses', at the 369 Gallery in Edinburgh. I wish to acknowledge the contribution made by Ms Douthwaite's drawings and by her accompanying notes to the pictures by which this sequence was inspired and I am grateful for her permission to publish the poems. I am grateful also to have the permission of Mr Robert Graves, who wrote the introduction to the exhibition catalogue.

The queen shrieks, cries, prays, tugs, entreats
her people. The people ring the captain round. The captain
leaves the king, retreats. He's grim, his feet
are on the beach. Hawaiians shout
and jostle him. The blue sky's pure, a swallow's there.
The human error builds. That island
you won't leave now, Captain Cook! –
won't leave living, won't leave whole.
Is there to be no understanding at all?
At the shallow-water rocks he stands
and gestures to the launch. His back
is to the islanders, Captain Fool, Captain Fool!
His back is full of daggers
and he's face down in the shallows
threshing faintly with his feet,
Captain Cook. The blood gushes, rushes, races
to discover the Pacific.

1974

'Cook in Hawaii' and 'Chicago North Side' (p.577) both come from the
libretto of a music-theatre composition by George Newson, called
Valentine.

The Break-In

I took a mop and swabbed the burglar's blood
from windows, walls, and floor. The spray and trail
of arteries punctured by the shards of panes
he had himself broken, entering, and was broken on,
leaving, spread down three stairs and made the block
of flats a Hitchcock set, but real, so real
that as I knelt when my mop refused the stains,
and had to rub a grey rag into them
and get, through two cuts on my fingers, his
blood into mine, not knowing yet he was
a hepatitis-ridden addict, I
re-lived that cursing stagger step by step,
and spot by spot tried to but could not blot
the dark blood from my mind. A buttock jab
takes care of hepatitis; record-player,
radio, watch, cheque-book, kitchen purse
are mortal goods that come and go. Not there
the invasion, the invisible assault,
as landings forget neighbours' running feet,

and shocked rooms spring back slowly into place,
and walkie-talkies fade along the road,
and the uneasiest of sullen nights
comes down and wraps things in an aspirin throb
of memories and apprehensiveness:
the greater break-in was not through those walls
but into my reddened hands, into my blood.

1982

An Alphabet of Goddesses

Aphrodite

She tramps in long tight boots like a hussar.
Her girdle is a brace of promises.
The sea-foam has long left her and she brims
blinding out of crimson velvet and smoky mink
and she shakes like a tumbril, shocked and shocking
chockfull of longing but not forlorn,
red captain wrinkling on her gloves,
black captain flashing her epaulettes,
silver captain slipping her stole,
headless captain with flesh like lightning.
Her marathon is the coast of desire,
vast melon-slice of sugar and ginger.
She strides and strikes through the flushy strands!
She cannot know who follows her, kingfisher, queenfisher!
She cuts out thought, the love of gods and men.

Bacche

The hot slopes buzzed with honey,
the caves dripped with hives.
She swore the air livid over all Libya
as she set the honey-pot and the acorns and the mash of roots
at the feet of her skittish changeling,
her flop-eared half-horned stinking growing
goat-thing, her filthy four-legged foster-child,
her god-willed, god-wild
charge
and care.
Her nails were in shreds with digging the earth,
her black hair hung in dusty knots.

464

She raged down into Africa
for a child to give honey to,
and gave all gods to Gehenna,
and the goat-god to the pits below Gehenna
even as she fed him
from her commanded hand.

Circe

She thought she could live on the capital of weather-hard Odysseus
having stacked his shield and spear at her door
and scampered in her bed that long time,
but now she has grown old there seem to be
no sunny days on her alder-dark island,
no fleets of sailors to entice ashore,
nothing but to chatter to herself by the stove.
What should a scrawny black marmoset
hold up her breasts to – men, mirrors, thunder?
She has got rid of all her mirrors,
and her best men are hogs that root among the thickets,
no longer able to rise on their hind-legs
and snout her with all they remembered of a kiss.
She remembers much, but it is going.
Her scrag-tail droops, her spells falter.
– Then she pulls on her black stockings, right up,
and screeches as she scrapes a nail
along the nylon like a welder's spark,
and pins on her old sphinx headdress from Cairo
with its mortal colours, immortal desires.

Demeter

When her daughter was taken she was distracted,
set fire to the silos, drowned cornfields in paraquat.
Travelling folk saw her looming blowsily
with her chainsaw among the oaks.
Her temples pounded, she was brown as the earth.
She cursed the burrs that clung to her back,
swore at the rolling fields. In her fury she was a queen.
The blood of many gods was stirred. She saw them
from the corner of her eye, their hands on their buckles,
their glances on her tatters. She changed herself
into a mare and watched them melt beyond the trees.
But she forgot there were gods too in the seas.
Poseidon laughed and splashed up like an octopus

and made himself into a hippopotamus
(too large) and a sea-horse (too tiny) and lastly
into a horse that met the case, and quickly
cantered through the marram-grass and covered her.
'It is not every day –' she mused
and nicely showed her teeth.

Eileithyia

Who is greater than Eileithyia?
Crossing, uncrossing her knees
in Chaos she brought Heaven
Earth and Love to birth.
Leviathan swims in her lap;
she snaps pods of men
and gods. Goddesses, women
cry to her; mare,
vixen, doe, ewe
lean into her back
once that hour strikes.
Childbearers, shieldbearers:
standing in their husbands' arms
in a quiet room, swaying
in water for the baby to pop
to the surface like a fish, crouching
in the foul rubble of a shelled
city with shudders too early,
caught without a telephone
in a rush of blood, they wait
on the mother of gods and men.
Run, Eileithyia, from the ends
of the earth. Terrible, be kind!

Fortuna

You want to keep your man? You want to catch your boy?
You want a raunchy bed? You want to give good head?
        She needs a little prayer,
        and doesn't ask a lot
        but better late than not.

You wish you were a geisha, with tea and tease and teeter?
You're set to be a stripper? Have champers in a slipper?
        She needs a little payment,
        she doesn't ask a lot
        but better late than not.

You must have two-way mirrors and a cache of bootleg videos?
You'd like a good address-book, a handy line in widowers?
> She needs a little patience,
> she doesn't ask a lot
> but better late than not.

And when you've got your gigolo, your gold taps, your jacuzzi O,
And are snug as a bug in your circular bed, with pots of caviar black
    and red,
> She needs some little praises,
> she doesn't ask a lot
> but safer late than not.

Gaea

When the earth had barely stopped being wild,
and the continents were grumbling down onto their day-beds,
the earth-mother could not contain herself
with the thought of life. She made the sky
give lightning, bluster, bruise, press, drench.
She had a fire cave. She whistled.
She ground the sea in a pot.
She hardly felt the monsters leave her
that were born to grieve her; guffawed
when she saw the first belly-knot,
but smiled at the second,
checked the third was there,
never noticed the fourth,
grew angry with the fifth.
A dozen roaring clumsy plated titans
scorned her dandling; towering one-eyed loners
roamed off, raised cyclopean forts; like walking redwoods,
hundred-handed giants flailed the groves.
What was she feeling for in her gross, careless prime?
Not giant times,
not beauty then,
not goodness yet,
but women, men.

Hecate

She does not love you. She is not good luck.
If there are forces of evil, she is high in their councils.
She does not like this world, but will use it.
She has made so much magic she has no shape.

467

Sometimes she has a dog's head and feeds on the dead.
Sometimes she is only your shadow, maybe.
What is pleasant to her, apart from slow limousines?
Gin; acid; bugles; and the moon shining on these.

Ismene

'Forgive me, Antigone my sister, I did not think
you were right to be so bold, and the tyrant so strong.
Now I see that even if you die
he has met his match in you, and I draw strength
from your strength and I mean to share your fate.
I thought of our poor brother's body naked exposed
to wandering dogs and carrion birds, in my mind
I was with you and helped you scatter dust.
It is not too late to tend a shoot of courage!
There is a desert where they will take us
and they will wall us slowly into a cave
– oh sister, hold me, hold me Antigone! –
and empty a wineskin before the last brick
while we try not to scream at the white sun
and suddenly the workman's brow and eyes
steady serious detached appraising
will fill the measured gap and at once
the brick will be scraped and tapped into the dark
and I shall not cry out or faint but put
my head on your shoulder, sister, if I may,
in that tomb.'

Jocasta

She had guessed long ago   but gave up the thought
as too grubby, too godless.   The green in his eye
had a family strangeness?   That failed to stick.
There were gaps in his story,   but so it goes.
Coincidence rules   in cradles not royal
as on couches in Corinth.   Kings command,
gods garble.   Pieces slip from the game.
Some said in malice   she might have been his mother,
but bitching throve   in bored Thebes.
She married him, cherished him,   gave him four children.
The great bedroom was blue   and blazing with gold.
Rain rang on the roof;   white sheets rustled.
When the sun was near   he would stretch naked,
fall on her at cockcrow   with uncooled force.

'et his mate was his mother,   as mouths had breathed
nd as she had half known   yet needed him the more.
Vhen everything was revealed   she veiled herself, vomited,
an with a rough rope   under the rafters
nd swung in purple   to be purged of her son.

Kore

In her forearms the faint
creak of wet hyacinths
as she ran across the field
brushed and diffused
a fresh, half-sick
pungent fragrance
that followed her, though
she would never touch
the tight sexy curls.
Spring became summer,
late brooding summer;
in the heat and heaviness
she let her flushed cheek
cool itself on petals
of a blood-red rose.
She would make love
to the very trees
when they turn yellow
and chestnuts thud
into the beech-mast.
She is bound for the underworld
and the creaking bed
of grim, strong, aged
pitiless Hades.
Through his cold thrust
wish her well.

Lethe

he has been lobotomized with Naomi Ginsberg but she does not
    forget.
he has been stoned in Khomeini's brickyard but she does not
    forget.
he has hung in a cage at Cumae wasting away but she does not
    forget.
he has burned in Israeli phosphorus for hours but she does not
    forget.

469

She has crackled in the market-place at Rouen but she does not
    forget.
She has been injected with kerosene in Belsen but she does not
    forget.
She has drunk the lees of Chappaquiddick but she does not
    forget.

> There is nothing you can pay her for the waters
> of oblivion. High in a glittering sieve
> she holds them, pans for grains of mercy.
> There is no ferry, no other life.
> Hunger and thirst after righteousness.

Medea

Snake-charmer, illusionist, aeronaut, chemist, chameleon,
multiple murderess; she had death and love
struggling under her black cowl like maimed eagles.
We are told that when she first saw pirate Jason
shaking his rings and squinting up into the sun
she got a superhuman shot from sardonic Eros –
the arrow blasted into her right to the feathers.
And when Jason left her for Creusa,
she put on a pleasant mask and ran up a little white dress
which she sent as a wedding-gift, and when Creusa
had stepped into it and her maid zipped it up tight
it was like striking a match: up she went
in flames, and it stuck to her like napalm
as she ran through the palace, setting fire to others
in a chain of charred vengeance.
And she who had dismembered her own brother for Jason,
and for Jason had seethed his usurping uncle in a cauldron,
now made a sacrifice of the two sons Jason had given her –
the altar's crimson shouted her dry eyes.
And she pulled on her hood, and wrote in her diary:
'I am not accountable. Gods are not grocers.
The arrow is in my side. I got the golden fleece.'

Nemesis

She will have you on a plate with two forks.
She knows the bad apple in the barrel.
She is the crab that comes at you the wrong way.
Her teeth grind exceeding small.
She controls the roulette-wheel – but don't bet on it.
She holds the ladder for you, and kicks it away.

Don't cry, How tragic! She loves comedy.
Don't laugh your head off; she might keep it.
One thing, though: never try to deceive her.
Propitiation is her *bête noire*.
But you must hold yourself in readiness,
and put your advisers on a slow train.

Oreithyia

In the beginning she swirled up naked
out of Chaos, before anything was made.
Out of Chaos she made a sort of wild sea and
over it and on it she skimmed and splashed with delight.
Over it and her she pegged up a sky:
it was blue, grey, black, as wild as the sea, and
it was to ward off infinity.
It was then between the sea and the sky she felt
almost at home, though alone,
almost able to dance, and she did dance
all the more wildly in her loneliness,
all the more intently in that wildness.
Arms flew, hair flew, breasts flew,
a vortex for Boreas. And the north wind rushed on her,
eagerly entered her, endlessly
impregnates her, plays with her, presses her, dances with her
in wildness and in order,
in order to make earth and stars,
animals and people
and everything that can be made.
Auroras dance over them; they mate for
aeons. And swelling, gorgeous, bloody, a
universe kicks
itself out.

Pasiphae

'Why should Aphrodite keep us down,
trudging about as servants in our dim robes,
testing her wine for poison, tracking her lost veils,
traipsing for rouge, combs, fans, roses, toothpicks?
The three Graces are the three Stupid Ones, sisters!'
– So she tore off her moth-brown jellaba,
and put on a topless feathery wool tunic
and strutted like a Sumerian temple harlot,
and then she spread out her arms and made them into wings,

flapped them and danced in quick angry swoops
until her feet became claws and as a bird
she could scold at Aphrodite and cast a shadow over her.
But Aphrodite plunged in the palace pool like a seal
and came up sleek glittering august invulnerable unmatchable
while jealous Pasiphae stood and screamed like a peacock,
and scuttered among the garden herms with her desperate lament,
sawing the impotent air.

Queen Alcyone

Halcyon days are calm and strong.
She hears and loves the sailors' song.

She watches for the sudden storm
and guards her captains free from harm.

She sees the snake-like waterspout
and shares the rowers' trembling shout.

She raises up her great winged head,
interposing dread for dread

until tornadoes hiss and turn
and sails regain the timid sun.

Sometimes her wings are blue in blue
as sea and sky melt in and through

her brooding stillness to a scene
unimaginably serene

where hurricanes have never been
and Alcyone is queen.

But mostly men must grip the rail
and hope they will not roar or quail

when crashing lumps and darkness rise
to pound and drown one more poor prize.

Rhea

'What was it like while you were a snake?'
'You mean when he was a snake too?' 'Who, Zeus?'

472

'Zeus, who else! Well, it was different.
It was certainly slitherier, if you like that;
very close, since nothing gets in the way.
I thought I would never go back to crude hugs
the first time I felt the slow travelling ripple:
it catches every inch of you in its squeeze
but in succession, severally, subtly, not
with one blunt anthropomorphic gasp
as four limbs fall on you dumped on a bed.'
'But – ?' 'But, yes, well, it palls.
You don't really seem to get any nearer.
What it lacks is purchase, resistance.'
'Can't you anchor your tails – a tree, a rock?'
'No, we tried, but there was no grip.
You don't exactly have a tail, you are all tail.'
'He made it, though?' 'Oh yes, after a deal
of threshing and twisting about, he made it.'
'Your son.' 'What do you mean my son?'
'Zeus is your own son.' 'Zeus was a snake
and I was a snake. *That* never came
out of my womb. Use your imagination.'
'I wish I had seen it. He must have coursed you
like a spaceship, you are both such titans.
You must have tangled like arms of nebulas,
or two galaxies passing through each other,
signals for some millennial dish.'
'I'm a goddess again. Make me a wish.'

Sphinx

What has the head and breasts of a woman and the
    hungry body of a lioness and the wings of a bird of
    prey and the long tail of a snake lashing slowly from
    side to side as it lies crouched on the branch of a tree
    on a busy boulevard and keeps asking pedestrians
    what is the square root of minus one and what was
    the song the sirens sang and why is it easier for a
    rich man to ride his camel into heaven than for three
    million unemployed to pass through the eye of a
    needle and how long would it take for the genetic
    mutations following an all-out nuclear attack to pro-
    duce a creature with the head and breasts of a woman
    and the hungry body of a lioness and the wings of
    a bird of prey and the long tail of a snake lashing
    slowly from side to side as it lies crouched on the
    branch of a tree on a busy boulevard asking pedestrians

endless questions and when they cannot answer
swings round its huge hungry lion-haunches and
strangles them with its sphincter?

I give up.

Terpsichore

She has made a jukebox video and is really jumping.
Her image flickers in the wired-up lay-bys,
gives you a charge in airport concourse bars.
In the twenty-first century AD/BC AC/DC she
is a body-stocking of poetry and pleasure, a kick
of fervent music in very very dark red,
with gloves, studs, belt of rarest Ravenscraig steel
and a lacquered helmet blond as corn.
She is not programmed, but she has a programme,
and that is to dance heaven down into your arms
with showers of gold direct
or alternating, rippling
like the wind.
And she will dance to heaven and you,
and you to her, and heaven to the two;
behind you soft mock-Tiffany lamps,
in front of you the whole laser-show,
and a gantry scarlet with hyperlager,
and a well-sprung floor and a welter of decibels,
the waves and shouts of day-glo nights,
the waves and shouts of day-glo nights.
– With what slow pain she will then draw it all back,
scarcely moving, drifting like a mime,
putting a finger to your lips,
binding the feet of heaven.
The paraphernalia roll off like tumbleweed.
Cameramen hold their ground. She looks at them.
They make her most beautiful video
of dawn, and the dying dance.

Urania

There was a raven on Mount Ararat
who came when he was called; she pampered him.
She also loved to watch the choughs that skim

474

these highest terraces; even a bat
would take her fancy. For it was all flight,
flight, flight! The white observatory dome
opened and shut as if it was her home,
but she was out there, in eternal night!
Her headdress was a comet, and the sands
of Mars were sown into her streaming robes.
Astronomy is not for hausfrau hearts!
Her signals travelled on a million bands,
and when she launched her own Olympian probes
it was to star and brim the starless charts.

Vixen

The Vixen of Teumessus, red-haired rager,
sniffs and barks and yelps for youths.
She is stronger than any trap.
Her sleeves never snag on brambles
as she runs through the woods
where young men saunter.
She marks her victim where he leans on a tree.
With a growl she pinions him, ties him to the trunk,
bares her breast, takes out her whip,
lashes him carefully, slowly, painfully,
loosens her skirt, draws his blood steadily,
moans with him, lets her long tongue dangle,
excites him with her rank hot breath,
lashes him quickly, sharply, deeply,
till at last with a cry he jerks at the ropes,
stains the ground red and white together.
          'And so he will release,' she said,
             'the lushest groves in Greece,' she said.
                But nothing more grew there
                than came from rain and air.
                So she was overthrown
                and turned to stone.

Wisdom

Wisdom-Titaness Metis, first wife of Zeus,
sitting motionless massive unsmiling in her grey tunic,
her pale feet on a cloud shaped like a globe,
her arms at rest in her lap, her eyes unblinking,
will suddenly be on her feet, in profile, kicking
the cloud down limbo, staring at a new thought,

her robe gone black, or white, a hand at her ear
to cup and amplify the faint spidery grating
of a nebula's arm as it goes akimbo in Cygnus,
and as suddenly again dive down silently
into the watery universe like a ziggurat in Atlantis.
Does she know everything? What she knows, she knows.
Does she know everything? She is a time queen;
millionaires with trembling piggy-banks
mean nothing to her, she does not sell.
Does she know everything? She is a woman
and she knows gross bold Jove waits at her side
to cut her exponential empire,
to divorce her troubling wisdom,
to devour her threatening knowledge,
but she does not know when.
She spreads her arms along the back of her throne.

Xenaea

She said if she saw him still two-timing her
she would make sure he never saw again.
He was tired of her tantrums and told her so.

When she watched how he settled the woman into her cloak
at the end of the next party, she knew they were lovers,
even if their obvious happiness had not told her so.

She said nothing, but went into her kitchen
when the servants were absent, and picked out a strong skewer
which she found she could conceal in the sleeve of her dress.

At their next meeting he seemed vaguely contrite,
brought her some pretty violets, but it was too late.
She had hardened her heart, and when he sat beside her

she rose quickly and without saying a single word
plunged the skewer into his eyes in turn.
It was only at his pitiful screams she began to shake,

and in the pain of love blinded herself,
standing in front of the grandest of bronze mirrors
any goddess ever held up to grief.

Youth

Trays and pitchers, glasses, flagons at the high table!
Cupbearer Hebe, youth-goddess, happy, all grace!
Flash of her white napkins, clack of her quick sandals!
The torches flickered, her shadow painted the floor.

The torches flicker, her shadow paints the floor.
White staring stiff and cold she is carried
into the deadly fields, takes no drink and gives none.
Her merry heart is only memory.

Her merry heart will be the memory
of youth that passes, and if it could last
would lose its happiness. Pitchers pour
without stint when they make us say they do,

in glasses on the changing changeless table.

Zeuxippe

Hyperborean ponies
followed her; she could not have enough of them.
She had sugar for a troop.
'Hey!' and 'Whoa!' and 'Holaho!' she would cry
as she scoured the stubble
or stood on knowes and mounds
and counted manes.
She had no care for power,
had long left palaces, been written off,
her name almost forgotten.
But when she sniffed the north wind
she knew her own country,
and ran with her horses along the broken strand,
the wild gusts blowing off to the horizon
her 'Hey!' and 'Whoa!' and 'Holaho!'.

From the Video Box
1986

Acknowledgement is due to the concept of the Video Box, where viewers can record their reactions to television programmes, as shown in Gus MacDonald's Channel 4 programme, 'Right to Reply'.

From the Video Box

ad te, ut video, comminus accessit
Cicero, *Letters to Atticus*

1

I saw that Burning of the Books, in China
I don't know how many centuries B.C.
If anything was compulsive on the set,
that was. You could almost feel the heat,
and when you saw the soldiers and flunkeys dancing
like demons against the glare, bending and lifting,
lifting and throwing, throwing and grimacing through the sparks,
and when you heard the crackle and spit of the wood
going off like fireworks, and they had fireworks too,
or I think they had, it was hard to be sure,
but anyway the bonfires getting bigger and bigger
and those gongs looming and booming in the smoke,
when you'd seen and heard all that,
I thought it was the best the old classics
had ever done for them, to warm a few hands
in a freezing night like that: there were no long faces,
I noticed, and no one ran with tongs
to snatch a few analects out of the flames.
This was first-class entertainment.
That emperor had the right idea.
That's really all I wanted to say.

2

I have just watched that fearful programme
of the burning of the Library at Alexandria.
I rushed to the box – I am still shaking –
to record my disgust that any producer
should foist such barbarous philistinism –
without introduction, without discussion –
on a million homes. Accident, arson, act of war –
I don't care what the miserable excuse is
for showing the death of books, live, on screen.
Men, I could understand; but books! –
all right, call them rolls, scrolls, codexes –
not one, not ten, oh no, but tens of thousands,
irreplaceable, perishable, unprinted, unique!
That was the grandeur that was Rome did that.
Then they had the nerve to show us an epilogue
when anything that was left six centuries later
was burned by the Arabs as pagan trash.
I shall certainly write straight to the Authority.

481

There are limits to what an ordinary man
can stomach, or should stomach. I admit my wife
was not worried, but then not everyone is a reader;
I'm sure she supports me though. Well I think that's it.

3

This is the first time I have ever recorded
my reaction, and I speak with some diffidence,
but surely the display of that conflagration
which laid the new British Library in ashes
must rate as quite unusually riveting.
The interest is greater in that every device
known to technology, heat detectors,
sprinkler systems, flameproof furniture,
fire doors, foam-capsuled mosaic floors
proved powerless to stop the hungry spread.
I thought to begin with it must be *son et lumière*
on the grand scale, but then the whole building
glowed bright orange through the firegrate of itself
and sent fireflies up into the north London night
that were soon to be charred falling flakes
of bindings, catalogues, incunabula.
The popping of the terminals, the melting of the fiches
presented future film-makers, I guess,
with such a lurid viable store of image and sound
I could see the library burning and toppling again and again.
On the old Bloomsbury site there was never
a spectacle as all-enfolding as this.
Silent now the dead tongue in 11375.cc.13!
Scandals of Cup.1000.c.7. all at rest!
And 12452.w.3. quavering in his sprightly grave!
Whoever was responsible for this show
was a person of imagination, and bold almost to excess.

4

I never believed in legendary heroes
till I saw that scratch video of Tantalus
video of Tantalus how could they get it
it was no actor no actor there he was
tall and muscular severe very swarthy and sad
naked but for shining leather sandals
shining leather sandals and a bronze fillet
round his black his black hair it was the way
he ran through the dust storm parched panting
it was the way he ran into that bright fresh river

fresh river to plunge and slake but the water
sucked itself back so that he could not reach it
stretched up through the heady air parched panting
to the overhanging orange-trees that jerked away
orange-trees jerked away it was the way
he suffered hope deferred jerked away
oh I know we were told he had stolen
Zeus's cupbearer to wait at his own table
and more but it was the way he stood
way he stood in that ruthless stream
that made me shiver and so feel for him
when the image of Ganymede flashed through the spray
for if he was allowed to touch it it was a shade
if it was real he was not allowed to touch it
if it was a shade he was allowed to touch it
if he was not allowed to touch it it was real
it was the way he ran it was the way
he stood severe very swarthy and sad

5

I am not here to talk about a scratch
video I am here to make a scratch I am
here to make a scratch video to make
tape-recorder on *a young man of mysterious*
appearance coming towards me fore-edge
painting flip a friend did this flip of me
jumping flip from bank to flip bank
like the force of enchantment miniature home video
watch it miniature home video I am bounding
into fields and woods back back I am
bounding from the door towards the fields
I am moving towards the door a friend
took this *I was now a justified person*
watch this close-up in the woods I fan
a batch of polaroids like a fore-edge painting
I fan a batch of swimming to the farther bank
and rising shaking water everywhere
the clothes were the same to the smallest item
and my clothes are still damp as you can see
my clothes are still damp with I think a
think a hint of steam in this hot video box
this singular being read my thoughts in my looks
I have nothing more to show the camera
anticipating the very words that I was going to utter
to show the camera after I have let
you see my friend who has been

behind me all this time
all this time and here he is
beside me now here we are
thank you thank you

6

my friend and I watched that scratch that scratch video
last night we watched that last night I was
on the black chesterfield and Steve was on the
black chair not that that will interest viewers
interest viewers but I want to be authentic
on the black the black chesterfield just as the sun
went down reddish outside and I could switch
from the set to the sky and back sky and back
and back back there was a squeezed sunset
on the set between gables and a helicopter cut
through the reddish screen like a black tin-opener
while suddenly a crow flew suddenly a crow
a crow flew through the real red outside what we
call the real red and tore it silently it silently
a scratch in air never to be solved scratch
in air Steve said never solved as inside
back went the helicopter to start again
to start again I said those gables don't
grow dark those gables don't grow dark
that's what I want to say they don't grow
dark those gables on the set

7

It is hard to know what it is I saw.
I had been switching through a score of channels
in that disgruntled and half-idle mood I'm sure you know,
a gloomy winter's evening with the curtains open,
the streetlamps on and the cars racing home,
and gusts of wind that shook the house,
raced off with armfuls of showers to the river.
Who can be happy? Not I. But the search
goes on, even through that flurry of switched images,
as if a picture, if at least it moved, could move
the sluggish heart. Everything happens, perhaps.
There was suddenly something growing on the screen
that could kick-start hope racing forward
into I don't know what roads of years.
There were no images, that's the hardest part.
The whole screen was a swirling dirty grey

that churned and churned and held the attention
only to wonder what it was; but there in the middle
it seemed to split like a skin, a thin
horizontal streak of blue flashed out –
no, it did not flash, that was only the surprise
of the contrast, it was too pure a blue,
an eggshell blue, a sky blue, blue
of an innocent eye, not harsh or icy,
not brooding dark or royal,
not feeble pastel either,
but clear and steady, beautiful and true.
It grew, like a rift in the clouds after rain,
or like the slow opening of an eye,
until the grey clouds, the grey lids, gathered
their hideous strength and grain by grain
joined seamlessly together once again.
Wherever I go I see that patch of blue.
Did anyone else watch it? Is there happiness?
Hope in things that come and go?
Why should we not know?

8

This is the most ridiculous thing I ever experienced
and I hope whoever is listening will take note.
I am not paying good money for such stupidities.
There is something wrong with Channel 49.
I was settling down last night for that old film,
I tell you I was just settling back with a sandwich
and a can of lager when the screen went pink,
then rosy, then red, absolutely red,
no announcement, no music, no captions, no anything.
It was very late. It was very quiet. The family
were in bed long ago. Here I am
waiting for my all-night movie and the set,
I almost said the bloody set, goes red.
I shook it, switched it off, on; still red.
Well, I sat and watched it! What would you have done?
It got deeper, darker, seemed to glisten.
I crushed the empty can, got up and threw it
in the kitchen bin, came back,
touched the set on an impulse,
pressed the screen or stroked it,
I don't remember, only an impulse,
and stared at my hand, it was wet
and sticky and red as blood or red with blood,
who knows, what sort of programme was that

and who lets these things happen?
Look, I didn't wipe it off. See that, camera.
You think I'm crazy? Think again.
I know we get our mail through the set, bills,
bank balances, but blood is ridiculous.
I want a clean dry screen from now on.
Let them bleed elsewhere, whoever they are.

9

At last, a programme for the colour-blind!
Here we come, tail-end of so many minorities
but never mind: congratulations all round.
It was a stroke of genius to use Kerouac's friend,
that red-green colour-blind wild Neal Cassady
who worked on the railroad and drove a train
through as many signals as would have crashed
the push of a less charmed supercharger.
We saw how he cheated at the Ishihara,
got the job to show man can do anything.
Well, that's all right. I don't admire him
to distraction, but I do admire
the secret film he made
for his fellow colour-blinders. All you out there
with your green green grass and your red red rose
saw your conventional story,
a bar, a shoot-out, a car-chase,
as my friends tell me,
but we saw something different,
oh, very different, and it is something you will never know
unless we tell you, because you cannot see it –
it is the same film, but strain as you will,
your lovely normal eyes will never figure
that carpet, our carpet,
rolled out from its orient.

10

I never really took to Shakespeare
until I saw that extract of the death
of Ragozine. We were not told
what play it was. The cell he lay in
was windowless and would have been black
but the half-kind jailers had left him a candle
because of his sickness. I thought the way
the fever made him toss and turn so much
that the candle-flame was never still

and threw a twisted shadow-play of his misery
on the old rough dripping graffiti'd walls
was a good touch. Everything flickered
like an ancient film, while his sweat seeped
into the paillasse: pirate's malaria
shook him, racked him worse than any rack,
hallucinated him till he shouted
he had brought a whole bastard boarded golden
Turkish argosy back limping to Ragusa
and could count his coins for life –
the bey was trussed, the scimitars were piled,
the bey was piled, the scimitars were trussed,
and he was the pirate of the western world –
oh I liked that. And the last moment
when his chest heaved right up, and his hand tried to,
his right hand, for the left one had been shot,
and his one gold earring flashed in the candlelight,
and he cried out in what was more defiance
than desperation before he slumped back dead,
I thought the entire prison must have shivered
as I did. But no, nothing so obvious.
Soon there was that sturdy singing executioner
rattling the bars with his axe and roaring,
I want a head! Where is that villain? I need his head! –
strode in, tore off the earring, struck.
And the staring head was stuffed in a bag,
swinging off as the credits rolled.
If that was Shakespeare, he's my man.

11

Poor Barbary! I must tell you
I switched off. I knew she was going to die.
I mustn't blame the programme-makers
but I saw myself there as she pined away.
It was a good scullery, quite bright,
where she scoured the pots, but nothing could hide
her sharp high shoulders and pinched cheeks,
she was almost a shadow as she hung up her cloth
and stared out listlessly at the canal.
When she took a chair
to sew and mend, nearer the window,
she could hardly drag it, or the basket
filled with her good mistress's stockings and kerchiefs.
She had stopped eating altogether since her lover went mad,
carted off to Bedlam. I have stopped eating altogether
since my lover jilted me for the army. It seems the same.

Scour pots; sew; faint; be put in sheets; end it.
Shakespeare knew when some can live
without the other and some have not the luck to.
Her song was terrible
when she laid the needle aside,
sing all a green willow,
her hair falling down like the willow
towards the flags of the floor.
I could take no more.
I cannot ask anyone
except the millions
out there, you,
what I have to do.

12

Oh the sheer power of that witch, that bitch, that
bit and talon of what universe, that Sycorax!
I had to come and say I love it when
there's no morality left, not a chink or a cheep
from damned good or damned evil we keep
hearing about, nothing but a screen
brimmed up with pure force and nothing lagging
in the energy not a stint in the energy
it pushes into our veins like acid.
I watched all those Shakespeare scenes, but this
beat the sentiment straight out of the rug, hung it up
like a felucca's grandmother, winds and tempests
could only batter it better and better. What a beast
she was as she scoured the brush of the island,
bent like a hoop but pregnant too, her eyelids
fuel-blue, her mouth crushed red with berries,
arms all whipcords, straining at last
like a wombed Samson between two pines.
She never brought the sky down but she brought
thunder down without a groan as she straddled
her slippery man-child brought down
wawling in a squall and squelch
of monsoon rain. She reigns,
bitch-queen, batch-quern, grinds out
pure nature, calves icebergs, makes archipelagos,
and I saw her suddenly in a final shot
solid with her thighs about the world,
frowning at a thousand twangling instruments
that to her were neither here nor there.
How good it is to have a set for that one!

13

I don't watch television,
but I was passing the box
and I would just like to say
if anyone is interested
that I really think
John MacLean is the greatest.
The Nationalists will never
win without Labour,
and Labour is useless
sitting in London.
They've all sold politics
for a mess of pottage
called economics.
They want more jobs
and that's all right,
but they never say republic
and that's all wrong.
My father told me –
and he knew MacLean –
'If people look at you
when you swear by the bones
of Baird and Hardie,
don't explain,
but don't forget.'
Neither I do.
It's as simple as that.
But somebody has to say it.
Well, I must move on.
Your box is quite nice.
Remember what I said.

14

Wait noo, wait a minute. Right.
Howzzat, eh? Big yin, innit?
See when it gets hard, thir a bend in it.
Yeah. Wait. Therr ye go. Yeah. Weird.
Lassies never complain but.
Hope yir camera's good at close-ups? Therr noo.
Well, that's yir loat. I'll away.
Ma mates are waitin. Wave
goodbye, Willie. Right,
in ye go. Yeah. Christ
it's a tight fit in thae jeans.
Never mind, that's me wan a tenner.
Auf wiedersehen, pets.

15

I know you won't mind if I use your box
for a *cri de coeur*. My, cat, has, gone,
vanished without a trace, I have not seen him
for a week, and I am *quite distracted*.
He is a marmalade cat called Robertson,
he is big and beautiful and an absolute *bumper*
of a creature, you could not miss him,
he is *sui generis* and *sine qua non*.
There *is* a tiny tiny tiny nick
in his left ear which I would *not* mention
but for the identification; he is *all cat*.
And he should be wearing a
smart smooth polished dark brown real leather collar
which was *so* carefully chosen
to go with that *lovely* lovely fluffy warm gold fur,
and his name and address are on it.
To those who are watching – I don't say he's been *abducted*,
it's just he has such a trusting trusting nature,
he would go with anyone for a kind word,
or a *little* fillet sole, he does not *gobble* or snatch,
and he purrs at your legs like a *percolator*.
Well what more can I say,
Robertson is a treasure, a dear, a *rara avis*, a gift –

and if any of you have him I want him back *pronto*.

16

There may be a case for subliminal images
but whatever backroom mandarin thought it could be made
by showing, or rather not showing, the Big Bang
was off his cosmic top. Technical triumph
I grant you, if we are to believe the programme-makers,
since there they were plugged into the very beginning,
the very first stir and flutter, the evulsion of nothing,
instead of their usual toytown graphics. They told us
we must watch out for it, the programme would not help.
There was only one window, one moment they could use.
It was some messy story about the Borgias,
all tiger-striped galleries with grille-filtered light,
and lean figures darting among pillars, and silks
hissing suddenly with skirts gathered up;
and pictures, bronzes, fountains, altars, footmen,
girls with cushions, boys with greyhounds,
dwarfs with pisspots, shrieks from birdcages,
great bangs from studded doors crashed shut

were flung about the screen
like counters in a game.
There was never a second when nothing was happening.
If you were not quick you missed the nod,
the heel-scrape, the thumb-twitch, the slipped veil,
you saw the doused torch, not the glow of the phial.
I reckon it was ninety per cent subliminal,
so why add more? I saw nothing,
my friends saw nothing. Just once perhaps,
in the banquet scene, when the servant
set down a purple pitcher of wine
which turned out to be the only one not poisoned,
and the camera looked straight down into the wine
to make us think it really had been poisoned –
it was that sort of film – I thought I saw a tremor
on the dark surface that was not caused
by the careful placing of the vessel on the table.
I recorded it, and played it again.
I said I recorded it, and played it again.
I played it slowly, and I played it again.
Well, there was nothing. It seems the duke
had gently banged the table for his chaplain
(one of the chief villains) to say grace.
Mind you, the nature of things is so sly
that the two tremors could be timed as one.
Be that as it may, and thank you very much,
but I am still waiting for the universe to begin.

17

That was so strange last night –
I thought I saw my son
who was lost overboard in a storm
off Valparaiso – five years gone –
I know he was drowned, his body
was washed up on the rocks
and brought back home to Gourock
where I can see his grave.
There are no ghosts. What I saw
in that split-second flash
was an image only a mother
could be sure to be her son,
to have been her son surely
since he was no longer there.
It came in a blizzard of images,
a speeded mosaic of change
in the Americas, I watched

491

half bored, irritated
by the strident music, ready
to switch channels – then!
– not in his seaman's cloth
but a camouflage jacket,
looking straight at the camera,
his fist in a revolutionary salute,
a letter sticking from his pocket
with writing I saw as mine.
Oh how little we know
of those we love! Perhaps
it was sabotage, not storm,
that sank his ship – perhaps
that broken body after all
was not – oh images, images,
corners of the world seen
out of the corner of an eye –
subversive, subliminal –
where have you taken my son
into your terrible machine
and why have you peeled off
my grief like a decal
and left me a nobody
staring out to sea?

18

There is one word
that should never be seen
except when you think you may have seen it
but are not sure.
It should never be lingered over or built up
or allowed to hang heavy and ornate
and should only be like lightning in summer,
the next thing to an absence.
No bustling presence
can move men, the sun, the stars –

There is one message
you must not spell out,
but let it slip like a smolt
beween weeds and vanish,
or like a quicksilver lizard
freeze on the rock.
Give it between shots
if you will, if you may, if you can. And yet
remember there is nothing rosicrucian about it,

492

it is not for adepts,
it gives everyone joy
in the flick of a tail,
the flicker of a tongue –

Neither noun nor verb
rules; what is
needs what does.
Let it in and let it go – so
quickly – programme-makers,
seed-sowers in the burning screen!

19

I was galloping down through Patagonia
on a breakneck nag a fortnight back,
prospecting a bit, rumbling the sierras,
paddling and pottering in some salty lagunas,
keeping a swarm of baas at bay
and wishing I could shear the mineral fleece
from the humpbacks and the crags –
well all that's by the way, but not entirely.
Clattering east along a dried-up watercourse,
I switched on my wristwatch television
(and I should add that these jewelled creatures
are my delight, as they are today to so many)
and caught in its amazing unflickering clarity
an astronaut probing some Martian rille –
I groaned as he twirled up his subsoil sample
of red-veined if not red-blooded riches –
and the fool's clear voice came over saying
'Once water, always water' – he was searching for life!
Good God, we've got life galore –
twenty million sheep in Patagonia –
while the mountains are sleeping on nations' ransoms.
I could take the pick from my saddle-bag and
strike not water from the rock like idiot Moses
but rock, and rock again, and coal, and silver, and shale,
and whistle down to the coastal corridor
my little tuneless clinking hoofbeaten song
of mineralogy and materiality.
Pusillanimous Mars-prodders I can switch off,
did switch off. But such a fine coincidence
I had to tell you about. I was reinforced.
I had it all on my wrist like a gulf-man's hawk
and I sent it off right back to Mars.
The picture winked, as well it might.

493

I sold my horse, boarded a flight
from Comodoro Rivadavia,
and here I am. Bless TV, bless video.
You think I don't mean it but I do.
Did you ever have my type in your box?

20

'Video wall, video wall,
which is the fairest of them all?'
I am sure the great video wall debate
will not be resolved by my participation,
but here is what I think: there are walls
and walls, and a wallful of videos seen
on the small screen is virtually de-walled
and pretty pithless, even if it is pretty.
Leave it for connoisseurs of the pretty,
paperweight-fanciers, home-birds, page-turners, chintz-persons.
I want wall video to be all wall.
I want to be there and to feel wall-ness.
And I don't mean a straight flat look-this-way wall either,
with me in the middle, three metres back, staring,
lacking nothing but a Victorian neck-clamp.
No, I need a total mobile wraparound,
a dome of many-coloured glass, in fact,
that will not only stain the white radiance
of any eternity there may be but
oh, oh,
positively dance round the
threescore, fivescore wedded, embedded
screens of talk, tale, trail, and trial.
You think it's over the top? A touch of Sardanapalus?
'Everyone knows a plain background's best for pictures.'
Not a bit of it!
Try my wall,
climb into my shell,
sell your house, bring your family,
sharpen your eyes and your wits until
the dance is story and the story dance,
and as you run forward you feel time run forward
to fetch the age of gold. Oh
you would never be ill or old
if I could build my hall, my video wall,
no, never at all.

494

21

Against my will, and I emphasize that,
I bought one of those portable chameleon televisions
which were going to revolutionize viewing.
Revolutionize my epidiascope!
You take the thing into a field of cows –
you've got the news read in a field of cows.
You take it skin-diving – oh yes it's waterproof, it's everything –
and the string quartet saws through giant kelp.
I had mine in Glencoe – there was a film about Glencoe –
it disappeared.
The brochure spoke of
'melting the boundaries between art and reality',
'hilarious or sinister juxtapositions',
'a set that can never bore'.
I have put it next to the microwave
in the hope of precipitating an identity-crisis
and if it results in mutual self-destruction
it will be worth it.
It really is time I went back to find out.

22

I put up the biggest dish in Perthshire
and all I got was ВРЕМЯ, ВРЕМЯ, ВРЕМЯ.
I do exaggerate, of course. I also had
a brief harangue from Tripoli, from a tent if you please,
all swags and carpets and bits of brass –
had to argue closely with my wife
who thought the man was charming.
How can you say he is charming, I asked her,
when you don't understand a word of Arabic?
It's his eyes, she said. What can you do?
Language is the devil. We keep hearing
about the wonders of science, and satellite TV
will 'bring the world into our living-room',
but these chaps in Moscow will not speak English,
I can't think why, since it's the best language,
but they won't. So where are the translation-machines
up in the satellites, why can't we hear
all those little Japanese beavers using
the language Shakespeare wrote and Churchill spoke?
That's my first complaint.
The second is interference.
I had painfully managed to home in
on a splendid meeting of those new men
of the right in Paris, and was beginning to follow

something of what they said, from words like 'France'
and 'pays' and 'tradition' and 'responsabilité',
when suddenly everything dissolved in a welter
of crocodiles threshing about some muddy shallows
while tribesmen shouted and beat drums.
It was sickening.
In Perthshire we like a job well done.
If there are teething troubles, get working.
If I need a larger dish, tell me.
If your satellite is foreign-made – I shall find out.

23

It is grand and fine to think
how the satellites in their places
are waiting to receive and give
it all. What shall we live to see?
White dish, listening eye:
if objects can be poetry,
you are. When you filled my screen
with a slow swoop over the masts
of America's Very Large Array
I thought between you you might bring
non-existent neumes and breves
from the long-exploded spheres.
You know my friends are hard on me,
that say it's a sin to be naive
and not a sign of innocence.
When did you last see a star suffering,
they ask me, or a dish writing,
or a V.L.A. making deserts bloom?
Why bounce trash from a great height?
Soaps are soaps even in Greek.
What is *Agamemnon* but a soap,
I try to reply. They miss the point.
Yes I've seen rubbish – violent
American rubbish, high-minded French
rubbish, hysterical Italian rubbish,
dignified Russian rubbish, silly
English rubbish, smiling Chinese
rubbish, maudlin Scottish rubbish –
but don't tell me I haven't seen
the dearest listeningest large array
where Adam covers half Iraq
and Eve in clouds bends over him,
and they are like a group, with stars.
What channel was that? The raucous laugh

496

rings round the yard: a hollow sound
to me. Think about it, viewers.
I shall go back, climb into my dish
and curl up like an oyster there,
swept by tides from everywhere.

24

Hullo there. That's my hamster, by the way,
in my breast-pocket, not my handkerchief.
He's the tamest creature you saw in your born days,
loves cameras too, so don't be alarmed.
What I came to say was
I won a satellite dish in a competition
which so far is a dead loss.
I tuned to a whaling epic from California,
but whenever a whale was harpooned
it turned into a baby, and some hydrophone
magnified the screams: they nearly split the house;
the blood was gallons, whale's blood, boiling out
till you got a puckered shrunken thing like a punctured doll.
Then the ship rocked in huge pressure waves,
and the set shook too; it did.
Now if I want protest I'll ask for it.
If I want excitement I want excitement.
See my hamster:
anyone that tries to harpoon him
gets a Stanley knife in his guts.
You can see from the look of me I mean that.
Well, you can see the knife too: there.
All I'm saying is
I hate arty-farty stuff,
and if that's the best you can do
I'll take down the dish and make
a swimming-pool for the hamster.
I like things straight. That's about it. All right?

25

If you ask what my favourite programme is
it has to be that strange world jigsaw final.
After the winner had defeated all his rivals
with harder and harder jigsaws, he had to prove his mettle
by completing one last absolute mindcrusher
on his own, under the cameras, in less than a week.
We saw, but he did not, what the picture would be:
the mid-Atlantic, photographed from a plane,

497

as featureless a stretch as could be found,
no weeds, no flotsam, no birds, no oil, no ships,
the surface neither stormy nor calm, but ordinary,
a light wind on a slowly rolling swell.
Hand-cut by a fiendish jigger to simulate,
but not to have, identical beaks and bays,
it seemed impossible; but the candidate –
he said he was a stateless person, called himself Smith –
was impressive: small, dark, nimble, self-contained.
The thousands of little grey tortoises were scattered
on the floor of the studio; we saw the clock; he started.
His food was brought to him, but he hardly ate.
He had a bed, with the light only dimmed to a weird blue,
never out. By the first day he had established
the edges, saw the picture was three metres long
and appeared to represent (dear God!) the sea.
Well, it was a man's life, and the silence
(broken only by sighs, click of wood, plop of coffee
in paper cups) that kept me fascinated.
Even when one hand was picking the edge-pieces
I noticed his other hand was massing sets
of distinguishing ripples or darker cross-hatching or
incipient wave-crests; his mind,
if not his face, worked like a sea.
It was when he suddenly rose from his bed
at two, on the third night, went straight over
to one piece and slotted it into a growing central patch,
then back to bed, that I knew he would make it.
On the sixth day he looked haggard and slow,
with perhaps a hundred pieces left,
of the most dreary unmarked lifeless grey.
The camera showed the clock more frequently.
He roused himself, and in a quickening burst
of activity, with many false starts, began
to press that inhuman insolent remnant together.
He did it, on the evening of the sixth day.
People streamed onto the set. Bands played.
That was fine. But what I liked best
was the last shot of the completed sea,
filling the screen; then the saw-lines disappeared,
till almost imperceptibly the surface moved
and it was again the real Atlantic, glad
to distraction to be released, raised
above itself in growing gusts, allowed
to roar as rain drove down and darkened,
allowed to blot, for a moment, the orderer's hand.

26

What was the best programme?
Oh, it was Giotto's O.
I don't argue the case
that it really was the past,
tapped under conditions
made suddenly favourable.
But how could any actor
so unpreparedly, so
swiftly yet so surely and
so gloriously seize
a sheet of pure white paper
and with a black loaded brush
paint a perfect circle?
The camera was so close
that no trick or device
could have stayed undetected.
No, it was Giotto's O.
The papal envoy, I observed,
crossed himself at the sight –
needlessly, there was no magic
either black or white, it
was only the life of a man
concentrated down
to his finger-tips in the great
final ease of creation
which in its silence and
no longer laboriously
circles round and out.

27

The programme that stays most in my mind
was one you called the Dance of the Letters.
The graphics here was altogether
crisp and bright and strong and real.
First that gallows, with the dust
whirling across the square to sting
a blackened and unfeeling face
and tear at the unreadable placard
pinned to its slowly twisting chest
resolved itself into a T.
Then the car, in bird's-eye view,
crawling through narrow streets to bang
its bomb-load and its girl martyr
into a crowded market-place
stopped, became a fiery H.

Mothers, children, grandfathers, all
knew how to line the desert dirt-road
in a few black rags, and stretch out bowls
in their twig arms or hold out only
arms, till their appeal froze
in stifling fly-black heat to form
an E. But then another E
was gently, tentatively drawn
from the hard, half-shining prongs
of a rake; the gnarled gardener
was keeping his patch clean and rich,
weedless and airy, able to deliver
the vegetables of the year.
In a courtyard, shaded with awnings,
where a tethered, slew-mouthed camel chewed,
one red earthen water-jar
as old as history waited in its stand,
turning at last into an N.
A fisherwoman, pregnant, walked
slowly along a rocky shore,
but then transformed into a ship
with blowing spinnaker sailed out
in her whole woman's life to break
silence only with the whipping
of the sheets and with the song
she or the wind threw back to us.
She left us, melted into the white
of a D that rang out through the blue.

from Themes on a Variation
1988

Acknowledgement

In December 1986 Edwin Morgan and Peter McCarey began 'reconstructing' som fairly well-known poems. The series was initiated by Peter McCarey, who worke first on each poem, Edwin Morgan countering with his own contribution; th whole sequence was published in *Verse* (4.2). Edwin Morgan's half is reprinte here, pp. 527-30.

The Dowser

With my forked branch of Lebanese cedar
I quarter the dunes like downs and guide
an invisible plough far over the sand.
But how to quarter such shifting acres
when the wind melts their shapes, and shadows
mass where all was bright before,
and landmarks walk like wraiths at noon?
All I know is that underneath,
how many miles no one can say,
an unbroken water-table waits
like a lake; it has seen no bird or sail
in its long darkness, and no man;
not even pharaohs dug so far
for all their thirst, or thirst of glory,
or thrust-power of ten thousand slaves.
I tell you I can smell it though,
that water. I am old and black
and I know the manners of the sun
which makes me bend, not break. I lose
my ghostly footprints without complaint.
I put every mirage in its place.
I watch the lizard make its lace.
Like one not quite blind I go
feeling for the sunken face.
So hot the days, the nights so cold,
I gather my white rags and sigh
but sighing step so steadily
that any vibrance in so deep
a lake would never fail to rise
towards the snowy cedar's bait.
Great desert, let your sweetness wake.

1986

Variations on Omar Khayyám

1

The caravan-master rose and clapped his hands.
The camel-men dashed out their coffee-dregs,
cracked whips, cried, cracked jokes, slapped, coaxed,
loaded, prodded; the beasts rose, groaned,
unknelt, rocked upright, stood, snaked their necks,
showed their teeth, splayed their toes,

softly stamped the cool dawn sand.
The master strapped on his gauntlet, his falcon flapped,
he spoke to it, it shook its bell, he strode, the whole
long line swayed off, set out, awake, slow, cheerful, steady,
robes loose, mongrels yapping, brasses bright,
banter of women, jingle of bangles, till the sun rose

and fed on them from red to orange, orange
to yellow, yellow to white, swallowed
the last black distant dots and filled the screen
where they had filed past, almost like life,
in close-up or in long-shot, wound off a reel
in the dark archive bay. Outside the ship
asteroids sparkled, hurtled; behind it the train
of its flotilla swung past Mars, all space
its battered caravanserai. The crews were wild,
half-trained, had stashed tequila, zithers, mescal,
hamsters, revolvers, the captain had macaws with headphones,
a cook was ejected, exploded, but still the majestic
tattered drove tried the universe.
Burnt-out computers, pushed from airlocks like blackheads,
made a cindertrack across another screen
as the convoy diminished and disappeared

and that panel flickered, not crowded round
by angels, not in heaven, but hung one moment
in annihilation's waste, the console glowed
unplayed by fingers, the code changed
every instant, a cold wind hurried down the steps
and ruffled the fresh dark well of life;
to taste it, drink from it, human lips
will do if they will not hold back,
but they must hurry, they must run,
we must run with our thirst,
all must hurry with their water-skins,
all must not knock but go,
all must slake and store,
throats, pitchers, all we have
and that is not enough,
when stars are setting, and the well
brims one moment, and the caravan
starts out for the dawn
of nothing, nothing at all.

A hand rose above the marshes near Basra,
high and bold over the broken land.
Everyone saw it, there was no hiding it.
A cloud of mortar smoke? No no,
it formed itself too perfectly,
though none could agree on its colour.
It held nothing – what could it hold? –
but made as if to write, on that dark blue.
We saw its fingers crouch, and move,
and thought a cordite-haunted sky had little need
of messages, or any of the rolling dead young men
awash in the shallows, gassed in foxholes,
burnt at despairing angles, left for film-crews.
Shi'a against Shi'a? Ideology
makes good dust, fills in mass graves.
No message then? Q is not N,
and never think it is, either, in this world:
every iota, hamza, shibboleth
burrs the graver, snags the plane; rules.
What will you grow on scorched homelands,
brother? Scorched homelands, after a while.

The dead roll still. The moving finger writes,
moves on. It made an error? It
did not understand you? It
missed the background? What,
you want to lure it back, you want it
to rewrite – changes – ever so slight –
glosses – is that it? Or you think it
wrote like Satan from left to right: what,
up there? in space? Or you object
a text so bald cannot be pious? What if piety
is a vulture on the roof of a torture-chamber?
You will not alter half a line,
not half a word, of that high text,
that bald text, not half a letter
that has been written in that text.

Ah but those in veils, at tombs, have tears.
Is there not a figure of pity
moving like a half-seen shadow
under the windows of those waiting
for a letter, for a step?
There is a package of effects
with no pity; closed doors; only smothered cries
are safe. Wishes

would turn back time. The martyrs
stiffened on the mudflats at night,
were long unburied. Mother and wife
re-read the official word. If they should weep
for ever, they would not wash out that word,
but they must never weep for ever.

3

Disengage, and lie back each upon the sand
as we have done so many times and may do yet.
The desert like a breathing animal
burns and grows cold, burns and grows cold,
until one day we find its cold as unremitting
as our own, while the lizard warms his blood
above us unseen. Bind the place then
with marram grass, or do not, it is as good
to trudge to wells without a cumber and let
custom carry the jar to its cool zarf.
Markers for sultans, vanishing for us.

But lying back in the quick twilight we stopped
shading the sun with our arms, and shivered.
It really was a wilderness, and the solitary spring
made it no less, nor the gaunt scrub. Women in black
took water beyond the horizon. If you tire of me,
talk to scorpions. – When I tire of you,
scorpions will talk. – I know; it was a joke.
– Never joke about the desert. Let's have a fire.
We made a fire; the stars came out.
We had a loaf of bread left, we clouded up
some pungent arak with well-water, and you began
singing that wild wavering raucous song
that seemed to tell the planets, Here we are!
Vanishing is not for us! As the fire sputtered
I crackled it into joy with more sticks,
an old piece of harness, some half-buried pages
from a lost book: the curling letters
curled again in fire, and warmed us.
– Cover me. – What? – I said, Cover me.
Not the rug. Dear God. Cover me!
Shaft me, I want all that darkness.
I want to feel everything till I feel nothing.
I want to fix the Great Bear for good
with love.

The wilderness
seemed to lift us first in its stony arms,
then further higher we were on its back
between stony wings, never fled but slowly soared,
hovered, the unbelievable heaviness
rocking us with light ease. There is no paradise
(who could believe in such shadows?) but
what there is can be so nearly so
I'd give the wilderness no other name
if you were there. There is no paradise
but you, that's all I know, here or to come.

1984

Stanzas

1

How can I love you, is there any way?
The rain that almost drove the windows in
as November left the world
had nothing in its bluster left to say
but: warm in room need never roam to win.

You let me kiss you, but your silent arms
are by your side, but what I wrap is warm
and does not struggle there,
but au revoirs at doors are powerless charms,
but still you shoulder to me through the storm.

So I twist and turn, now on, now back.
Relentless quartz hums on the mantelpiece.
Well, we have had our times,
I ought to be content, but any lack
love feels is incompatible with peace.

The lack, and so the love itself, are fed
from your eyes; they look at me in ways
I have no words for, where
something hidden half smiles, half hoods its head,
totally haunts my unresisting days.

Your red hair in the doorway is like fire.
My arms are loath to let your kindness go,
but I must turn the latch.
You are warm as a bird, as a deer, as desire.
I look at you this time. I know you know.

I was thirty-eight when you were born.
You think I want a son? Of course I do –
or daughter – but that's not it,
not it at all. I'd rather have your scorn
than you should never know what runs me through –

yourself, you are the blade, the freeing light
that cuts imagined age to shreds, and doubts
from veins, and solitude
away, quite altogether, cuts day and night
until there's just eternity, and shouts

of wakened earthbound sleepers, metal horns
making cracks in doomed ramparts, songs
as tough as tundra, sails
tearing doldrums apart like white-hot thorns,
the chrysalis of rights, the dying wrongs –

I can never shrink back, I tell you that,
you've drawn me out on such an instant thread
I'm like a flower, sunned,
turning, glowing, thrusting the grubby tat
of rootedness deep in the garden bed

so we can soar if we should want to soar,
or make a marigold of the whole air,
of that entire bright place,
where pungent perfumes never known before
would wind the world up through them like a stair.

3

To be simple, to be clear, to be true –
the sweat and cost of it are surely such
that all must shut up shop.
Why buy, then sell, what metaphor can do?
What shoulder did metaphors ever touch?

I don't know; you're confusing me; come on.
Of course a poem doesn't seize lapels,
but can it seize the soul?
And if it does, why should comparison
not flush the ripples of a brace of bells

and flood the bays and oxbows of our hearts?
And where do these bells come from? How should I
know – carried in the wind –
I heard them, ice-cream vans, carols, parts
of dashboard Messiaen, churches even, why

can there not be bells in cities, no need
to skulk a provenance, any more than ask
the moon on Primrose Hill
if it was sailing at its cloudy speed
to see two sleepers sprawled without a mask.

All the same, it was simple to wake, to dress.
Good coffee, orange, rolls – is that not clear?
And only what is true
is harder, just a little, I confess,
except that happiness was hovering near.

4

They are not good, thoughts of the shortest day.
A vicious intermittent frequent sleet
turning to rain, not snow,
thickens from the low gloomy array
of cloud and squelches under hurrying feet.

Northern peoples take it as it comes
and even in the grey of noon can see
signs of the light that waits;
but now I only feel it as it numbs,
for you go home to him, and I to me.

Ring road buses hiss and lurch through slush,
churn kerbside mud and camouflage the street
with lumbering zebra'd drab.
The afternoon closes, and wraps the crush
of hunching anoraks and hurrying feet.

How different was that motorway return,
hour after hour, to talk, laugh, doze, to be
ourselves, clear evening, moon
and lighted towns all running like a burn:
but you went home to him, and I to me.

The darkest day at last deserts the year.
How can the sun and this earth ever meet?
I seem not to know that,
or how the fading of one haunting fear
could rid my nightmare of its hurrying feet.

5

Buffeted by every visit you make
I clutch the flying shrouds of reason, but
I need you more and more,
and anything that for resistance' sake
was rock is seething foam and floating strut.

Sometimes if we should hug or briefly cling
or lean, it is as if a furnace roared
to melt me down again
and forty years have slipped off like a ring
too tight, too gold, for this love to afford.

For it would be the simplest cost of all
if you would come to me in that exchange
no one could lose from, bind,
or stumble over, or ever miscall,
but of such a release, such ease, such range

we would ourselves be in a ring of joy
and rainbow the rough waters bright above
the earth as under it:
one springing circle linking star, bay, buoy
and the half-charted under-world of love –

love that rules, whatever we may say,
taking us to peaks and troughs new-found
where we may praise our stars
or plead on our bent knees against them, grey
hair or red, gone to earth, green as the ground.

6

The year dissolves in solid days of rain,
runs out, runs off with everything except
you, what you brought me,
gave without having to give, the pain
of the lit fire, the drawn resin that wept.

And I would have nothing other than that.
How the story will end, I cannot see.
You must take stock, take stock!
says the old year. I've scrubbed; shaken the mat;
changed calendars; touch of paint; house, so. But me?

I would have nothing other than what has changed.
You have peeled off some covering, some coat
I thought I needed, when
all I needed was to see it gone, estranged,
not mine, not me. I settled and I wrote

those lines, these lines, only to be true.
Let us be level-headed! With the head?
The head is like a bird,
all quick, hot, hungry, darting through the blue
or two eyes in a rainbush, shivering, unfed –

alive though! We live, we feel, we know
the truth's in feeling, and the openness
feeling must give at last.
Come on then buzz my door and shake the snow
from your padded jacket if January whiteness

drives wetness away; come in; the kettle's on,
the books are out, I die for your look, your talk.
You see how easy I am.
Good God how that Chalk Farm moon knocked and shone!
Have you not tried my heart? It has no lock.

                                                        1986

The Room

After René Magritte, Souvenir de voyage III (1951)

It was a blustery March day in the mountains
when she told him they had come to the end of the story,
she would not see him again, he should take a job
in the next village. As she looked up at him,
holding her hair back from her eyes, he shuddered
at a determination nothing would tug her from.
Daffodils bowed; twigs raced past; the sky
was in a ferment. She tugged her coat
and turned back quickly along the street.

He ran from that place, pounded the craggy paths,
threw oaths after the loose stones he kicked
into the chasm, choked back exclamations
the wind did not cut first. Abandonment
drove him forward and flew before him.
Blindly he made the straggling lower village,
slowed down, kept silent, picked an inn.
'Here is the key. You'll find the room all right,
on the first floor.' The dusty stairs seemed endless,
the landing clock could hardly bring itself
to tick, the greasy air he groped through
had gone viscous as at last he gripped the key
and slowly ground its tons of metal home.

And the room waited for the jilted man
to join it, for its life, like his, had stopped.
Its bare floor-boards, table, thick damask cloth
were already half-fossilized, and the same rock
they were becoming had invaded the book,
the bowl of fruit, the bottle and its glass.
Stone shutters opened on an airless world
of stone that pressed its twisted pinnacles
almost into the room. What balcony,
what garden, what sky? There was nothing
unpetrified, uncracked, unpitted, pitied.

Only the lock is not stone: slowly it turns.

1985

'Dear man, my love goes out in waves'

Dear man, my love goes out in waves
and breaks. Whatever is, craves.
Terrible the cage
to see all life from, brilliantly about,
crowds, pavements, cars, or hear the common shout
of goals in a near park.
But now the black bars arc
blue in my breath – split – part –
I'm out – it's art,
it's love, it's rage –

512

Standing in rage in decent air
will never clear the place of care.
Simply to be
should be enough, in the same city, and let
absurd despair tramp and roar off-set.
Be satisfied with it,
the gravel and the grit
the struggling eye can't lift,
the veils that drift,
the weird to dree.

Press close to me at midnight as
you say goodbye; that's what it has
to offer, life
I mean. Into the frost with you; into
the bed with me; and get the light out too.
Better to shake unseen
and let real darkness screen
the shadows of the heart,
the vacant part-
ner, husband, wife.

                                                    1987

Waking on a Dark Morning

1

If anything was ever even as at ease
As where they lay when it had made a scene
All but overgrown, a sole drop lost at once,
Whatever even took it from the wood
Prevaricating, although slowly, like to bounce
As clouds of clay could, thrown not to stick,
And gravity keeping a low profile might
Low even, rolling along to be milked
Of such leaden showers as can bear it,
Even for ever, even without the deference
Of a long arm, within interstices
However bright, ceilings however blue,
To carry ends however plain, if so,
It could do nothing for dry eyes, no,
Not even when they were raised right up, or closed
To run the moon's grey pack into the ground.

2

It is hardly impossible not to speak out,
Yet everyone thinks it is foolhardy to speak in.
Whatever way you come at it it goes.
The perch for anything that flies flies.
Whenever there was a void there was a move
Till everything fell forward and was seen gone.
Those that thought it was something, hardly more,
Bungled or not, blundered about all night
Till there was nothing gracious that had hardly crumbled
Before a wizening-up was seen never to be impossible
As long as nothing could change otherwise,
For all its blowzy bluster. To be winged,
Lying, a shout more than ever unheard,
With anything blood could speak, they knew better,
And the smoke was only curling into nothing
When things that might have made a ring were silent.

3

Every shot is dumped, for all the flare.
They imagined nothing like survivors,
The arrow was to keep in its side, the earth
Being as ready as it had always been.
Even if it was slow, they wanted it.
Their plumes are petrified into the causeway.
What armourers are at large for, august though it is,
Needed even less singing in its veins
When the dogs passed over like a wavering banner
Someone had sewn something darker in
Than any night it streamed through. For the fire,
No one who never saw it ever knew
What solemn canopies, melting in swags,
Were crowns, or jewels dropped on cheeks like eyes
Were only that, or ever felt the weight
Of one intolerable iron veil.

4

Even what was struggled for, if there,
Was anybody's, hardly more than the dark
But felt as smoke or mud or fog or fur,
While open-windowed curtains breathed like gills,
Half-seen in worlds half-thought, in seas half-sailed,
For anyone believes a heavy sheet,
And it was almost very cold, or colder;
Old glaciers new as they lurched inches, metres

Into the sound; nothing is far away; it snored,
The blowhole. Wherever they dived they thought
It could never really, or hardly ever, be darker,
Yet bands of it charged them, unrelenting,
Not even ever what they knew, not blinding them
But sending them all bound like mummies upward
Right into what could only laugh at drowners
Shouting to swim without a leg or arm.

5

No, it was only one; in the dream two,
In the nightmare many. The sleeper still sketched
His groaning wraiths in shapes of stars and seals
Though nothing ever shot an autumn sky
Or mewed, whatever might have been half-human
Or might have blazed and crashed or cradled omens
Was in the process, off the process, the profound
Could only ever even think it sounded.
Jetsam of a crumpled dogfish sea-purse,
The sleeper's pillow gave an ear a jolt,
A rasp of rusty sandpaper, his skin
Bled down the bed clasped by such last shagreen
As the most grave and desperate sharks of daybreak
Laboured to give, and any knew it was,
Whatever might be thought of dawn, like care,
Or pain, or even horror, not never, but now.

6

It was an early bus that wakened me,
Braking at the stop outside my window.
The thin curtains filtered an amazing light,
Half red, half silver-grey, into the room.
The amaryllis on the sill seemed ready
To take off with a cry, a bird the shadows
Were slipping from, and every last concealment.
I yawned, and stretched out like a starfish.
Memory threw up streaks of something dark.
I found I did not even want to know.
How quick the deadly shades are, to crowd back
As if they could not stand a waking man!
The night never wanted me to speak, did it?
But speak we will, and clearly too. The great
Rude day strides the roofs to rouse me. Rouse too
The friend I love who makes his star elsewhere!

1986

The Gurney

A gaunt, wasted, childlike bag of bones
was all they had to wheel in on the gurney.
One lover, one van-driver were all the procession.
They found a cardboard box marked ROCK HUDSON,
bundled the body in, slung the box onto the cot,
ran with it as pressmen banged the crematorium doors,
rolled their bungled parcel straight into the oven
and watched it burn so fast that the very body
was nothing, as its dignity was, as we all may be,
in an instant. No camera recorded
what can be written. Everyone needs someone,
when cot and box are waiting for their journey.

1986

The Bench

After Tom Phillips, Benches

Honey-brown varnish glistens: Easter hymn.
Even its WET PAINT sign sings out spring's here.
It's sturdy, foursquare, brown, abstract, and clear.
Nothing could make the backdrop tree buds dim
or undo wonder from the sharp fresh green
of daffodil strikes but this silent thing
that sits and shouts, a throne to kid a king,
and when he rises, nakedness is seen.
But nothing sticks except a twig, dropped there
by frenziedly building crows. The March wind
tugs at it, but it will not stir, or mar
perfection less by letting the air bare
its print. No caws, no nest, no brood is thinned.
The first to brush the twig off sees the scar.

One thing is certain, it is not abstract.
Who can see the wooden slats for five, six
people, a dog (seven!), pigeons, a mix
of life as warm in its midsummer fact
and midday pause as ever hit a park
with one moment withdrawn from every pain?
Crackle of crisps lost in hot blue space, brain
at a drowsy crossword, crumbs in an ark
of fingers held out (holy that too!) as

516

treasures for motley wings and scavengers,
mingled with 'I don't know, that's what he said –'
and '– wants one of those instant cameras'
and '– a nice bit of ham –'; those passengers
race in their happiness towards the dead.

Leaves die, but not the tree, not yet, not soon.
Red, yellow, crinkled, papery, they scrape
along the bench, collect at the slumped shape
of a tramp; they've nothing to say; forenoon,
afternoon he sleeps, stirs, shifts, mutters, feels
October probing sluggish arteries,
clutches his coat like a cloak. Batteries
of sleet wait to be loosed, not yet. With squeals
cut by rising gusts, children chase and dart.
There is a thud of chestnuts, and one breaks.
What a soft sheeny tender eye looks out
in wonder from its shattered shell! Take heart
it says. The old man stares at it. The rakes
rattle in sheds, there is a far-off shout –

never heard in the whiteness over all
and the seat quite filled with high-drifted snow
like a dust-sheeted hurdy-gurdy. Go
by it still, good winter walkers! The fall
of silent feet dislodges a few grains.
Whistle and breath might melt a dozen more.
But suddenly all flakes are in uproar:
a great floundering setter coughs and strains
and leaves his lead, flounces onto the bench
through wet white flying sprays and veils, and skids
wild claws along the wood at last, shakes, barks,
a snowdog breaking bonds, his boisterous wrench
shows sage winter callow. With white eyelids
he grins; his master laughs. They see lambs, larks.

1985

Nineteen Kinds of Barley

Acclaim was one of eighty thousand waving and bristling in the stadium; his ears crackled in the squeezing heat as he moved with the surge.

Celt was a harp of cobwebs; when they plucked him in the morning he yielded creaks and shivers, a scrape of pure mildew.

Corgi grew up on aircraft steps but never rooted well; his dwarfish habit came from too much handling.

Delta was seldom tracked down; she ran like quicksilver through the monsoons and left an India of children thrusting spears at the sun.

Doublet was woven tight and velvety and pulsed like a heart; they cut him down with pikes.

Flare came suddenly, like a moor-burn, a royal flush, a tenth wave; wild airs and rounded clouds jostled to solicit him.

Golden Promise shook his spiky hair and straddled the shore; cows' tongues rasped his belly when he turned white with salt.

Gold Marker strode over the hill's flank unfurling his strawy banner next to the hot yellow patch of rape; he whistled, and marched like mustard.

Golf had a rough time but grew stoic and hardy; prone on the headland he pricked his ears like flags.

Javelin struck hard and straight through the rain and shone; gloved harvesters swore as the steely beards drew blood and clanked down the chute for robots' bannocks.

Klaxon was so strong he made rutting stags stumble; brewed Thor's mash in Asgard.

Kym leaned lightly, listening; too far off her father Kandym stalked the wastelands, binding and rebinding the restless Kara Kum from his bag of marram.

Lina crouched in a tangled sea of tresses at the feet of Jesus; her roots moaned for the crop they had still to give.

Midas swaggered in a cave-mouth, lolled on couch-grass, played with bear-bones; now gapes, purple, staring, drowned in his seed-hoard.

Nairn was agoraphobic, itched to be malted, doze ten years in casks; a second life under ribs of men.

Natasha bent down her drear dark brows as the thousand-mile-old wind swept to her across the steppe; unbreaking bent down, bowed down, bore unbroken.

Piccolo piped the high meadows awake; his pink-shears gave the dawn chorus an edge.

Themis swayed to the left, to the right, courtly, with all her companions; a chorus of measure, the breathing of the earth, in a windless field.

Vista was a blue-eyed tundra-watcher, hard as nails; when the Yenisei came roaring through her bed she snapped her fingers and cast grain in his face, extending her empire north, towards the ice.

1984

A Trace of Wings

Corn Bunting	shy but perky; haunts fields; grain-scatterer
Reed Bunting	sedge-scuttler; swayer; a cool perch
Cirl Bunting	small whistler; shrill early; find him!
Indigo Bunting	blue darter; like metal; the sheen
Ortolan Bunting	haunts gardens; is caught; favours tables
Painted Bunting	gaudy flasher; red, blue, green; what a whisk!
Snow Bunting	Arctic flyer; ghost-white; blizzard-hardened
Basil Bunting	the sweetest singer; prince of finches; gone

from these parts

1985

The Hanging Gardens of Babylon

for John Furnival's 50th birthday

the hanging gravids of babyland
the happy gurgles of bath
the hassle gabblers of gath
the horrible gobblers of broth
the harridan guardians of barchester
the hapless gods of brecht
the hubble gargle of bubble
the hearty gaekwars of baroda
the hatter's gust of blawearie
the hunter's ghost of baskerville
the humming gullies of brum
the hazardous gasps of bellerophon
the heavy glums of brood
the hollow gums of cholmondeley
the hustling grunts of numb
the hungry guzzlers of slough
the hundred groans of caledonia
the hasty grooms of glory
the hallowed grubs of china
the harried gagsters of cuckfield
the hobbling gaffblowers of tirana
the horny golachs of wigtown
the hurricane galleons of duncansby
the hedda gablers of gloucester
the headless gardeners of kew
the handless gamblers of crewe
the hamfisted gasfitters of hyderabad
the hairy gaddings of sable
the hawthorn gatherers of woodchester
the handheld gardenias of wilts
the hyperactive geotropism of vainglory
the hyacinthine gorgeousness of samson
the holy guns of fun
the halfhearted garters of flannel
the heterogeneous galligaskins of folderol
the harmless gauds of fabulous
the hangdog gadroons of fallopia
the huddled gundogs of fenland
the hagridden gussets of fulvia
the hurdy gurdy of fux
the hidden gleams of furness
the hollied garments of hope
the hengest gleemen of furnivall
the hornbeam glades of fifty
the halcyon galleys of furnival

1982

520

A Bobbed Sonnet for Code Cobber

for Bob Cobbing's 65th birthday

climbing Popocatepetl with popcorn packets
humming Mahabharata humbly but unhurriedly
surfing through Sargasso with syntagmatic spinnakers
throwing tantrums at Antananarivo train-hoots

Zoroastrian asterisks satirized astutely
Athabaskan aubades ululated unabashed
ro-ro car-wash scrub-up freak-out
tsetse-zizzing isthmus-asthma

onomatopoeic articulation incomparably extrapolated
hubble-bubble hob-nob with heavy-breathing hobos
shaman's-salmon psalm for spawn-master's shawm

slaloming along shalom-hung swan-songs
simply spellbinding spielbonding spoolbending
loading London with logodaedalian lauds

1986

521

The Computer's First Birthday Card

many returns happy
many turns happier
happy turns remain
happy remains turn
turns remain happy
turn happy remains
remains turn happy
mains return happy
happy mains return
main happy returns
main turns happier
happier main turns
happier many turns
many happier turns
many happier turns
many happier turns
er turns er turns ?
happy er er happy ?
er *error* er *check* !
turn er pre turns !
many happy turners
+$?-+!=%0½^´*/£()&
many gay whistlers
no no no no no no !
many gainsboroughs
stop stop stop stp
happier   constables
010101010101010101
raise police pay p
ost early for chri
stmas watch forest
fires get well soo
n bon voyage KRRGK
many happy returns
eh? eh? eh? eh? eh? eh?

1966

Byron at Sixty-Five

The rumour of my death has long abated.
The Greeks still love me, but I don't love Greeks
Except for one – or two; I must be fated
To wander and to change; when the mast creaks
I smell the salt and know my soul unsated
Until it finds the language no man speaks.
And what is that? some simpleton demands
Who's never heard the seething of the sands.

No seething here, though, or not much; the plop
And gurgle of old timbers slowly walloped
By oily steamship wash is not the top
Of pleasure; no sea-horses ever galloped
A winning streak in muck; what made me stop
In Venice? Well, the curtain's nicely scalloped,
My dear contessa's maid has lit a fire,
And shut-out January re-lights desire.

Don't laugh; Childe Harold may be grey and paunchy,
A lame, ex-English, ex-Scottish ex-Romantic
Soon to be ex-everything, including ex-raunchy.
But still I'll have a gaudy night, not frantic
Like forty years ago; and at dawn she
'll re-tell, re-live, forgive each aging antic.
All right, it's comedy; but the comedy's high
You must admit: palazzo, contessa, and I.

Hear how the north wind batters at the pane!
A spot of grog's the thing for nights like this –
Not too much seltzer. Sailors in the main
Have grog for birthdays – victories – and Christmas –
And I'm a sailor – and I've no champagne –
So here's to Doctor Grog, and let's not miss
His therapeutic memories of sails,
And holystoning pigtailed tars, and whales –

Speaking of which, I've just read *Moby-Dick*
And think its author very enigmatic
But enigmatically great, one flick
Of that huge fluke and verse is in the attic,
Prose fills the morning-rooms and thrashes quick
About the hall, large, muscular, and vatic.
We poets must throw off our well-pressed laurels,
Let children play with chinkling beads and corals.

He said. But unresisting, took a rhyme,
Watched the floating bulk of language approach,
Rose up, and at the crucial tilt of time
Shot out that sharp harpoon and saw it broach
The stanza's shoulders to a ship-bell's chime.
And Melville needn't try to drive a coach
And horses through my case in his next book.
He uses metre in his prose, the crook.

But still, America comes on and on,
Land of the turkey, Edgar Allan Poe,
Clam chowder, telegrams, and Audubon.
I think I'll take a tour there, just to know
A New World now that this damned creaky old one
Has got itself a gout in every toe
And totters, more than marches, to the future,
Afraid to break its grim dynastic suture.

What do I care, they'll say, an exiled whiner,
A superannuated stateless has-been.
Victoria's not much of a Regina
In my opinion; let the age come clean,
And stop pretending everything is finer
Because the blood and sweat are seldom seen.
You twitch your skirt, but that still leaves the dust.
You pay, but you don't give, the workhouse crust.

O Forty-Eight, the year of revolutions,
Men on the streets from Budapest to Bradford,
We saw such rhetoric, such resolutions,
So many torchlight columns, but all baffled,
All gone into a night without solutions,
And storm-clouds burdening the vengeful scaffold.
Who would not think the tyrants had returned,
And all our boyhood hopes swept up and burned?

Marx and Engels wouldn't; I read their book,
Manifest der Kommunistischen Partei.
They say a spectre's haunting every nook
Of power in Europe, and that chains will fly.
If that is true, the printing-presses shook
Like thunder when these pages flickered by.
Who could believe them? Yet I read it twice,
And thought I heard the cracking of the ice.

I sent a copy off (in German of course)
To Wordsworth, with a pleasing dedication
'To our oldest living renegade'. The force
Of this last-minute well-meant operation
To save his soul proved to be over-coarse,
Or else the man was well beyond salvation.
Soon afterwards, he went to meet his Maker,
An unrepentant stupid Tory Laker.

Peace to all such! as parsons say – not me.
Stir up the fire, Teresa dear, it's dark
And wild outside. Mushrooms, olives, Chianti
Will keep us going in our little ark –
Not so little, I know – that sniffs the sea
And rots and shivers here beneath St Mark.
Every house moves in Venice, drifting down
Canals of blackness to a mirrored town.

How easily we slip into abstraction,
And thoughts of gloom and distant things, things lost
Or never won, the sour fruits of inaction,
And joys that jaded with relentless cost.
Our very loves are ivied, fraction by fraction
Crumbling loose at the onset of frost.
– It isn't so, my sweet contessa, is it?
Ovid lodged *Tristia*, ours are but a visit.

And any time I feel myself go tristful,
I write a stanza to my staunch Teresa.
Knowing her short of patience for the wistful,
I improvise a shivaree to please her –
Throwing up a palace, fistful by fistful,
Of crystal, smarter than pyramids in Giza,
Within the Hyde Park of my mind. O Paxton,
Houser of catalogues undreamt by Caxton,

Such cornucopias of imperial trash –
Bronze Gothic chairs – three-hundred-bladed knives –
Pudic statues – rhino horns – calabash
And collapsible piano – sets of tropic gyves –
Such ludicrously philistine panache
As millions never saw in all their lives,
Or loved as soon as saw, or had displayed
Before them in a threadbare horsy glade.

Horses! God, I'm so fat. What a front to flaunt!
I rode my last horse fifteen years ago.
Today I'd float, not swim, the Hellespont.
And every winter this damned foot eats crow
(As Yankees say) and drags me taunt by taunt.
I'm just a sack of gibes, milord for show.
But dinna fash, lassie (as we Scots say).
We'll sing to keep the mulligrubs at bay.

We're at the nameless bottle now; it's good.
Your rings wink in the gaslight as you pour.
Gas is the thing; I never understood
Why some still rig their dripping candles galore,
Parlours like altars, wax-ends in the food.
Electric's next – science to the fore!
I think I'm ready for some bread and cheese.
Don't get up. I have the pantry keys.

There we are. Now if only Ada was here –
You know I miss my daughter – she can talk
Like an angel on sine and cosine, severe
But winning with it, you could never mock
The hypotenuse in her company, or sneer
Your way into some asymptotic baulk.
She's working all out now with Charles Babbage,
And that's a far cry from roast beef and cabbage.

It seems they have the plan for a machine
To do computing, a thousand sums a minute.
This engine has not trundled on the scene
Yet, but d'you think there might be something in it?
They need a language that is not – obscene –
Or human – or Albanian – or Inuit.
Ada wants the very machines to confer.
Perhaps they'll name the language after her.

Babbage and Marx – can that be what's to come?
Machines to compute, and all the workers free?
My dear contessa, what a maximum
Of bliss it would be to come back and see –
To burn the dungeons that have made men dumb,
And wade whole rivers to the liberty tree.
Burns said *I guess an' fear*. Ah when we do,
Mark then and shape the new life thundering through.

How red the fire is now – let it go down.
We never tried the pine-cones Lisa left us.
I must look out. The canal is silver-brown,
Half slurry and half sleet. Weather's bereft us
Of distant towers. Gondoliers would frown
But there are none. Whatever angel cleft us
Out of the rock is gone. We are ours to keep.
Bed, my love; pop the gas; to touch, and sleep.

                                                    1985

Shakespeare: a Reconstruction

from Matthew Arnold, 'Shakespeare'

Others are open. You give a high smile
as you win the Prospero stakes, and silently
bury your books deeper than any auditor
could find them sound or unsound.
Did you 'die a papist', hate dogs, love swarthy
ironhaired women and fair flibbertigibbet men
or are the sonnets a load of. Cigarette foil
litters our searching and poring. You sit there
self-sustaining, a white cloud, while your wife
sews your new coat-of-arms *passim*. Better sew
than unpick! See Marlowe? Well.
All pains the immortal spirit must endure,
all weakness that impairs, all griefs that faze
rebels like him, you filched to salt your plays.

                                                    1986

To the Queen: a Reconstruction

from Tennyson, 'To the Queen'

Revealed in death, will you still hold
Some nobler office upon earth
Than powdered arms or braided girth
Could give the wanton queens of old,

O Liberace? Royal grace
Floated you on a thousand stages
With the diamonds of the ages
And irresistible embrace

Stretched out for all, such love, such care,
Dracula in white mink, no time
To make demands of modern rhyme
With candelabra everywhere;

Now – where your honeyed music wakened
A million matrons' stifled calls,
And palace-like piano-walls
Vibrated as the yearning beckoned –

Take, Sir or Madam, this quick song;
For if your faults were thick as dust
In well-closed closets, you can't trust
The future will be kind. How long

Will those who thought you ruled your blood
Take to cross off your natal day,
And tell their children you were gay?
'She had her secrets since the Flood;

'She held court in another scene;
Her aides that saw her eyelids closed
Thought she could die undiagnosed,
But better far this wasted queen

'Should have a shroud of truth, and get
Its gritty ice on, not its mink
On shoulders, rings on hands – and shrink
From freedom as if narrower yet

'She had to go, in that decree
Which struck her throne and raked her till
Of tokens of the people's will,
And poled her Iron Maiden to sea.'

1987

Chillon: a Reconstruction

from Byron, 'Sonnet on Chillon'

My God we must repel a plea for dungeons
even by the back door of mind over matter.
Anyone who says chained Biko's mind
was chainless underwrites tyranny.
Bonivard had it easy. A damp vault

six feet above lake-level? Dayless gloom
in 'really a spacious and rather airy vaulted room'?
Come on, I love you Byron, but that won't do.
What, Bunyan's Chillon was a holy place
because he begot his Pilgrim there?
That *Progress* never served progress!
Boethius left footprints too? *De Consolatione*
Philosophiae would suit Botha very neatly.
Let them appeal – it's quite safe – to God.

1987

True Ease in Writing: a Reconstruction

from Pope, 'An Essay in Criticism', lines 362-73

True ease in writing comes to art by chance,
as those move easiest who break the dance
slightly, and almost imperceptibly –
but not quite – swing the senses surely, ably
out of the lock of echo, thud of sound,
even when classic numbers mow the ground
flat.
High maze hedges hide – but not quite – the hat
of the six-footer tangoing bravely through:
no, it does not take two.
And if sharp-fanged Carmilla scours the plain,
it is by moonlight, by fits and starts, for blood, with might and main.

1987

On Time: a Reconstruction

from Milton, 'On Time'

I don't know about the snail, it's okay I think,
I don't envy it though. How could I,
having been to Lapland and back in a day,
stamping snowboots on Concorde steps
at tingling Rovaniemi with a New Year pack
of reindeer slices in my hand and
five hours of frozen river and pine
inside me, long or short
impossible to say.
Afterwards, that day seemed a week,

a fortnight, a world, Puck's world, a puck
birled across a void of sticks for luck.
Yet Concorde's a snail too,
I know it is. I'm number 102
in the civilian list for 1992's
space shuttle. Was, before the disaster. What year
will it be now? Like a supreme throne
high on time, the happy-making ship
half guides, half rocks me as I climb,
gross earth snail lapping broken glass,
never tired of stars, always longing to sit
in the brilliant cone, even with chance, even for a time.

1987

Not Marble: a Reconstruction

from Shakespeare, Sonnet 55: 'Not marble...'

A Sqezy bottle in Tennessee,
if you want permanence, will press
a dozen jars into the wilderness.
It's bright, misspelt, unpronounceably
itself. No one loves you! I guess
there's *amour propre* in a detergent not to be
called sluttish. Vulgarity
dogs marble, gildings; monuments are a mess.
Exegi this, *exegi* that. Let's say
I am in love, crushed under the weight
of it or elated under the hush of it.
Let's not just say. I actually am.
Hordes, posterities, judges vainly cram
the space my love and I left yesterday.

1987

Halley's Comet

I visit them from time to time, to see
their face and their state; seventy-six years
are in my sight but as a day. Old fears
have gone, they speed their little probes to me
but never guess that I might have a thought
to match. A ball of gritty slush, a tail

530

that whisks its gas about! They never fail
to measure what the measureless has brought,
and when it sails away from them they know
it must return. I have considered this,
and as I gulp their probes down I feel roused
and full of fire and eagerness to go
so far beyond them they will rage to miss
a torch so undemonstratively doused.

1985

The Gorbals Mosque

Archbishops, moderators, and ambassadors,
high doctors and imams, administrators
and highest persons of goodwill joined hands,
delivered words, prayed, smoothed their bands
and threw their smiles to cameras; Egypt,
Mecca, Pakistan, Strathclyde, which outstripped
which in high amity by the minaret?
At dusk, the dome glowed like an amulet
among the gap-site detritus, the inaugurators
had swept back to their stations, the doors
leaked light. Sightseers lingered but not
for long, as mock-muezzins howled a shot
across their bows, and one boy with some wit
shouted 'White trash!' and his companion hit
a capping relish with 'Renegades!' while they strode
and laughed and kicked the rubble of the road,
raucously ululating into town,
but yet not really wishing the bright mosque down.

1984

Rules for Dwarf-Throwing

1. If a dwarf is thrown through a glass window or glass door, he
    must wear gloves and a suitable mask.

2. If a dwarf is thrown through a burning hoop, extinguishers must
    be provided.

531

3. If a dwarf is thrown down a well, the organizers must ensur that the bottom of the well is dry, and is covered by leaves to depth of three inches.

4. If a dwarf is to be thrown across the path of an oncoming train the thrower must previously satisfy the organizers that he bear no personal malice to the throwee.

5. If a dwarf is thrown into a pond or river, he must wear a wetsui and need not be tightly bound.

6. If dwarfs are thrown at night, they may be painted with phos phorescent paint, so that the point of impact may be clearly established.

7. If a dwarf refuses to be bound in the usual way before throwing he may be put in a straitjacket of the requisite size.

8. If a dwarf utters any sound whatsoever, either in flight or at the moment of impact, the throw will be disqualified.

9. If a jockey impersonates a dwarf, and wins a competition because his light weight allows him to be thrown farthest, he will be liable to a fine of £1000 or three years imprisonment.

10. It is strictly forbidden, in dwarf-throwing literature and publicity to refer to dwarfs as 'persons of restricted growth' or 'smal people'.

1986

The Bear

Come here, come here, I'm really playful today,
don't be afraid, they've even made me a chair
or a hammock of sorts I love to loll in
and surprise my visitors. I am never hungry
since I took this part. No no, I don't mean him,
Antigonus. Good lord, as soon as we're off stage
we jink a little sweet rough tumble together
as like a dance as you ever saw, nothing
like death, nothing like death. I like that man.
He gives me herring from the brown barrel.
He gives me beer and honey once a week.
I could tear the lid right off that barrel

with a swipe and stuff myself stiff with fish
but I don't. I nuzzle the man. I get enough.
The only one I can't like is that Perdita,
she's a hussy in all that greenery-yallery,
with her pert stamping foot, his I should say,
these boys are a saucy pampered lot,
if they got some women I would really dance.
Antigonus though, he seems to like bears.
Strange man, but good. He won't change.
I love to creep up on him, hardly
breathing, stand at his back and tap
his shoulder. He never jumps,
just smiles. 'This is the chase,'
he says, 'we must go on for ever.'

                                                        1987

Save the Whale Ball

(heading in *The Times*, 2 June 1981)

Is the Whale Ball worth saving? That is the real question.
What is to be said for and against it? Let us recall
the history and origin of the Whale Ball.
Old people – very old people – will perhaps remember
the Decade of Demise, when whale sightings thinned out
year by year, and the end could not be delayed.
Even whales pampered in oceanariums by every art
drooped and refused to mate. It was as if
some once promising species had beached
on a shelf of evolution they were not made to master.
So all that time their skeletons were gathered and stored,
in hundreds and in tens, and the last few. The world
agreed about them dead if not alive, no
whaling nation refused to subscribe to the monument.
Two generations of schoolchildren have yawned through
official films of the building of the Whale Ball,
but I have heard old men with sticks and bright eyes,
in sheltered housing and hospice, or sitting by the shore,
thrill to the memory of that idealism
and that propitiation, that overplus of patience and skill,
that overkill, that gigantic hyperborean scrimshaw
perched on a scarp at Angmagssalik.
How many dozen trainloads of whalebones were compacted
and fused into a spherical mass where the World
Trade Center and the Sydney Opera House could be inserted

533

like mites in a cheese, and how many craftsmen and sculptors
fretted the sphere into a thousand ancient scenes
of hunt and storm, with frozen seas and drowning men,
and flukes that smacked the arctic air, again, in bone, in vain,
in galleries of unfalling spray, and how that ball
as if some Chinese ivory ball had taken root and grown
rose white and huge into the mists of Greenland
and in a ceremony was declared fit and whole,
the records tell. Better than any barrow
of Beowulf or Breca, it broods like a boulder
from the beginning of time, and those who have heard
blizzards whistle their music through it
have come back half crazed with wonder.
But the Whale Ball is crumbling; it is too far north;
its cracks are widening, and its carved kayaks
have joined real kayaks in the sound. Some say
all megalomania has its reward: the dinosaurs,
the whales, the Whale Ball. Some would like nature
to regain the scattered bones, and in its ruthless welter
slowly rub off all signs of man, and roll
those rounded fragments in the deep-wombed currents
where who knows what might not be made of the dead.
Some would re-cast it in stainless steel; others
would pulverize it for talismans.
Some say we should have saved whales instead.

1981

Dom Raja

If you cannot get your dead to burn,
if the wood will not take, and they are still there
accusing you mornings, evenings after,
if battering rain blurs the flame,
your work spent out in profitless smoke,
if your poverty cannot even steal
matches and oil, among the many waiting
to deliver ranks of other dead,
and flies seethe where fire should,
making the eyes move again and signal
they have an indomitable reproach
for you as you stand alive in the sun:
I will put an end to this if you call for me,
I promise I will make ashes if you need me,
I will leave your accuser without a tongue

if you can pay me, and if you believe
that I know the dead and their ways
and am their king.

I tell you they are not easy to destroy,
the dead. Sometimes with a rush they are back,
circling the camp relentlessly mourning
those that are dead to them, for you
are never as remorseless as they are,
they have no bread to bake or clothes
to wash or anything but time
to fill, and swarming through the bounds
they fall on you, they tear you, eat you,
spit you out to your terror as lacking
the substance they must have. The substance
they must have is not in you and can
never be, so why do they devour you?
I can tell you they are not unappeasable
if you will ask me to tell you. I could show you
how to harrow the little hell they march from
if you were good to me, a little.
You have only to take me aside
to see my kingdom.

Look how I have pushed the broken thing like an ark
burning straight down roaring to the water-line.
I dance, I am set on a throne, my torch
is never out. My suppliants put stones
on the bodies against jackals, and run
to search for me, they scuffle and pray
and ask me to melt their guilt to drops
of fat. The dead smell me far off.
I wrestle with them until they are black.
The Ganges reaches darkly seaward.
Look where I point: the smouldering riches
drift foul and slow, then rough and swift,
still fighting, still twisting towards the living,
still throwing indignations like anchors
to scrape and scour the frowning grief
that lines the banks. The dead are so restless
that even I have to drive them before me
with all my power, but if you want me to do so
– and how few there are who want me to do so –
I will keep them silent, weltering
at the feet of their king.

1986

The Change

For all its banks bursting with bullion,
    the land of injustice will not prosper.

The skyscrapers shine as if they could never
    smell black smoke or shake to thunder.

Tanks, whips, dogs, laws – the panoply
    cracks steadily, being built over a fault.

Of course there are battleships, communications,
    planes; but the sophisticated do not have it.

The spirit has it, the spirit of the people has it,
    townships, shantytowns, jails, funerals

have it. It is no use digging in,
    rulers, unless you dig a pit to be

tipped into. Ruling has gone on too long,
    will not be saved by armbands or the laager.

The unjust know this very well.
    They lay ears to the ground, hear hooves.

Beasts, one time; an express, one time;
    men, one time; history, one time.

Straighten up and pat your holsters.
    Self-righteousness and a ramrod back

will not help. The sun goes down with you,
    other fruits ripen for other lips.

                     1987

Vereshchagin's Barrow

With every war
Vereshchagin is trundled onto a dump of mammoths.
With every war
Goya is stuffed screaming into a geode.
With every war
Kollwitz lies buried in a terminal moraine.

'There in the permafrost you cannot
read, much of the night, or go south in the winter.
Thunder scurries over you faint as sparrows' feet,
cream-heavy fogs blunder and probe unseen,
blizzards howl no louder than feathergrass.
Lay the cold to your bones,
burrow in, past a few pressed shards and hooves,
you have hardly any dimension now, except time.
It is too late to try a sign, far less a cry.
You will never make that fossil tusk a horn
to rouse the dead or bring down walls
or even flute yourself to sleep –
fools without finger-tips,
lips drawn like packthread,
an arm crushed into a rib-case,
bellies full of peat.'

    Goya stirs a thumbnail.
    Vereshchagin stretches a toe.
    Kollwitz twitches an eyelid.

'Why should you burrow upwards through the deadly soil?
Why should you want to break sorrow?
If ever you did burrow up, do you know, do you know
you would not meet air but a layer
of more permafrost impacted
in a desolate tumulus, a tangle
of Etendards and Harriers, Exocets and Sea-Darts,
Sea-Kings and Skyhawks, destroyers and destroyers?
Think about a mound
of drowned men and melted aluminium.
Can you fight your way through white-hot steel?
Can you paint the paint that's scorched off hulls?
Paint-flakes drift into snow-flakes.
The only flying-fish is the Exocet.
Car-crusher time has pushed it all on top of you.
We call it Vereshchagin's Barrow.'

    Vereshchagin groaned, kicked the mammoths' bones to
        ninepins.
    Kollwitz drove her brow like a prow through the glacier.
    Goya gave a shout, split the geode, flashed quartz.

'Well, I see there is no holding you.
Can you not take oblivion quietly?
What do wars end in but peace?

Do you think brush or pen or graver
can put flesh on a pyramid of skulls
or get a torso on a tree to sit at supper?
Are you still enslaved by Owen's old lie
that it is not sweet and fitting to die
for a homeland? Don't listen to us.
Nothing can tell you whether we are Furies
or Eumenides. Go off. Draw war.
If you have cameras, give them care.
In this world from which we speak to you
we do not trust artists any more.
I know, I know.
All right then, go.'

A mother gave her dead child's thumbprint to Kollwitz
without a word.
A hooded figure rose and followed Goya
without a word.
Sea-fogs trailed their coats for Vereshchagin
without a word.

1982

Uncollected Poems
1949-1982

Acknowledgement

'Spell' is the libretto for a musical composition by Martin Dalby, later titled 'Col for the Hazel Tree'. It was commissioned by Electric Phoenix with funds from the Arts Council of Great Britain (1979).

'The Triumph of Life': a Conclusion to Shelley's Poem

'Then, what is life?' I cried. 'What is this vast
Harrying along the inescapable road
Of figures into deepest sadness cast,

Regret, regression from the glory of good,
Battered and spent to phantoms in that air
Where once their hope the very winds outrode?

Does time outlast the virgin's blazing hair
And thwart the youth with death of dancing days:
Can sun and moon smother the hour of the fair?

Are yearning, effort forceless as the gaze
Bent through a dubious concealing dusk
On some impossibly beloved face?

I do not see the lover fall through lust,
Or the great heart through penury of feeling;
I do not see the soldier buy his dust

Except with pain, and his passion is the revealing
Of trust as dumb as running blood has been;
I see the flush and flash of life go stealing

From child new-born, for grief never to wean:
How can we name the folly or failing, the sin
That rises silently to intervene

Between first breath and last, so early in
And so invisible to mortal eyes?'
That spirit answered slowly then, 'To win

Beyond the loss, the wound, the fury, the cries
Such knowledge as you ask of why these are
And why all men these still disparadise

As if forepunished under Adam's star,
Nothing but time and death you need demand,
As I with narrowed lids gazing afar

Even from my poor eminence command
Half-glimpses of the answer sought by us all.
If you are eager still to understand,

Come with me now to the heights where those crags fall
From regions of the solemn clouded storm
To this green bay of grass, where eagles call

Across the air from fell to fell and arm
Their liberty with the incredible white sun,
Where lightning and the quick tornado form

That shatter cedars and oblivion,
Men with the brawling rock and oak-top thrown
To fell in dusty fields, their singing done.

Come, follow me as I lead up alone
From all the press and clamour, let the shout
Of revellers and sadder souls be borne

Like music ever more faintly blowing out
On the wind away, and make this sharp ascent,
Which may resolve or feed your heavy doubt.'

We rose, and climbed, and in the fierce wind leant
Into the body of the naked bluff.
I think the congregated blasts were sent

From the peak down with labour and mission rough
To scatter our presumption in the vale,
But we had heart and handhold firm enough

And clasped at last the ragged crest, kneeled pale
In the great roaring of the summit, but he indeed
Far paler, tugged by more than earthly gale,

And gathering strength, stood up. 'If you now lead,'
I said, 'my eyes as you have led my steps,
O let them into every quarter speed

Where to your clearer sight the world reflects
Images of that tranquillity surmised.
The air grows cold; the terrible sun sets

With stained and angry mass slowly excised
From drowsing sky; my prayer is for your haste,
Guide if you are, and friend, so characterized

By what you were, and as I read your face.
O Rousseau, soon to darkness I must wake
As the last bloom and fleck of day are chased

From this strange earth, and all my thirst reslake
At fountains of a custom-rich despair.
Temper this time with kindness for my sake!'

He raised his head into the blowing air
And spoke, against it and his weariness.
'Look down on the dusty valley lying there

So far below us that its keen distress
Swirls and travails in silence to our sense,
Remembering the reckless bitterness

Of minds from pleasure and magnificence
Snatched in the brow of manhood perilous;
Of beauty's useless shoring last defence

Against the ravager of majesties,
Of powers and prides, of true and painted cheeks
And the most beloved and the most illustrious

Blood that lip of lord or leader bespeaks;
Of poorer souls by worldly honouring
Whom chance impounded, and from years to weeks

Cut down by unjust laws their dreaming spring,
To winter banished back, widow-like mourning
For what returning time can never bring;

Of eager wayfarers in a golden morning
Whose journey night and tempest wrapped away;
Of lovers as the blessed stars adorning

The night and gloom of life, who could not stay
But cast their crying glory to the earth
And broke the precious fragments of a clay

Too fiercely fused to bear that second birth;
Of these, and more, whom mortal loss and grief
Drive like the leaves from stations of high worth,

Honour, devotion, and delight, to mad relief
Within the chariot's prancing minstrelsy
And songs far wilder than the driven leaf

Hears through October's whistling, or wretchedly
To slavelike trudging at the chariot-wheels,
Dulled, senseless but to oppressive misery

And what the heart of long-fled joy still feels.
Look down, and see in that dark cavalcade
The witless hate religion's rhetoric deals,

The smiling priest with soul as stiff as jade,
Hierarchs bland with mercy, blind with pride,
Adepts in meekness, ministering undismayed

Beneath the shadow of Christ while far and wide
They fan the dexterous demon of this world
To split minds with hot rancour, and divide,

Where they should brighten into love, and hold;
The statesmen, glib in million-pawn debate,
Who live to lie when youth and faith are hurled

From battlefields their moving pens create,
Signing indelible annihilation,
The justice of their word becoming fate;

The servile scientist, sophist in evasion,
Whose sweating zeal is lavish to destroy
Men, and men's works, beyond my indignation,

Whom savage force and statecraft now employ
Conscienceless, a prevaricating voice
Swept up with that resistless bad convoy

Bearing the nations to be smashed like toys;
And all the rest: prophet and profiteer,
The pseudo-pauper whom maudlin never cloys,

Soul-bankrupts, blackmailers of the earth's austere
Who batten on the vices of good lives,
The simulate-swearer, the tool-artificer of fear

Whetting his white-heat-hammered slander-knives,
And there the simple, there the saintly mind,
Samaritan, servant, spirit endeared which drives

From night the hearts that seemed to night assigned;
See how in one grey multitude confused
Along that path of stumbling human kind

All follow what birth and grain of growth infused
Into their incomprehensible condition,
Endlessly willing till their flesh is used

That end of which all gain their different vision,
To good or evil vowing energy,
Dreaming a happiness in this creation.

Before the everlasting lethargy
Of death, all seek what space and time can give,
And of that search see now the imagery

Below you through the twilight made to live:
The plunging timbers of the chariot,
The flashing steel and gold, the falling cliff

Whose rubble to the road's pale dust is wrought
By feet and years, by dancing and by time,
Those slavelike forms whose pleasures dearly bought

Force them the selfsame stair forever to climb,
And those bright soaring souls who stooped too soon
To scorn the harshness of temporal hail and rime

Equally with Milton and Shakespeare's mortal moon,
Caesar and Socrates and Alexander
And all the gardeners of Babylon

Wheeled through the breathless arcs of dusk to wander
Over time's plain, along its dusty way,
And dust to dust more ancient still surrender.

See where the winding road, as far away
As sight can follow, bears the stream of those
Who crossed the gulf of bodiless night to day

And took the same divinity as the rose
Before their sleeping children's faces became
Withered and sunken sadly at the close;

On this grey road all go, from womb to fame
Or to no name at all, but all know death:
Unhappy everything that hears that name

And feels the dread rebellion of the breath!
Night to the eye, how miserably sent!
Paralysis, how fell! Some rend the earth

Reckless with imprecations, some intent
On the warm minute stealing from the sun,
And some too loudly and too late repent

545

For crimes all time can never see undone.
On sense the full and polar cold must fall;
Life must be fought for, lifelessness be won.

So like some darkling-hectic funeral
You see these thousands pass across the plain
Washed in such golden poured recessional

Of light as in the west is left to flame;
Yet as they journey to that glittering west
See how the features become sharp and plain

Picked out in fire and gloom, the gilded crest
Of the high chariot, the bright reins and faces
Move into a semblance unexpressed

Of brilliant and angelic countenances
And emblems more of paradise than decay.
And as the main with moonlight moves and dances

So this long valley's long farewell to day
Seems crowded with innumerable glories
Brighter than any that have passed away.'

'But still,' I cried, 'what surer histories
Remain beyond my hunger to recall?
You blazon twilight rich with mysteries,

But why be blazoning that shield at all
If the smooth face keeps nothing of such art?
Although these splendours day and night should fall

Across the moving figures, part by part
Investing luminously with that fire,
Surely the fire disdains to touch their heart?

Each marvellous jewelled face we here admire
Is surely of the same dark substance made
Though sparkled over with light, nor any higher

Flown the mind from its deep inward shade
Because a brow receives the tide of the sun?'
That spirit replied, 'Yet all is well arrayed,

In rags or in the sunlike robes all one;
According as the light of thought can strike,
Its lightning shows the magnitude and sum

Of mazed Orion in a simple cheek,
As lovers on this earth most surely know.
And if the effulgence here is not unlike

Some meditation swept from heaven so,
Some bending thought upon the affairs of men,
What wonder that all this wretched world below

Into pure blaze and dazzle should stray again
As once in Eden when that thought all day
Brooded on rose and man and woman without stain?

Remember always how those glories play
About the millions moving to their peace
As the sun sets on even this rough way,

But never forget what things will never cease,
Still unassuaged in that warm benediction.
The fires that burned for Bruno must increase,

Sleepless are the barbarisms of Goya's malediction,
Stephen is stoned although his name grows dim,
And demons need no superseding fiction;

The wicked sin and know no interim
Years or the grave can offer, infecting still
Their redegeneration in life and limb.

Remember that no glory need bend the will
From working grief and havoc in the world
Where grief and havoc flourishing lusts fulfil;

No sigh the less, and no reproach less wild,
No juster remonstration against fate,
No good to be less desperately willed,

No happiness to fall at merit's rate,
Nothing to sweeten ancient fortitude,
Nothing of joy heavenlier than what our state

Has seen in perplexed hours of gratitude
Scattered along the years; nothing you should hope
Suaver than what you bear in your blood's mood,

Tainted when Eve called paradise to stop.
Such as things are, see with undarkened eyes;
Let those who will after forgiveness grope,

Reward, reversal, vengeance, clear assize!
Could we go higher here, you would then see
Far broader landscape, vaster sky arise,

Mountains and rivers huge, the plains, the sea,
A hundred forests, waves of dancing wheat,
And every wide green sweeping heath and lea

Lapped in the circle of the wind and of the heat,
Rocked in summer and on the whirlwind's breast,
Rained on by the sunshine and the sleet.

And if all round you saw from east to west
While time and empire filed through poring sight,
You would see many roads like this addressed

Towards the mauve distance and the bed of light
All with innumerable figures thronged
Of men and women in tears and in delight,

Seized with some wonder, startled, faithless, wronged,
Flailing the dying day with fevered arms,
Cursing the bearing womb; some poem-tongued

Stilling the very dust with witchlike charms
And their companions to acceptance whole
Of what all still must suffer; and thought alarms

Others who cringing in that processional
Ward off invisible terrors from their hearts;
But all move on, soul struggling after soul

For knowledge not the wisest ever imparts
And happiness subsisting but untold;
And all the lunging load-hung chariots

On all those roads with thunders onward rolled
Milled round by the imploring human flood
Surge forward till the foaming roans behold

Before their brilliant hoofs a sea like blood
Flashing with thousands of reflected fires
And splendid as Antares swung unflawed

Among the starry and immeasurable shires;
And all the black roads thick with dusty men
That fate upon the world of pain requires

Run from the first circumference of pain
Converging on this centre where all lie bright
Plunged in those gulfs I pray to see again,

Blessed and resolved in the immensity of light.'
He paused, and that proud ringing left the air,
And soon I saw we must be parted in night.

Huge shadows lay behind us, the hemisphere
Of the great west was livid with the end;
Stars pricked the sky; the air was chill and clear.

'Whatever all things are,' he said, 'defend.
For all move onward in unseen order bound
Until that adored centre is attained

Where God by every voyager is found.
And there the tears man's oldest sorrow shed
Are lost, rocked in the light-drenched broad profound

And swelling main that washes all the dead.
Foamed in those glimmering acres armies lie,
Chariots and congregations forever led

Out when their triumphs here have faded by,
Into the boundless splendour of that Lord,
Sounding a thrall of trumpet, lyric, and cry

Praising him manifest in invincible accord
Seen through his works and purpose surely known
Triumph, to glad acknowledgement restored.'

Now far above me the night's stars were sown,
And as that ghostly radiance downward shone
I started up to find myself alone

On the dim crag, my guide and the sun gone,
And knew that I must waken from that hill
Soon into life, but in such harsher dawn

Amidst my sighs his words were moving still,
And when I felt the weight upon my breast
Again of day's heavy unquiet and ill

Some sea within me breathed in perfect rest.

1949

549

Making a Poem

Coming in with it
from frost and buses
gently burning
you must prepare it
with luck
to go critical.
Give the hook your scarf,
the chrome hook, maybe,
your green scarf. Say
Smoky Smoky
to the cat, set him
on his cushion, perhaps
a patch cushion
from old Perth.
Put the kettle on,
go to the window,
mist the glass
dreaming a minute lightly,
boys on the ice,
rows of orange lamps.
And go cut
white new bread.
Make tea like skaters' leaves.
You're never free.
It's blue dark night again.
Below the panes
in quietness.
Take a pencil
like the milkman's horse
round and round.
But you must agree
with it, and love it,
even when it grows
too fierce for favour.
It comes, and the cat shines.
And make the poem now.

1968

550

Dogs Round a Tree

ow!
wow!
bowwow!
!bowwow
w!bowwo
ow!boww
wow!bow
wwow!bo
owwow!b
bowwow!
wow!
ow!

1963

Instant Theatre Go Home

a
HA!lf
Ping
PENny
ING
in
Pen
ang

pong

1964

551

A Child's Coat of Many Colours

love	head	eyes	bawl	bend	wake	feet	wink	soap
come	yell	nose	soul	rest	tell	wash	poop	bath
rose	kiss	look	bell	days	howl	wind	sulk	talc
baby	rusk	lips	arms	mole	neck	back	tail	talk
hand	hold	room	gaze	want	wall	tale	seat	mama
		blue	bird	purr	burp	dada		
		toys	crib	pram	tree	walk		
		milk	suck	pins	grin	pink		
		hair	pond	bark	crow	wish		
		dogs	wait	mash	glad	slop		
		last	home	ring	next	road		
		feed	wean	fire	this	shop		
		that	bead	poke	soft	tear		
		push	risk	wipe	blub	hoop		
		rash	clap	skip	lull	sing		
		skin	doll	girl	lift	song		
		ears	boys	slip	star	trip		
		moon	park	rain	roof	boat		
		fist	gate	ball	leaf	duck		
		step	grip	sand	bite	dusk		
		take	pail	dawn	gums	chum		
		wave	noon	stir	fork	shoe		
		toes	gold	stop	warm	blow		
		give	puss	call	pony	wail		
		turn	knee	slap	puke	suds		
		lean		open		shut		
		year		dear		fall		
		wrap		rock		down		
		good		snap		mine		
		week		true		trot		

1968

The Fleas

ho

yf

m

w

a

n

le

a

a

r

s

e

k

a

m

i

n l

g

o

v

e

n

o t

he

ol

db

a s

e r

i

k

u

nr

g

1970

Warning Poem

this poem is going to be cut off by a
this poem is going to be cut off by
this poem is going to be cut off b
this poem is going to be cut off
this poem is going to be cut of
this poem is going to be cut o
this poem is going to be cut
this poem is going to be cu
this poem is going to be c
this poem is going to be
this poem is going to b
this poem is going to
this poem is going t
this poem is going
this poem is goin
this poem is goi
this poem is go
this poem is g
this poem is
this poem i
this poem
this poe
this po
this p
this
thi
th
t
tr
tri
tria
trian
triang
triangu
triangul
triangula
triangular
triangular s
triangular sh
triangular sha
triangular shar
triangular shark
triangular shark's
triangular shark's f
triangular shark's fi
triangular shark's fin
triangular shark's fin b
triangular shark's fin bi
triangular shark's fin bit
triangular shark's fin biti
triangular shark's fin bitin
triangular shark's fin biting
triangular shark's fin biting i
triangular shark's fin biting in
triangular shark's fin biting int
triangular shark's fin biting into
triangular shark's fin biting into i
triangular shark's fin biting into it

1975

The Moment of Death

```
unite
 unite
unite
 unite
    unite
  unite
    unite
        unite
      un tie
      unite
     unite
     unite
   un tie
    unite
  un tie
     unite
     unite
       un tie
       un tie
      un tie
      un tie
      unite
      un tie
        un tie
        un tie
       unite
       unite
       un tie
       un tie
       unite
       un     tie
       unite
       unite
       unite
      un     tie
       unit
       u n     ti e
       uni
      u  n       t ie
       un
      u  n        t ie
        u
u    n              t  i                              e
```

1968

Blues and Peal: Concrete 1969

1

dying is daunting
dying is concrete

concrete is daunting
concrete is dying

crying is concrete
crying is daunting

dancing is concrete
dancing is trying

concrete is dancing
concrete is trying

karting is daunting
karting is tiring

dying is karting
dying is tiring

trying is tiring
trying is crying

karting is dying

dancing is tiring

trying is daunting

concrete is krang

2

whaling is catching
whaling is stunning

stunning is cunning
stunning is concrete

concrete is stunning
concrete is cunning

cunning is catching
cunning is winning

curling is concrete
curling is sweeping

concrete is whaling
concrete is sweeping

winning is cunning
winning is catching

catching is concrete
catching is sweeping

curling is stunning

whaling is cunning

sweeping is catching

concrete is whing
1969

By the Fire

That night I was your father and mother, I broke
your solitude, I cradled something that you became.
You cried my name.
How wildly we had turned! I smoothed
your brow where we lay in the glow,
kissed you so deep, so long, it was
as if I had moved a key
in the door of desolation,
you were almost weeping
thinking of your dead brother the apple of your eye
crushed in that torn car-metal, your dead sister
grotesque on the black ice, your mother in her grave –
your years of waiting, half life, half death –
your diffidence, your fear –
but I was then your brother and your sister, in
the dance of the fire with your head in my arms.

I will take all the black ice of Lanarkshire
from the heart that only needs love.
What I give you, give me,
and break me free.

1963

The Furies

Still breathing – we are still here, my furies –
think up whatever you can quickly –
the world is turning and the moon
is in the camera's eye, we shall be there soon –
don't tear up my side with less than steel or fire –
for we have got up into a place
where the mind takes hope
from ages to come: turning now
out, into them, like its world and mentor –
the world that makes the mind move, slow, from
ruts, diffidence – itself incredulously
holding anguish in breaths of new joy,
like a new time born.

Still the sheets of flame, the ambulances,
shadows of planes: what orphan's not a sage
or lawgiver, dead politics like a scorched field:

558

remain. Yet to insult with hope
is to confer with sufferers. Without power
we shall make power come. Old woman,
you must gather the sticks and rags, life is
the sticks and rags our furies cannot stomach ever,
left in the dust. You must steal from the dust.
Crude fury loves despair, waits for that in you,
can't see the patience in a patch of sorrow
under the wind. When the shriek follows
exploded metal he prances, but only
when the remnant in their desolation
cry if this is living they want no more
he pounces. Old woman of dust and grass,
breathe still by your dead sons!

1966

Trilobites

A grey-blue slab, fanned like a pigeon's wing,
stands on my record cabinet
between a lamp and a speaker.
Trapped in a sea of solid stone
the trilobites still almost swim;
the darker grey of their backs,
thumbnail-sized and thumbnail-shaped,
gives out a dull shine as I switch on the lamp.
I have eight of them; half are crushed, but
two are almost perfect, lacking nothing but the antennas.
My fingertip, coarse and loutish
tracing the three delicate rows of furrowed plates,
tries to read that paleozoic braille
as vainly as the blast of Wagner at their ear
searches for entrance five hundred million years
and a world of air too late. But I would not trade
my family torn by chance from time
for Grecian urn or gold Byzantium.

1979

An Arran Death

When the canon lay dying on the island
in his long strength at ninety-four
and his closest friend came to visit him
after many years, and sat by his head
in the stormbound cottage, and talked,
the old man gazed at him
while rain beat on the sea
patiently, said at last,
I want to thank you for everything you've done –
especially the crucifixion.

The shutters banged. He lay staring at his friend.
1967

Heron

A gawky stilt-
ed fossicker a-
mong reeds, the
gun-grey-green
one, gauntly
watchful cold-
eye, stiff on
single column a
brooding hump
of wind-ruffled
feather-brain
feathering the
blue shall-
ows with one
scaly claw
poised drip-
ping –
    wades
the pebbled lake,
prints the mudflat,
scorns the noi-
sy fancy oy-
stercatchers' talk,
stalks, tall, to
his flat ramshack-
le nest or shack

560

of slack sticks
with three dull
greeny eggs
by a bul-
rush grove –

till the snaky neck
coils back
and strikes, beak
darts and spears
quick fish,
fish, fish
silvery-rich
fisher-king dish –

and then in the lone-
ly white lazy
hazy afternoon
he rises slowly
in a big zig-
zag heavy over
sultry fens
and windmill vanes,
flapping silently
in the land of wings.
                    1968

Blackbirds

Uncertain darkness
and a blackbird sweetness
are the best of day.
It is not to be measured
when I am lonely
staring out
at each squeal of brakes
as the buses pass
and you are not there.
The beauty strokes
the rooms I prowl through
with such pain,
at the end of day.
And I groan to no one,
crouch by the window

as two blackbirds swoop
by the darkening grass
in their gladness.
What use is my house
when the light is gone
from the hearth
and I have no shame
crying your name,
no shame praying
for your return,
and for your safety,
and even for whatever
you could wish or lack
in this world, my love,
to leave me or
to find a better.
I cannot find
a better one.
I'm in this place
till the shameless tears
on my cheeks are dry
and the night breaks up
and you are on your way
with the sun – my best of day.

1967

Blackbird Marigolds

It's morning
with five marigolds
in a dewy tumbler
the sun shines through
as I hold it high
from the long grasses

– You can't come in
I'm not –
– Oh yes I can
with my wet marigolds
dripping on the floor
and stand behind you
fold you round
to smell the faint
fresh cut gold
petals –

my head in your hair
the window open
the door open
coffee on the stove
the garden all
one song of blackbirds
1970

The Blackbird

I dreamed I was a child again,
the bedroom dark and still.
A blackbird began whistling
from old trees by the wall.

The notes came out so clearly
in phrases long and sweet
I though he must be speaking
to some listening mate.

But he was never answered
as the day grew slowly grey.
I crept up to the window
thinking surely I'd see

one solitary songbird,
but though he sang and sang
with such half-shy persistence
I never glimpsed a wing.

I stole back to the bedclothes,
turned over; it was five.
I woke, and heard a blackbird
clear and loud and live.

He filled me with his freshness,
more sweet because more real.
Yet he had set me dreaming,
if to wake, and feel.
1980

563

The Dolphin's Song

Man is a fool
as a rule
but we must humour him in school.
So far he only plays with hoops
but we suspect he talks
and every time he looks
at us we blow our tops
and surface laughing – really
we must try to communicate
before it is too late
with the silly
suicidal but engaging skate.

1970

Northern Nocturnal

Heaven rises massive with its stars over
Hekla, Quinag, the smoke and cloud, the gloom
Naked in Striven, the glade of deer, of human
Crofts the half-lost glen and dereliction.
North the glacier, north the broch; and the voices
Struggling from boat and peat and granite street.
Cassiopeia as if sempiternally
Studs with faintest crystal the Pole's crust.
The blue and crawling floe stiffens in the cold,
The dolphin glides with brow of ice. Glasgow
Stands like a mailed tomb where the full flood of bronze
Palls the million of the living in strong and perdurable folds.

Winter and midnight! It is a still beauty.
I whisper, and the frosty steeples prickle.
One great word might speak this city awake.
How many hopes buried in its cradling stone,
Atom by atom with girder, glass and gable
Retain their cries, and when the heart recalls them
Cry out again, from their vision buried in vain!
Treasures of things made everlasting, joys
Liker fire than light, shouting and phoenix dayspring
Breaking the lagging calm of common years –
How could life bear so much desire! Meagre and mute
In its youth seemed life, yet life devoured desire. Moonlight

564

Is silvering the stark Necropolis,
The pavement glitters like a river, space
Is turned to time. Back, back! Where are your ghosts
O miseries, and O anxieties
Show me those unappeased, your ancestors!
The silent tenements breathe deep. Night moves.
No brick, no grave, no gutter lies so silent
As the gaunt arteries and walls of the heart
Immense in its desertion, a dead city
Inert and icy, defiant, whole and solitary.
Hidden it lies like a great diamond, and only this haunting
December hour of stars evokes its ghostly glancing.

Who walks its flashing roads? Who laughs and sings?
Who turns the corner of time? This face I know,
Those outstretched arms, the smile – sun, moon, wind, friends
Cling, plucking the flying rags, cry
Remain and remember, blow with their lips to fires
Extinguished, till the love leaps up in pain
From sleep to speech through flame. Black lay the bridge
Above its drowned lamp-images; it shakes:
A late train blazes and shrieks past. I watch
As its train of sparks rides off into the darkness
Among the freezing stars, and over the Clyde's dark streams
Falls through those trembling wakened struts of wintry steel.

When all is dark indeed: the whirl, the luminance
Clouded from identity, the glimmer on slate and cobble
Faded, and the wan flash of windows gone,
The streetlamp and the Plough; when all is quiet
As dust in dead waves on the Sea of Showers,
As tranquil and as noiseless as those years
The voyaging universal radiance divides;
When all is cold as cavern-flume, sea-floor,
Jupiter, or Pluto in the Thule of the sun:
And then to blackness, silence, cold, my sense
Chokes blind in breaking death, death like this night will free
My fire and shower of desire to the stone and the steel and the sea.

1954

The Glasgow Subway Poems

The Budgie

Spirit of the place,
mascot of the enterprise,
lurking in the tunnels,
flashing past windows
or riding on the roof,
perky yet shy,
talkative but elusive,
she's a ball of gold
like a light's reflection,
a chatterbox
you think you heard
but turn your paper
and shake your head
as the train gathers speed.
The guard is her friend
and drops a few crumbs.
She picks, pecks, turns,
a magic bird,
a clockwork orange.

The Cat

The subway cat
just loves to sing.
You cannot miss him
as he struts on the platform
in his red leather boots,
inflating his chest
and stroking his whiskers,
gets the key on his moothie
and renders his favourites,
'O Flower of Cessnock'
and 'Hillhead the Brave'.
Girls come to pat him,
boys shake his paw,
and once he was kidnapped
by an impresario
from Bakerloo
but he sprang his basket
and soon he was back
to yodel at West Street
and dance at Cowcaddens.

The Giraffe

The subway giraffe
keeps its head down.
It has a special joint
in its neck. Its mother
is known to have been friendly
with an excavator.
It feeds on old tickets,
a cold chip or two,
makes do with cigarette-ends
but shivers with pleasure
at a scatter of rings
torn off from cans,
smacks its lips
as the metal rattles
down to its stomach.
The neighbours nod wisely:
'Favours his da.'

The Piranhas

Did anyone tell you
that in each subway train
there is one special seat
with a small hole in it
and underneath the seat
is a tank of piranha-fish
which have not been fed
for quite some time.
The fish become agitated
by the shoogling of the train
and jump up through the seat.
The resulting skeletons
of unlucky passengers
turn an honest penny
for the transport executive,
hanging far and wide
in medical schools.

1982

567

let gallows languish
let gas flurry
let glowworms fetch
let galluses flash
let geggies launch
let galoshes fish
let gasteropods munch
let gashes flinch
let glass vanish
let gases flush
let gaggles nourish
let goggles crunch
let Gagool fumble
let assegais frolic
let cargoes lurch
let Owlglass shuffle
let laughter urge
let lassies fudge
let lashes fash
let laggards finish
let Gardners furnish
let glasses varnish
let Gogol lunch
let grasses worry
let gags fashion
let sago bunch
let gorgeous tundish
let garages burnish
let gorges brandish
let gargoyles forage
let gaffers ravage
let gavels hurry
let gravel crush
let gunwales crash
let grannies touch
let gurges famish
let gambols clinch
let gutters rush
let galaxies usher
let starfish grumble
let fungus gush
let gasmen gamble
let lurchers shamble
let gundogs fadge
let gasbags fuddle

let flunkeys gargle
let flags garnish
let Brasso furbish
LET GLASGOW FLOURISH
1974

The Han Princess

'Redesign me, unalign me.
I'd be better off without me.
I've a target I can't fly to,
all the ways I'm going blind to
make me tell you I've a mind to
leave you while you build another.
Oh I'd never be your lover
while I stumble through the forest
of your favours, and the lichens
crust me over as if moving
was a nightmare, my delight is
at a standstill. Break me down then,
take me down into my essence
if it's essence, breach the cell-walls
if it's cell-walls, and disperse me
far from the descent of blessings.
What? you want a smaller labour
as I whiten into fainness?
Or you want me to reward you
for the purchase of a patent?'

'She's raving. Is the jade suit ready?
Hold her down and get it on her.
Let her shriek into the jade for
two days, three days? and begin then
marching to the dusty kingdom.
In the smiling middle kingdom
send me, gods, a queen of silence.'
1973

From Cathkin Braes: a View of Korea

This is a quiet ridge.
The stars come out, and the city
In its streetshine and smoke below me
Vibrating composes the dying
Day to order and calm.

On broken far-off Bloody
Ridge history stiffens
Slowly among the stained snows.
The ice creeps from yesterday
Into a stony truce.
The glittering craters are fixed,
Taut, sheeted, blank
Like shell-blinded earth-
Tears only thaw can shed
And roll down ravaged lines
In spring, upon the dead.
Can history make more
Of all that is held in this cold
Than: hordes who sleep in elegy?
Than: a night of flares and blood,
Shadows, the shriek of jets
And men like shadows running
From thicket to stunted thicket
Gaining a tree, an ambush,
An outpost, a shelter, a bullet,
Or down in some crawling convoy
Spattered by the blasting rocket-
Shots' disintegers, or lumbering
Wounded in doomed ambulance
To the rut that roofs a mine,
Or with white frostbitten hands
Gripping a truck-side, a flamethrower,
A rifle, a letter, or shoulders
Of a friend at the threshold of death,
Or worst this side of the atom
To be caught in the awful napalm
And wrapped in that inquisition
And blanket of secular fire
To scream unheeded to the stars
What man now hardly hears,
Since man has hardened man,
Contemning order and calm.

'This place was Bloody Ridge,
This place was Heartbreak Hill.'
As for the men, and the land,
They lie in the order of valour,
And desolation is its calm.

1951

Friendly Village

firefly uneasy purple flute low
flicker chiffon laggard teahouse
horn dark delta
drone roof
avert

alert lead mirror ricefield shadow
puddle bamboo skirt silhouette
running black violet
black indigo
black

eyes wary dog ricebowl eyes
sparrow chopsticks green silence
lamp shadow drone
swing dark
door

roofscape tangled swifts wakeful smoke
flutter chiffon shelf strings
drone candle avert
drone candle
drone

shadow village zoom joystick accident
lazy map mauve delta
drop fire lazydog
kick stick
skies

cries chiffon flame shrapnel christening
cradle charring eyes mother
running silhouette flame
Mekong moon
silent

silent accident cry meritless furnace
silent accident man cry
silent cry woman
furnace bearing
children

1969

Black and Gold

Olympic Games, 17 October 1968

Better a thousand times their black
glove, a fist to the anthem, a
flag unregarded, than the gold
ring of the president's widow thrown
on that shipping-master's ledgers
against a frieze of smiling colonels.

1968

Hunger

in that room there is a mirror
and in that mirror there is a room
and in that room there is a land of candles
and in that land there is a lake of coffee
and in that lake there is an island of ananas au kirsch
and in that island there is a spring of prunelle de bourgogne
and in that spring there is a log of hanche de chevreuil
and in that log there is a sap of givry clos st pierre
and in that sap there is a node of petite fondue
and in that node there is a drop of juliénas
and in that drop there is a cell of pochouse seurroise
and in that cell there is a gel of rully blanc
and in that gel there is a nucleus of galantine de jambon
and in that nucleus there is a stain of mâcon lugny
and in that stain there is a map of skin
and in that map there is a land of rags
and in that land there is a room of bones
and in that room there is a mirror
in that mirror there is a room

1978

Spell

Grommm. Hraammm. Vrawvv. Kraavv.

Rawmmm. Krzhaak. Grzaammm. Grzhoommm.

Vragak. Romnoon. Krawvosh. Zoovgam.

Volagram. Azbekesh. Groozaman. Krazhagav.

Grovv. Rozz.

Wovv. Wozz.

Was. Was. Was fore. Was before.

I was. I was. I was before.
I was before the world.
I was a sound, a wish, a thought, a blush
Of hydrogen, a streak of particles, a crash
Of atoms, a hush
Breaking, a signal seed.
I made a little space for the universe.
See me as I grew and hear me as I flew!
My roots are in the rock wherever you may walk.
My branches take their stations in the constellations.

Was. Was. What was. I was.
I was what was. I was that.
I was the comet that had kings quaking.
I heard the creaking Himalaya go up.
I pushed the continents apart.
I helped Christ out of his spaceship.
I was a fly on the shroud of Lazarus.
I was the mammoth in the ice-block.
I was the tear in the tear-bottle.
It was I who made Pandora's box.
It was I who drove the camel through the needle's eye.
I was the first sheet of paper.
I was the last passenger pigeon.
I was the evening and the morning star.

> Boaster! Liar! Lucifer's creature!
> Back to your roots, back to your mud!
> Get your chains on in the galleys.
> Run too slowly for the streams of lava.
> Lose your path on winter fells.

573

When were you ever with the lepers in the forest?
When did your flesh turn black on the gridiron?
Where were you when the new bride died?
Where were you when the old man had his vision?
When the boy walked into the quicksand
                 you were threading silk.
When the Appian Way was bright with human torches
                 you were teasing your lover with grapes.
We know you by your absences,
                 as much as by your terror.
We fear you on your high bright wheels
                 crossing our plains like a dragon.
We have stopped sending you messages
                 which are torn to pieces by your eagles.
We know you in the desert
                 by the dried-up oasis.
We know you by your sculpture
                 when the tower-block collapses.
We are building a bottomless dungeon
                 and we mean to find a decoy
Whose name is the last secret
                 you will never find.

All the secrets of heaven and earth
Wash over me as I lie on the lake.
My ears are labyrinths drumming with wonders.
I trail my fingers through empires and archives.
My hair swirls out beyond Vega.
In my lips are computers. I am
Beyond your wit. I am. I am.
Let me play with your secrets to pass an evening.
A is for atlas, but I am not in it.
B is for beehive, but I have the honey.
C is for cheesecloth, but I shall not materialize.
D is for Darwin, but I am a mutation.
E is for ecstasy, beyond your apprehension.
F is for fools – how are you, my friends?
G is for gunfire, all in the day's work.
H is for high altitudes – for some.
I is for invisibility – see?
J is for jailer, but mine is not born yet.
K is for knell, but mine is not tolled yet.
L is for law, but I have none.
M is for mantra, but mine is silent.
N is for nature, but I am beyond it.
O is for owls, but wisdom is for me.
P is for plot, and that you have not got.

Q is for quick, and you had better be.
R is for rust on your trap – look!
S is for sweetness I stole from the stars.
T is for truth, terrible as fire.
U is for untruth, an old yellow tooth.
V is for veil, and mine is of iron.
W is for war, but I do not advise it.
X is for xerox, but I have no copy.
Y is for you as you sink into the grave.
Z is for zero, and that's all your secret.

> Let us gather in the dark
> Like the roots round a tree.
> Let us stare into the blackness
> And join hands to sing
> Our last incantation
> And a spell to bind him
> Which is the spell to free him.

>> By the roots of things,
>> By the grit at the root,
>> By the blood and the grit
>> Drawn under ground
>> Together, and the worm
>> Bringing air to the soil,
>> By the crocus shoots
>> Or spread of clover,
>> By the shining beech
>> Or the dear brier
>> Or wheat most dear;
>> By the human grain
>> In the wood of things,
>> By the human cry
>> In the sound of things,
>> By the loaf of bread
>> In the severed hand,
>> By the water-skin
>> Riddled with bullets,
>> By the grass hut
>> On fire, on fire;
>> By the broad oak
>> Where the elders sit,
>> By the giant redwood
>> You drive right through;
>> By water and wind,
>> By dusty sparrow,
>> By mossy wall,

By ricey shallow,
By the seed of the poor
And the fruit of the good
Be bound, be free!
Be bound! Be free!

I struggle in a storm of trouble.
The rain lashes my face.
What is that star? Where is this?
What are these branches over my head?
I can hear some roaring, far away,
Like rapids, or an avalanche, or else
It is great crowds. What crowds,
What roaring? Or is it only in my ears
As I stand buffeted here? Is it pity?
I never heard it till now.
The trees are closer, thicker.
I must make my way with no shelter but theirs.
This is an impossible forest, but I am in it.
Beech, pine, palm, oak, elm.
And that star, that rainy star.
Hurry, hurry! Lightning and the crash
Of timber behind me, and yet I am like lead,
I drag myself through a whirlpool of leaves,
I am sucked down to the earth.
My armour is heavy, I must take it off.
How strange it is to feel the leaves and rain!
It is not cold now in this grove.
And there are so many voices. It must be birds
As well as rain, and that far-off human roar
That washes and recedes like waves.
I feel so light I'm almost free.
What happened to my dragging feet?
Nothing moves now except sound.

* * *

The blackbird swoops and sings through his sweet place,
The rainbow trembles where the downpour ended.
The air is clear, but clearer is my song
Now that my heart falls open undefended.

I thought that earthquake and typhoon alone
Had backs to bear the power of my riding.
The breeze that scarcely shakes the summer grass
Has brought some other power out of hiding.

576

The window is half open in the sun.
I lean out as a dog barks in the clearing.
I cannot think in this simplicity
Of the hill shadows veering, disappearing.

They disappear, and the light disappears.
I sit in darkness on the porch, and listen.
A thousand sounds are stirring, like my song.
In starlight I can see a snail-track glisten.

If there is any kindly dream to come,
If there are worlds of mercy, woods of peace,
Let the rain fall, let the wood-pigeon call,
And bind me in the bonds that bring release.

1977

Chicago North Side

Seven men waited in a dingy garage
For a bootleggers' truck to be sent from Detroit,
But someone sent them a valentine.
For death came first
With a machine-gun burst
As they squirmed and they cursed –

Reinhart Schwimmer, Alfred Weinshank,
Adam Hyer, James Kashellek,
Peter Gusenberg, Frank Gusenberg,
And John May
Died that day
The Al Capone way.

Capone had an alibi but the hoods were his,
Hot Sicilians raked the seven
With brothels and breweries, shysters and speakeasies,
Chains of protection and hijacked taxis,
And bullets for each
Just to teach
Them Capone could reach

Reinhart Schwimmer, Alfred Weinshank,
Adam Hyer, James Kashellek,
Peter Gusenberg, Frank Gusenberg,
And John May

To make them pay
And die that day,
Sweet St Valentine's Day,
The Al Capone way.
1974

'Cook in Hawaii' (p.462) and 'Chicago North Side' both come from the libretto of a music-theatre composition by George Newson called *Valentine*.

The Demolishers

This combination of poetry with on-site recordings of demolition workers in Glasgow was broadcast on Radio 4, 19 May 1978, 'Voices and Verses'.

In the beginning there were no cities
but the cities of the ants,
or coral cities in the seas,
or cities in clouds that would not stay.
But towers rose in Nineveh,
and domes and spires in Kiev and Rome,
and roof by roof the intricate patterns of protection,
like red scales and grey scales
of a creature breathing and growing,
its clusters of active cells and its hidden life
massing and stirring, a thousandfold,
a hundred thousandfold, a millionfold,
great webs of shops and banks and homes and smoke and souls.
The city is hard to kill,
like Jericho's eight thousand years.
Its life is not in a row of columns, or a frieze,
or that bronze horse in the square,
or the obelisk of a conqueror,
or the town hall of exquisite proportions.
Rebuilt a dozen times, it rises
over bones and ghettos, unexploded mines,
rocket-casings, cannon-balls, arrow-heads, dinosaurs.
It lives with those who live in it,
sparkling, arrogant, delicate, dull, shabby, decaying,
a hundred storeys or falling asleep.
Its life shifts, moves, migrates, returns,
the winking lights of its speeded-up history
like a message always changing and always the same.
Tenements crumble; fires leave shells; dogs hunt in packs;
windows are boarded and streets are deserted.
The wind howls for what is lost,

the new blocks rise slowly.
The skyline is half bristling with cranes,
half slashed with ruins and gap-sites.
The rain browns the new concrete,
the young trees shiver, but make it.
Sudden clouds of dust puff up here and there,
as walls crash to the bulldozer.
It is Glasgow '78. A squad of demolishers
scramble through the wreckage, shout, whistle, joke,
pause, have a view of things. Glasgow – ?

    We're entitled to change it, it's due a change.

Due and overdue, so long due
that change is painful when it comes.
The solid, filthy walls resist, the beams
groan as they splinter, the chimneys
are huge, formidable, like art objects.
But there is a time for everything under the sun.

    Just goany happen intit, it's goat tae come doon.

And the people who lived there, what do they think
of the men who are tearing their rooms to pieces
and flinging their doors in the rubble?
What do they think as they pass the loaded skip?

    Not before time, that's all they dae, it's not before time you're
    starting this.

Are they all so realistic? Have they no regrets?
When they see layer upon layer of wallpaper
exposed and tugged by the wind, is there no past
they'd weep to lose, exposed and tugged
like the cheap, carefully chosen paper?

    They don't like leaving the auld hoose, but I think they would
    like tae improve the country and improve their homes, because
    all these auld houses are all rotten. And that's it.

Some have lived there many years,
all their lives, till they're used to
what others can't bear to see.

    Well, some of them don't like it, the auld wans.

The desolation of the cleared site.
Showers beat on the low piles of rubbish,

579

the postman looks for a street-name,
the panda car hurries through.
What if the change is a new desolation,
a cemetery of expressways and car-parks?

Changes here is just absolutely terrible, all you see is big empty
spaces, then it becomes car-parks, no houses, no shops,
nothing, you've to go down town and that's it. It's mibbe for
the best, not in my time but. I goat a new house, it's nice, so
I better no say too much.

Change is eternal division, a Janus coin
that spins a jaundiced and a jaunty side,
and who would bet on any one man's view?

I think it's very good, is getting these auld hooses all away,
very good. All these new roads they're making, I think it's a
very good idea, good wide roads an aw, I think it's a very good
idea to knoak these auld houses down, but I've goat a new
house now, I stay up in a new house, they're reconditioned
houses and they're really good wee houses, warm. The one I
left was damp, I would say about three feet, and the wall was
pure dampness and that was for eight years I lived in that
house, it's a corporation house of course, they've re-let it again,
you see they're goany remodel it in aboot five years time they
say, but ma house is still damp, terrible damp, now I goat
arthritis through it, terrible damp house.

But who is the demolition man,
cutting a swath through broken landscapes,
bringing down the past and singing with it?
Who is the necessary destroyer?

Really desperate for a joab actually, and they know nothing
aboot it, aboot twelve years ago I started, started aff just usual,
lifting floors, things like that y'know, then I started to steadily
work ma wey up, to foreman . . . Start fae scratch, y'know, start
as a nipper, then ye work yer wey up, ye always go oanty a
labourer, then as a top-man, y'know that's a block that works
for heights, roofs, chimneys an aw that . . . Y'don't actually need
a skill, y'know the longer ye're there the more skilled ye
become, and as A say efter a certain time you're called a top-
man, your next step from there is a gaffer.

Labourer, top-man, gaffer – floors, storeys, roofs –
they climb through ceilings, end in silhouette
against the sky, lean briefly on a jagged coping

to stare down at the shrunken street,
come down themselves as the building does,
and start again. A head for heights
is learned on the way, or never learned.

> No everybody can dae the heights, y'canny send a man up a
> height that canny dae it, that disny feel like daein it. You'd tell
> them well the wey ye go doon. Some come up, they learn
> y'know, this is the wey the boay learned, an then when they
> learn, at the end up they enjoy it, they know whit they're
> daein. But there's naebdy that'll come up a height that's no
> allowed up a height, they canny do the joab so that's right
> enough, they're in the street to watch the street, watch for cars
> and people passing by, direct them over to the other pavement,
> y'know this kinna thing, ye've goat tae be there a few year
> before you can go up a height.

Tarzan in a jungle of rafters – not that, but
not a tea-party either. Part knack and practice,
part patience, part brute strength, a job
that's not for all, scaffolding or no scaffolding.

> It's hard working, it's awright, y'know, ye dae a loat a work,
> there more work involved, y'know the kinda job we do, it
> varies, ye could be inside lifting flerrs, y'could be doing a roof,
> y'could be burning, which A dae, a bit burning y'know – pinch-
> ing the stonework in, loading steel, ye see it's an everyday
> thing in the demolition . . . It's quite a hard game, y'know A'm
> talking aboot when A first started, it wis a wee bit hard, y'know,
> but now y'just go up a scaffold, pinching away, y'know A think
> it's still a wee bit hard, y'know tae the ordinary man that canny
> dae a height, y'know it's really hard work . . . When a supervisor
> gies me a new man, A dae ma report, mibbe, in a couple days,
> two or three days, A've goat tae explain whit like he is, if A
> think he can do it. If A say he canny do it, A tell him an he
> finds him another joab, suitable for him, like.

Whatever men do is interesting.
The interest is in the detail, in the specific
bend or balance of arm or leg, the gesture
of placing, the pressure of pushing or levering,
the gauged step, the jump across a gap,
the measuring eye, the catching hand.
There is a process, an order, in tearing down.
Demolishers are builders in reverse.

581

When you're oan the ground wae a machine you've already done your work to the building, y'know you've been up and took so many levels that they're building up, y'know you've pinched aw the brickwork down, tae it's a safe height y'know tae be pulled wae a machine, y'know pushed in, this is how you're oan the ground, well you've goat tae dae aw that work before the machine can really move in, y'know take the wood out, lift the flairs, leave the building mair or less like a shell, y'know in the inside, this is how you start, your roof off, the flairs first, your roof, everything out. Pinch the front in tae it's a safe height, when the machine moves in, and then crashes it doon.

Detail in work, detail in tools.
When is a pinch not a pinch?
In England they hack obliquely with a pick,
in Scotland the straight pinch jabs into the bricks.
What could more neatly suggest national difference?
Ah well, but in England the demolisher's ball
swings free, but in canny Scotland
does its damage in swaddling-bands.

A went doon tae Leicester and goat a joab in a demolition, and it wis the usual pinching doon, they didny even know whit a pinch wis, they used picks. I find it strange working wi a pick, trying tae take a building doon wae a pick, but when ye dae it wae a pinch ye find it a loat easier, it's easier tae work wae, ye've only goat a straight bar, wae a pick you've goat tae dig doon the wye, a pinch we can work through the wye. In England they can use a ball, tae ball it builders builders canny use it up here, y'can only drop ball up here it's goat tae be controlled, wae a drag line. Y'have to have a dragline – as Jim says, it's jist straight balling, y'know, up and down, there's nae side swings, everything's goat tae be controlled wae a ball and a dragline.

Remove the romance of the wide-swung ball
and you have safety; safety grows;
conditions change; men watch; the foreman
watches for his men, and he knows why.

There's quite a bit of danger attached tae it tae, but of course that's wur first, that's wur main thing, safety that's wur main thing, that's doon tae me or the general foreman, you've goat tae keep that going all the time, it's safety aw the time, you've goat tae watch what you're daein aw the time. That's where the safety comes in, I've goat tae watch the like o thaim tae.

You know, the men…When I first started there wisny such a thing as a safety officer, like, but noo they've clamped doon on the safety aw the time. There never was such a thing as a scaffold, we never had a scaffold, no in a building, when you went oan a building there was no scaffold, there wis only y'know you worked oan the building itself, noo you can work aff a scaffold, where the safety is a loat greater. When I first started y'know that wis five years ago A've been in this job now, as I say everything ye do now you've goat the safety helmets, your gloves, y'know if you don't drink the job's right. If ye think there's a wee bit danger ye jist consult the foreman, or the general foreman, they tell you whit tae do, how to work it, m'mm whenever there's a cran on a joab for the last few years now, ye git aw that y'know, this is everything, it's aw safety, really which is a good thing noo.

Safety implies danger, and danger is the background
to be dealt with, shrugged off, acknowledged,
half-friend, to keep the respect for chance,
great enemy that strikes in flashes
or is remembered even as a dark wing
passing over without hurt.

Once A wis takin doon a crane in Millerston Street, y'know wan o thae big, kinny overhead things. I was frightened then right enough, apart from that it disny bother me much, you know.

Beyond the danger is the accident,
the cry, the fall, the blow, the fracture,
the hospital bed or worse. Like climbers,
pilots, acrobats, demolishers who fall
are in a continuation game that cannot stop
and they must climb again at once
or lose their nerve and job. Their job
is something that tells them this. Learning
the hard way is still learning – to go on.

Accidents, aye there's been a few, ma brother wis up in the roof, we were lifting a…an a chimney came doon in tap o him, put him right through the building, damaged his lungs an that, he wis aff for three year, and the following week ma wee mate fell, hunner and oad feet, he was aff for three year, he he started back then he fell again, no that long ago, he went aff again, and he's still off. I've no fell that yit, A fell aboot twenty feet, broke an airm, damaged some ribs an that, that's aboot aw, y'know nothing really serious y'know, quite lucky that

583

way. But the first thing you do, if you fall, ye git up again or you'll never go up again. As soon as ye stay doon that's you, you'll never go up again. That's the first thing you dae when you go back, get up.

They don't forget, though. Who could forget
the warning shout, the panic moment,
the crushed arm half off, the head
driven through a door like a bullet?

There's three o iz up taking this front down, y'know big coping stanes, but there was a big heavy lintel, instead o jist lintels between the butts, this wis a full length yin, a twelve by twelve. An two boays were at wan end, levering it up an A wis at the back, pinching it, next thing the boays shouted at me, Alex, an A looked back thinking he wis kiddin on... oan the scaffolding, then A seen the gaffer running oot the bothy, he ran roon tae get him... him doon. Well... for aboot hauf an oor efter that, his airm got stitched up, hauf hinging aff, he broke his leg, his back, he got a right good sore, y'know. He wis aff for months and months. It wis only that time, anither time, anither block fell... that wis when A first started, A never actually seen him faw either, he musta fell, whit saved him, wis a door, y'know the panel o a door his heid went through that, if it wisny for that he wid of went right through the rubble, he gied his sel a right sore yin, he wis aff for two years, right enough.

It must be done without excess,
without extravagance of feeling, there must be
a sense of being where you are
as if you'd always been there, saw no reason
to lurch sideways into destiny.
It's what you do; it's where you are; that's all.

Whit it really feels like tae me, I'm jist merely standing on the ground, working away, A dareny look round, bit it disny actually bother me, I'm jist working oan the ground, if you have tae slip, well that's it. You might have a harness or if ye wanta wear that. Some people prefer tae work without it, but A've never actually fell or anything like that, I've always kept ma balance, it's dangerous to a certain extent, let's say, the miners they're getting their money and us I wouldn't mind going down a mine, nae bother, that wouldn't bother me. Most of the people say it would be dangerous but as for maself A'm used tae it, I like ma work anyway, keep coming back, I've been away and A've come back, A've always come back to it. I like ma joab.

The wind's on your face; there's sun, or rain,
and passers-by, and cars and lorries, and never
two days the same, two walls the same.
There's dust and skelfs and cuts, but
jokes and taunts and wit,
and you're a team.

> Tried working inside factories an A canny stick it, need intae
> the fresh air an that, widny make any difference in the winter
> or the summer, summer is the best right enough, yer moaning
> aboot too hoat in the summer and being too cold in the winter.
> If you didn't enjoy it, you widny be doing it, ye get a good
> laugh, wi the crowd o boays yer working wi, that makes a
> difference too, I think.

They clear a space for the future.
The city breathes and sighs, settles, is restless, is furious,
is knee-deep in rubble, is renewed.
Buildings are – works of art, tombstones,
machines for living in, punctuation-marks
in history, legends, targets for stones,
pyramids, wonders, too old or too new,
ugly and indestructible, beautiful and disposable,
drowning like Venice's palaces,
crowding like Hong Kong's modules,
dreaming like Brasilia's monoliths,
guidebooked like Edinburgh's terraces,
poised between death and life
like Glasgow's closes and courts.

1978

The Morning

Dependence – warming fire!
Not to be through with being free
but that you know me.

And dangers hidden
with wild care
won to streets, letters, lighted windows, air.

Fog and gravel go,
railings dripping by dead sheds, a hand
combing the scuppered land.

585

Wind blows the stony lot to hell.
The pit rolls out
a tongue and takes the filth for a shout.

And river warehouses,
cracked like wardrobes,
try the probes

of light. What particles
fly in the light mist,
the curtain at my wrist.

A thrust of gold, and birds crying
loud, so easy, so near.
Not that it was day, but that there was no fear

was why I laid my head on your arms
and kissed your hands that crept
to my face as you slept.

1967

A New Book by Wittgenstein

How nice to read a new book by Wittgenstein!
But how much nicer to read 'A new book by Wittgenstein
will naturally be felt to illuminate
whatever topic or subject it treats of.
Not that the present offering is exactly
a new book by Wittgenstein:
for it is not a book by Wittgenstein at all.
"The first thing to be said about this book
is that nothing contained herein
was written by Wittgenstein himself."'
Oh, reading about Wittgenstein,
even when it is not exactly about Wittgenstein,
is so much better than reading Wittgenstein himself!

1966

The Little White Rows of Scotland

whitewhitewhitewhitewhitewhitewhitewhitewhite<u>meigle</u>
whitewhitewhitewhitewhitewhitewhitewhite<u>macadam</u>white
whitewhitewhitewhitewhitewhitewhite<u>rizzio</u>whitewhite
whitewhitewhitewhitewhitewhite<u>faslane</u>whitewhitewhite
whitewhitewhitewhitewhite<u>napier</u>whitewhitewhitewhite
whitewhitewhitewhite<u>duntulm</u>whitewhitewhitewhitewhite
whitewhitewhite<u>yarrow</u>whitewhitewhitewhitewhitewhite
whitewhite<u>curling</u>whitewhitewhitewhitewhitewhitewhite
white<u>maxton</u>whitewhitewhitewhitewhitewhitewhitewhite
<u>alloway</u>whitewhitewhitewhitewhitewhitewhitewhitewhite

1967

The Day the Sea Spoke

mhl mhwl mhwwwll mhwll mhl
   mmmmmmwm hwm mmmmmmmp
        vvvvvrrfffmm rfffm rfm fm mmm
          ffffvvvwwwmmmmmmmmmmmm vwm vwm vwm

    fshshshshllm hlllm fshshlm hrrrm
     shrfr shrfr shrfr shrfr shrffffff
    ffsssssss shrfr fsssss shrfsss fss sss

      hrgl plsss hrgl plsss hrglp llsssss
      glp mp glp mp glp lp lp mp lp
      plm plp plp plm plp plm plp plm

  hhhhwwwwwwwmmmmmmmmmm
     hhhhhhhhhhhhhhhhhhhhh
   hhhhhhhhshshshshshshsh
 hhhhhhshshshshshshshshshsssssssssssss
      hhhhhhhhhshshshshshshshshsssssssssss
   hhhhhhhhhhhhhhhhhh

here are your

mmmmwwwshshshshwwwhhhhhhhhhhhhhhhh

1968

587

Found Poem: the Executioner

The old king was led to the low black seat,
and there solemnly and reverently beheaded.
His head was wrapped in a black cloth;
his blood was caught in a golden cup;
  both were placed with his body in the first coffin.

One after another, the other two kings
and the three queens submitted with silent dignity
to the same fate. Then the black executioner,
preparing to withdraw, was himself beheaded,
  and his head placed with his axe in a little shrine.

1970

[From *The Chymical Wedding of Christian Rosenkrantz* by Valentin Andreas,
tr. Foxcroft (1690), in the modernized version by Margaret Bennell & Isabel Wyatt
(Stroud, Glos.: Michael Press, 1965:)]

Found Poems

MY UNCLE

He trembles upon the verge
of fourscore. A white hat with a yellow lining
is no indication of wisdom
suitable to so great an age.
He can go but one step farther
in the road of impropriety
and direct his executor to bury him
in it. He is
a very little man
and had he lined his hat with pink
instead of yellow,
might have been gathered by a natural mistake
for a mushroom
and sent off in a basket.

MY DOG

My dog, my dear, is a spaniel.
Till Miss Gunning begged him
he was the property of a farmer

588

and while he was their property
had been accustomed to lie in the chimney-corner
among the embers, till the hair
was singed from his back, and till nothing
was left of his tail but the gristle.
Allowing for these disadvantages
   he is really handsome.

MY GREENHOUSE

I am pleased with a frame of four lights,
doubtful whether the few pines it contains
   will ever be worth a farthing;
amuse myself with a greenhouse
which Lord Bute's gardener could take upon his back
   and walk away with;
and when I have paid it the accustomed visit
and watered it and given it air
I say to myself, This is not mine,
it is a plaything lent me for the present;
   I must leave it soon.

                                (1971)

[From William Cowper's *Letters*]

Found Poem: Glasgow

We entered Glasgow last evening
under the most oppressive stare a body could feel –
When we had crossed the bridge Brown looked back
and said its whole population had turned
to wonder at us –
we came on till a drunken man came up to me –
I put him off with my arm –
he returned all up in arms, saying aloud
that 'he had seen all foreigners bu-u-ut
he never saw the like o me' –
I was obliged to mention the word
Officer
and Police
before he would desist – The city of Glasgow

I take to be a very fine one – I was astonished
to hear it was twice the size of Edinburgh –
It is built of stone
and has a much more solid appearance than London.
1971

[From John Keats's *Letters*]

Found Poem: The Awakening

Electrified, bewildered consciousness!
God died in Eden without a sigh.
What it was to live while the first kingdom
died, not knowing every sorrow sweet!
Lies, beatings: life is sweeter there.
Faint soul, proud in a maiden name
whose one amen was traced in sand, pass
below. Manhood is the rose calyx, blown
in, in; reader of the other; he
with his thought of a flower and of air.

1973

[Rearrangement of the words of David Gray's
poem 'My Epitaph']

Found Poems

SMALL HOLDINGS

Small Holding of Black Cock
old ruined Holdings and homesteads
rectangular area
a rectangular trench
lazybeds for potatoes
spade and pick and hard labour
home-grown fare raised by hard toil
brawny, brainy

ROUGH NEUK QUARRY AND POND

quarry of Rough Neuk, noted for fossils
corals and numerous shells in the mudstone
Amiens offensive in August 1918
intelligent black horse dragging the trunks zigzag to a sawmill
under the grey withering branches at the base of the brae and
    bordering the pond
waterhens had hid their nest
a Kilkerran or Kirkoswald anchorite
placid pond
sun-flecked forest
buzzing of flies
faint tolls of Maybole old kirk bell
the original cathedral
a grand cathedral
tender green duckweed so relished by rabbits
belt of long horsetails, rushes, meadow-sweet
scented water mint
encircled by brackens
wood sorrel, mosses, shaded by pines, larches, and firs

STA' O' STABLE

glass of warm wild-herb milk
a sheep farmer, sauntering in the stable
'Losh he's no' a tramp'
the manger
'Steek the door, an' ye'll be gie cosy'
fresh-scented hay
snug, restful and grateful as one might be in a bed of eider-
    down in Hotel Cecil
curlew, peewit, and corncrake calling
mountain breeze sighing
the mountain lambs and sheep bleating and breaking the stillness

EVANDALE GLOW-WORMS AT NIGHT

low round ridge
Evandale
Evan water gurgling over greywacke bouldery bed
glow-worms
stems of grass

fire-flies
trail to Prince Albert
buffalo skins
canister
two inches in diameter
mantelpiece of my bedroom
circle of bright light, about 2 feet in diameter
waned
fortnight later
body is dusky red
female is wingless and its phosphorescent light
near its tail
light is yellow
cast of green
attracting the male
inactive
night advances
lamp again begins to burn

DUNBAR HIGHWAY AT NIGHT

10.30 p.m.
en route for Dunbar
last of the drunks
worth of his money
long roll of breakers
vast, moaning, melancholy main
'diamonds in the sky'
guarding angels twinkling good cheer

'JOCK TAMSON'S BAIRNS' AT DAWN

a mile south
first human voices
birds at 1.40 a.m.
daybreak
'A' Jock Tamson's bairns'
amid big, awesome, silent mountains
brown, stalwart gillies
John Barleycorn
raced
jing-go ringed
'good morning'

GOWRIE IN THE GLOAMIN'

sauntered up the calf park
trees silhouetted on the yellow
dark wooded Kinnoull Hill
slept soundly
sunrise reddening the Carse and the Kinnoull Hill
full of memories
'truth in love'

1973

[Taken from *Tramps across Watersheds* by A.S. Alexander
(Glasgow, 1925) – phrases italicized in original text have been
put together in separate lines, without additions or omis-
sions; titles taken from sections of original text.]

Epilogue: Seven Decades

At ten I read Mayakovsky had died,
learned my first word of Russian, *lyublyu*;
watched my English teacher poke his earwax
with a well-chewed HB and get the class
to join his easy mocking of my essay
where I'd used *verdant herbage* for *green grass*.
So he was right? So I hated him!
And he was not really right, the ass.
A writer knows what he needs,
as came to pass.

At twenty I got marching orders, kitbag,
farewell to love, not arms (though our sole arms
were stretchers), a freezing Glentress winter
where I was coaxing sticks at six to get
a stove hot for the cooks, found myself picked
quartermaster's clerk – 'this one seems a bit
less gormless than the bloody others' – did
gas drill in the stinging tent, met
Tam McSherry who farted at will
a musical set.

At thirty I thought life had passed me by,
translated *Beowulf* for want of love.
And one night stands in city centre lanes –
they were dark in those days – were wild but bleak.
Sydney Graham in London said 'you know
I always thought so', kissed me on the cheek.
And I translated Rilke's *Loneliness
is like a rain*, and week after week after week
strained to unbind myself,
sweated to speak.

At forty I woke up, saw it was day,
found there was love, heard a new beat, heard Beats,
sent airmail solidarity to Saõ
Paulo's poetic-concrete revolution,
knew Glasgow – what? – knew Glasgow new – somehow –
new with me, with John, with cranes, diffusion
of another concrete revolution, not bad,
not good, but new. And new was no illusion:
a spring of words, a sloughing,
an ablution.

At fifty I began to have bad dreams
of Palestine, and saw bad things to come,
began to write my long unwritten war.
I was a hundred-handed Sindbad then,
rolled and unrolled carpets of blood and love,
raised tents of pain, made the dust into men
and laid the dust with men. I supervised
a thesis on Doughty, that great Englishman
who brought all Arabia back
in his hard pen.

At sixty I was standing by a grave.
The winds of Lanarkshire were loud and high.
I knew what I had lost, what I had had.
The East had schooled me about fate, but still
it was the hardest time, oh more, it was
the worst of times in self-reproach, the will
that failed to act, the mass of good not done.
Forgiveness must be like the springs that fill
deserted furrows if they wait
until – until –

At seventy I thought I had come through,
like parting a bead curtain in Port Said,
to something that was shadowy before,
figures and voices of late times that might
be surprising yet. The beads clash faintly
behind me as I go forward. No candle-light
please, keep that for Europe. Switch the whole thing
right on. When I go in I want it bright,
I want to catch whatever is there
in full sight.

1990

595

Index of Titles

598

600

601

Index of First Lines

602

605

606

608